GLOBAL CITIZENS

GLOBAL
CITIZENS

The Soka Gakkai
Buddhist Movement in
the World

Edited by

David Machacek
and
Bryan Wilson

UNIVERSITY PRESS

OXFORD

UNIVERSITY PRESS

Great Clarendon Street, Oxford OX2 6DP

Oxford University Press is a department of the University of Oxford.
It furthers the University's objective of excellence in research, scholarship,
and education by publishing worldwide in

Oxford New York

Athens Auckland Bangkok Bogotá Buenos Aires Calcutta
Cape Town Chennai Dar es Salaam Delhi Florence Hong Kong Istanbul
Karachi Kuala Lumpur Madrid Melbourne Mexico City Mumbai
Nairobi Paris São Paulo Shanghai Singapore Taipei Tokyo Toronto Warsaw

and associated companies in Berlin Ibadan

Oxford is a registered trade mark of Oxford University Press
in the UK and in certain other countries

Published in the United States
by Oxford University Press Inc., New York

British Library Cataloguing in Publication Data

Data available

Library of Congress Cataloging in Publication Data
Machacek, David W.
Global citizens: the Soka Gakkai Buddhist Movement in the world /
David Machacek and Brian Wilson.
p. cm.
Includes bibliographical references and index.
1. Soka Gakkai—History. I. Wilson, Bryan R. II. Title.
BQ8412.8.M33 2000 294.3'928—dc21 00–057107
ISBN 0–19–924039–6

1 3 5 7 9 10 8 6 4 2

Typeset by Hope Services (Abingdon) Ltd.
Printed in Great Britain
on acid-free paper by
T.J. International
Padstow, Cornwall

Foreword

Phillip E. Hammond

SOKA GAKKAI INTERNATIONAL is at once ancient and modern. Drawing upon thirteenth century Buddhist teachings, the movement founded by Tsunesaburo Makiguchi in the 1930s in Japan essentially disappeared during World War II when the founder and his disciple were imprisoned for opposing the war. Makiguchi died in prison, but the disciple, Josei Toda, emerged and began anew. His success was great; by the time of his death in 1958 the Soka Gakkai had grown to three-quarters of a million members.

Daisaku Ikeda followed Toda as a leader, and it was his decision to evangelize outside of Japan that led to the addition of the word "International" to the movement's name. Branches of SGI are now found in many countries of the world, especially Brazil (which had large numbers of prewar Japanese immigrants) and the United States. As the chapters in Part II of this volume testify, SGI has been successful in establishing chapters in many places. In just half a century, then, the Soka Gakkai has become a world religion.

The contributions brought together in this book represent the work of scholars who have studied Soka Gakkai in various parts of the world where the organization is experiencing growth. While sharing a generally sociological interest in the movement, each contributor brings a unique perspective to the volume. Thus, this anthology achieves a certain internal consistency while also demonstrating the rich diversity of theoretical approaches that can be brought to the study of new religions.

While the book speaks to a broad audience, contributions are written primarily with an academic audience in mind. Scholars of new religions, in particular, should be gratified to find here a representative sampling of current research on a single religion—a novel departure from the usual miscellaneous collections of research on new religions.

Contents

Contents

List of Tables

List of Contributors

Hiroshi Aruga is Professor Emeritus of the University of Tokyo and Professor of Political Science at the College of Law, Nihon University. He has specialized in the history of political thought in Europe, especially relations between politics and religion.

Dayle Bethel is Dean and Professor of Education and Anthropology at the International University in Kyoto and Honolulu. He has written widely on the role of education in the formation of persons and societies. His books include *Compulsory Schooling and Human Learning: The Moral Failure of Public Education in America* (1994), *Makiguchi the Value Educator* (1973), and *Education for Creative Living* (1989)—an edited volume of Makiguchi's educational writings, which has been translated into several languages. Dr Bethel has been an active participant in movements for holistic educational alternatives both in Japan and in the United States.

David Chappell is Professor of Religion at the University of Hawaii at Manoa.

Peter Clarke is Professor of the History and Sociology of Religion at the University of London, King's College. He is founding and present co-editor of the *Journal of Contemporary Religion*. He has researched contemporary religions in Africa, Brazil, Japan, and Western Europe. His books include *Japanese New Religions in the West* (ed., 1994), *An Annotated Bibliography of New Religions in the West* (1997), *New Trends and Developments in the World of Islam* (ed., 1998), *An Annotated Bibliography of Japanese New Religions in the West* (1999), and *Japanese New Religions in Global Perspective* (1999).

Karel Dobbelaere is Emeritus Professor of the Catholic University of Leuven and the University of Antwerp, where he taught sociology, sociology of religion, and sociological research. He is a member of the Royal Belgian Academy of Sciences, Letters, and Fine Arts, and a member of the Academia Europaea. He has published books and articles on religious involvement, pillarization, sectarian and new religious movements, and secularization. He is co-author of *A Time to Chant: The Soka Gakkai Buddhists in Britain* (1994).

Phillip E. Hammond is the D. Mackenzie Brown Professor of Religious Studies at the University of California Santa Barbara. He is the author of numerous books on the sociology of religion, including *Soka Gakkai in America: Accommodation and Conversion* (with David Machacek, 1999).

Jane Hurst is Professor of Philosophy and Religion at Gallaudet University, where she has taught these subjects simultaneously in voice and sign language since 1981. Dr Hurst has been conducting field research on Nichiren Shoshu and the Soka Gakkai since 1972. She is the author of *Nichiren Shoshu Buddhism and the Soka Gakkai in America: The Ethos of a New Religious Movement* (1992).

David Machacek is a Lecturer at the University of California, Santa Barbara. He is co-author of *Soka Gakkai in America: Accommodation and Conversion* (with Phillip E. Hammond, 1999), and author of several articles on religion in America.

Maria Immacolata Macioti is Professor of Sociology of Institutions and of Sociology of Religion at the University of Rome, La Sapienza. She is co-editor of the quarterly magazine *La Critica Sociologica* and is on the editorial boards of *Religioni e Società*, *Journal of Contemporary Religion*, and *Anthropology and Philosophy*. She has published extensively in the areas of general sociology and qualitative methods. Her books include, *Il Buddha che e in noi. Germogli del Sutra del loto* ("The Buddha who is Inside Us: Blossoms of the Lotus Sutra") (1996) and *Teoria e tecnica della pace interiore* ("Theory and Technique of Inner Peace") (1980).

Daniel Metraux is Professor and Chair of Asian Studies at Mary Baldwin College in Staunton, Virginia. He is currently Visiting Professor at Doshisha Women's College in Kyoto. Dr Metraux has published widely on postwar Japanese religion and politics. He is author of four books on the Soka Gakkai Buddhist movement, including *The Soka Gakkai Revolution* (1994) and *The Lotus and The Maple Leaf: The Soka Gakkai Buddhist Movement in Canada* (1996).

Kerry Mitchell is a Regent's Special Fellow and doctoral student at the University of California, Santa Barbara, where he recently completed his master's degree in religious studies. He has delivered several papers on religious conflict.

Noriyoshi Tamaru is Professor Emeritus of Religious Studies at the University of Tokyo. He served as president of the Japanese Association for Religious Studies between 1984 and 1996. He is an honorary life member of the International Association for the History of Religions. Professor Tamaru specializes in theoretical issues in religious studies and the history of Eastern religions. His books include *History and Problems of the Study of Religion* (1987) and *Religion in Japanese Culture* (co-author, 1996).

Atsuko Usui is concurrently a Lecturer in Religious Studies and Religious Sociology at Kanda University of International Studies, Tokyo University of Foreign Studies, and Toyo Eiwa University. She was Research Fellow of the Japan Society for the Promotion of Science at Ochanomizu University Institute for Gender Studies between 1991 and 1993. She has published several papers on women in contemporary religions, including Tenrikyo and the Soka Gakkai.

Takesato Watanabe is a Professor of Journalism, Media, and Communication Studies at Doshisha University.

Bryan Wilson is Reader Emeritus in Sociology at the University of Oxford, Emeritus Fellow of All Souls College, Oxford, and a Fellow of the British Academy. His various books include *Magic and the Millennium* (1973), *Contemporary Transformations of Religion* (1976), *Religion in Sociological Perspective* (1982), *Social Dimensions of Sectarianism* (1990), and (with Karel Dobbelaere) *A Time to Chant: The Soka Gakkai Buddhists in Britain* (1994).

Introduction

Bryan Wilson and David Machacek

I T is a commonplace of history that when, in particular periods, a society enjoys hegemony of economic, scientific, and technological enlightenment, its intellectual and social elite will also exult in the distinctive customs, mores, and values of their society's way of life. In these conditions, even the common people, following their leaders, tend to attribute their nation's relative success not solely to advanced technical expertise, but to the patterns of social control and discipline that their country's particular ethos has inculcated. Their manifest superiority to other peoples in respect of material culture confers credit on the ideological, moral, and spiritual tradition they have inherited or evolved. In such circumstances, those most committed to sustaining and diffusing such values have tended to regard it as incumbent upon them to communicate their special and superior ethic to peoples less "advanced" than themselves. Rome sought worshipful tribute for its deified emperors; Catholic religious orders were specially charged, using the Inquisition as their device, to save people from heresy; eighteenth and nineteenth century Europe and America sought to disseminate Christian virtues to all as yet "benighted" peoples, readily crediting to Christian influence the success of Western civilization. Given such examples, it should not therefore be surprising that from a revitalized and booming postwar Japan, emissaries should have gone forth to propagate the distinctive message and moral ethos of Japanese religions.

The particular circumstances of religion in Japan after World War II imposed some differences between Japan's and earlier, explicitly Christian, missionary activity. Christian missions often enjoyed wide popular support and were consciously organized and under the direction of professional "experts"—namely, priests or (in the case of Protestantism) stipendiary ministers. The spread of

Japanese religions, virtually all of which were relatively new, was initially a less consciously organized affair. The manual workers who migrated in the first half of the twentieth century were not so much the carriers of distinctive Japanese religions as the creators of Japanese communities overseas, which became obvious spawning grounds for those religions once these movements had established their bases in the Japanese homeland. Later, businessmen setting up overseas, the spouses of Western businessmen working in Japan, and the brides of (especially American) servicemen stationed in Japan became the principal agents for the diffusion the new religions—Soka Gakkai by no means least among them.

The spread of Japanese religions was essentially the contribution of lay people. It was not, as with nineteenth century Christians, undertaken by professionals—missionary priests, sent out in an organized fashion by religious organizations "back home." It was a much more spontaneous manifestation of lay commitment. In the case of Soka Gakkai it was not in any way the priests of Nichiren Shoshu who sought to further the growth of Nichiren's Buddhism overseas: it was, rather, the ordinary believers, the members of Soka Gakkai. Thus, overseas, the movement that was known as Nichiren Shoshu was always more effectively the operation of the lay body, Soka Gakkai. The movement's dependence on lay initiative and lay enthusiasm proved to be an advantage in a world in which disenchantment with institutionalized priestly religion was an increasingly common phenomenon.

Of the various twentieth century religious movements—whether Japanese or other—that have acquired an international following, few have achieved that position as rapidly as the Soka Gakkai. Its success as a lay Buddhist movement in Japan, and as the most prominent Japanese "export" religion to draw significant numbers of non-Japanese converts in various countries around the globe, in itself demands scholarly attention. Beyond this, however, examination of the reasons for its phenomenal success reveals aspects not only of the religion, its ideology, and organization, but of the social environment that illuminate the changing place of religion in contemporary world.

Perhaps the most notable feature of this Buddhist movement is a distinctive reform orientation. The object of reform has changed since the movement's origins, shortly before World War II, when a Japanese educator, Tsunesaburo Makiguchi, organized a group of like-minded teachers in an attempt to infuse humanistic ideals into the Japanese educational system. When, after the war, the movement's second leader, Josei Toda, reorganized the movement as a lay organization affiliated with the Nichiren Shoshu sect, the object of reform was extended to the whole of Japanese society. To Makiguchi's humanistic educational philosophy, Toda added a populist political dimension that seems to have had a distinctive appeal in the confused and stressful situation that followed Japan's defeat in the war. However, it was the ideology of "human revolution," articulated by Soka Gakkai's third president, Daisaku Ikeda, which constituted the movement's primary source of appeal, not only among the Japanese public, but also to individuals worldwide who were experiencing the processes of social change taking place in the late twentieth century.

The concept of "human revolution" encompasses goals of reforming institutional structures, but asserts that the way to reform social institutions—to improve education, promote tolerance, protect the environment, and end war—is through individual enlightenment. Thus, reform is directed foremost to individual lives and by extension from individual lives to communities, nations, and the world. The process of becoming a Soka Gakkai member illustrates the idea very well.

Soka Gakkai commends itself to recruits as a means of happiness and success in this world. While testimonies collected in studies of conversion to Soka Gakkai indicate that newcomers are attracted foremost by the friendly dispositions of the people who are already members, these members themselves attribute their overall well being to their practice of chanting. The primary activity of Soka Gakkai Buddhist practice is to work on improving one's circumstances in life, whilst receiving encouragement and guidance toward this same end by participating in meetings. At meetings, too, the member will be presented with opportunities for involvement in worthy causes—efforts to clean up local parks, to educate the public about important social issues through performances and exhibitions, and to make the world more beautiful by participating in the fine arts. As is apparent in the chapters that follow, involvement in these social causes is seen not only as a means of reforming the external social world, but also as an opportunity for self-improvement. By participating in an exhibition to raise public awareness of human rights issues, one becomes more educated about these issues oneself; by participating in a musical performance or stage play, one also introduces the fine arts into one's own life. Participation in worthy causes, collectively identified in Soka Gakkai as efforts for world peace or building the "third civilization," becomes a context in which individuals may improve themselves. Such, furthermore, is the Soka Gakkai understanding of karma—the inseparability of cause and effect, self and environment.

To understand how this philosophy of religious self-determination might appeal to individuals living in advanced industrial societies, one has only to compare this philosophy with more traditional Christian and Buddhist notions of salvation. In both cases, salvation was conceived as a release from the matters of this world, and to this end both religions prescribed a certain kind of ascetic self-denial. In Christianity, committed self-denial and even the ready acceptance of suffering came to be perceived as positive virtues. The world was full of sin and temptation to sin, which the Christian should avoid in hope of a better life to come in heaven. Classical Buddhism charted a "middle way" between the extremes of indulgence and self-mortification that prescribed detachment from worldly things as the way to break the karmic cycle of birth, death, and rebirth, and the suffering that inevitably attended this process.

While the Buddhism of Soka Gakkai maintains the classical notion of karmic reincarnation somewhere in the background, the philosophy expounded by Daisaku Ikeda considers enlightenment (salvation) as a way of engaging with the world, rather than liberation from it. The world is only as good or evil as we cause it to be, and the only delusion is the idea that forces bigger than ourselves, and therefore beyond our control—gods, natural laws, or history—determine our chances for a life of suffering or enjoyment. Hell or heaven, delusion or enlightenment, are not conditions imposed on us, but states of being.

Clearly, such an understanding speaks to the experiences of people living in contemporary, urban, industrial environments. Compared to traditional social systems in which one's family name, class, or guild determined more or less the kind of life experiences one could expect, life in contemporary society is uncertain, dependent largely on the merit of choices made by the individual himself. Such self-determination can be confusing and alienating, but Soka Gakkai Buddhism teaches that it need not be so. The religion prescribes a ritual response to troublesome areas in one's life that serves to focus attention on possible responses and potential outcomes, turning problems into opportunities, or, as Soka Gakkai members are fond of saying, "turning poison into medicine." The act of chanting is not an empty ritual, but a means of focusing one's attention on one's own contribution to problem areas in one's life, and thereby a means of realizing potential responses. In addition to the practice of chanting, Soka Gakkai offers small group meetings in which the member might receive "guidance" from other members. That guidance might take the form of specific suggestions or it might be no more than mere advice to continue chanting about the matter, or to hear testimony from other members who have successfully negotiated similar hurdles themselves.

Beyond the basic understanding that every individual contains within themselves the potential for enlightenment and that chanting the title of the Lotus Sutra, *Nam-myoho-renge-kyo*, is the means of unlocking that potential, it may be noted that such a pragmatic philosophy is somewhat removed from the teachings of Nichiren, at least as handed down through the priestly Nichiren Shoshu sect. Compared to the rather pragmatic and individualistic orientation of contemporary Soka Gakkai, Nichiren taught a form of Buddhism that, while distinctively this-worldly, was much more priestly and sacramental. In his major writings, Nichiren makes clear that he understood the evils experienced by Japanese society during his lifetime to be the result of widespread teaching of false doctrines, and more acutely, the establishment of false religions by the Japanese government. He called, therefore, for the establishment of his own form of Buddhism as the official religion of Japan and the construction of a national high sanctuary both to symbolize the centrality of this Buddhism and to support a class of priests charged with maintaining the tradition on behalf of the government. Only when this was accomplished would Japan experience an end to poverty, crime, disease, and war.

Such a religion would be perhaps ill suited to the circumstances of contemporary Japan, and certainly it is not suited to the circumstances of other countries where the movement has achieved a following. The Japanese constitution specifically prohibits the establishment of religion, and despite impressive rates of growth outside of Japan, nowhere does the Gakkai constitute a following sizable enough to make religious establishment a realistic goal. Indeed, in its current manifestation, Soka Gakkai would vehemently oppose such establishment, now that religious tolerance has come to be upheld as a positive value.

Indeed, an anti-establishment position is altogether more congenial to Soka Gakkai's philosophy of personal and social reform. Traditional, establishment religions cannot do other than view change as decay—evidence the caution of former religious establishments worldwide toward social change, or even their outright condemnation of it. The call for social change, reform, or revolution amounts to a rejection by the new generation of recipients of whatever is handed down (the meaning of the Latin root *traditio*) to them. World-reforming religions such as the Soka Gakkai are, in a sense, inherently anti-establishment, viewing change with much greater optimism.

This quality of the Soka Gakkai Buddhist movement may, in fact, partially explain why it has experienced such success in countries where former religious establishments are losing their hold on the public; countries such as the United States, Brazil, and Great

Britain, indeed Japan. It certainly helps us to understand the appeal of Soka Gakkai to people living in contemporary industrial societies where change is the order of the day.

Indeed, it would be difficult to understand the rapid spread of this Buddhist movement except in the context of more encompassing social change. The nascent movement emerged amid the processes of democratization and industrialization in postwar Japan and found its earliest adherents among those most affected by these currents. The spread of the Soka Gakkai Buddhist movement went hand in hand with the expansion of the Japanese economy into the international realm. New patterns of international migration and cultural exchange made possible the growth of an originally parochial movement into a global presence. Emerging concerns about human rights, the impact of technology on the environment, the destructive potential of military technology, and problems of ethnic tolerance and understanding gave Soka Gakkai a *raison d'être* beyond the promotion of a particular sect of Buddhism, and without which the 1991 schism would almost certainly have spelled the death of the movement.

Contemporary researchers into the activities, organization, membership, and social purposes of Soka Gakkai cannot but be conscious of the powerful consequences for the movement of the 1991 split from the Nichiren Shoshu priestly sect. That episode has been likened not only by scholars (such as Jane Hurst, Chapter 3 in this volume), but also by Soka Gakkai leaders themselves, to the Christian Reformation. Clearly, many of the specific issues were different. Soka Gakkai had no Luther. It did not, in the first four or so decades of its activity, condemn the ritual aspects of priestly performances (for example, in the important role of priests at funerals), although at the time of the schism it likened memorial services and monuments to the sixteenth century Catholic sale of indulgences. Its ethos, whilst stressing personal responsibility, endorses neither the concept of the calling in a typically Lutheran way, nor the austerity of the Calvinist conception of work as embraced in the Protestant ethic. But there are certainly similarities, and without attempting here to enumerate those or to press further the comparison, it may be emphasized that the break from the priestly sect has turned out to be a liberation of energy for Soka Gakkai, giving a strong fillip to activities for social welfare and a reinforcement of its this-worldly orientation.

There is one other sense in which the split between the priestly sect and the lay movement militated to the advantage of the latter. In earlier, more harmonious times, Soka Gakkai members collected sufficient funds to present to the Nichiren Shoshu an impressive structure known as the great Main Temple, or Sho Hondo, built at the priests' headquarters at Taiseki-ji. For many of the faithful (perhaps including many priests) this architectural monument was identified as the Kaidan, the high sanctuary of Buddhism, regarded as the third "Great Secret Law," in which was housed the *Gohonzon*, and from which the truths of *kosen-rufu* were to be promulgated to protect mankind in the disastrous age of *mappo*. In 1998 the chief priest—still pursuing his vendetta against Ikeda seven years after the schism—had the building demolished, despite the international protest of architects, critics, and artists who acclaimed it as a great work of architectural art of worldwide importance. By any standards, and without partisanship respecting the issues that induced the schism, the chief priest's order for demolition was an act of appalling philistinism.

Yet even that destructive gesture had consequences that may well be positive for Soka Gakkai. Some traditional religions, and even some movements which are themselves not ancient but which have adopted the structures and styles of ancient religions, have sacralized a given structure or location, conceiving it as a point of origin or a place of destiny—an *axis mundi*. Among traditional religions one sees the importance of Mecca to Muslims. Among modern movements the Mormon temple in Salt Lake City held a monopoly of sacrality until, in the face of worldwide expansion of Mormon membership, the radical decision was made to build other temples to cater to the demands of those who could not journey to Utah for vital rituals. Considering the new religions in Japan, mention may be made of the importance to adherents of Tenrikyo of the *jiba*, conceived as the center of the world.

However, in modern times the global diffusion of religious ideas and the democratic ethos of equality has tended to induce demands for parity of treatment for believers, wherever they might be, and hence to bring into question the constraints imposed on a living faith by the sanctification of one particular sacred place above all others. Sacred geography is no longer of such importance in the affirmation of ideological and moral consensus, and Soka Gakkai may not—in the longer perspective—be disadvantaged by the enforced abandonment of Taiseki-ji and the implied dominance of specifically Japanese culture it represented. A worldwide religion with global appeal may need to review the role of such singular centers of sacredness with their investment in one specific cultural tradition. They may rather seek to adjust their faith to diverse cultural contexts, and accommodate locally the needs of devotees by pursuing a pragmatic policy of building well-distributed, rationally organized, functional facilities rather than devoting resources to arbitrarily designated, sole centers of sacred power. The sad demolition of the Sho Hondo may have had the incidental consequence of enhancing yet further the autonomy of national branches of Soka Gakkai International (SGI) throughout the world.

Appropriately, the present volume is the product of cooperation by an international group of scholars who have studied this Buddhist movement in various parts of the world. The chapters gathered here by no means exhaust the research on SGI that various scholars have undertaken, but we believe it to represent much of the best of current studies. Readers who are interested in learning more about the movement are referred to the Further Reading, for which we thank Jane Hurst.

The anthology was made possible by a grant from SGI headquarters in Tokyo. The project was coordinated at the Center for the Study of Religion, and the grant was administered by the Institute of Social, Behavioral, and Economic Research—both at the University of California in Santa Barbara. In this regard, the editors are indebted to Phillip Hammond, who handled the administrative aspects of this project. The editors were accorded complete discretion to select authors, determine the contents, and edit the manuscript as they saw fit.

The chapters are arranged roughly in historical order, so that reading this volume from beginning to end would provide the reader with a sense of the pattern of Soka Gakkai's development. Chapters 1 and 2, by Tamaru and Bethel, provide a historical account of the emergence of Soka Gakkai and its development into a lay movement of the Nichiren Shoshu sect. Hurst's chapter then documents the growing autonomy of the Soka Gakkai movement and its eventual separation from the priesthood. Aruga and Metraux (Chapters 4 and 5), from the complementary perspectives of a Japanese and a foreign scholar, chart the entry of Soka Gakkai into the realm of Japanese politics and bring the reader up to date on the current status of the Komeito, the political party founded by Soka Gakkai. We are very pleased to include Usui's chapter (6) on the changing status of women in the Soka Gakkai, the often quiet but irresistible force that constitutes much of Soka Gakkai's strength. Watanabe's chapter (7) gives a keen and critical evaluation of the relationship between Soka Gakkai and the news media in Japan, the implications of which extend to all other modern societies in which the media constitute a major force influencing public opinion. Finally, in Part I Dobbelaere describes Soka Gakkai's peripheral institutions in light of pillarized structures comparable to those that have evolved in some of the religiously divided European societies.

The chapters in Part II of the book document the spread of the Soka Gakkai Buddhist movement beyond Japan to North America, South America, Europe, and other Asian countries. Machacek and Mitchell (Chapter 9) highlight the critical role of Japanese migrants in spreading Soka Gakkai, and discuss the changing status of ethnically Japanese members in SGI-USA. Chapters 10 and 11, by Machacek and Chappell, then develop the story of organizational growth and change in the United States, first from a macrosociological perspective and then on a more localized level. The relationship between the Soka Gakkai Buddhist movement and the surrounding religious culture is an important topic in the study of new religious movements generally, and this theme runs through the next three chapters (12–14) on the Soka Gakkai Buddhist movement in Brazil (Clarke), Britain (Wilson), and Italy (Macioti). Finally, Daniel Metraux (Chapter 15) discusses the emergence and appeal of Soka Gakkai in Southeast Asia, the most recent development in the story of the movement's progress.

A volume devoted to reviewing the progress of a new religion in various diverse cultural contexts might all too easily concentrate on the statistical and organizational characteristics of each locale. Macioti and Metraux have skillfully avoided any such tendency. Their chapters—the one produced by qualitative methods of participant observation, and the other largely by interviews—reveal the distinctive flavor of Gakkai meetings in widely different social milieus. Clarke, furthermore, focuses on the extent to which various Japanese new religions have sought to accommodate the cultural particularities of Brazilian society. His chapter makes apparent that even the more exclusivistic of the Japanese imported faiths, including Soka Gakkai, whilst disavowing syncretism, have made conciliatory gestures toward indigenous Catholicism. Those looking in this book for ethnographic aspects of this missionary movement, and who want to know "what it feels like to belong to Soka Gakkai" might find what they are looking for in these chapters.

Throughout the book, one may get the sense that the meaning of ethnicity, nationality, and religion and the relationships between them that once served to give people a sense of identity and place in the world are growing more and more complex. There is much to be learned from this examination of the Soka Gakkai Buddhist movement, but there is one lesson that stands out: the blurring of religious, ethnic, and national boundaries necessitates the development of new ways of thinking about ourselves in relationship to others. The old lenses are too small, limiting our ability to perceive the reality of our interconnectedness with other people living on this globe, indeed with the planet itself. The Soka Gakkai Buddhist movement challenges us all to think of ourselves less as temporary residents on the planet and more as global citizens, and to embrace responsibility not only for ourselves but also for the impact of our own lives on others, as the term "citizenship" implies.

I

Origins and Changes in Japan

1

Soka Gakkai in Historical Perspective

Noriyoshi Tamaru

ALONG with the accelerated trends toward "globalization" in the postwar years, many religious groups have developed extensive missionary activities in areas outside their home countries. Japanese religions are no exception to this, and the Soka Gakkai International (SGI) may be regarded as a typical example of a successful overseas mission conducted during the last few decades of the twentieth century. Formally established in 1975, it is now estimated to have branches in more than a hundred countries or areas, and counts a considerable number of non-Japanese members. Of the religious groups stemming from Japan, it is certainly among the very few to have acquired a multinational character.[1] Although it has become international in this way, SGI continues to bear the mark of its Japanese origin: the very name Soka Gakkai (Value Creation Society) is Japanese, and its basic tenets and practices would be utterly unintelligible without recourse to the context of Japanese religious history that helped to formulate them. For an adequate interpretation of this remarkable movement, therefore, a careful examination of its background, course of development, and relationship to other strands of Japanese religions is indispensable.

---

[1] In his extensive survey of the overseas mission of Japanese religions, Inoue distinguishes two types: the branch office type, which is mostly based on Japanese immigrant communities, and the multinational type. He counts SGI among the latter. See Nobutaka Inoue, *Umi wo watatta Nihon shukyo* ("Overseas Mission of Japanese Religions") (Tokyo: Kobundo, 1985).

The following exposition is based on a few key themes. First, since Soka Gakkai (and its antecedent, the Nichiren school) brought about an important transformation in the previous forms of Buddhism in order to accommodate to changing circumstances, special attention must be paid to the social milieu in which it emerged. Second, these movements were started not by mere chance, but at the initiative of outstanding individuals whose creative ideas and deeds should be given due recognition. It is equally important, third, to focus on the contents of their teachings and corresponding practices and, finally, to grasp the organizational traits and structures that the movements came to exhibit in the course of their development. Such a combination of intellectual and social history will enable us to delineate the basic features of these movements and locate them correctly in the sociocultural setting to which they originally belonged.

The Buddhist Tradition in Japan

Soka Gakkai may reasonably be regarded as a unique contemporary form of Buddhism in the broader sense. This statement corresponds not only to the explicit self-understanding of the adherents, but also to the observation of many outsiders. To what extent, then, is it traditionally Buddhist, and in what respect is it new and contemporary? To answer this simple question, it is necessary and convenient first to recapitulate the essential characteristics of Buddhism as a religion, the course of its permeation into Japanese society, and some of its major schools and their doctrines.

Buddhism was founded some 2,500 years ago in India by Gautama Siddharta (or Shakyamuni, the "historical Buddha"). At the time of inception, it represented a kind of innovative movement while inheriting some typical elements from the preceding stages of Indian religion. In the course of several centuries, however, it was gradually transmitted to people living in the wide areas of South, Southeast, and East Asia, eventually becoming the common and universal religion of this region. As is the case with other universal religions, the process of expansion and indigenization necessitated a series of transformations in teaching and practice. The decisive turning point in this whole process was no doubt the rise of Mahayana Buddhism.

Broadly speaking, Buddhism in its initial form was an order of mendicant monks who forsook the ordinary way of life to concentrate on meditative practices with the aim of attaining enlightenment. To all appearances, these monks represented a rather small minority in Indian society of the time, and we may safely assume that they formed a circle of religious elites. In other words, early Buddhism was what Max Weber once termed "virtuosi religion." Certainly there were a number of lay people who sympathized with its teachings and supported the monks, but they in no way belonged to the core of the order. This "monastic" form has been retained, with more or less modification, in the Theravada Buddhism of the South and Southeast Asian countries.

Mahayana, by contrast, was lay-oriented and popular, and led to a shift of emphasis in the religious system. As regards the elements of belief, the concept of the buddha, which originally meant an enlightened person, came to assume an increasingly supernatural trait, finally resulting in the formation of a peculiar pantheon of many buddhas and bodhisattvas. In the sphere of practice, another group of values necessary for ordinary social life superseded the strict discipline prerequisite to monastic life. In addition, Mahayana produced a multitude of sutras (sacred texts) wherein these new ideas found literary expression. The Lotus Sutra (Sanskrit *Saddharma-pundarika-sutra*; Japanese *Myoho-renge-kyo*, often abbreviated as *Hokekyo*: the Lotus of the Perfect Law), which later was given a central position in Nichiren's teaching, was, besides the so-called Pure Land sutras and esoteric texts, one of the most representative scriptures of this class.[2]

Buddhism was officially introduced to Japan in the first half of the sixth century CE. As to the route of transmission, Japanese

---

[2] It is a historical fact that the Lotus Sutra, disregarding the problem of its authorship, has played an eminent role in Japanese culture. See George Tanabe Jr. and Willa Jane Tanabe (eds.), *The Lotus Sutra in Japanese Culture* (Honolulu: University of Hawaii Press, 1989).

Buddhism may be regarded as a branch of the Northern school, and as to its overall features, it clearly represents a variation of Mahayana. It should be noticed, in this connection, that it embraced almost all the elements of doctrine and practice that had developed during the centuries since its inception in India. In other words, the Buddhism brought to Japan was a sum total of the higher religious culture flourishing on the neighboring continent at that time, and the apparent variety of Japanese Buddhism in terms of its basic forms of belief may be attributed, at least partly, to this historical circumstance. Furthermore, it determined the way Buddhism took root in Japan. When it was introduced, the country was in the process of political consolidation, uniting various local groups, and Buddhism—together with other elements of Chinese civilization such as Confucianism, Taoism, legal institutions, and the Chinese system of writing, etc.—was accepted as an ideology to support the whole endeavor.[3] As a consequence, Buddhism in Japan, especially during the ancient period until about the beginning of the ninth century, came to have a close relationship with the state, a trait which has often been described as its particular quality.[4] In its initial phase, Buddhism was adopted primarily by the circle of the political elite and only gradually permeated the wider strata of the population.[5]

[3] For an overview of the general framework of Japanese Buddhism, readers are referred to my article "Buddhism in Japan," in Mircea Eliade (ed.), *Encyclopaedia of Religion*, ii (New York: Macmillan, 1987).

[4] See e.g. Shoko Watanabe, *Japanese Buddhism: A Critical Appraisal* (Tokyo: Kokusai Bunka Shinkokai, 1968), the Japanese version of which had a large audience in the postwar years. In order to avoid misunderstanding, however, it must be added that in no period of Japanese history did Buddhism possess a monopolistic position within the public institution of the state. Even during the Nara period (CE 710–794), when it came very close to being a "state religion," it coexisted with the indigenous Shinto cults. Seen in this light, Japan may be regarded as having been religiously pluralistic from early times until the present.

[5] For this reason, the history of Japanese Buddhism has often been depicted as a development from an aristocratic to a popular, mass religion. This also is the title of a very useful exposition by Daigan and Alicia Matsunaga, *Foundations of Japanese Buddhism*, 2 vols. (Los Angeles: Buddhist Book International, 1974–6). On Nichiren and his followers, see esp. vol. ii: *The Mass Movement*, ch. 3.

Over the following nearly fifteen centuries there were a number of important movements, which broke new ground in Buddhist doctrine or practice and had a lasting influence on its future course in Japan. Of these, the "New Buddhism" that appeared during the years of transition to the Kamakura period (1192–1333) deserves special attention, since Nichiren, on whose teaching Soka Gakkai depends as its sole basis and source of inspiration, was clearly a representative figure in this whole development.

In Japanese historiography, the Kamakura period is generally regarded as inaugurating the second major stage of the Middle Ages—the age of feudalism. Internal power passed from the hands of the landed aristocrats, living mostly in the areas around Kyoto, to the class of warriors whose base was in the provinces, especially in eastern Japan. Parallel to this sociopolitical upheaval, several new trends appeared in Buddhism and gradually gained ground. Whereas the "old" schools, already an integral part of the establishment, were supported mainly by the aristocrats and geared above all toward *chingo kokka* (protection of the state), the new Buddhism addressed itself to the individual or, in a sense, personal needs for salvation.

How did this come about? In addition to the social changes just mentioned, the restructuring of the religious system that took place alongside them needs careful examination to account for the new trends. It has been noted that the Buddhist system introduced to Japan encompassed diverse elements deriving from the long process of development and transmission among other Asian peoples. However, this did not immediately result in diversity at the organizational level, at least in the Ancient period directly after its arrival. Japanese Buddhism during these centuries was closely connected with the state and was patronized, as well as controlled, by it. For instance, the monks, its chief agents, became government officials of a sort. Their behavior was subject to strict legislation, and it was absolutely essential that monks be ordained at one of the few *kaidans* (platforms for ordination) in order to receive the title. Facilities for this purpose were first erected in the ancient capital of Nara and, somewhat later, in the monastery on Mt Hiei, near Kyoto (two other minor ones may be disregarded). For a long period these two functioned as the principal training centers for Buddhist monks.

Within this rigid institutional framework, the study of Buddhist teaching and, consequently, the training of monks enjoyed more freedom. Broadly speaking, a monk in those days was expected to study all the various doctrines and disciplines to become well versed in the whole of Buddhist teaching. In other words, this system was basically synthetic, and its synthetic character was apparent especially at Mt Hiei, the headquarters of the Tendai school established by Saicho (764–882). Founded by the Chinese monk Chih-i (538–97) at the Mt T'ien-t'ai monastery and introduced by Saicho, this school laid special emphasis on the Lotus Sutra, regarding it as the culmination of all the other forms of Buddhism. Indeed, on Mt Hiei meditative practice, which from the beginning was of central importance, was taught together with a whole-hearted belief in the saving grace of Amida Buddha, mingled with lofty philosophical speculation and esoteric ritualism.

It is worth noting that most leaders of the Kamakura New Buddhism were once trained in the Tendai center on Mt Hiei: Honen (1133–1212) and Shinran (1173–1262) representing the Pure Land piety, Dogen (1200–53) stressing the Zen discipline, and Nichiren (1222–82). However, in contrast to the synthetic approach of the preceding period, they chose, each in his own way, a specific motif from among the wide variety of Buddhist teachings and made it the sole basis of their practice, rejecting all the rest. In other words, their orientation was fundamentally selective rather than synthetic and aimed at a simplification of religious life. To that extent the term *senju* (single practice), which Honen used as his motto, was apropos for all the new trends.

As a natural consequence of this selectivity, each of the new movements put forward a definite type of religious life as its ideal. Thus, the Pure Land group stressed the necessity of sincere faith in Amida Buddha, representing a sort of pietism. The Zen group held that the austere practice of sitting meditation was most fundamental, following the spirit of mysticism inherent in Buddhism from the outset. For these two major trends, it is possible to find proto- types either in India or in China, from which they derived their basic ideas. The third important movement—that initiated by Nichiren—exhibits a typically "prophetic"[6] character without precedent in Buddhist history, and may be regarded as a uniquely Japanese phenomenon.

Though usually grouped together under the heading of New Buddhism, each in fact had a clearly different orientation. Moreover, as their activities developed over a period of more than 100 years, quite naturally there was a gradual change in the atmos- phere around them. More concretely, in their early stage the new movements were not necessarily in direct conflict with the estab- lished schools. However, as they grew in influence and began to attract a following, the orthodox schools in Nara and on Mt Hiei felt the need to resort to legal measures to suppress the new wave, and this eventually led to the persecution of the Pure Land group during the last years of Honen. Somewhat later a similar clash with the established authorities repeated itself in the life of Nichiren.

Nichiren: Life, Teachings, and Followers

Among the leaders of the new movements, Nichiren appeared rather late on the scene, and his teachings had a somewhat different character from the other groups. As mentioned above, each of these groups chose a specific element from among the

6 In this context, the term "prophetic" is applied strictly in the sense for- mulated by Friedrich Heiler in his classical work *Das Gebet* (Munich, 1918), 248 ff., and adopted widely by students of the history of religions, namely as indicating one type of the higher, universal religion. As such, it is characterized by an explicit commitment to the historical and social realities and opposed to mysticism, which is basically introverted. Nichiren, in the course of his career, became increasingly convinced of his mission to fight for the cause of the Lotus Sutra, and this conviction seems to have been strengthened as he suffered repeated persecution. In the latter half of his life he called himself a *gyoja* (lit- erally, practitioner) of the Lotus Sutra. An excellent biographical account from this perspective is Masaharu Anesaki, *Nichiren the Buddhist Prophet* (London: Oxford University Press, 1916; repr. 1966).

ample spiritual resources of Buddhism and made it the core of their doctrines. This is clearly illustrated in their choice of sacred texts as the source and the norm of their respective views. Although a great number of texts were produced and codified in the course of Buddhist history, they did not always possess the status of a canon in the strict sense. In practice, each Buddhist school or group took some texts and declared them to be authoritative for their doctrine. Thus, the Tendai school regarded the Lotus Sutra as the final message of the Buddha (for this reason, it was formally called the Tendai-Hokke school); the Pure Land school replaced it with the Three Pure Land Sutras; the Zen group went even further and insisted on a "direct transmission outside the scriptures."

At this point the essential feature of Nichiren's teachings comes to the fore. Instead of discarding the Lotus Sutra on which Tendai orthodoxy rested—the mainstream of Japanese Buddhism at that time—Nichiren pursued a new path by according it an absolute meaning and making it the sole object of personal commitment. In this sense, his movement may be interpreted as an attempt at reform or revitalization from within the Tendai tradition. However, the extreme simplification of doctrine, the strong sense of mission, and the exclusivist tendency in his ideas and deeds indicate unmistakably the qualitative difference that separates it from the synthetic eclecticism of the established schools.[7] His movement, no doubt, took its shape in the turbulent atmosphere of those days, but it also bears a strong imprint of his personality, for among the major schools of Japanese Buddhism only this one is named after its founder.

Nichiren was born in 1222 in the village of Kominato in Awa province (the present Chiba prefecture), facing the Pacific Ocean.

[7] Like other founders of the major schools, Nichiren has so far been interpreted in a variety of ways. His position *vis-à-vis* the Tendai orthodoxy has been one of the crucial issues in this discussion. Without going into details, Hoyo Watanabe's view may be cited here as being most representative: "Although Nichiren remained fundamentally within the Tendai tradition, he is known as a reformer, if not a radical, who departed from many of the teachings of Saicho . . . he virtually reduced the Tendai doctrines to the sole practice of chanting the *Daimoku*" ("Nichiren," in Mircea Eliade (ed.), *Encyclopaedia of Religion*, x (New York: Macmillan, 1987), 425).

As he later recounted, his family was engaged in fishing and other local businesses. His eventful life may be divided into two halves by the year 1253, when he seems to have established his own views. The first half was the period of training and preparation, and the latter half the years of public activities when he unceasingly tried to bring his conviction to the people. This latter half, comprising thirty years until his death in 1282, has also been subdivided into two periods: before and after his exile on the remote island of Sado (1271–4). By this time his harsh criticism of and attack on other Buddhist schools and the secular authorities had nearly come to an end, and the remaining years were spent chiefly in summarizing his teachings and caring for his disciples and followers.

As a talented youth, in 1233 he was sent to the nearby Tendai monastery of Seichoji (Kiyosumidera) to receive formal education. In 1237 he became a monk and started his training in Buddhism. Two years later he visited Kamakura in the neighboring province, then thriving as the seat of the military government. He seems to have studied Pure Land Buddhism and Zen, which were gradually gaining ground in the city. From 1242 to about 1252 he studied extensively in the centers of traditional Buddhism on Mt Hiei and in Nara. Convinced through these experiences of the inadequacy of the Buddhist teachings of the day, especially of Pure Land Buddhism and Zen, he returned home to Seichoji and, in April 1253, began publicly to denounce them and to advocate a wholehearted faith in the Lotus Sutra. At this time he also began to call himself Nichiren (meaning Japan and lotus).

According to his own testimony, he was deeply troubled from his youth by doubts about the cause of the natural and social calamities that plagued the nation. The years of study brought him to the conclusion that they were caused by the disappearance of true Buddhism. In order to restore the social order and secure the welfare of the people, therefore, he thought it was urgent to reinstate what he believed to be the true Buddhism. To bring this view to a greater audience, later in 1253 he settled in Kamakura, where he began to preach to passers-by, standing at the crossroads. In

1260 he wrote his treatise *Rissho ankoku ron* ("Establish the Right Law and Secure the Nation") and presented it to the government authorities. In it he urged the rulers to ban false teachings, and warned them that rebellions and foreign invasions would result from their failure to follow his admonition.

It is no wonder that such drastic behavior offended his opponents, and the government, which ignored his proposal, was finally forced to take measures against him. In 1261 Nichiren was exiled to the province of Izu (Shizuoka prefecture). Though pardoned after two years, he was exiled again in 1271–4, this time to the island of Sado, in northern Japan. Life in exile was harsh and full of dangers, but it proved to be a fruitful period, for during these years he not only acquired a small but dedicated following, but was also able to accomplish major works summarizing his basic ideas, including *Kaimokusho* ("Opening of the Eyes") and *Kanjin honzonsho* ("The Object of Worship by Introspection of Minds"). Soon after returning to Kamakura, he retired from public activity and went into retreat in Minobu (Yamanashi prefecture). He died in 1282, surrounded by a few disciples, on the outskirts of modern Tokyo.

In the history of Japanese Buddhism Nichiren's teachings occupy a unique position. They are distinguished from other schools by their pre-eminently political orientation, bringing Buddhism into the realities of social life, and by the firm sense of mission to achieve this goal by any means. It is a mentality rarely found elsewhere in the Buddhist world and may be called "prophetic" in the proper sense of the word. Indeed, in the latter half of his life Nichiren came to regard himself as a prophet of the Lotus Sutra; a bodhisattva who had been commissioned by the Buddha to propagate the true teaching. This conviction seems to have been strengthened by the repeated persecution he suffered. This activist spirit is clearly an integral portion of his legacy and can be found in a number of his followers, including the founders of Soka Gakkai.

His conviction was based upon his perception of the Lotus Sutra as the final message of the Buddha. In its usual form this sutra consists of twenty-eight chapters: the first fourteen deal mainly with the sermons of the historical Buddha; the other fourteen give the discourses of the eternal Sakyamuni, the Truth itself, of which the historical Buddha was only one of numerous manifestations. In doctrinal terminology, the first part was called the *shakumon* (section of manifestations), and the second half was called the *honmon* (section of origin). Of these two, Nichiren decidedly gave priority to the latter and summarized its contents into the Three Great Mysteries of *honzon*, *daimoku*, and *kaidan*. *Honzon*—a Buddhist term designating the chief object of worship, by which he originally meant the eternal Buddha as revealed in the Lotus Sutra—was applied later to the peculiar mandala he made during his retreat in Minobu, showing the *daimoku*, the sacred title of the sutra. As the *daimoku* was the quintessence of the sutra and hence the absolute truth, its recitation, *Nam-myoho-renge-kyo* ("Adoration to the Lotus Sutra") was obligatory. And he seems to have planned to establish a special *kaidan* to instruct people in this true teaching apart from the extant ones in Nara and on Mt Hiei.

In addition to these ideas, *shakubuku* (literally, "break and subdue") was an important aspect of his activity, which he both practiced and recommended to others as a means of persuading nonbelievers and opponents. He held that an attack on false doctrines was an effective means of leading people to the absolute truth, and throughout his life he never ceased to criticize severely the Pure Land and Zen schools, to which Shingon esotericism and Ritu (*vinaya*) were later added. This intolerant spirit is doubtless a characteristic inherited by his later followers.[8]

---

[8] Nichiren regarded *shakubuku* as a method required in the age of *mappo* (final and declining days of Dharma) and in a country opposed to the true teaching such as Japan. A perusal of his writings reveals, however, that they leave some room for diverging interpretations. In later centuries his followers did in fact take different stances toward other schools of Buddhism or the secular authorities and sometimes fought each other on that account. In this sense Nichiren Buddhism has never been monolithically exclusivist, as Stone has shown; see Jacqueline Stone, "Rebuking the Enemies of the Lotus: Nichirenist Exclusivism in Historical Perspective," *Japanese Journal of Religious Studies*, 21/2–3 (1994), 231–60.

Finally, we may note a certain ethnocentric tendency in his teachings. It is well known that in *Kaimokusho* he took the vow to become "the pillar, eyes, and ship of Japan."[9] On closer analysis, this ethnocentrism reveals an implicit feeling of inferiority—Japan being far removed from the homeland of Buddhism. In any event, it is clear that this aspect of Nichiren's thought exerted a far-reaching influence on nationalistic leaders in modern Japan—such as Chigaku Tanaka (1867–1939), who founded Kokuchukai (the Pillar of Nation Society).[10]

The teachings of Nichiren, which started as a new movement outside the established schools, gradually took root in Japanese society and have by now become firmly institutionalized. In fact, it constitutes one major sector of Japanese Buddhism together with the earlier groups of Tendai and Shingon, and the Pure Land and the Zen groups, which arose almost simultaneously.[11] Like other sects, it is divided into nearly thirty subschools. The reasons for

[9] "I will be the Pillar of Japan, I will be the Eyes of Japan, I will be the Ship of Japan, and I will never forsake it" (*Selected Writings of Nichiren*, ed. Philip B. Yampolsy, trans. Burton Watson (New York: Columbia University Press, 1990), 136).

[10] In the modern period since Meiji, Nichiren has exerted a far-reaching influence in society outside the traditional clerical circles. His teaching inspired poets like Kenji Miyazawa (1896–1933), but its impact has been most conspicuous in the sphere of political ideology. This may readily be explained as a natural consequence of his basically realistic orientation aiming at an improvement of the world order. It must be noted, however, that his ideas could be utilized to support a nationalistic policy, as was the case with Chigaku Tanaka, as well as an antinationalistic, pacifist endeavor such as Sinko Bukkyou Seinen Domei (the New Buddhist Youth Federation, 1931) of Giro Seno (1889–1961). Tsunesaburo Makiguchi's espousal of Nichiren Buddhism, too, reinforced his resistance to the nationalistic trend of his days. In brief, the teachings of Nichiren have an ambivalent political implication. The campaign for world peace that Soka Gakkai has been promoting since about the 1970s must be interpreted, at least partly, in this historical context. See also Christina Naylor, "Nichiren, Imperialism and the Peace Movement," *Japanese Journal of Religious Studies*, 18/1(1991), 51–78.

[11] This conventional grouping is employed also in the *Shukyo nenkan* ("Religion Yearbook"), which has been published since the 1950s by the department of religious affairs of the agency for cultural affairs and is the only available source of official statistics. In this yearbook most "new religions" are classified according to their background. For instance, Reiyukai and Rissho Koseikai are subsumed under the heading of Nichiren Buddhism.

this fragmentation are numerous: in the earliest phase it was primarily caused by an internal dispute about leadership; later, this was
outweighed by dogmatic differences. At this juncture, because of
its relationship to Soka Gakkai, one of the subschools, Nichiren
Shoshu (the True Nichiren school), needs to be mentioned.

According to tradition, on his deathbed Nichiren entrusted six
main disciples with disseminating his teachings and taking care of
his tomb in Minobu. However, soon afterwards a difference of
opinion arose in this circle concerning the legitimacy of worshipping at Shinto shrines. As a result, Nikko (1246–1333), who tried
to keep the purity of his master's teachings, parted from the others
in 1288 to form his own school. Two years later he left Minobu
and founded his temple, Taiseki-ji, near Mt Fuji. This Fuji school
was the precursor of contemporary Nichiren Shoshu.

Nichiren Shoshu may be regarded as the most radical among the
subschools of Nichiren Buddhism in terms of doctrine. As mentioned above, Nichiren himself saw the *honzon*, the first of his
Three Mysteries, in the eternal Buddha as revealed in the Lotus
Sutra. Later on, however, there arose a tendency among his disciples and followers to accord central significance to the unique
mandala that he made toward the end of his life showing the sacred
title of *Nam-myoho-renge-kyo* surrounded by the names of a few
buddhas and bodhisattvas. Since it was in the possession of
Taiseki-ji, the school insisted on its supremacy over other groups.
The emphasis on this object of worship at the same time induced
people to think of Nichiren, its author, as a manifestation of truth
even greater than the historical Buddha Shakyamuni. Chanting the
daimoku, too, came to be interpreted as the realization of *jyobutu*
(enlightenment).[12]

---

[12] Recent research tends to interpret the whole of Nichiren Buddhism—
Nichiren himself as well as later schools like Nichiren Shoshu—as a variation
of the *hongaku shiso* (original enlightenment), which had developed within the
Tendai circles and represented a special form of "world affirmation," minimizing the difference between the religious ideal and the realities of life. However,
since the key term "original enlightenment" remains somewhat equivocal, the
issue needs further exploration.

The Soka Gakkai movement has been, from its beginning until quite recently, closely related to Nichiren Shoshu. This connection at first was formed, so to speak, by a historical incident. But repeated conflicts between the two bodies, leading to the final "schism" of 1990–1, show that this alliance between an essentially clerical organization and a new lay movement has been somewhat precarious from the very beginning.

The Emergence and Development of Soka Gakkai

Soka Gakkai is generally counted among the "new religions" in contemporary Japan, and it is certainly one of the most successful. Though exact statistics are not available, there are good reasons to think that at present it has a membership amounting to several million in Japan and some tens of thousands abroad. Part of the reason for this enormous growth, no doubt, lay in the rapid process of urbanization that occurred in Japan during the postwar decades and heightened the mobility of population. But its development needs also to be attributed to factors inherent in the movement itself. In order to spell out its peculiarity, therefore, the general background and some common features of the new religious movements must first be briefly mentioned, followed by a description of the major stages of Soka Gakkai's development and a tentative analysis of its basic teachings and organization.

In the history of Japanese religions, the term "new religion" is generally applied to movements that started during the last two centuries. The earliest group appeared toward the end of the Tokugawa period (1600–1868). In Japanese society at that time, whose equilibrium was artificially maintained by the policy of national seclusion and the ban on Christianity, the new religions represented a natural outburst of the religious aspirations of people who could not find fulfillment within the narrow confines of established Buddhist schools. Broadly speaking, they emerged on the periphery of or outside the extant organizations, absorbing various ideas and ritual elements from two major sources—namely such publicly acknowledged systems as Buddhism and, to a lesser degree, Confucianism on the one hand, and syncretistic folk beliefs on the other. Their activities were especially conspicuous during the decades around 1900 and after 1945.

Though often grouped together under the rubric of new religion and discussed in a general manner, a closer look reveals that these movements differ considerably from each other in size and content. Accordingly, scholars have attempted to classify them into several major types to facilitate further investigation. Perhaps the easiest way to deal with their great variety would be to group them together by the religious strands that formed their respective backgrounds. By this standard, new religions in contemporary Japan may be distinguished by their affiliation either with Shinto (including folk Shinto and some syncretistic forms) or with Buddhism—new movements with a Christian background being almost negligible (excluding some recently imported ones such as the Unification Church and Jehovah's Witnesses). Remarkably, the great majority of movements with a Buddhist background belong either to esoteric Buddhism or to the Nichiren tradition, a circumstance indicative of some kind of congeniality of the teachings of these schools to the new movements.

This leads to another typology based on the characteristics of their teachings and practices. Susumu Shimazono recently proposed a classification of the new religions in Japan into four types: (1) groups founded on the basis of indigenous beliefs, (2) intellectual–ideological types, (3) movements aiming at the moral improvement of individuals, and (4) mixed types. According to this typology, many new movements affiliated with Buddhism may be regarded as belonging to type 2—the intellectual–ideological type— while such early cases as Tenrikyo or Konkokyo clearly represent type 1—those founded on indigenous beliefs. Moreover, these Buddhist movements may again be subdivided, depending on the proportion of constitutive elements in their doctrine and practice, into semitraditional; syncretistic Buddhist; and an intermediate type.[13] Soka Gakkai belongs to the semitraditional Buddhist type.

[13] See Susumu Shimazono, *Gendai kyusaishukyo ron* ("Salvation Religion in the Contemporary Age") (Tokyo: Seikyusha, 1992), 67–70, 88.

As they generally appeared outside the established institutions, the new religions have often been called "popular" movements. This is not altogether mistaken, since most Buddhist new religions were initiated and supported by lay believers rather than by professional clergy. However, upon closer analysis it becomes clear that sometimes not only the populace but also intellectuals and people related to established schools played an important role in the inauguration or development of a new religion. This may also be a characteristic feature that distinguishes a proportion of new movements appearing in Japanese society where, especially since the early modern period, literacy and education were eagerly promoted and steadily maintained at a rather high level. Soka Gakkai is a good example.[14]

The foundations of Soka Gakkai were laid by two impressive personalities: Tsunesaburo Makiguchi (1871–1944) and Josei Toda (1900–58). As master and disciple, they together gave birth to this powerful movement and led it as the first and second presidents, respectively. Indeed, its emergence and development would have been inconceivable without their initiative. Originally both worked as elementary schoolteachers, and in their endeavor to improve educational practices current in those days they happened to come into contact with the teachings of Nichiren and embarked on their religious quest. Thus, the fundamentally intellectual–ideological vein that distinguishes Soka Gakkai from other groups—and continues to the present—was nurtured in the process of its formation.

Born in Niigata prefecture in northern Japan, Makiguchi finished his course in the teachers' academy with a good record and entered his career as an elementary schoolteacher in Hokkaido. Later on he was appointed the principal of a number of schools in Tokyo and remained in this profession until retirement. As a devoted teacher he was concerned with the promotion of his

---

[14] In addition to the classification by historical backgrounds or contents of their teachings, new religions may also be divided into several types based on such sociological traits as the degree of organization, the form of leadership, or the size and distribution of their membership.

pupils' abilities, and incessantly sought the most effective means to achieve this goal. Above all he spent much effort on teaching geography, which he tried to reorganize on the basis of pupils' experiences in their "native places." His first publication, *Jinsei chirigaku* ("A Human Geography," 1903), was a result of these teaching experiences. Incorporating many insights and practical suggestions accumulated during his more than twenty year career as principal, in 1930 he published the first volume of his *chef-d'oeuvre*, *Soka kyoikugaku taikei* ("A Theory of Value-Creating Pedagogy"), to which three further volumes were added in a few years. This is usually regarded as the formal foundation of Soka Kyoiku Gakkai (the Value-Creating Educational Society), the precursor of contemporary Soka Gakkai. In fact, however, it was not until 1937 that the activities of this association started fully.

How, then, did Makiguchi come to embrace the teachings of Nichiren? As he himself later recounted, although his parents' family was affiliated with a Zen temple and his foster parents (he was adopted at the age of 3) with a Nichiren temple, he accepted neither of them. In his youth he was deeply influenced by his teachers and friends, who were mostly Christians, but did not convert to this new faith. He clearly was not content with the conventional Confucian morality still very much current in Japanese society and searched eagerly for another principle that could afford him a sense of integrity.[15] On this spiritual journey, about 1916 in Tokyo, he had a chance to hear the lectures of Chigaku Tanaka, who then had a high reputation, but he found Tanaka's nationalistic interpretation of Nichiren's teachings repugnant. The decisive event that led Makiguchi finally to the Nichiren Shoshu faith was a meeting with Sokei Mitani (1887–1932) in 1928. Mitani, also a teacher, and principal of the Mejiro Gakuen School in Tokyo, had joined the circle of adherents of a Nichiren Shoshu temple about 1915–16 and was then engaged in literary activities to propagate Nichiren Buddhism.

[15] Tsunesaburo Makiguchi, *Makiguchi Tsunesaburo zenshu* ("Collected Works"), viii (Tokyo: Daisan Bunmeisha, 1984), 405–17; Koichi Miyata, *Makiguchi Tsunesaburo no shukyo-undo* ("Makiguchi Tsunesaburo's Religious Movement") (Tokyo: Daisan Bunmeisha, 1993), 72.

In this way, Makiguchi came into contact with Nichiren's teachings rather late in his career, but accepted them as the culmination of his lifelong intellectual quest. His published works, accordingly, show a unique combination of his own thinking and the doctrine of traditional Buddhism, or an attempt to reinterpret the latter by means of the former. The key concept in this combination is "the theory of value," which became the motto of his whole movement. To elaborate, he first examined the system of values proposed by German neo-Kantian philosophers and often referred to in Japan, but replaced it with a new one. Instead of the neo-Kantian system of "truth, goodness, beauty, holiness," he proposed "beauty, profit, goodness." In this formula beauty represents aesthetic values connected with individual, or partial, life. Profit refers to the values of individuals as living totalities. Goodness means values of society as collective life. Especially noteworthy is that this argument completely discarded the value of holiness as pertinent to the religious sphere *per se* and sought to derive it from other values—goodness, in particular, which is therefore called "Great Good." This implies that he saw religion as being not separate from, but identical with, the actual life of individuals in society, so that the efforts to create values in mundane life obtained a religious foundation. At the same time it must be noted that his thinking was thoroughly pragmatic and empiricist rather than idealistic.

Thus, Makiguchi's personal endeavor came to have the dual character of both a reform movement of school education and a religious movement. In time, of course, the latter aspect gradually prevailed. Soka Kyoiku Gakkai, which he founded to promote his reform program and probably consisted of only a few dozen members, grew to comprise some hundreds of people by 1940. However, in 1943 it was violently effaced by the wave of nationalism that overwhelmed wartime Japan. Faithful to Nichiren's teaching, which held Buddhism as superior to everything else, Makiguchi refused to worship at the Ise Grand Shrine—the tutelary shrine of the imperial family—and advised the members of the society not to visit Shinto shrines. In July 1943 he was arrested, together with other staff of the society, for *lèse-majesté* and for breaking the law for the preservation of national security. He died in prison on 18 November 1944, leaving the task of reestablishing the movement to his disciple and collaborator Josei Toda.

Toda, like his master, was born in the northern part of Japan and grew up in Hokkaido. Having received the license of an assistant teacher, he came to Tokyo in 1920 and encountered Makiguchi. This encounter determined his future course of life, for, starting his profession as a deputy teacher under Makiguchi's guidance, he thereafter shared everything with his master. He was an assistant, a devoted colleague, and a fellow lay believer of Nichiren Shoshu. In fact, the first volume of *Sioka Kyoikugaku taikei* (1930) was prepared by Toda as editor and publisher. Besides his professional career, Toda showed his talent for management in running private classes for pupils. During World War II he was also arrested and imprisoned, and suffered severe treatment until his release in the early part of July 1945, shortly before the end of the war. After recovering his health, he set to work reinstating the movement. In January 1946 he began to appeal to former members, using a slightly changed name for the organization, Soka Gakkai, and on 18 November 1946, the anniversary of Makiguchi's death, he convoked the first general assembly in Tokyo to resume its full-scale program.

As may be easily seen from this rather sketchy description, the Soka Gakkai movement was almost completely disrupted by the war, and its progress after 1946 was comparable to a new beginning from nothing. However, under Toda's leadership it grew rapidly from a small group consisting mainly of teachers to a nationwide organization. In 1951, when he succeeded his master as president, it probably had a membership of some 500 families (Soka Gakkai used to give its size not by individual believers but by families). He then resolved to get 750,000 more families as members—a goal seemingly reached by the time of his death in 1958. For the purpose of effective management, in 1955 the growing body was reorganized on the basis of area blocks. Aimed at establishing a closer network among its members, this system was first introduced in the Tokyo branch.

Enormous growth in the postwar years was also achieved by some parallel groups derived from Nichiren Buddhism such as Reiyukai, which was founded in 1930, and Rissho Kosei-kai, which split from Reiyukai in 1938. In the case of Soka Gakkai, however, growth was greatly promoted by the practice of *shakubuku*, the vigorous method of proselytism inherited from Nichiren. Actually this objective was pursued mainly in small discussion groups where members tried to persuade nonbelievers by personal confrontation. In order to make this procedure more effective, in 1951 Toda edited and published the *Shakubuku kyoten*, a catechism of Soka Gakkai doctrine, and strongly recommended that members join "the great *shakubuku* march." This handbook is now out of use, but it indicates the basic ideology of Soka Gakkai in a very impressive way.

Toda was certainly an able leader and organizer who reinstated the nearly disbanded group and helped to make it the largest new religious organization in contemporary Japan. His achievement, though, was not limited to this. He also provided the movement with two central ideas that inspired people in his generation and elicited their commitment. One was the doctrine of *obutsumyogo* (the union of worldly matters and Buddhist teaching), which he combined with the proposal to establish a "national *kaidan*" as a place to instruct people in Buddhism; the other was the "philosophy of life" as the quintessence of faith. In the former, it is not difficult to see that it was a formulation of the preeminently sociopolitical intentions inherent in Nichiren's teachings. Because of severe criticism from many quarters in postwar Japan, however, it finally had to be withdrawn. The second element, which restates another important motif of Nichiren Buddhism in modern language, remains the basic principle for all the activities of Soka Gakkai to the present (see below).

After Toda's death, Daisaku Ikeda (1928–) succeeded him as president in 1960. Though he resigned this post and became honorary president in 1979, under his leadership the movement continued to grow and consolidate its presence both at home and abroad. Before surveying these recent developments, its characteristics in terms of both doctrine and organization may be briefly summarized.

Features of Doctrine and Organization

As we have seen so far, Soka Gakkai was initiated as a reform campaign for school education by Makiguchi, Toda, and their confederates. In the course of further development, however, it came to adopt the teachings of Nichiren, as interpreted by Nichiren Shoshu, as the highest principle of its activities and gradually turned into a distinctively Buddhist movement. This religious aspect was conspicuous particularly during and after the period of rapid expansion in the postwar years. Nevertheless, it has retained something of its original concern and shows an intellectual–ideological trait when compared with other new religions. In other words, it has the peculiarly dual character of both a religious and an ideological movement.

Such a statement, of course, arouses the complicated question of where to draw the demarcation line between religion and other spheres of life. At this juncture suffice it to say that, at least in Japan, the borderline fluctuates and that, especially since the early modern age, there has been a series of teachings of similar nature.[16] But whereas these systems of thought, which combined practical guidelines for life with an implicit world view, usually remained within relatively small circles, Soka Gakkai was able to grow into a mass movement. This remarkable difference may be explained with reference to the contents and form of the message each group intended to convey. That is, in order to become popular, a teaching must not only meet the needs of the people, it must also be

[16] In Japan, since early modern times, several teachings appeared besides the established Buddhist schools that tried to show practical guidelines of life incorporating the ideas of Confucianism, native beliefs, and Buddhism. The Singaku movement of Baigan Ishida (1685–1744), discussed in detail by Robert N. Bellah in his *Tokugawa Religion* (Glencoe, Ill.: Free Press, 1957), was a typical example. A careful examination reveals that such religio-ethical teachings have played an important role in shaping the religious situation in modern Japan, and this may be an intriguing topic for further investigation.

stated in a widely accessible style. In the case of Soka Gakkai, this can be demonstrated by comparing the discourses of Makiguchi, who led the movement during its initial stage, and Toda, who led the postwar stage, when growth was most rapid.

During most of his career, Makiguchi incessantly sought a supreme principle to render his life meaningful. For him as a modern man, such a principle could not be offered by an external authority, but had to be appropriated according to the standard of reason. Thus, he avoided becoming a member of traditional religious groups. His "theory of value," expounded in the second volume of *Soka Kyoikugaku taikei* (1931), stipulates that values, like scientific truth, should first and foremost rest on reason and evidence. Second, values should have the form of "law" instead of "person." And third, religious value should also comprehend morality and science.[17] Applying these criteria, Makiguchi concluded that the teachings of Nichiren, especially the Nichiren Shoshu version to which he happened to have been introduced, represented the ultimate truth. Such criteria, he often pointed out, were exactly what Nichiren himself had recommended in the three evidences of true religion: reason, empirical facts, and sacred scriptures. To this, Makiguchi added that these criteria of truth were completely in accordance with the spirit of modern science.

Makiguchi's interpretation of Buddhism, with its emphasis on compatibility with modern science, is at least partly in line with the views of Enryo Inoue (1858–1939), who developed a rationalistic apology of Buddhism against Christianity. Possible relationships between the two thinkers and other related issues must be reserved for further exploration. More importantly to the present discussion, it is clear that Makiguchi's exposition was too intricate to be readily accepted by people on the street. Toda's "philosophy of life," by contrast, which he outlined at the beginning of *Shakubuku kyoten*, was more intuitive in nature and could serve as a basis for mass indoctrination. Indeed, "Life" (*seimei*), or "Great Life,"

---

[17] Makiguchi, *Makiguchi Tsunesaburo zenshu*, v (1982), 359–60; Miyata, *Makiguchi Tsunesaburo*, 74–6, 119–20.

remains one of the key terms that often recur in the publications and statements of Soka Gakkai to this day.

Toda had many things in common with his mentor, and this was also the case with his conversion to Nichiren Shoshu. However, his harsh experiences in prison seem to have modified his understanding of Nichiren Buddhism in a subtle way. During his incarceration he set about enquiring carefully into Nichiren's writings and sutras. This led him to the realization that the Eternal Buddha of the Lotus Sutra, so crucial in Nichiren's teachings, was nothing but "Life". According to Toda, this means "the fundamental power of the Universe," and the Universe itself is Life, even before living creatures appear in it. He thus advanced a panvitalistic vision that equated Buddha, Universe, and Life as being mutually identical. Furthermore, this vision, far from being a mere metaphysical speculation, had a practical implication. He insisted that this fundamental power, Life, could give people happiness, and it was the duty of human beings to appropriate and transfer it to others. Happiness was nothing other than a harmonious relation between us and the Buddha-life, and it could be achieved by sincerely believing in the Three Great Mysteries as formulated by Nichiren and by the chanting of *daimoku*.[18]

Though Toda put forward these ideas in close connection with the traditional doctrine of Nichiren Buddhism, it was stated in a somewhat different language. For instance, the key term Life, or some equivalent, did not occur in dogmatic literature. Makiguchi certainly mentioned it a few times in his "theory of value," and suggested its relevance for human happiness, but did not necessarily accord it a central position as his successor did. In short, Toda seems to have added something of his own to the traditional teachings and to the system of his mentor.[19]

[18] About Toda's "philosophy of life" an illuminating analysis may be found in Susumu Shimazono, "Shinshukyo to gensekyusai shiso" ("New Religions and the Idea of This-Worldly Salvation"), in Jikido Takasaki and Kiyotaka Kimura (eds.), *Nihon bukkyo ron* ("Essays on Japanese Buddhism") (Tokyo: Shunjyusha, 1995).

[19] In this context, the recent attempt by several scholars interpreting the "vitalistic world view" current among the Japanese populace from earlier times

Having discussed a few issues related to the basic doctrine of Soka Gakkai, I turn next to its organizational features. Its development into a mass organization was doubtlessly prepared for by the structural changes of society in postwar Japan. Not only were the many restraints of government legislation removed, a considerable part of the population became dislocated by the accelerated process of industrialization and urbanization—fertile soil for new religious movements. Taking account of these circumstances and Soka Gakkai's relationship to other domestic bodies, the sociologist Tsutomu Shiobara distinguished four major stages in the structural development of Soka Gakkai: (1) an initial stage of ideological movement in a small circle led by Makiguchi, (2) the stage of a militant socioreligious movement, mainly under Toda's leadership, (3) the stage of a religiopolitical campaign aimed at the realization of *obutumyogo* by means of a dual organization, and (4) the stage of institutionalized movement trying to adapt to the social milieu.[20]

The doctrine of *obutumyogo* was formulated by Toda, incorporating a central motif in Nichiren's teachings. To implement this, Soka Gakkai began, in the second half of the 1950s, actively to engage in election campaigns, first on the local and later on the national level. In 1961 Komei Seiji Renmei (the League for Clean Government) was established as a political tool. It was succeeded by Komeito (the Clean Government Party) in 1964. In 1967 Komeito started to send members to the House of Representatives, and by the 1970s it had become the third largest party. As it is the first political party in Japan with a definitely religious background, it surely deserves special attention. However, it is equally obvious that the proposal to establish a national *kaidan* was not only contrary to the modern principle of the separation of

as a background of many new religious movements deserves special attention. See Michihito Tsushima, Shigeru Nishiyama, Susumu Shimazono, and Hiroko Shiramizu, "The Vitalistic Conception of Salvation in Japanese New Religions," *Japanese Journal of Religious Studies*, 6/1–2 (1979), 139–61.

[20] Tsutomu Shiobara, *Soshikiundo no riron* ("A Theory of Organized Movement") (Tokyo: Shin'yosha, 1976), 400.

state and religion, it was also incompatible with the Japanese tradition of religious pluralism. These and other considerations probably led the third Soka Gakkai president, Ikeda, to declare "the separation of Soka Gakkai and Komeito" and the withdrawal of the plan for a national *kaidan* in 1970. This was clearly a turning point in its development and marked the beginning of the abovementioned stage 4.

A new religious movement must face, sooner or later, the problem of how to shape its relationship to the surrounding world, and Soka Gakkai was no exception to this rule. However, there was another structural factor that can rarely be found in parallel cases—that is, its connection with the clerical order of Nichiren Shoshu. Like other groups that derived from Nichiren Buddhism, such as Reiyukai and Rissho Koseikai, Soka Gakkai has been and remains a fundamentally lay organization. But while the others developed almost independently of traditional Buddhist schools, Soka Gakkai defined itself as a *ko* (adherents' organization) of Nichiren Shoshu from the very beginning. More concretely, it often—if not always—received instructions concerning important matters of belief and practice from professional clergy. Since the *Gohonzon* was in the possession of Taiseki-ji, this could not be otherwise. Indeed, this headquarters of Nichiren Shoshu came to assume the character of a sacred place for the members of Soka Gakkai, and mass pilgrimages to this center were eagerly recommended and conducted as a major activity of the organization.

In brief, Soka Gakkai was dependent on the traditional school, which possessed the central symbol of faith. However, Nichiren Shoshu also depended on Soka Gakkai in several respects, especially as regards its finance. As the members of Soka Gakkai became adherents of the traditional school and willingly contributed the means to build new temples, the small school, which had consisted of only a few dozen temples, grew to nearly ten times its original size by 1990, and the living standards of professional priests improved notably. In this way there emerged a complementary system wherein the traditional order legitimized the new movement and the new movement supported the traditional order from without. As can be easily understood, the functioning of this remarkable system rested on a subtle, and somewhat unstable, balance between the two parties. Seen in this light, the schism of 1990–1 was an unavoidable result of the dilemma built into their mutual relationship. Although it was surely a severe trial for both, it was unavoidable because, as stated above, Soka Gakkai leaders have been trying to reinterpret the teachings of Nichiren in a way to render them more relevant to the modern situation.[21]

The Latest Trends

Soka Gakkai exhibits an undiminished dynamism in its activities even after the critical event of the schism. The years of Ikeda's presidency were a period of continued growth and active commitment to Japanese politics as a means to implement its religious program.

It is noteworthy that almost simultaneously with this change of course, a new development was initiated—its overseas mission. Soka Gakkai, until then an exclusively domestic body, established a branch in the United States in 1960 and expanded its mission to various other parts of the world. Soka Gakkai International was formed in 1975. At the same time, Soka Gakkai began to put more emphasis on social–cultural activities. For example, in 1971 Soka University was opened, and in 1974 the peace campaign started with the publication of antiwar memoirs. At present, "peace," "culture," "human revolution," and "renaissance" are among the key words that, together with "faith," occur most frequently in newspapers and magazines circulated among its members.

More than sixty years ago Soka Gakkai was inaugurated as a reform movement of education—and, by implication, of living—by a small circle of intellectuals. In the course of its development it adopted the teachings of Nichiren and, especially in the severe

---

[21] Bryan Wilson and Karel Dobbelaere, *A Time to Chant: The Soka Gakkai Buddhists in Britain* (Oxford: Clarendon Press, 1994), app. A: "The 1990–1991 Schism of Nichiren Shoshu and Soka Gakkai." See Daniel A. Metraux, "The Dispute between the Soka Gakkai and the Nichiren Shoshu Priesthood: A Lay Revolution against a Conservative Clergy," *Japanese Journal of Religious Studies*, 19/4 (1992), 325–36.

social circumstances of war and the ensuing years, became an emphatically religious movement. Today, Soka Gakkai is trying to extend its activities in society and culture to achieve a unique combination of Buddhism and modern mentality. Whether this proves fruitful and whither the whole endeavor will lead, certainly, can only be answered by events in the coming decades.

2

The Legacy of Tsunesaburo Makiguchi: Value-Creating Education and Global Citizenship

Dayle Bethel

IT has been my privilege and joy, during the past twenty-five years, to talk and lecture about "value-creating education" both in Japan and the United States. The discussion periods that followed the lectures and seminars were, for me, particularly stimulating and challenging. At the same time I often left those encounters with a feeling of unease and dissatisfaction. For a long time I could not put my finger on the cause of this uneasiness. Then one day a few years ago, after a particularly intense and far-ranging seminar, the problem suddenly dawned on me.

The problem was one of divergent images and perceptions. Some members of the audience—and these tended to be the most eager to engage in dialogue and ask questions—seemed to perceive value-creating education as a specific, clearly defined body of knowledge. They perceived value-creating education as a kind of magic formula, which had issued forth from the mind of Tsunesaburo Makiguchi. It was something already completed and finished. Understood and applied correctly, Makiguchi's formula would resolve all our educational and social problems. In my role as an "expert" in the field of education and of Makiguchi's life and thought, it was expected that I would confirm and strengthen this magical image of Makiguchi's work. This was my dilemma. I could not, in all honesty, support this perception of Makiguchi and his life. Moreover, I began to realize that some of my own writings had undoubtedly served to strengthen this understanding of Makiguchi's legacy.

Value-creating education is not a magic formula for the "correct" conduct of human learning and human life. Makiguchi himself would have objected to such an interpretation of his work. Time and again he made it clear in his writings that his ideas and proposals should not be interpreted as pronouncements of absolutes. In fact, he repeatedly warned of the dangers of absolutist thinking and of "one-track beliefs and attachments."

Makiguchi would be more accurately perceived as one of a company of dissident scholars who understood and deplored many of the educational practices that evolved in industrial societies following the Industrial Revolution in Europe, and proposed more organic and holistic approaches to the learning process. Some— such as Kunio Yanagida, Kumazo Tsuboi, Shigetaka Shiga, Inazo Nitobe, Lester Ward, and John Dewey—were Makiguchi's contemporaries; others—Rousseau, Pestalozzi, Herbart, and Froebel—were long since dead and known to him only in books.[1]

This, I am confident, is how Makiguchi would wish to be remembered and honoured: as a contributing member of a company of educational reformers whose members span many generations, including our own. Value-creating pedagogy constituted Makiguchi's attempt to express his insights into the nature of human learning and growth, and to summarize those of fellow dissidents.

We, in our time, are the beneficiaries of these dissident forebears, who sought to provide nourishing, humane ways of

[1] Various names have been used to express the insights and philosophical principles of this tradition: humanistic education, natural education, progressive education (in its original meaning), education for life, to name a few. Makiguchi chose to express these insights and principles in terms of value creation and his value-creating pedagogy represents a major contribution to that tradition. Today's dissident educators speak of holistic education and student-centered education when referring to these educational ideas and principles. In keeping with current usage, I will hereafter use the term "holistic education" when referring to the ideas and proposals within this tradition, including those of Makiguchi.

teaching young people. But there is an important difference between their situation and ours. Each of these earlier holistic educators, including Makiguchi himself, tended to be lone voices of dissent within their culture at the time. Dominant, often hostile, interests within their respective cultures easily marginalized them. Alternately, contemporary dissidents are a part of an emerging global movement of holistically oriented people—parents and lay people as well as educators—who are beginning to redefine not only education but all of our social institutions.

In order to understand and appreciate value-creating pedagogy, we must recognize the manner in which these dissident educational thinkers built upon the insights of those who had gone before. It is equally important to recognize the cross-fertilization of ideas that occurred among contemporary members of this company of dissident educators. Makiguchi repeatedly acknowledged his indebtedness to Yanagida, Shiga, Dewey, Ward, and other contemporaries. In like manner, the keen insights being expressed by today's dissident educational thinkers and critics are possible because of the rich heritage left to us by Makiguchi, Dewey, Pestalozzi, and many others.

Two factors have contributed to a new situation today. One, just noted, is the rich heritage of those earlier dissidents. The other is the crisis of moral decay in contemporary industrial societies created by the excesses and flaws built into those societies. Background understanding in both areas is prerequisite to assessing the significance of value-creating pedagogy for the twenty-first century.

Societal Realities

Westerners, particularly Americans, have grown up with a culture that posits change as not only normal, but also progressive. A steady stream of technological innovations, from computers to advances in biomedicine, suggests that this aspect of the American belief system is still intact. And what is true of Americans is also true of the Japanese. In fact, it is precisely this aspect of American culture—an unshakable faith in change as benign and progressive—that has been most closely embraced by Japanese people.

Both Japanese and Americans have failed to realize for the past hundred years, however, that this faith in progressive change applied only to technology and material culture. Changes in other areas of life have been perceived as threatening and, thus, held at bay. Social and psychological changes, so essential to the well-being and survival of the earth and its inhabitants, have been effectively stifled. This situation has led, first, to the misuse of the democratic decisionmaking process, which was supposed to have enabled human societies to govern themselves intelligently and effectively. Second, it has resulted in a massive buildup of unsolved social–psychological–ecological problems that now threaten human survival itself. One holistic educator, James Moffett, observed: "The many interlocking problems of this nation [the United States] and this world are escalating so rapidly that only swift changes in thought and action can save either."[2]

Moffett suggests that the generation about to enter schools during the final decade of the twentieth century may be the last generation that can still reverse the negative megatrends, which are now converging. But, for these children to learn the new ways of thinking that are needed, the present generation in charge of human societies must set up a kind of education that this generation never had. It must, in other words, arrange to reeducate itself at the same time. This is the challenge we face at the end of the century. The insights, understandings, and proposals of Makiguchi and other dissident educators are valuable resources for meeting that challenge.

The Dissident Tradition

For my present understanding of the dissident tradition, I am indebted to the work of many contemporary educators. Among these, within my own culture, the writings of Ron Miller, David

---

[2] James Moffett, *The Universal Schoolhouse* (San Francisco: Jossey-Bass, 1994), p. xii.

Norton, James Moffett, and Ivan Illich have been particularly helpful. In Japan, I have found the work of such contemporary educators as Yoshio Kuryu, Ikue Tezuka, Atsuhiko Yoshida, and Yoshiharu Nakagawa helpful and inspiring. An analysis of the integrative studies of these modern scholars, in conjunction with the writings of earlier dissident thinkers, suggests that there are basic principles of human learning that can be expressed in the following terms:

1. Education must nurture a sense of wonder, awe, and appreciation for life within each learner through interaction with the natural and social worlds.
2. Education should enable discovery of self.
3. It must support learners in the actualization of innate potential—the source of a sense of purpose and personal destiny.
4. Education involves a natural, organic relationship between generations.
5. It is rooted in a sense of place, and a spiritually nourishing traditional wisdom.
6. Education should nurture an appreciation of and love for work.
7. It places responsibility on the learner to choose the what, where, and when of learning. And,
8. It takes place in the context of a local community, whose resources provide the curriculum for learning and whose members actively participate in the learning process.

These ideas and approaches to learning constitute the core of the dissident educational tradition, from which Makiguchi freely partook and to which he made an important contribution.

Beyond a shared understanding of basic principles of human learning, two other factors have united dissident scholars since the beginnings of the Industrial Revolution. One is a realization that the factory model of compulsory schooling created by industrial capitalism and economic nationalism leads inevitably to cultural, intellectual, and spiritual damage. The other is a sense of urgency in searching for and implementing more holistic, democratic, and humane approaches to children's learning. Makiguchi, as he came to realize what was happening in his own culture, became obsessed with these two overriding concerns. And these concerns served as the driving force in the formulation of value-creating pedagogy.

Makiguchi's Legacy for the Twenty-first Century

Among the many valuable insights contained in Makiguchi's major writings, three seem especially important as start a new century. Each of these goes to the heart of contemporary humanity's deepest problems and deepest needs.

The Need for Human Bonding with the Natural World

During the last half of the twentieth century the single-minded pursuit of profit by the world's industrial elite, led by the United States and Japan, brought the planet, on which all life on earth depends, to desperate straits. The seriousness of the resulting ecological devastation prompted 102 Nobel laureates in science and 1,600 other scientists from seventy countries to sign the "World Scientists' Warning to Humanity" in 1992. That document reads in part:

Human beings and the natural world are on a collision course . . . If not checked, many of our current practices put at serious risk the future that we wish for human society and . . . may so alter the living world that it will be unable to sustain life in the manner that we know. Fundamental changes are urgent if we are to avoid the collision our present course will bring about.

We the undersigned, senior members of the world's scientific community, hereby warn all humanity of what lies ahead. A great change in our stewardship of the earth and the life on it is required, if vast human misery is to be avoided and our global home on this planet is not to be irretrievably mutilated.[3]

---

[3] David Orr, "So that All the Other Struggles May Go On," in *Wild Duck Review*, 4/2 (1998), 3.

Just one hundred years earlier Makiguchi had foreseen the ultimate ecological possibility toward which his country's headlong rush to embrace American style industrialism would lead—the possibility that is now ecological reality.

That vision of an ecologically devastated Japan galvanized Makiguchi to undertake his first major work, *Jinsei chirigaku* ("A Geography of Human Life"),[4] written during the final decade of the nineteenth century and published in 1903.[5] But *Jinsei chirigaku* was motivated by more than fear of ecological devastation. Fundamentally, it was a celebration of the natural world; an expression of love, appreciation, and responsibility for the earth. The earth, for Makiguchi, was a miracle. Life was a miracle, and he saw life vibrating and pulsating through all phenomena. And early in his professional career Makiguchi called his fellows, particularly young people, to an awareness and appreciation of the earth and the life pulsating through it.

In *Jinsei chirigaku* we are confronted with what to Makiguchi was the ultimate question: "How, then, can we observe our sur-

---

[4] Translations of *Jinsei chirigaku* contained in this chapter are from a translation of the work into English undertaken by a team of translators working under my direction as editor during the years 1992 to 1995 (*A Geography of Human Life*, forthcoming). The members of the team were: Katsusuke Hori, Satomi Nishida, Yukiko Summerville, and Mariko Takano.

[5] The first edition of *Jinsei chirigaku*, consisting of approximately 1,100 pages, was revised by Makiguchi several times and went through numerous printings in the ensuing years. The book was approved by the ministry of education and during the early decades of the century was widely used as a text in Japanese schools for teachers seeking certification to teach geography. By mid-century, however, it had fallen into disuse and was little known in Japan during the post-World War II era. Between the years 1971 and 1980 a revision of the 5th (1905) edition of the book was published by Seikyo Press, in Tokyo, in five volumes with a total of 1,392 pages. The Seikyo Press revision sought to make the book more accessible and readable by adding commentary and explanations, further information on scholars and sources cited by Makiguchi, and phonetic symbols to aid in the reading of difficult Chinese characters. Some changes in the numbering of chapters were also included in this revision. Quotations from *Jinsei chirigaku* are from the Seikyo Press edition. In the course of the work of translation and editing, the editorial staff used as the basis for the English edition both Seikyo Press's revised edition and a reprint of a 1908 edition published by Daisan Bunmei Publishing Company, Tokyo, in 1976.

roundings? How can we make contact with the earth? We are born of the earth; we are inspired by the earth; we die on the earth; the earth is our home."[6] We should, he wrote, think of ourselves in community with the environment:

[We should] regard people, animals, trees, rivers, rocks, or stones in the same light as ourselves and realize that we have much in common with them all. Such interaction causes us to feel, if not consciously think, "if I were in their (or its) place, what would I feel . . . or do?" Sympathetic interactions occur, therefore, when you regard or feel another person or object that you are in contact with as a part of yourself or as one of your kind. You share experience with that person or object and are able to place yourself in the position of that person or object.[7]

Perhaps more than anything else, it was this reverence for nature, this sense of wonder and appreciation for life, this sense of being intimately connected with our natural environments, that Makiguchi longed to communicate to his students and fellow beings. The development of such awareness and appreciation was, he believed, of crucial importance both for nature's sake and for the development of people of moral character.

Makiguchi tells us in the foreword of the book that the desire and compulsion to share these insights with his fellows became so strong that "they occupied my whole being. I could not think of

---

[6] Makiguchi, *Jinsei chirigaku*, i (Tokyo: Seikyo Press, 1971), 45.

[7] Ibid. 55–6. It is instructive to compare the view of nature held by Makiguchi with that of Western peoples prior to the Scientific Revolution. Note, for example, the following observation by Morris Berman in *The Reenchantment of the World* (Ithaca, NY: Cornell University Press, 1981), 16: "The view of nature that predominated in the West down to the eve of the Scientific Revolution was that of an enchanted world. Rocks, trees, rivers, and clouds were all seen as wondrous, alive, and human beings felt at home in this environment. The cosmos, in short, was a place of *belonging*. A member of this cosmos was not an alienated observer of it but a direct participant in its life. His personal destiny was bound up with its destiny, and this relationship gave meaning to his life." According to Berman, this intimate view of nature and of the cosmos as a place of belonging were sacrificed as Western peoples came under the domination of the modern ethics and the exploitative view of nature spawned by the Scientific Revolution of the 16th and 17th centuries.

anything else. I could not even work to make a living."[8] In response to this inner compulsion and in order to free himself from it, he jotted down notes over a period of ten years. The notes included ideas, insights, observations, and his personal feelings about the natural world and the relationship of human beings to it. An edited collection of these notes came together under the title, *Jinsei chirigaku.*

As the passages above suggest, Makiguchi was convinced that the development of a sense of interdependence and interrelatedness with the natural world, of which he perceived humans a part, is central to being human. Not only is this holistic orientation the most pervasive theme of *Jinsei chirigaku*, it became the central theme of Makiguchi's life. Consider the following, for example:

being aware of the rich variety of phenomena that influence my life, I cannot help thinking of the way the whole earth operates. I look around and, although my eyes can reach only a few kilometres in any direction, my heart and mind is filled with excitement and wonder and curiosity about the earth and about the relationship between the earth and our lives on the earth. I begin to realize that if we would seek deeper understanding of this relationship, we must prepare ourselves to make observations and inquiries into several different aspects of the planet, such as its topography, dimensions, movements, and structure.[9]

Such was Makiguchi's invitation to young people in particular, and to all his contemporaries in general, to join him in a journey to

[8] We may better understand the depth of Makiguchi's conviction and his obsession with the need to share his ideas by noting Berman's conclusions as to the significance of modern Western culture's world view (ibid. 17): "The logical end point of this worldview is a feeling of total reification: everything is an object, alien, not-me; and I am ultimately an object too, an alienated 'thing' in a world of other, equally meaningless things. This world is not of my own making; the cosmos cares nothing for me, and I do not really feel a sense of belonging to it. What I feel, in fact, is a sickness in the soul." Translated into everyday life, what does this disenchantment mean? It means that the modern landscape has become a scenario of "mass administration and blatant violence." Jobs are stupefying, relationships vapid and transient, the arena of politics absurd. In the collapse of traditional values we have hysterical evangelical revivals, mass conversions to the church of the Revd Moon, and a general retreat into oblivion provided by drugs, television, and tranquilizers.

[9] Makiguchi, *Jinsei chirigaku,* i. 86.

explore the wonders of the earth and life born of the earth. *Jinsei chirigaku* is something like a "ship's log" or diary of that journey. But it was also intended as a handbook or travel guide for others who are motivated to take the journey themselves.

In Makiguchi's thought, to live as a human being meant to love, understand, and appreciate the earth. A central tenet of his writings and his life was that through our spiritual interaction with the earth the characteristics we think of as truly human are ignited and nurtured within us.

The Need for Community

The writings of Tsunesaburo Makiguchi remain meaningful today because Makiguchi dealt with the central realities of human existence. They are especially meaningful at the present time because one of the realities that was central for him has been lost to contemporary life. I refer to his preoccupation with human-scale, self-reliant, local communities. The human individual can experience the full development of her humanness and her potential only in intimate, nurturing, caring, reciprocal relationships with other humans in community—especially in the early stages of life but in some degree at all stages. In Makiguchi's words:

it is our nature as human beings to form societies. No one can live totally alone. It is through association in society that we can provide not only for our basic needs and security, but for everything that makes our lives fulfilling and rewarding. This realization leads to the universalization of sympathetic feelings that were initially toward a specific individual or object. Growing awareness of our indebtedness to our society gives rise to feelings of appreciation and a sense of social responsibility within us. Beginning in our very personal relationships . . . our sympathetic concern and appreciation expands to include the larger society and, ultimately, the whole world.[10]

The indivisible interconnection between nurture in a caring, intimate geographic community and the development of fully alive,

---

[10] Ibid. 56.

socially and morally responsible, self-actualizing (value-creating) individuals is a common theme running through all of Makiguchi's major writings, from *Jinsei chirigaku* at the turn of the century, through *Kyodoka* ("Community Study") in 1913, to *Soka kyoiku-gaku taikei* ("A Theory of Value-Creating Pedagogy") in the early 1930s.

There are some matters that must be clarified in order to understand what Makiguchi meant by community. First, we must recognize the importance of "rootedness" in human growth—both of individuals and of societies. Rootedness involves a special relationship between a person and a place—a sense of appreciation for the land in which one is rooted and feelings of responsibility toward it. Interaction with one's natural environment in the context of human-scale communities is, according to Makiguchi's thought, the source of integrity in human beings:

I arrived at a conviction that the natural beginning point of understanding the world we live in and our relationship to it is that community of persons, land, and culture, which gave us birth; that community, in fact, which gave us our very lives and started us on the path toward becoming the persons we are. In other words, that community which has given us our rootedness as human beings. The importance of this rootedness and personal identity given us by our native cultural community, our homeland, can scarcely be overemphasized.[11]

Our loss of community in modern life and the rarity of integrity as a personal characteristic in modern society stem from our loss of love and respect for the land. As Aldo Leopold observed half a century after Makiguchi wrote *Jinsei chirigaku*:

We abuse land because we regard it as a commodity belonging to us. When we see land as a community to which we belong, we may begin to use it with love and respect. There is no other way for land to survive the impact of mechanized man, nor for us to reap from it the aesthetic harvest it is capable, under science, of contributing to culture.[12]

[11] Makiguchi, *Jinsei chirigaku*, 29–30.
[12] Aldo Leopold, *A Sand County Almanac* (New York: Oxford University Press, 1964), p. ix.

We are belatedly, as the twenty-first century dawns, realizing how much we have lost by our modern tendency to perceive the natural environment as just another "thing" to be possessed and exploited.

As previously noted, the need in every person's life for intimate ties with the land is a major theme underlying *Jinsei chirigaku*. Makiguchi was driven by his insights into this reality of human existence. He sensed that the social, economic, and political conditions developing in the Japan of his day threatened the existence of community and the natural world. He feared for his society and its people, especially its children, if Japan were to lose the intimate, interdependent connections between people, their communities, and the land.

This conviction of the indispensability of community and rootedness in human experience is shared by a growing number of people today. David Orr, a contemporary educator, points to the difference between an *inhabitant* and a *resident* to emphasize the significance of rootedness in human life.[13] An inhabitant, Orr writes, is rooted in a place, in a community, whereas a resident is a rootless occupant. An inhabitant and a particular habitat cannot be separated without doing violence to both. The global environmental crisis, Orr believes, and Makiguchi feared, has been created by the virtual disappearance of inhabitants rooted in communities, while contemporary society mass produces residents to take their place. This is because the inhabitant and a place mutually shape each other. The resident, on the other hand, "shaped by forces beyond himself, becomes that moral non-entity we know as a 'consumer', supplied by invisible resource networks which damage his and others' places."

John Gatto, winner of New York City's Teacher of the Year Award in 1991, expresses similar convictions. "One thing I know," he wrote, "is that eventually you have to come to be a part of a place, part of its hills and streets and waters and people—or you will live a very, very sorry life as an exile forever." And of communities, he writes, "an important difference between communities

[13] Ron Miller (ed.), *New Directions in Education* (Brandon, Vt.: Holistic Education Press, 1991), 91.

and institutions is that communities have natural limits, they stop growing or they die."[14]

The loss of community and the experience of rootedness in a particular habitat has had far-reaching consequences for human beings and their societies. The recovery of community is central to any hope for a peaceful world order. As M. Scott Peck begins one of his books: "In and through community lies the salvation of the world."[15] This is what Makiguchi was saying one hundred years ago.

But it is one thing to recognize that our way back to psychological and social health is through community. It is quite another thing to understand how this can be accomplished. Our present society and its institutions have become unimaginably complex and interdependent. Thus, if we want to back away from the abyss that looms before us and create an alternative, more humane world, we must realize that there are no quick or easy answers; there will be no "quick fixes." A better and healthier world, if we succeed in creating it, will come into being only through honest efforts to rethink our central values and a deep commitment to the task of creating new communities and new social structures.

In order to recover community, and the personal and social health that can come only through community, it is essential to gain some understanding of the reasons that community was lost to modern life in the first place. What led to the breakdown of community and the estrangement from nature that is part of that breakdown? Increasingly researchers, social analysts, and scientists of every type are coming to agreement in this regard. They are concluding that primary factors in the breakdown and disappearance of community in modern life are the two institutions that we have long considered to be the chief underpinnings of the good life— mass compulsory schools and free trade in international markets.

It is not possible here to consider fully the implications of this assertion, but let me note, first, Makiguchi's observation on the

[14] John Gatto, *Skole*, 9/2 (1992), p. i.
[15] M. Scott Peck, *The Different Drum: Community Making and Peace* (New York: Simon & Schuster, 1987).

development of modern schools. In *Soka kyoikugaku taikei*[16] he wrote:

In the days before there were schools, the prevailing method of guiding young people to the proper roles in the general scheme of life was an extended home life, whereby one apprenticed at the family trade through-out one's formative years, with this training supplemented by things learned from the local community. Then came the Meiji period (1868–1912) with its modern education and the spread of schools . . . Everyone was taken by the hand and dragged off to schools, and soon the other two schemes of learning fell into disuse. This was the age of the school reigning unchallenged and omnipotent. Only in recent years have we seen the grave error of our ways and tried to fill in the gap with various kinds of adjunct education and youth groups for extra-curricular activity . . . From this point on, school education must be aware of its own share of the educational role . . . It must co-operate with the other two areas of education, the home and the community, each with its own expertise . . . These three areas of education must link together in an orderly system of mutual complementarity.[17]

As Makiguchi noted, the development of the modern school was the beginning of the breakdown of community life and the creation of societies of "rootless consumers" that we know today.

This process of community disintegration, which began with the creation of modern schools, was extended and accelerated by the rapid spread of the free market system, which even today is considered around the world—particularly in industrially advanced countries—as a sacred cornerstone of democracy and freedom. Chet Bowers has noted that the disintegration of community is a requirement in order for free markets to function successfully:

---

[16] The translation of *Soka kyoikugaku taikei* ("A Theory of Value-Creating Pedagogy") into English, referred to in this chapter, was done by a team consisting of Alfred Birnbaum, translator, and Dayle Bethel, editor. The material thus translated and edited was published under the title *Education for Creative Living: Ideas and Proposals of Tsunesaburo Makiguchi* (Ames: Iowa State University Press, 1989).

[17] Ibid. 181.

There is a statement in Kirkpatrick Sales' recent book, *Rebels against the Future* (1995), that is especially useful in clarifying the shared lineage of a vision of how the world's cultures need to be transformed. The success of the Industrial Revolution, Sales notes, required that all that community implies—self-sufficiency, mutual aid, morality in the market place, stubborn tradition, regulation by custom, organic knowledge instead of mechanistic science—had to be steadily and systematically disrupted and displaced. All of the practices that kept the individual from becoming a consumer had to be done away with so that the cogs of and wheels of an unfettered machine called "the economy" would operate without interference, influenced only by the invisible hands and inevitable balances . . . of the benevolent free market system.[18]

Not all trade is injurious and detrimental. For a clear distinction between beneficial trade and trade that is injurious and community-destroying, we can turn to no other than one of the fathers of modern economic theory, John Maynard Keynes. Notably, those who speak so glowingly of the benefits of free trade never quote Keynes's most important insight: "Ideas, knowledge, art, hospitality, travel—these are things which should of their nature be international. But let goods be homespun whenever it is reasonable and conveniently possible; and, above all, let finance be primarily national."[19] Though advocates of free trade never mention this aspect of Keynes's economic theory, that is not because it is outdated. It is as true today as the day he wrote it. And, it is, as students of Makiguchi's writings will recognize, in harmony with his economic insights. In one of the concluding chapters of *Jinsei chirigaku* Makiguchi noted that a major threat to the well-being and survival of local communities was the runaway growth of cities. One of the most serious problems posed by cities, he contended, is that they lead to the decline of the industry, enterprise, and culture of local communities:

[18] Chet Bowers, "An Open Letter on the Double Binds in Educational Reform," *Wild Duck Review*, 4/2 (1998), 7.

[19] Herman E. Daly, "The Perils of Free Trade," *Scientific American* (Nov. 1993), 50.

There is no greater threat to our societies than this. William Cobbett (1763–1825), an English journalist, likened the city of London and other cities like it to warts because they suck nutrition and strength from the nation, just as warts suck nutrition from a living body.

Clearly, we must face the problem of the runaway growth of cities. We cannot afford to permit the decline of our primary industries. Although their decline could be compensated for by engaging in foreign trade, the loss is permanent while the compensation is unstable and temporary. Furthermore, there is no way to calculate the overall loss. If the health of the nation is jeopardized or the productivity of the land is sacrificed, the entire society will be affected, and recovery will be difficult.[20]

Thus, while acknowledging that cities are essential, and that their contribution to the enrichment of human life and culture is important, Makiguchi contended that we must learn how to control their growth. Cities can be permitted to expand only up to the point at which they become a threat to the society's primary industries. Beyond that point they must not be permitted to grow.

We have not, obviously, controlled the growth of cities. There has been almost no attempt upon the part of modern societies to do so. We have not protected the economic base of local communities. There has been in every part of the world steady erosion of the power and resources of local communities and local institutions as a combined consequence of schools, corporate business activity, and the emergence of a global market. This breakdown of local identity and cohesiveness has, in turn, had a devastating impact on the lives of individuals and families, just as Makiguchi foresaw that it would. If hopes for peace and well-being for the earth and the human race are to be more than glittering generalities, we need to give serious attention to rebuilding and strengthening our communities.

The Need for Character-Nurturing Education

Makiguchi's insights and convictions pertaining to land and community provide the context within which he sought clarity and

---

[20] Makiguchi, *Jinsei chirigaku*, v. (Tokyo: Seikyo Press, 1980), 148–9.

understanding of two related concerns: the development of people of moral character and of social institutions capable of nurturing people of character. He saw that the two must go together. In other words, good institutions can only be created by people of good moral character, but good institutions are a prerequisite for the development of people of character. Thus, he wrestled with the question: What kinds of learning experiences nurture people of moral character and social responsibility? His efforts to answer that question led him to a basic assumption that there is something within every person—an inborn potential—that is unique, unrepeatable, and precious. He was convinced that every person, at birth, possesses potential for greatness and goodness. But it was one of the tragedies of life in his day, he observed, that this inborn potential remained dormant and undeveloped in most people. Most people "see" only on a surface level. They never develop the capacity for direct and intimate communication with natural phenomena. They tend to become a slave to books. Unfortunately, even after reading thousands of books, they remain ignorant of the really important insights and understandings needed to live fully and creatively. Their lives become stunted and their potential greatness lies unchallenged and unrealized.[21]

Makiguchi believed that the schools of his day were among the causes of this deplorable condition. In one passage in *Soka kyoiku-gaku taikei* he describes what he observed happening to children in his society's schools:

The detrimental effects of force-feeding a small child can be easily seen because of the small body's inability to metabolise more than it can digest. The excessive bulk passes through the child's system, an undigested waste. Or worse, it may lodge in the digestive tract, slowly putrefying and poisoning the whole system. Unfortunately, the effects of psychological toxification in children caused by the forced learning of masses of unintelligible information are not immediately visible. Consequently, the detrimental effect of this poisoning process in children's lives is not recognized. The situation is serious, but when we search for the causes of the problem, we are faced with the paradox that teachers and parents alike see them-

[21] Makiguchi, *Jinsei chirigaku*, v. (Tokyo: Seikyo Press, 1980), i. 41.

selves as providing for the future well-being of their children even though they make them miserable in the process.[22]

He believed the schools of his day to be guilty of ignoring and violating the most basic principles of human learning. The aim of education, he maintained,

is not to transfer knowledge; it is to guide the learning process, to put responsibility for study into the students' own hands. It is not the piecemeal merchandising of information; it is the provision of keys that will allow people to unlock the vault of knowledge on their own. It does not consist in pilfering the intellectual property amassed by others through no additional effort of one's own; it would rather place people on their own path of discovery and invention. The words have been resounding in the ears of educators like ourselves since the days of Comenius and Pestalozzi, but they have yet to be put into real practice.

Education consists of finding value within the living environment, thereby discovering physical and psychological principles that govern our lives and eventually applying these new-found principles in real life to create new value. In sum, it is the guided acquisition of skills of observation, comprehension, and application.

Thus, if one possesses the keys to unlock the vault of knowledge, it becomes possible to obtain for oneself all the learning one will ever need in life without having to memorize endless volumes of scholarship. . . There is no reason to overload our lives with mountains of useless and trivial information that we may never need.[23]

Makiguchi was therefore pointing to a fundamental shift that had taken place in both the purpose and the practice of education. Prior to the introduction of mass compulsory schooling the purpose of education was to create meaning or, in Makiguchi's words, to create value. Education was a natural, organic process that occurred in the learner's family and community. However, in Makiguchi's day education had shifted to the mass transfer of knowledge in schoolrooms segregated from the community, without regard to meaning and without regard for the individual personality of the learner.

---

[22] Bethel (ed.), *Education for Creative Living*, 21.   [23] Ibid. 168.

John Dewey, in the United States, writing at roughly the same time, expressed similar concerns:

If one attempts to formulate the philosophy of education implicit in the practices of the new education, we may, I think, discover certain common principles amid the variety of progressive schools now existing. To imposition from above is opposed expression and cultivation of individuality; to external discipline is opposed free activity; to learning from texts and teachers, learning through experience; to acquisition of isolated skills and techniques by drill, is opposed acquisition of them as means of attaining ends which make direct vital appeal; to preparation for a more or less remote future is opposed making the most of the opportunities of present life; to static aims and materials is opposed acquaintance with a changing world.[24]

In India this concern about miseducation and its effect on the growing personalities of children was a deep concern of Mahatma Gandhi. In 1945, shortly after Makiguchi died in a Japanese prison, Gandhi wrote, "Education for life does not mean education for the duration of life, but education for the sake of life . . . education is a matter of teaching the art of living. A man who masters the art of living has become a complete human being."[25] Half a century later, Joseph Chilton Pearce would write in a similar vein:

The first thing I would like to say about any true educational system is that it is not founded on the notion that we are preparing a child for life. The theory we are preparing the child for life, or for the future, is a terrible travesty which betrays every facet of the human being. We don't prepare for life, we equip the child with the means to live fully at whatever stage they are in. The idea we're going to train a child at seven to get a good job at age twenty-seven is a travesty of profound dimension. It makes for a world where every 78 seconds a child is attempting suicide, as is true today. It is this kind of terrible despair we breed in our children when we

[24] John Dewey, *Experience and Education* (New York: Simon & Schuster, 1938), 19–20.
[25] Marjorie Sykes, *The Story of Nai Talim: Fifty Years of Education at Sevagram 1937–1987* (Sevagram: Nai Talim Samiti, 1988), 51.

don't see the difference between preparing and equipping our children to be present to life.[26]

Any person willing to examine the evidence can understand the psychological and spiritual damage experienced by children who undergo the kind of age-grade, segregated schooling that so concerned Makiguchi, Gandhi, Dewey, and Pearce.

Makiguchi believed that the sole aim of education was to enable every person to become a joyful, self-confident, self-directing, self-actualizing, socially conscious member of society. In one instance, he called attention to an admonition of Buddha to "heed the law, not persons." This, Makiguchi suggested, is the greatest guidance that Buddhism has to offer to the advancement of humankind. "Here," he wrote, "we are shown the way up from dependence to true freedom, from living in obedience to charismatic power figures to living in unison with universal order. To blindly follow the will of others is a form of personality worship." In our unthinking worship of and obedience to charismatic power figures, Makiguchi contended, we are "self-sold into bondage."[27]

Especially dangerous, in Makiguchi's view, are those religious leaders who offer exclusive truth to their followers. People who respond to such claims, he warns, have

no chance to rise above a life of person dependence. Just like the lover who has no eyes for anyone but his love, the devotee of a personality cult has not the least inclination to assume an objective scientific stance to calmly compare the various religions, hail the greater similarities, and reject the trivial differences.

Erich Fromm, writing in our own time, supports Makiguchi's insights in this regard when he describes the psychological and spiritual emptiness that leads a person to follow blindly the will of another person or group. He first observes that faith, whether in a religious, political, or personal sense, can have two entirely different meanings, depending on whether it is used in the having mode

---

[26] Joseph Chilton Pearce, "An Interview with Joseph Chilton Pearce," *Wild Duck Review*, 4/2 (1998), 28.

[27] Bethel (ed.), *Education for Creative Living*, 84–5.

or in the being mode. In the being mode, faith is, in essence, an inner orientation, an attitude. It is a healthy, thoughtful, caring approach to every aspect of life. It is life lived lovingly and mindfully. Faith in the having mode is quite the contrary:

[It] consists of formulations created by others, which one accepts because one submits to those others—usually a bureaucracy. It is the entry ticket to join a large group of people. It relieves one of the hard task of thinking for oneself and making decisions. One becomes one of the *beati possidentes*, the happy owners of the right faith. Faith, in the having mode, gives certainty; it claims to pronounce ultimate, unshakable knowledge, which is believable because the power of those who promulgate and protect the faith seems unshakable. Indeed, who would not choose certainty if all it requires is to surrender one's independence?[28]

This kind of person dependence, and the blind, unreasoning behavior it produces, leads inevitably to catastrophe for both people and societies. How, then, can person dependence and rule by people be avoided in human experience? For Makiguchi, the answer to this question was very clear. Every human being, he believed, needs to be awakened to consciousness of an underlying order and a commitment to rule by law rather than by people.[29] In this "awakening to consciousness" Makiguchi saw hope for the future of humankind. And the key to this awakening, he maintained, is education—not the twisted education of his day, which he deplored and cited as one of the causes of widespread person dependence in Japanese society, but holistic education capable of producing creative, aware, responsible members of society. Thus, Makiguchi states,

as we move through the process of acquiring ever more knowledge, the subjective emotional elements give way to more rational considerations. We gain a certain distance from the charismatic figure as our consciousness of an underlying order grows more pronounced. The realization dawns that even that person we had so revered only shortly before is but

[28] Erich Fromm, *To Have or To Be* (New York: Bantam Books, 1976, 1981), 30.
[29] Bethel (ed.), *Education for Creative Living*, 85.

one ordinary human being. At that moment, like a sunrise outshining the stars that appeared to gleam so brightly, the focus of that consciousness driving our very being shifts from persons . . . to the natural order and social laws that work equally for all without favour or discrimination.[30]

Rule by people, Makiguchi believed, leads ultimately and inevitably to divisiveness, egocentric individualism, and strife in human affairs. But, he wrote, "as ordinary people—through creative, learner-centered, holistic educational experiences—gain awareness of their alienation from the power that is rightfully theirs and realize the impotence of a divided, non-collective existence, they will be able to unite to seek release from their former bondage."[31]

Efforts to transform education should be viewed and understood in this context. Our present educational systems were intentionally designed to strengthen and perpetuate rule by people and the elite groups those people form to achieve their aims, even though on the surface they honor and proclaim the merits of rule by law. Our present educational systems serve to produce nonthinking individuals capable of obediently and mindlessly carrying out the desires and wishes of those they recognize as their superiors. Not only Makiguchi, but more recently Alvin Toffler, Yoshio Kuryu, and a host of other scholars and researchers have made this crystal clear and have described how it was accomplished in the early history of the industrially advanced societies, particularly Japan and the United States.[32] Makiguchi's counsel to "heed the law" and the basic principles of physical and spiritual health and well-being is especially relevant at this juncture in the history of human civilization.

To emphasize a central tenet of value-creating education again, direct learning of natural systems in children's immediate, physical community is crucial because growth of moral character, attitudes of appreciation and wonder toward the natural and social systems

[30] Ibid.   [31] Ibid.
[32] See Alvin Toffler, *The Third Wave* (New York: Bantam Books, 1981), 29–30; Dayle Bethel (ed.), *Compulsory Schooling and Human Learning* (San Francisco: Caddo Gap Press, 1994), pp. xi–xv, 79–87.

that sustain life, and a sense of responsibility toward those systems are indispensable for individual happiness and social health. These outcomes can be nurtured in no other way.[33] Makiguchi charged that the indirect, secondhand learning system that had developed in his country was the height of folly. Primarily a product of implantation from Western cultures, that system of education, he charged, confined learners to classrooms and forced them to go through a meaningless routine of "memorizing and forgetting, memorizing, forgetting, and on and on."[34] Furthermore, it severed the learners' ties with the natural systems making up their environment. Makiguchi contended that long continuation of such a superficial system of learning would lead to unhappiness for individuals, serious problems for society, and destruction of the environment.[35] The sense of urgency he felt stemmed from his convictions about the dangers of this form of education, predominant then is his country.

Beyond its implications for education, Makiguchi's work raises intriguing questions about the beginnings and development of contemporary societies. Was the type of industrialism that originated in the West, and that in ensuing years has come to dominate all the cultures of the earth, inevitable? Or could there have developed industrial societies with a different face? There has been a general tendency on the part of the world's people, at least within the industrially advanced countries, to view the rise of industrial

[33] This should be kept in mind while reading Makiguchi's discussion of industrial societies. He writes hopefully and optimistically of the possibilities of an industrial society in which the needs and well-being of all society's members would be provided for. But this could only happen, in Makiguchi's understanding, through the development within the society of leaders of high moral virtue.

[34] Makiguchi, *Jinsei chirigaku*, i. 39.

[35] In this connection, see David Korten's contention that the social and ecological crises we faced at the close of the 20th century could be traced to the long historical processes by which the human species has become increasingly alienated from community and nature. The prevailing "economics of alienation," he writes, must be replaced with an "economics of community." (*In Context* (Fall 1993), 19–20). See also Alfred North Whitehead's observation that "first-hand knowledge is the ultimate basis of intellectual life" in *The Aims of Education and Other Essays* (New York: MacMillan, 1967), 51.

societies as an inevitable outcome of impersonal social, economic, technological, and political forces. Christopher Evans has written, for example, that "once the process of the Revolution was fully under way, its dynamic growth was remorseless, and no power, no man or combination of men, could set it back against its course."[36] Makiguchi's works suggest the possibility, however, that industrialism in Japan could have taken other forms and developed in other directions.

Makiguchi's writings suggest that he attempted to respond to realities in Japan as he saw them. Although he admired and approved many aspects of Western industrial culture, he counseled against wholesale adoption of the Western model and offered to his countrymen a vision of a uniquely Japanese industrial society that would draw on the strengths and assets of Japan's geographical situation and cultural heritage. Morris Berman's contrast between enchanted and disenchanted worlds is relevant here. Makiguchi probably did not foresee the full extent of our modern dilemma or comprehend the potential for moral and spiritual bankruptcy to which our Western, scientistic industrialism has led. I believe, however, that he sensed its dangers intuitively, and committed himself to work for the development of an industrial society that would not sacrifice the "enchanted world" he loved.[37]

How different the world might be today if the Japanese had, in fact, developed a brand of industrial society based on Makiguchi's perception of the environment and of education, and if that Japanese model had spread over the earth instead of the American-fashioned Western model! As we look back over the history of the twentieth century from our vantage point in the next century, we recognize and accept the fact that the people of Japan during the century's early decades rejected Makiguchi's vision. As Americans had, during the early years in the development of their industrial system in the United States, rejected alternative models of industrial development that were available to them, the Japanese

[36] Christopher Evans, *The Micro Millennium* (New York: Washington Square Press, 1979), p. ix.
[37] See Berman, *The Reenchantment of the World*, particularly pp. 23 and 46.

rejected the alternative proposed by Makiguchi.[38] Japanese society followed the American model of industrialism with only slight variation, based as it was on unrestricted exploitation of the natural environment and less technologically advanced human populations. We are now forced to recognize the many negative consequences of the choices made during the formative stages of these two industrial giants.[39]

This recognition, and the clearer historical understanding it fosters, can also bring to our awareness the realization that we, too, are living in the formative stages of a new cultural epoch. People who seek now to lay the ground work for a better and more humane twenty-first century—in education, in business, in all of society's social institutions—will find in Makiguchi's writings insights worthy of consideration and a wealth of ideas and practical methods to aid them in their efforts.

[38] See Ron Miller, *What are Schools For?* (Brandon, Vt.: Holistic Education Press, 1990), 24; Douglas D. Noble, "The Regime of Technology in Education," *Holistic Education Review*, 6/2 (1993), 4–13.

[39] With regard to the Japanese case, see Koji Nakano, *Seihin no shiso* ("The Concept of Honest Poverty") (Tokyo: Soshisha, 1992).

3

A Buddhist Reformation in the Twentieth Century: Causes and Implications of the Conflict between the Soka Gakkai and the Nichiren Shoshu Priesthood

Jane Hurst

T HE essential Buddhist practice taught by Nichiren Daishonin (1222–82) is chanting the Hoben and Juryo chapters of the Lotus Sutra and its title (*Nam-myoho-renge-kyo*) to the Supreme Object of Worship, the *Gohonzon*, a sacred scroll inscribed with prayers and sections of the sutra. When the Soka Gakkai brought this practice to the United States in 1960, it brought with it copies of a small book, *The Liturgy of Nichiren Shoshu*, called the *gongyo* book by members. In it were the Japanese characters with a phonetic translation into the Roman alphabet so that American converts could chant without learning Japanese first. The Order of Recitation included silent prayers of gratitude to the *shoten zenjin* (the guardians of Buddhism), the Three Great Secret Laws (including the *Dai-Gohonzon*, *daimoku*, and the high sanctuary of true Buddhism), and for Nichiren Daishonin and the successive high priests. Prayers were then to be offered for the attainment of *kosen-rufu* (the spread of Buddhism throughout the world) and for the deceased. The textured cover of the *gongyo* book became a testimony to the member's faith. The more worn it became, the more the member had been chanting. A member would treasure the *gongyo* book, carrying it constantly as a reminder of the Buddhist practice that was transforming his or her life.

The exact content of the silent prayers changed with the fluctuating relationship between the Nichiren Shoshu priesthood and the Soka Gakkai organization responsible for the worldwide propagation of Nichiren Daishonin's Buddhism. From 1976 to 1978, when the relationship was at its high point, the fourth silent prayer included the phrase "I pray for the Soka Gakkai to flourish and accomplish the merciful propagation of true Buddhism," and the fifth included specific thanks to the first two Soka Gakkai presidents, Tsunesaburo Makiguchi (1871–1944) and Josei Toda (1900–58). After open conflict between the priests and the laity erupted in late 1978, these sections of the prayer were omitted by the priesthood from *gongyo* books.

After the permanent split in 1991, when all 11 million Soka Gakkai members were excommunicated by the Nichiren Shoshu priesthood, two different *gongyo* books were printed. The priesthood version is still called *The Liturgy of Nichiren Shoshu*, and the prayers remain as they have been since 1978, with no mention of the Soka Gakkai. The Soka Gakkai version with the SGI symbol on the cover is called *The Liturgy of the Buddhism of Nichiren Daishonin*. What Soka Gakkai considers to be the intent of the fourth and fifth prayers has been restored, with prayers for *kosen-rufu*, Soka Gakkai's role in fulfilling it, and with gratitude for Presidents Makiguchi and Toda. The third prayer has a glaring omission from the past version. The section thanking the first three high priests has been retained, but the section offering "praise and deep gratitude to the successive high priests" is nowhere to be found.

In these small but significant changes we see ritual evidence of the split between the Nichiren Shoshu priesthood and the Soka Gakkai. The more than fifty-year cooperation between the largest Nichiren sect, Nichiren Shoshu, whose head temple, Taiseki-ji, stands at the base of Mt Fuji and houses Nichiren's greatest material legacy, the *Dai-Gohonzon*, and the Soka Gakkai lay organization came to an end in 1991. The practitioners of Nichiren's Buddhism were faced with a choice. Most stayed to practice with the Soka Gakkai organization that had recruited them. Others, disenchanted with Soka Gakkai, had been practicing at the temples for a long time and stayed there. Some left Soka Gakkai at this point to practice with the temple as part of a Hokkeko group. These latter two groups became the most hardened advocates of the priestly point of view. And finally, some practitioners simply abandoned their practice and gave up their devotion to the Lotus Sutra.

However it was perceived and experienced, the split between the Nichiren Shoshu priesthood and the Soka Gakkai brought with it dramatic changes. In 1998 the head temple, Taiseki-ji, called the Sho-Hondo, which had been built from the donations of nearly 8 million Soka Gakkai members, was demolished at the request of High Priest Nikken Shonin. The Sho-Hondo had been constructed as the fulfillment of Nichiren Daishonin's third Great Secret Law, the Hommon-no-Kaidan (the True Sanctuary). Nichiren taught that this would usher in the age of *kosen-rufu* and bring peace to the world. It was eighteen stories tall at its highest point, with more than 110,000 square feet of interior space. It cost $100 million to build.

The Nichiren Shoshu priesthood said that the Sho-Hondo had begun to deteriorate from within, just as Nichiren's Buddhism had been corrupted by the Soka Gakkai and Daisaku Ikeda. The demolition was necessary "out of serious concerns for safety in the event of an earthquake."[1] To the Soka Gakkai, destruction of the Sho-Hondo and the art works within it was an expression of the high priest's megalomania, since he intends to build his own version of the True Sanctuary on the site. In spite of international protests by architects, historic preservationists, and Kimio Yokoyama, the

---

[1] From an online discussion by Nichiren Shoshu lay practitioners at <coyote.accessnv.com/tamonten/discus/index.htm>. There are limited official Nichiren Shoshu sites in English. See Further Reading: Internet Sources, for an explanation.

project's chief architect, the demolition started in 1998 and by 1999 was completed—a cause for joy to some priesthood supporters and deep sorrow to some Soka Gakkai members.[2]

The split between the Nichiren Shoshu priesthood and the Soka Gakkai lay organization can be traced to two major religious issues. First, the Soka Gakkai emerged at a time of great cultural, economic, and technological change. The changes they have brought to the practice of Nichiren's Buddhism are a reflection of the changes of the late twentieth century. Second, the religious needs of these twentieth century converts are quite different from those of the thirteenth century Nichiren Shoshu priesthood. The pragmatic, goal-oriented, this-worldly focus of the Soka Gakkai lay believers conflicts with the priestly, mystical, other-worldly focus of the Nichiren Shoshu priesthood. In light of this, it is remarkable that the cooperation between the two from 1951 to 1991 lasted as long as it did.

This chapter will compare the Nichiren Shoshu–Soka Gakkai split to the split that led to the divergent paths of Roman Catholicism and Protestantism within Christianity. The parallels between this twentieth century Buddhist Reformation and the sixteenth century Protestant Reformation are striking. When we explore the causes and results of the Protestant Reformation, we see quite similar themes emerge in both the dramatic cultural, economic, and technological changes of sixteenth century Europe and the resulting change in the religious needs of Christians at that time.

Since 1973 I have carried out research on the then united group (known as Nichiren Shoshu Academy and later Nichiren Shoshu of America (NSA) and Nichiren Shoshu–Soka Gakkai of America (also NSA)) using the technique of *participant observation*. Although I never became a practicing Nichiren Shoshu Buddhist,

[2] Mary Jordan, "A Major Eruption at the Foot of Fuji," *Washington Post* June 14, 1998, G1, 5. For one Nichiren Shoshu view, see <www.coam.net/~kuvera/>, a site that shows scenes of a destroyed Sho-Hondo while "Ode to Joy" plays in the background. For the Soka Gakkai view, <www.starless.com/photo_framee.html> and <www.save-shohondo.com>.

I attended weekly Soka Gakkai meetings for nearly three years, as well as the 1976 NSA Bicentennial Convention in New York City, and occasional meetings in the years since. Since the 1991 split I have continued my research through many conversations with both Nichiren Shoshu temple Hokkeko practitioners, and members and leaders of SGI-USA.

The Nichiren Shoshu and the Soka Gakkai

In thirteenth century Japan a new school of Buddhism was born from the writings and teachings of Nichiren. His self-chosen name, meaning Great Teacher of the Sun-Lotus, indicates the single-mindedness of his work—to teach about and disseminate a focus on the Lotus Sutra as the most important Buddhist teaching. Nichiren himself was a reformer. He studied the various Buddhist schools of his day and was not satisfied. Nichiren found the Lotus Sutra and its title, *Myoho-renge-kyo*, to be the essence of all Buddhism. Not interested in the story of the Buddha's enlightenment, the Four Noble Truths, including the Eightfold Path, or more traditional forms of meditation, Nichiren believed that chanting *Nam-myoho-renge-kyo* alone would bring enlightenment.

Nichiren was not content to teach his truth to the faithful. His understanding of compassion meant that he must show the truth to those who did not yet accept it. He alienated other Buddhist sects and the government as well by his forceful insistence that the Lotus Sutra alone was *the Truth*. His personal difficulties caused by those who did not accept him, his exile to Izu peninsula and Sado Island, and a death sentence that was miraculously stayed by the sudden appearance of a comet did not trouble him and were taken as proof of the power of his teachings. Nichiren was a millennialist and taught that he was the True Buddha of the final stage of history called *mappo*. The transient teachings of Shakyamuni Buddha could now fall away, and the teachings of true Buddhism could come to the fore. His vision included the conversion not only of Japan but of the rest of the world as well.

Nichiren was a contentious person, inspired as he was by his conviction that through him true Buddhism could now be taught. His method was *shakubuku*,[3] in which his followers would forcefully convert others to the Truth.

"The practice of the *Lotus Sutra* is *shakubuku*, the refutation of the provisional doctrines." True to the letter of this golden saying, the believers of all provisional teachings and sects will ultimately be defeated and join the followers of the king of the Law. The time will come when all people, including those of Learning, Realization, and Boddhisattva, will enter on the path to Buddhahood, and the Mystic Law alone will flourish throughout the land.[4]

During his lifetime he was available to interpret this truth and hold his followers together. At his death Nichiren Daishonin left a legacy as a teacher that included his writings and calligraphic interpretations of the Lotus Sutra. What he did not leave were clear instructions on who was to have the authority to lead Nichiren Buddhism. Over time thirty-seven different Nichiren sects were formed. Nikko Shonin established one of these in a temple at Mt Fuji that enshrined the *Dai-Gohonzon*, a mandala of passages from the Lotus Sutra. This group became the largest of the Nichiren sects, Nichiren Shoshu, and it traces its legitimacy back to the second high priest (after Nichiren), Byakuren Ajari Nikko Shonin, who is regarded as "the great leader of the propagation of true Buddhism who received its pure lineage from Nichiren Daishonin."[5]

Nichiren Shoshu was for centuries one of the many sects of

---

[3] Although one possible translation of *shakubuku* is "break and subdue," this has been most often used by critics of the method. One Soka Gakkai leader told me, "The 'break and subdue' translation of shakubuku is misleading, perpetuating the unsubstantiated accusations of violent proselytization which affected Nichiren himself and the Soka Gakkai centuries later. Even the word 'forceful' suggests physical, rather than moral, strength. Shakubuku does mean to refute (break) another's attachment to provisional Buddhist views and to remove (subdue) the suffering, which accompanies such attachments."

[4] Nichiren Daishonin, "On Practising the Buddha's Teachings," *Major Writings of Nichiren Daishonin*, i (Tokyo: Nichiren Shoshu International Centre, 1979), 103.

[5] *The Liturgy of Nichiren Shoshu: The Taisekiji Version* (Tokyo: Nichiren Shoshu Temple, 1979), 40.

Buddhism which seem to coexist so well in Japan. Despite its insistence that it alone taught true Buddhism, the lay members associated with Nichiren Shoshu temples did not attempt to proselytize to any great extent. This changed in the twentieth century when Tsunesaburo Makiguchi founded a new lay organization called Soka Kyoiku Gakkai in 1930. Makiguchi and his friend and protégé Josei Toda took up the mantle of Nichiren Daishonin and intended to reform society based on his teachings. Their faith-inspired refusal to cooperate with the Japanese wartime government landed them in prison. Makiguchi died there, martyr to Nichiren Buddhism.

Josei Toda, now the second president of the renamed Soka Gakkai, took heart from the courageous death of the founder and chanted *Nam-myoho-renge-kyo* 2 million times in prison. At this point he was inspired by a "true, clear vision" of the Truth and dedicated his life to the spread of true Buddhism through *shakubuku*. Perhaps in other eras this would not have been successful. In postwar Japan it seemed a perfect answer to the collapse of meaning and structure that followed the defeat in World War II. With the dropping of the atomic bomb on Hiroshima and Nagasaki, it was no stretch of the imagination to believe that the world had come to the age of *mappo,* the final stage of history.

As a result of the war an upheaval in Japan's social, governmental, and economic structures had occurred. How to negotiate a new life from the ashes of prewar Japan? For many millions in the 1950s and 1960s, Soka Gakkai provided an answer. Its teachings were simple, but to the members they were life-changing. Each member would enshrine a copy of the *Gohonzon* in his or her home. In what seemed to be a mutually beneficial arrangement, Nichiren Shoshu priests would make the *Gohonzon*, empower them with an Opening of the Eyes ceremony at the head temple, and present them to new members in a Gojukai ceremony. Members would in turn give financial support to the priesthood, which included building new temples and maintaining them. Each member would enshrine the *Gohonzon* in the home, make offerings of fruit and incense, and chant *gongyo* each morning and evening.

According to Nichiren Daishonin's teachings, the *Gohonzon* is the Supreme Object of Worship, the material manifestation of the Law in Buddhism. By reciting the Lotus Sutra daily to the *Gohonzon*, the Nichiren Buddhism practitioner builds a relationship with the eternal laws of cause and effect and is able to experience life in the flow of that Universal Law. Individuals might "chant for" something, such as a job or a boyfriend or a new car. In the process, the job, the boyfriend, or the car might turn up or might not, but the practitioner feels that by being part of the eternal law he or she gets exactly what is needed. In any case, life is sacralized and made meaningful. That perfect job does not come along by chance, but as a manifestation of changing one's karma as influenced by one's faith and the practice of chanting. The smallest things in life have eternal implications. Our busy, materialistic, and often alienated world is made into a deeply meaningful place for one's karma to be played out. The fractured quality of modern life is made whole by the individual's relationship to the *Gohonzon*.

During the time of its association with Nichiren Shoshu, Soka Gakkai members had minimal contact with Nichiren Shoshu priests. Priests conducted marriage ceremonies and funerals, led the chanting ritual during pilgrimages to the head temple at Mt Fuji and periodically at local temples, and of course bestowed the *Gohonzon* on new members. They also, with Soka Gakkai participation, edited study materials and editions of Nichiren's writings. On the other hand, Soka Gakkai members had intense contact with Soka Gakkai leaders. In the late 1960s and early 1970s, the Soka Gakkai community center could become the focus of the member's life, with almost nightly activities including community events and *shakubuku*. Soka Gakkai members formally prayed for all the Nichiren Shoshu high priests from Nikko Shonin to the present in their daily chanting ritual, but it was for the third president of Soka Gakkai, Daisaku Ikeda (1928–), that they felt the greatest respect and admiration.

President Ikeda, a teenager during the war, saw the possibilities for fulfilling Nichiren Daishonin's teachings in the postwar period. Not only would Nichiren's Buddhism spread throughout Japan, but conversion of new members would also become a global mission. In a way, President Ikeda's vision of spreading Japanese Buddhism to the world was parallel to the vision of Japanese businesses in their plans to make Japan part of a global economy. In 1960, before the first Toyota or Datsun rolled onto American shores, Daisaku Ikeda had formally established the organization, Soka Gakkai, that would disseminate the teachings of Nichiren Daishonin in North America. It was the first successful Japanese import not only to the United States but also to countries throughout the world. Soka Gakkai's description of its practice, "world peace through individual happiness," made it clear that its focus was global.

Through the years of Soka Gakkai's expansion it maintained its symbiotic relationship with the Nichiren Shoshu priesthood. Soka Gakkai recruited members, who in turn built temples and made financial contributions to support the priesthood. The priesthood, with its claim of authority going back to Nichiren, the first high priest, and the second high priest, Nikko Shonin, in the thirteenth century, conferred legitimacy on the Soka Gakkai. There were some signs of strain through the years, though these were mostly behind the scenes. In a 1973 edition of the Soka Gakkai publication *Seikyo Times* the completion of the new head temple at Mt Fuji was celebrated jointly by the then high priest Nittatsu Shonin and President Ikeda. Pictures show them smiling at one another as they greet dignitaries and bless the fountains with water from a sacred spring. At that point it seemed to be a peaceful coexistence.

An open conflict erupted in 1978 when President Ikeda was ousted as Soka Gakkai leader and replaced by Hiroshi Hojo. Mr Ikeda became honorary president of Soka Gakkai and full-time president of Soka Gakkai International (SGI), an organization he had founded in 1975. President Ikeda's picture was taken down from meeting rooms in members' homes and community centers, though within a year it had been put up again. It must be noted that, although Soka Gakkai has always called its leader "president," he has not been democratically elected by the entire membership, as few religious leaders are. Rather he is elected by the board of directors, currently seventy-two individuals representing thirty different countries, although in the past it was completely Japanese. The president is then considered to have authority by virtue of this designation. President Ikeda's charisma, both then and now, reinforced his official status.

In 1978, from the point of view of the priesthood, President Ikeda and other Soka Gakkai leaders had deviated from their own commitment to the Nichiren Shoshu faith as originally established by second president, Toda, in 1950. They had broken their promises to serve the head temple for the advancement of *kosen-rufu*, to have all Soka Gakkai members register at their local temples, to adhere to the doctrines of the head temple, Taiseki-ji, and to honor the Three Treasures of Nichiren Shoshu—the Buddha (Nichiren Daishonin), the Law (the *Dai-Gohonzon*), and the priesthood as embodied in the successive Nichiren Shoshu high priests.[6] By breaking these original promises, the Soka Gakkai leadership had deviated from true Buddhism. President Ikeda and Vice-President Tsuji apologized to the high priest in a *tozan* during pilgrimage at the head temple on 7 November 1978, with Vice-President Tsuji stating, "for a number of years, the Soka Gakkai cultivated the idea that President Ikeda should be held in high esteem. While this feeling may come naturally, we must exhibit restraint, so that this kind of expression does not become excessive."[7] President Ikeda, who, unofficially, some members had felt to be a reincarnation of Nichiren Daishonin himself, was not to put himself in competition with the high priest. His apology was accepted by the Nichiren Shoshu priesthood. In fact some hundred priests who still felt the Soka Gakkai to be in error, the Shoshinkai group, were themselves disciplined and expelled from Nichiren Shoshu in 1980 for failing to accept the reconciliation.

In retrospect, though, the Soka Gakkai leaders' apology was insufficient to heal the deep-seated priesthood–laity conflict. From the priesthood point of view, that apology was hypocritical and

---

[6] "Gego—The Outside Protector of Buddhism," xeroxed typescript essay distributed by the Nichiren Shoshu Ashuzan Myosenji Temple, Washington, June 26, 1991, 4.

[7] Ibid. 5.

never sincere; from the Soka Gakkai point of view, the apology was necessary to maintain even a semblance of cooperation with the priesthood, but it was never truly accepted by them. The issues of disagreement at this point, focusing on such diversions of the faith as integrating Western music into Soka Gakkai culture festivals, were picayune and served to mask the fact that the priesthood just simply did not share Soka Gakkai's vision of how to accomplish *kosen-rufu*. The ensuing conduct of the high priest strained relations to the breaking point.[8]

The Split between the Nichiren Shoshu Priesthood and the Soka Gakkai

In the late 1980s tensions between the Nichiren Shoshu priesthood led by High Priest Nikken Shonin and the fifth Soka Gakkai president, Einosuke Akiya (1930–), had once again begun to build. Issues of authority, finances, and interpretation of Nichiren Daishonin's teachings proved insoluble, and in 1991 the high priest excommunicated the Soka Gakkai.[9] Nichiren Shoshu priests would no longer perform weddings or funerals, or bestow *Gohonzon* through Soka Gakkai. Nichiren Shoshu temples, including the head temple at Mt Fuji, were made off limits to Soka Gakkai members. Soka Gakkai members would no longer support the priesthood with loyalty and monthly donations (*zaimu*). The relationship that had given mutual legitimacy to the Nichiren Shoshu priesthood and the Soka Gakkai was at an end.

The split between the Nichiren Shoshu priesthood and the Soka

[8] It is interesting to note that, at this time in America, a group of disgruntled former members centered in the New York area were not satisfied with either the Soka Gakkai apology or the official priesthood acceptance of it. Led by Revd Kando Tono, they recommended disbanding Soka Gakkai and centering all lay Nichiren Shoshu worship at the Nichiren Shoshu temples. Four hundred and twenty-five Nichiren Shoshu believers sent a petition to the head temple and the SGI leadership in Japan to that effect. They now exist as a separate Nichiren sect led by Revd Tono.

[9] Technically, he excommunicated the organization, I was told, but individual members would be free to practice at the temples if they renounced Soka Gakkai.

Gakkai was cataclysmic for both sides. From the priesthood point of view, Soka Gakkai and its members were showing supreme disrespect for the legitimate legacy of Nichiren Daishonin in their refusal sufficiently to honor the high priest and his authority as one of the Three Treasures. The Soka Gakkai leaders, especially President Ikeda, seemed to want to usurp the high priest's position as ordained carrier of Nichiren Daishonin's true Buddhism. The doctrines they taught were disobedient, as was their faith. As a religious corporation they were slanderous and had betrayed the priesthood.[10] Their new members were worshipping counterfeit *Gohonzon* issued by SGI, which would bring great misfortune, or at least no benefit, to those who practice with them. The Soka Gakkai "cannot be the foundation for the Buddhism of Nichiren Daishonin."[11]

Soka Gakkai members felt that their many years of efforts to support the priesthood had resulted in their excommunication. They felt as if the Nichiren Shoshu priests were trying to exert their authority where it ought not to be—into the personal practice of chanting the Lotus Sutra to the *Gohonzon*. The priesthood had become corrupt with increasing demands for money from the laity to support lavish lifestyles. For the Soka Gakkai members, the teachings of Nichiren Daishonin have the ultimate authority in Nichiren's Buddhism, and the Soka Gakkai is true to the teachings. In this, the organization itself represents the Sangha, the correct Third Treasure of Buddhism. Nichiren had intended to transform the world with his teachings, and SGI was dedicated to that aim with members in 128 countries and a global mission.

The Nichiren Shoshu priesthood and the Soka Gakkai lay

---

[10] *Dai-Nichiren (Special Edition): On the Soka Gakkai Problem*, iii (n.p.: Nichiren Shoshu Bureau of Religious Affairs, n.d.).

[11] *SGI "Gohonzon": Source of Misfortune*, Nichiren Shoshu Broadside (n.d.), published in response to the 1993 Soka Gakkai decision to reproduce *Gohonzon*, sent to me by a lay temple practitioner. This document accuses a former Nishiren Shoshu priest of reproducing the *Gohonzon*, though Soka Gakkai says that they are doing it directly themselves without the participation of any priest.

believers still shared what had originally brought them together: a deep and abiding commitment to the practice of the teachings of Nichiren Daishonin, the True Buddha for our times, the age of *mappo*; his teachings on the Lotus Sutra and the Three Great Secret Laws (*Dai-Gohonzon*, *daimoku*, and the high sanctuary), and the spread of those teachings, *kosen-rufu*. However, as Wilson and Dobbelaere have suggested, it should be no surprise that a culturally conservative Japanese priesthood built on ideas of hierarchy, ritual, and traditional custom should conflict with a global lay movement built on ideas of egalitarianism, active faith, and rational adaptation to the modern world.[12]

These two viewpoints result in doctrinal differences with significant implications. Nichiren Shoshu regards the Three Great Treasures of Buddhism (Triple Gem) to be the True Buddha (Nichiren Daishonin), the Law (the *Dai-Gohonzon*), and the Priest (specifically the high priest who carries Nichiren's lineage). The Soka Gakkai interpret the Three Great Treasures to be the True Buddha (Nichiren Daishonin), the Law (the *Dai-Gohonzon*), and those who practice Nichiren's Buddhism in the way taught by the first three Nichiren Shoshu high priests.[13] At issue is whether or not the ritual power of the priesthood conveys anything special that is not accessible to believers in their own personal practice. Nichiren Shoshu insists that priests are necessary to carry the pure lineage. The Soka Gakkai feel that priests are not necessary and, since 1991, have developed ways to practice Nichiren's Buddhism without them.

The two groups also differ on their interpretation of the master–disciple relationship. Is this meant to be a hierarchical relationship built on rules of respect and deference, as the Nichiren Shoshu priesthood insists? Or is it meant to be like a teacher or coach who encourages the faithful and, by doing so, keeps them from unnecessary mistakes and suffering, but who is essentially equal in

[12] Bryan Wilson and Karel Dobbelaere, *A Time to Chant: The Soka Gakkai Buddhists in Britain* (Oxford: Oxford University Press, 1994), 243–4.

[13] Note that this latter formulation is much closer to what the majority of Buddhists mean when they refer to the Buddha, the Dharma, and the Sangha.

the practice of Buddhism—the Soka Gakkai view? And what does this say of the high regard in which President Ikeda is held by the members? In the early days of the American movement, some believed he was the reincarnation of Nichiren Daishonin, though this was never official. This certainly implies hierarchical thinking. The structure of the organization was intensely hierarchical, with management clearly on a top-down model. The official position of the Soka Gakkai, however, is that all believers are equal before the *Gohonzon*, including President Ikeda. "Personal practice makes benefit and transformation happen, and thus balances the power of the master–disciple relationship," one leader told me. "We worship the Law in each person, and not the person, and this balances out the possibility of corruption."

A fundamental disagreement between the two groups is over the issue of what is the proper way to promote *kosen-rufu*, the spread of Buddhism to the world. When Nichiren Daishonin taught this concept in the thirteenth century, it must have seemed an absurd dream, considering Japan's isolation from the rest of the world and the limits of transportation and communication at that time. As the twenty-first century begins, intercultural contact is inevitable—the hallmark of our era. To the Nichiren Shoshu priesthood, *kosen-rufu* will take place when others see the merits of Nichiren's Buddhism. They do some proselytizing, and since the split they have made efforts to convert both former and present Soka Gakkai members. However, the priesthood's eyes remain firmly focused on Japan. Nichiren Shoshu priests are all of Japanese birth.

To the Soka Gakkai, the activities they design to promote Peace, Culture, and Education will spread the essential values of Nichiren's Buddhism. New members may join the group by being attracted to these aims, as well as by the attraction of the positive life condition of individual members. Soka Gakkai has already spread around the world, and it embraced diversity before the idea became commonplace. According to its charter, members are "world citizens" and not merely citizens of their respective countries, though cultural differences are to be respected and honored in SGI. The entire world is their home.

We see, therefore, a profound difference of opinion on the essential purpose of promoting Nichiren's Buddhism. To the priesthood, it seems to be the protection of its own traditions, temples, and especially the *Dai-Gohonzon*. The purity and legitimacy of the lineage is a paramount concern. They see the Soka Gakkai as a heretical sect practicing a counterfeit religion. A recent publication, *Refuting the Soka Gakkai's Object of Worship: 100 Questions and Answers*, explains the reasoning behind this view. Soka Gakkai is called "Ikedaism." To the Nichiren Shoshu, the fact that the Soka Gakkai has not been destroyed by its own evil actions and illegitimate practice is proof of the duplicity of its leaders, who have misled the faithful to make them stay in the organization. As a result, lay believers who practice at the Nichiren Shoshu temples in Hokkeko groups are still angry with the Soka Gakkai. They have neither forgiven nor forgotten the offences committed against them and the priesthood. They have watched the Soka Gakkai's actions and freely criticized them. They have not made any great changes in their organization in the last six years. They are essentially conservative of tradition, and they deeply believe this to be Nichiren Daishonin's intent.

To the Soka Gakkai, the split from the priesthood resulted in an incredible sense of freedom. They are free to express what they have always believed—that the power of the *Gohonzon* is separate from any priestly authority and that "the Daishonin inscribed the *Gohonzon* for all people throughout the world" without regard to rank or financial considerations.[14] The organization has been free to reinvent itself, as its charter, adopted on October 17, 1995 shows. The themes of world citizenship, support for freedom of religion, respect for cultural differences and diversity, care for the environment, and promotion of education are seen as a blueprint for the twenty-first century. The democratization of the structure of SGI has reaffirmed these themes. SGI members are as enthusiastic as they were in the early *shakubuku* days, but without

[14] *Reaffirming our Right to Happiness: On the Gohonzon Transcribed by High Priest Nichikan* (n.p.: SGI-USA, 1996), 12.

the high pressure tactics and intolerance. Although there is some residual pain and anger,[15] they have moved into a middle age of respect for all and commitment to the Buddhism that has given benefit and meaning to their lives. SGI regrets the split from the priesthood, but only because of the hard feelings and pain it has caused. There is some anger and negativism toward the Nichiren Shoshu, and some have called it "the Nikken sect," but they cannot and would not go back. The positive effects for SGI are too great.

Comparison of the Nichiren Shoshu–Soka Gakkai International Split and the Protestant Reformation

At this point we will shift gears and put the split between the Soka Gakkai and the Nichiren Shoshu priesthood into a larger historical context by comparing it to the sixteenth century Protestant Reformation. Catholic and Protestant historians do not exactly agree on what took place during the Reformation. "Catholic scholars have viewed the Reformation as a religious and theological aberration and (as regards its historical significance) the cause of modern secularism. Protestant historiography, in turn, has depicted the Reformation as the restoration of authentic Christianity."[16] Whatever the case, a series of historic changes led the way for Martin Luther and others to develop the ideas that started the Reformation. Luther and his followers could no longer find religious satisfaction in a priestly religious orientation and sought to reinvent Christianity with a pragmatic religious orientation.

In the late fifteenth and early sixteenth centuries Europe was undergoing a transformation of its economy, its social and political structure, and its understanding of itself and its place in the world. The movement of populations from the farms to the cities

[15] See < members.aol.com/watchbuddh/link.htm > for links to sites where personal opinions on the split are expressed outside the official Soka Gakkai view.

[16] Hans J. Hillerbrand, "Reformation," *Encyclopaedia of Religion*, xii (New York: MacMillan, 1987), 244.

with the rise of businesses and trade guilds opened up individual opportunities for advancement and self-determination. A middle class grew as a result. The rising power of nation states reduced the relative power and influence of the Church. The technological breakthrough of the printing press made books widely accessible for the first time in history. The Bible, translated into vernacular languages, could be widely read by the laity for the first time in Christian history. The discovery of the New World in 1492 opened up the globe to Europeans, and consequently their ideas about their place in the world were for ever changed. The ocean, which had formerly been a limit, became a route to possibility and opportunity.

For individuals at this juncture in history, such changes must have been simultaneously exhilarating and terrifying. The opportunity to rise beyond the place in life assigned by the circumstances of birth can be seen as wonderful, in that it allowed the individual to succeed according to his or her own efforts. However, the comfortable structures that gave meaning and understanding to the self in relationship to others were slowly being dismantled. Not all sixteenth century Europeans immediately felt the impact of this change, and perhaps it was acted out most dramatically by those who emigrated to the New World and reinvented themselves, but certainly many members of society experienced a profound anomie as a result of the socioeconomic changes taking place.

Against the backdrop of these deep cultural changes, the Roman Catholic Church took a defensive posture. It may be in the very nature of institutions to react slowly to change and, in many instances, react directly against it. In any case, the medieval Church in the early sixteenth century was unable to adapt to the new era. Centerd in Rome, it had a kind of myopia and looked at the world from the isolated viewpoint of Italian culture. Thus the extent and depth of the changes sweeping the rest of Europe went almost unnoticed.

There is also no doubt that corruption had entered into the face-to-face dealings of the Church's priests and their agents with the faithful. The most infamous example of this is the sale of indulgences. Church teaching of the time held that every sin must be paid for, either before or after death. The Church, as the agent of Jesus Christ on earth, could decide what the punishment would be during life. These punishments could be redeemed by paying a Church official, a pardoner, and receiving an indulgence and for-giveness of the sin in return. The opportunities for exploitation are obvious. Ironically, little of the money raised in this way found its way to Rome. The fifteenth and sixteenth century papacy was chronically short of funds.

The Church misjudged its own power and did not perceive the loss of its influence as the nation states gained power. It attacked its critics as it had always done and dealt with Martin Luther severely, excommunicating him in January 1521. In the past this would have taken care of his heretical teachings, but the matter did not end there. Rather, it served as a turning point, and many thousands of Catholics left the Church to follow Luther's understanding of Christianity. They were also leaving the Middle Ages and its meaning system for a new era and a meaning system that reflected individual effort, responsibility, and self-determination.

Theologically, this was reflected in the doctrine of the "priest-hood of all believers." Authority came from the Bible alone, and the Roman Catholic Church traditions were stripped of authority. Salvation, for Protestants, came from God's grace alone and could not be the result of human action (especially the sacrament of con-fession). Faith in God was a necessary condition for salvation, but was no guarantee. The Roman Catholic view was that both faith and good works led to salvation. With the Reformation, individu-als were free to invent their own institutions rather than to accept them as given. This sort of thinking led to the end of the Middle Ages and the beginning of a great era of cultural, economic, and political change in Europe, an era in which institutions were not ordained by God but created by human beings to meet their social needs and to reflect their chosen values.

The similarities between the sixteenth century Reformation in Europe and the 1991 split between the priesthood and the laity in Nichiren's Buddhism are striking. The conflict between priestly

religion and pragmatic religion is the same. The key issues of contention in both reformations are:

- a conflict between priestly authority and lay creativity;
- hierarchical versus egalitarian organization;
- an emphasis on sacrament and ritual versus an emphasis on
  the faith of the individual;
- a focus on tradition as the key to understanding scripture,
  compared to a focus on scripture alone;
- a view of religion that is local, conservative, and mystical versus one that is global, progressive, and rational; and
- an other-worldly spiritual focus, as opposed to one that is
  engaged with the world.

These theological issues do not appear in a vacuum. Both of
these reformations appeared in times of great technological, economic, and cultural change. Human beings had recently revised
their cosmic self-understanding—for the Reformation period with
the discovery of the Americas, and for our time with the landing
on the moon. More specifically, for Japan the global interconnectedness of the late twentieth century opened up a new world. Both
eras had experienced wars in the previous century, and plagues
were a sad reality.

When the world changes, social institutions must adapt or fail.
In the sixteenth century the Roman Catholic Church was slow to
respond to the new era, though the Counter-Reformation that followed in a few decades accomplished that feat. By adapting, the
Church ensured its own continuity. In Nichiren's Buddhism in the
twentieth century we have yet to see if the lay Nichiren Shoshu
temple groups will make a similar adjustment. There are signs that
this may be so, and if they wish to survive, it will be necessary.

In both the twentieth century and the sixteenth century cases we
see an essential conflict between *priestly* and *pragmatic* forms of religion.[17] Priestly religion sees its purpose as relating people to a
divine, mysterious world accessible only through precise tradi-

---

[17] For the inspiration for this section I am indebted to Bryan Wilson's discussion of the Nichiren Shoshu–Soka Gakkai split in his book with Karel

tional ritual. It is conservative at its heart, because it believes that only through tradition will the connection with the sacred world be maintained. The weakness of priestly religion is that it can become hollow ritual with hierarchies that exploit their position. It can ignore the real needs of believers while focusing on the tradition it feels obliged to maintain. It can become myopically focused on its own continuity and ignore its cultural context.

Pragmatic religion has its focus on the transformation of this world through faith. Individual faith creates the connection of the secular and the sacred, and individual action puts it into practice. The aims of pragmatic religion are to make things better in the here and now based on the values of its particular faith. Its weakness is that it can become a debased subjectivism, in which the lack of authority blurs its religious purity. If each believer can be a priest, then what each preaches can stray far afield and corrupt the teachings at the core of the religion. In addition, its explicit disavowal of hierarchy makes pragmatic religion naive about the perils of charismatic leadership unchecked by institutional limitations.

It is not surprising to find conflict between these two divergent forms of religious expression. Over time Christianity has made great strides toward Protestant–Catholic reconciliation, although it seems unlikely that a full reunification of the Christian Church will ever occur. Will this happen in Nichiren Buddhism? Will a dialogue ever open up between the Nichiren Shoshu priesthood and the Soka Gakkai? To answer these questions we look at the impact of the split on each group.

Changes in the Nichiren Shoshu Priesthood since the Split

Since the aim of the priesthood in excommunicating Soka Gakkai members was to uphold tradition and prevent change, there have

Dobbelaere, *A Time to Chant*. He makes the distinction between Nichiren Shoshu's organizational form and innate tendencies as compared to those of the Soka Gakkai. From this I have developed the idea of two innately different forms of religious expression, the priestly and the pragmatic, as seen through the experience of the believer.

been few changes in the Nichiren Shoshu priesthood since the split. If anything, the Nichiren Shoshu priesthood has become more entrenched. Official numbers are not available, but, according to a group of Nichiren Shoshu reformed priests, out of 1,300 Nichiren Shoshu priests at the time of the split, 600 now practice with one of three separatist groups called Domei.[18] There is no indication in the official priesthood writings that anything is amiss. From the publications that are available in English, it appears that High Priest Nikken Shonin intends to carry on with his plans to build his own True Sanctuary.

The overseas temples, built by the Soka Gakkai members of those nations, have stayed in control of the Nichiren Shoshu priesthood, including the six in the United States. Each one has a lay organization called Hokkeko that practices at the temple. These are small: the Washington, DC area temple claims about 300 to 700 lay members; the New York Temple is supported by about 1,000 households. In all, there are probably no more than a few thousand Hokkeko members in the United States and an unknown number in Japan.

All of this suggests that the financial support of the Nichiren Shoshu temples has changed dramatically, as has the intensity of activities of the priesthood. Even given an optimistic number of several hundred thousand Hokkeko members, their needs for weddings, funerals, naming ceremonies, and conferral of *Gohonzon* would be much less than the needs of the many million lay Soka Gakkai members lost in the split. There must have been some major adjustments at the head temple, though these have not been publicized.

If the Nichiren Shoshu priesthood's aim in excommunicating Soka Gakkai members in 1991 was to maintain the *status quo* in their centuries-old practice of Nichiren's Buddhism, they have succeeded. They stood firm in upholding their understanding of Nichiren's doctrines. They created a loyal and dedicated lay membership at each of their temples. Some former members left SGI

[18] For information on these groups, see < members.aol.com/domeinews/ nichiren-shoshu/reformation/domei.htm >.

for the temple; others left the practice of Buddhism altogether. If, however, the priesthood expected a mass exodus of members from SGI, this has not occurred and is not likely to. A "last chance" to return to the temples and give up SGI membership was issued by Nichiren Shoshu in the fall of 1997 with a November 30, 1997 deadline. Although some may have taken advantage of this offer, it seems likely that, after so many years, positions are entrenched on both sides.

To dedicated lay practitioners associated with Nichiren Shoshu temples, what Soka Gakkai does or does not do is not their major concern. Although one Hokkeko member told me, "Nothing is more desirable than for mistakes to be corrected and things to go harmoniously on," he does not expect it to happen soon:

The tremendous growth of the lay association in six years [in New York from twenty-two to 1,000 households] is cause for optimism. So is the growth of the members' personal faith and practice. The value of this practice is the difference it makes in daily life and vitality and wisdom. My decision to stay with the temple has made a tremendous positive impact on my life.

Changes in Soka Gakkai International since the Split

In retrospect, changes in SGI since the split from the Nichiren Shoshu priesthood were inevitable. Globalization of the movement pushed it beyond the limits of Japanese culture and tradition. The late twentieth century was a time of immense cultural and economic change, and around the world we saw a movement away from authoritarianism toward democracy, albeit not without considerable problems along the way. This surely has had an influence on SGI. The women's movement during these decades was progressively successful, and any organization with institutional sexism has been challenged again and again. The very numbers of SGI as a lay movement may have given it power in relation to the priesthood. The aging of the members may have brought other influences as well.

Most important, for the SGI Nichiren Buddhism practitioner, the core of a good life is the personal relationship with the

Gohonzon through chanting the Lotus Sutra. If anything is possible with the *Gohonzon*, if anyone can tap into the mystical law of cause and effect through this practice, then at heart it is essentially democratic. Even when organizational power might flow to members from the top down, the unlimited power of the *Gohonzon* is available to anyone who chants *Nam-myoho-renge-kyo*. In time, this could be expected to transform any organization whose members practice Nichiren's Buddhism. This is certainly the intention of members, who believe that world peace can be built on a foundation of individual happiness. It is also what appears to have happened with the SGI organization.

The influence of President Ikeda is the key. In the early decades of his leadership he seemed to be an intense, sincere, and driven leader, and at times his enthusiasm and single-mindedness in working for a transformation of the world through true Buddhism seemed almost sinister. Certainly outsiders perceived him that way. Members honored him as their *sensei*, their spiritual master, and when 10,000 members sang "Forever Sensei" in his honor at the 1976 Bicentennial Convention, they did so from the heart. He certainly has the ego of any successful CEO who has watched his organization grow. It is remarkable that as he has matured as a leader, he has chosen the moral high ground.

Rather than giving in to the temptation to exploit his power as a leader of a now 12 million member organization, Mr Ikeda has instead worked to see that organization become more democratic. Many of the reforms since the split from the priesthood have been on his initiative, and others are a result of democratic structures he put in place. Power in SGI has not stayed centered in Japan but has spread throughout the world in the various organizations that SGI has founded to promote its aims of peace, culture, and education (more specifically, disarmament, racial tolerance, care for the environment). SGI's status as a registered nongovernmental organization with the United Nations Economic and Social Council reaffirms this.

In America the changes have been dramatic. The authoritarian, male-dominated central leadership of the 1960s and 1970s has

been replaced by a standing 147-member central executive committee. It includes equal numbers of men and women, youth and
older members, and membership rotates on a cyclical basis. The
members represent the SGI communities throughout the United
States, and they meet four times a year, with timing depending on
the needs of the organization. The central executive committee's
job is to make organizational policy and ensure that the organization conforms to the practice of Nichiren's Buddhism. This move
toward democratization is evidenced in the SGI-USA newspaper,
the *World Tribune*, which now features letters to the editor. The
goal is to "keep our self-reflection and to continually purify the
institution." In other words, these changes are seen as part of a
process to ensure member participation in leadership decisions.
Members now take part in a four-year study program designed to
demystify Nichiren Daishonin's teaching and make it accessible to
all.

The relationship between leaders and members has also
changed. Guidance, the communication between leader and member, which was sometimes understood in the context of the
master–disciple relationship, has become much more open and less
vulnerable to leaders' eccentricities. The leader is responsible for
responding to the member's needs and protecting his practice.
This means that support is offered in times of illness or personal
difficulty, but based on the bonds of friendship and trust rather
than the more coercive style of *shakubuku*. What seemed to be pressure to practice in the past is now understood in the true sense of
encouragement. The practice of *shakubuku* itself has changed, and
should take place on the basis of preexisting relationships or natural affinities with other people. This has made the group more
genuinely open to friendships with outsiders, who in the past
might have been seen only as "potential members." The model for
understanding is to engage in dialogue, to talk as equals and
respect differences, while focusing on the common cause of making the world a better place.

A further development has been SGI's interest in interfaith
understanding. Rather than insisting that it has the one Truth that

all others must accept—an attitude of the old high-pressure conversion days—SGI now wants to be accepted as one representative group in a broader community of faith. To this end, it has worked with various Jewish, Christian, and Muslim groups for mutual understanding and toward other common aims such as interracial communication. Symbolic of this was President Ikeda speaking at the Simon Wiesenthal Center and SGI's sponsoring of the first exhibit on the Holocaust to appear in Japan. In Washington Soka Gakkai is the only Buddhist member of the Interfaith Council.

SGI-USA and other Soka Gakkai-affiliated organizations, especially the Boston Research Center for the Twenty-first Century, have fostered dialogues and various conferences. Among them:

- a lecture cosponsored by the Research Center and Columbia Teachers' College called "Thoughts on Education for Global Citizenship" by Daisaku Ikeda;
- a conference of the Society for Buddhist–Christian Studies in Chicago on the theme "Socially Engaged Buddhism and Christianity";
- a conference on "Global Accords for Sustainable Development";
- a consultation along with Boston University on the subject of "Religion and Transnational Civil Society in the Twenty-first Century";
- a series of workshops called the Massachusetts Conference on Women: Bringing Beijing Home to commemorate the Beijing women's conference;
- a traveling multimedia exhibit entitled "Ecology and Human Life"; and
- a program called "Gandhi and the Future of Non-Violence."

Furthermore, representatives attended the annual meetings of the Society for the Scientific Study of Religion and the American Academy of Religion Conference in New Orleans. The themes of care for the earth, nonviolence, abolishing war, and the Earth Charter dominate the work of the Boston Research Center. In addition, local SGI-USA communities sponsor their own interfaith events, as well as programs on nonviolence, the environment, and disarmament. For example in the Washington, DC area SGI has presented "Exploring the Ethical Dimensions of Environmental Conflict in the Twenty-first Century" (1996) and "Ecology and Human Life Exhibit" (1996).

On a more practical note, the functions of the priesthood have been taken over by lay members, who volunteer for one-year terms as a minister of ceremony. They legally represent the organization for marriages and funerals. They are prohibited from accepting money for their services, including expenses for travel. Clearly we are observing what Martin Luther called a "priesthood of all believers." One leader told me that, as laity, "we don't need priests. You worship the Law, not the person, and therefore all are equal in their Buddhist practice." Another leader pointed out that "Nichiren never had a temple, because he did not want those who chanted the Lotus Sutra to the *Gohonzon* to become an isolated group." He expanded, "if the goal is for the individual to transform suffering and create greater value and happiness in life for self and for other people," no temple was needed to achieve it.

Nichiren Shoshu priests not only take care of the rituals of daily life, they also confer a *Gohonzon* to each new convert, which becomes the focus of personal *gongyo* and *daimoku* prayers in his or her home. Without a priesthood ritually manufacturing and conferring these *Gohonzon*, the Soka Gakkai was unable fully to initiate new members for several years following the split. This situation was resolved when Nichiren priests who were members of the reformist Domei began to make personal *Gohonzon* based on one originally transcribed by the high priest Nichikan in the 1720s. For Soka Gakkai, this is the final step in their liberation from the Nikken-dominated Nichiren Shoshu. This was also liberating for some of the former Nichiren Shoshu priests. In a 1994 SGI interview Chief Priest Yugo Narita said, "In the priesthood everything was closed and dark. Now I feel great joy. I practice for the entire world."[19]

[19] *Seikyo Times*, 394 (May 1994), 41–3.

SGI has been in the vanguard of working toward diversity. Its meetings are a patchwork quilt with people of all colors. Its culture festivals are celebrations of artistic expression from a variety of cultures. Between 17 and 20 percent of SGI-USA members are African American, giving it the largest percentage of such members in an American Buddhist group, and there are also a high percentage of Latino and Asian members. When SGI approved of a same sex "partnership ceremony" in 1995, it made explicit what had been an implicit policy of acceptance of alternative lifestyles for years. As early as 1968 some Soka Gakkai Districts had memberships that were almost exclusively gay, and because there was a teaching of "no moral rules" apart from those imposed by one's own karmic debts, this occasioned no official comment.

The SGI-USA organization of 1999 is hardly recognizable to those who joined it twenty or even ten years ago. Though the basic Buddhist practice is the same, the energy of the community is quite different. Any kind of exclusivism and feeling of "specialness" is gone. SGI members now tend to see themselves as having chosen their path because it suits them and not because it is the only truth. Those who left the organization years ago with complaints about overbearing and dictatorial leaders would not, say SGI officials, find the same problems now.

As SGI moves toward the twenty-first century, we can observe a consistent commitment to putting its ideals into action. Its charter states, "We, the constituent organizations and members of the Soka Gakkai International . . . embrace the fundamental aim and mission of contributing to peace, culture, and education based on the philosophy and ideals of the Buddhism of Nichiren Daishonin."[20] SGI's publications, activities, and leadership all point to an organization that is engaged in healing some of the wounds caused by the twentieth century and moving toward a greater future for all. Their goal is to "enable all people to cultivate

---

[20] "SGI Charter," in Soka Gakkai International, brochure (Tokyo: Soka Gakkai International, 1996), 1.

their individual character and enjoy fulfilling and happy lives,"[21] and each member's efforts contribute to its accomplishment.

SGI has translated the essentially democratic practice of chanting into social and political action that respects each individual as an equal member of society. What in the past some considered to be an "unintellectual" mass movement now looks like a model of diversity with a stable membership from all of America's ethnic groups. What had been criticized in the past by adherents of more meditative forms of Buddhism as simplistic and materialistic can now be seen as a model of "engaged Buddhism" in which personal practice leads to solid social reforms. Under the leadership of President Ikeda, SGI has had at least one foot in the twenty-first century for several years now.

Conclusion

Can we expect a reconciliation of the Nichiren Shoshu priesthood and the Soka Gakkai organization? If you ask lay members of Nichiren Shoshu, this would require individual Soka Gakkai members to admit their mistakes in following a false path and sincerely to agree to practice under guidance of the high priest. Some have done so, and it is not impossible that more will do so still. However, those who support the priesthood see Daisaku Ikeda's leadership as sinister and corrupting, and think that no good can come of the organization as long as he is at its helm. Worse, those who have stayed to practice Nichiren's Buddhism with Soka Gakkai are believed to be worshipping a false mandala (the Nichikan *Gohonzon*), and this rejection of true Buddhism will bring upon them a fate worse than death. They have committed the worst slander of all in rejecting the true teaching and should expect some karmic consequences.

Soka Gakkai members and leaders do not expect reconciliation to occur. SGI members believe they have returned to the true teachings of Nichiren and feel a sense of liberation as a result of

[21] "SGI Charter," in Soka Gakkai International, brochure (Tokyo: Soka Gakkai International, 1996), 1.

their separation from the priesthood. One publication states, "we can confidently say that by being excommunicated by Nikken, the Soka Gakkai has actually liberated itself from the shackles of the priesthood and its authoritarianism. This also means that the Daishonin's Buddhism has been given the grand opportunity in this time period to be taught exactly as it was by Nichiren Daishonin."[22] They see themselves as doing quite well without the association with the priesthood; they can now focus on the efficacy of Buddhist teachings to bring peace to the world. They do not want to be removed from the world, but rather to be engaged in its reform. The priestly model does not appeal to them. They do face a challenge when President Ikeda steps down, and some leaders feel that he is already working to ensure an orderly transition of leadership so that the organization outlives him. His efforts at democratization and decentralization of power are seen as evidence of this.

They perceive in their movement a dynamic tension of the mystical religious impulse, the individual's relationship with the eternal law developed through chanting *Nam-myoho-renge-kyo* to the *Gohonzon*, and the pragmatic engagement in the world that the Soka Gakkai organization represents. "If there is value in Buddhist practice," I was told, "that value should be transmitted to lessen the suffering of society." This vision of *kosen-rufu* is rooted in Nichiren's teaching of *esho funi*, the inseparability of spiritual and material conditions. As the individual improves his or her spiritual condition, this becomes a basis for social transformation as well. Nichiren's Buddhism, as understood by Soka Gakkai practitioners, sacralizes participation in the secular world.

It can be expected that the American SGI movement, with its long experience in representative government and social and economic freedom, will have a growing influence on the Japanese organization. Already, for example, the equality of the American women, both in SGI-USA and in American society, is seen as a model by Japanese women. There has even been talk of moving

---

[22] *Questions and Answers on the Temple Issue* (Santa Monica, Calif.: Soka Gakkai International-USA, 1997), 6.

SGI's international headquarters to the United States, though there is no definite plan to do so at this time. We can predict that as Japan opens up to the world, so will SGI. This will enable it to fulfill its role as a training ground for global citizens who, based on their practice of Nichiren's Buddhism, will help create a world of ethnic diversity, environmental care, disarmament, respect for all cultures, and educational progress.

After 400 years, will these two groups work toward reconciliation and mutual understanding, as Roman Catholicism and the Protestant denominations have done? It is almost impossible to imagine the world four centuries from now, and to imagine the religious realities of those times is equally difficult. The struggles to define the relative importance of priestly authority and lay creativity, tradition and scripture, ritual and faith, conservation and progress, hierarchical ranking and egalitarian organization, the mystical and the rational in religious practice, appear to be constants in the history of religions. It is probably safe to predict that, since religions have historically changed through cyclical reform movements, there are more changes to come for Nichiren's Buddhism. This is a testament to the vitality and endurance of his teachings.

4

Soka Gakkai and Japanese Politics

Hiroshi Aruga

T HE Soka Kyoiku Gakkai (Value-Creating Education Society) embraced goals that differed significantly from those that this same organization espoused after World War II, when it became Soka Gakkai. In his work, *Soka kyoikugaku taikei* ("A Theory of Value-Creating Pedagogy"), Makiguchi emphasized a "system of learning based on methods to nurture capable people who will create value as befits a purpose in life"; or to be more precise, the society advocated the reform of educational policies and educational methods. Accordingly, the membership in the early period was overwhelmingly composed of educators, and the Soka Kyoiku Gakkai was only minimally involved in political activities. Both Makiguchi and Toda were believers of Nichiren Shoshu Buddhism, which was considered heterodox by the more traditional Buddhist community. Their religious beliefs undoubtedly had a primary influence on both men and, consequently, on the organization itself. However, it was not until the later Soka Gakkai that this Buddhist philosophy gained more prominence in the organization's goals and activities.

In the years preceding World War II, it appears that the society became involved in politics only incidentally. During this period, in which Japan was becoming increasingly militaristic, it was impossible for the educational reforms proposed by Makiguchi to be accepted by the government. Indeed, circumstances were such that Makiguchi would be forced to resign from his position as principal because of his strong stance on educational reform. Makiguchi realized that the period in which he was living was the world of *mappo*, or the Latter Day of the Law.[1] Consequently, he began to direct his energies into activities for *kosen-rufu*, which aimed at widely spreading and communicating a correct understanding of Buddhism. In this way, the society, which was initially centered on educational issues, started to attract members from diverse backgrounds. At the end of 1941, before the start of the Pacific war, it is thought that the membership numbered 3,000. However, with the onset of the war and its prolonged duration, the military and the government, mutually supported as they were by state Shinto, proceeded to control religions and ideologies. Thus, the arm of oppression also began to close in on the Soka Kyoiku Gakkai. In response to this, Makiguchi, faithful to the teachings of Nichiren, claimed that now was the time to reveal the errors of the political leaders with regard to the gravity of the state of the nation and to urge the leaders that it was indispensable for them to base their actions on a correct understanding of Buddhism. In this way, the Gakkai found itself gradually pulled into the real world of politics.

In July of 1943 in Izu, where he was visiting for the purposes of propagation, Makiguchi was arrested on suspicion of *lèse majesté*

---

[1] *Mappo* refers to a period in which Shakyamuni's Buddhism (i.e. the "Law" or "Dharma") begins to lose its effect and eventually dies out. Much like eschatological theories in Europe, there are various hypotheses regarding the exact beginning of the age of *mappo*; however, in Japan there is a general consensus that the period in which Nichiren (1222–82), the founder of Nichiren Shoshu, lived was already the age of *mappo*. Asserting that the day in which he lived was indeed the age of *mappo*, Nichiren believed that the prevalence of natural calamities, famine, and epidemics could be attributed to the widespread acceptance of erroneous teachings and misleading claims. For this reason, Nichiren wrote the *Rissho ankoku ron* ("Treatise on Securing the Peace of the Land through the Propagation of True Buddhism"), in which he emphatically stated the need to establish True Dharma, or True Buddhism and correct practice. This treatise was submitted to the Kamakura government of his time, but was rejected. Following this remonstration with the government, Nichiren was assailed and exiled by the government on two separate occasions. These experiences surely led him to become even more convinced that this was indeed the age of *mappo* and strengthened the idea that only through reform of politics or with constructive cooperation with authority figures of that time could True Buddhism be firmly established.

and violation of the Maintenance of Public Order Act,[2] and sent to prison in Tokyo. On the same day Toda was also taken into custody from his home and incarcerated in the same prison. In the subsequent period, until March 1944, a total of twenty-one Soka Kyoiku Gakkai leaders were arrested. Several months later, in November of 1944, Makiguchi passed away from old age and malnutrition.[3] By the time the war came to a close, the Soka Kyoiku Gakkai was on the verge of dissolution.[4]

Josei Toda played a critical role in the reconstruction and development of the Soka Gakkai after the war, and his later actions appear to have been greatly influenced by the legacy of the Soka Kyoiku Gakkai as summarized above. Toda had served as the general director while Makiguchi was president, and as reflected in his efforts to support the Gakkai in both its financial and organizational aspects, it seems that he was more a man with entrepreneurial and organizational skills than an educator. His persecution at the hands of the state authorities most likely served to further deepen Toda's belief in Nichiren Buddhism, and Makiguchi's death in prison led Toda to vow in his heart to succeed his mentor in making the widespread propagation of "True Buddhism" a reality. When Toda was finally released on bail in July 1945, he was greeted by Japan's defeat in the war and the confusion that followed in its wake—truly the most terrible manifestations of a society in the age of *mappo*.

In the midst of such circumstances, Toda changed the name of the Soka Kyoiku Gakkai to Soka Gakkai in March 1946 and, making the society both in name and reality a religious lay organization of Nichiren Shoshu, vigorously initiated activities toward the goal

[2] This law was actually a pretext used by the increasingly militaristic government to control freedom of expression and thought.

[3] As Japan became an ultranationalistic stronghold, it was common for individuals accused of thought- or religion-related crimes to be held in prison, even though their guilt or innocence had never been determined.

[4] Most of the leaders who were arrested during the war were released as soon as they renounced their belief in Nichiren Shoshu Buddhism. In this sense, with the sole exception of Makiguchi, there are no martyrs in the Soka Gakkai.

of *kosen-rufu*. As a result of his efforts, the membership, which was virtually nonexistent after the war, gradually grew in number. By 1951 it is reported to have consisted of approximately 5,000 households.[5] In the same year Toda was elected as the second president of the society (first president since the name was changed to the Soka Gakkai). As president-elect, Toda announced that he would increase the membership to 750,000 households within his lifetime. To achieve this goal, he poured his energies into the development of the organizational structure and emphasized the importance of studying the teachings of Nichiren among the members. Thereby he laid the foundation for propagation activities on a nationwide level. According to the official figures given by the Soka Gakkai, the goal of 750,000 households was accomplished by the end of 1957, several months before Toda's death the following April.

Making matters more complex, however, was the fact that the Soka Gakkai had started to make a move into local assembly politics in 1955. With a presence in the public arena, the religious activities of the Soka Gakkai also started to attract attention. As the seemingly assertive propagation activities, called *shakubuku*, continued to advance, they came under strong attack from other religions and the mass media. Nevertheless, this did not affect the movement's further development, and the Soka Gakkai experienced amazingly rapid growth to an official membership of 6 million households by 1966. In the subsequent years various issues arose, as will be discussed below, which put a stop to the explosive rate of growth. These obstacles notwithstanding, by 1971 the membership grew to 7.5 million households, with the numbers increasing in small increments ever since. Today, the official membership stands at over 8 million households.[6]

[5] Within the Soka Gakkai the household is used as the unit for tallying membership. This method may have been adopted because one of the criteria for membership is to have a *Gohonzon*, and also on the assumption that, in general, an entire household prays to the same *Gohonzon*. Because of this usage, the exact membership figures probably cannot be ascertained, even by Soka Gakkai itself.

[6] Although it is quite complicated to try to estimate the number of active

In order to understand the relationship between the Soka Gakkai and Japanese politics, it is first necessary to examine what actually constituted *kosen-rufu* and, in this regard, to examine the diverse factors that brought about the rapid growth of the Gakkai. From such an analysis, a more distinct picture of the "politics" with which we are concerned should emerge.

Economic Development and *Kosen-rufu* in Post-War Japan

The period of Soka Gakkai's most rapid growth was from 1951 to 1970, which happened to coincide with a period of rapid development of the Japanese economy. Although the Japanese economy suffered a period of dire need and chaos for several years following World War II, by the 1950s signs of reconstruction were becoming apparent. The special procurements called for by the Korean War further spurred postwar recovery, so that from the late 1950s to the early 1960s it became clear that Japan had entered a period of high growth. It was not until the 1970s that the prospect of continued growth began to wane, and with the first oil shock of 1973, the Japanese economy entered a new phase. The growth of the Soka Gakkai proceeded as if following the pace of the economy—rapidly from 1951 and, from the 1970s until the present, at a more subdued rate.

The Soka Gakkai's sudden spurt of growth spanned a twenty-year period and stands out in contrast to that of other religious groups. Many new religions surfaced in the chaotic aftermath of the war, and many of the religious groups that had existed before the war had also been revived. However, many of these new religions disappeared as the postwar confusion began to subside, and even those that remained never gained a large following. The only exception, other than the Soka Gakkai, is probably the Rissho Kosei-kai, but even its growth cannot compare with that of the

members based on the official membership figures, when taking a multitude of factors into consideration, one might venture to say that the number of active members after 1970 is roughly half of the official figures.

Soka Gakkai. Why is it, then, that the Soka Gakkai was able to achieve such a spectacular growth during this period? The answer is complex. It is essential, first, to examine aspects of doctrine and organizational structure, for in these two aspects the Soka Gakkai exhibits characteristics not found in the other new religions.

First, with regard to doctrine, the Soka Gakkai was established as a lay organization of believers who maintained faith in Nichiren Shoshu. The teachings of Nichiren had characteristics that distinguished it from both the conventional religions and the various religions that arose during the Kamakura period (1185–1333). Buddhist concepts traditionally associated with concerns of one's own individual life—such as life after death, metempsychosis, or *satori* (moments of awakening)—were prevalent in these religions. In Nichiren Buddhism, however, these concepts were played down. Emphasis was placed instead on establishing a correct understanding and practice of Buddhism in this life, both for individuals and in society. Moreover, inasmuch as the world in which Nichiren lived was in the age of *mappo*—an age of confusion and delusion—it was difficult to expect everyone in society to embrace True Buddhism, regardless of efforts put forth by Nichiren and his followers. For this reason, Nichiren was convinced that the ideal society according to Buddhism would have to be realized through people in influential positions—that is, through politics. The *Rissho ankoku ron* ("Treatise on Securing the Peace of the Land through the Propagation of True Buddhism"), a pivotal work by Nichiren, can be understood as a proposal to create a peaceful and prosperous land based on such an awareness.[7] In other words, the "salvation" at issue for Nichiren clearly meant the salvation of society and of those who lived amidst the realities of this world. In this sense, one could say that the postwar activities of the Soka Gakkai were true to the spirit and teachings of Nichiren. While actively promoting *kosen-rufu*, of which politics is a part, the Soka Gakkai

---

[7] The word *koku* (country or land) as used in the title *Rissho ankoku ron*, differs from the English words "state" or "nation," and can be interpreted in several ways. In this particular case, it should probably be understood as a society that includes the political realm.

has also made headway in the realms of education and culture in its efforts to realize a peaceful and prosperous society.

According to the explanations given by the Soka Gakkai, *kosen-rufu* means to build a society based on the Buddhism expounded by Nichiren, to bring about the rise of a humanistic culture, and to establish firmly a lasting peace. In addition, the Buddhist practices of the believers in the age of *mappo* include converting those who hold erroneous beliefs to embrace the "true" Buddhism (*shakubuku*). By widely spreading and communicating Nichiren's teachings (*kosen-rufu*), they seek to save a society, a nation, even the world. While many religions, including Christianity, ultimately seek the salvation of individuals, the doctrine followed by the Soka Gakkai considers that the self and the environment (other people, society, nature, etc.) are mutually intertwined and, together as one, shape reality. Thus, in conjunction with one's own transformation and salvation, the surrounding environment will also change and be saved, which in turn will again have an impact on one's own transformation. Consequently, the basis for judging what constitutes true Buddhism and what constitutes an erroneous belief is not the notion of an absolute god as in Christianity, but rather is subjectified as something of this world. In this way, it is also possible for individual believers to connect Buddhist practices with the pursuit of secular gain.

In the summer of 1951 the Soka Gakkai announced that it would conduct a "Great Propagation Campaign" and proceeded to accelerate its propagation activities in order to achieve its goal of religious reformation. By emphasizing that the postwar Japanese period was exemplary of the age of *mappo,* and by opposing the existing order and its degeneration, this propagation activity was highly successful. The Soka Gakkai membership rapidly increased, mainly among those who were of the downtrodden classes in large urban areas and who were excluded from the benefits of the upward swing during the reconstruction period of postwar Japan.[8]

---

[8] Before the economic takeoff most self-sufficient agricultural communities in Japan remained stable compared to the large urban areas. One could say they were spared the social turmoil experienced in large cities.

Accordingly, a certain image of "reform" became attached to the Soka Gakkai at this time. On the one hand, this "reformist stance" had a refreshing appeal to those citizens who were dissatisfied with the existing order. On the other hand, when this image was combined with an exclusivist religious nature, a large number of people sensed a kind of fascism in the Soka Gakkai. However, when one takes into account the uniquely Japanese traits of the Soka Gakkai, one can see that there was never really a threat that it would move toward fascism. Still, these kinds of propagation activities gave the impression of authoritarianism and rigid discipline.

The Soka Gakkai's basic organization, the structural development of which had achieved some stability by 1952, consisted of a pyramid, at the top of which stood the headquarters, then several regional chapters, which in turn were organized into districts, groups, and subgroups, with leaders appointed at each of the levels. At the same time the organization of the youth division, the standard-bearers for this Great Propagation Campaign, evolved separately from that of the pyramidal structure of the Soka Gakkai, with the youth division members belonging to different units. Thus, the main structure and the youth division units pursued propagation activities separately. Indeed, it was as if the structural development of the youth division was an attempt to form the core in a religious reformation movement. The young men and young women's divisions, which took on key responsibilities in the propagation activities, were initially organized in a format that bore some semblance to the military. A unit leader was appointed to each of the units within the youth division and also received a unit banner from the president. Soon after the units were established, an advisory committee was designated for the youth division, including staff members responsible for strategic planning. Whether it be the basic organization of the Soka Gakkai or the unit structure of the youth division, the representatives at each level most likely held a corresponding amount of authority, with the president as the focal point. As for the actual propagation activities, they were conducted with a certain competitiveness between the chapters and the various youth division units. Yet, because the new members who had been introduced to this Buddhism by the youth division were placed in subgroups, which were the smallest units of the chapters, the organization as a whole experienced exponential growth.

As for the sociological composition of the people who were newly introduced to this practice, it is often thought that the main body consisted of the lower to lower-middle stratum of large urban centers. To be more specific, one might say that these were employees, managers, or owners of small and medium-sized businesses that included the manufacturing and service industries. If one were to situate these individuals in postwar Japanese society, one could probably identify two distinct groups. The first consisted of those who, upon observing their circumstances amid the postwar chaos, found a living environment almost identical to that before the war. For these individuals, a decisive difference between their prewar and postwar experiences lay in the fact that they had been firmly rooted in their surroundings before the war—previously, there had existed communities in which they even served as "district commissioners."⁹ As the turmoil of democratization set in, these communities were destroyed, at least to all appearances. Hence, a strong sense of estrangement from postwar society developed. The second group, which for our purposes is more significant, consisted of young working class laborers who flocked to the city in droves during the revitalization of postwar capitalism. Since these were individuals who had no stable base in their daily lives and tended to be mobile, they differed fundamentally from the first group. However, one could discern a number of commonalities as well. For instance, people in both of these groups had difficulty adjusting to the "isolating individuation" of the urban centers, and in many cases they felt what might be called a kind of "nostalgia" toward the community. Above all, they were among

⁹ Since people from this socioeconomic background were not recent urban transplants, they tended to occupy prominent positions in their local community. As the war intensified, the "neighborly assistance" system evolved. People from this class were often appointed to leadership positions, thus assuming key responsibilities in the management of their communities.

those who were excluded from the prosperity that was generated by economic development. With these points complementing each other, it seems inevitable that a strong sense of alienation should set deeply in their consciousness.

If, indeed, the bulk of the membership originated in these groups, then it is not necessarily surprising that the Soka Gakkai developed rapidly from 1951 onward. To this feeling of dissatisfaction and frustration, the Soka Gakkai offered a sense of returning to a communal order, an understanding of Buddhist philosophy, and the possibility of obtaining benefits in this lifetime. As mentioned earlier, the act of propagation consisted of tireless efforts to convert those who held erroneous beliefs, and this necessitated a pyramidal structure and regulations. Consequently, becoming a member signified a definitive return to a communal order. Furthermore, the results achieved through the act of propagation fostered a sense of satisfaction for the individual as a member of a group. In this way, it may be said that this constituted a logic of direct action, which did not necessarily entail a religious and internal satisfaction. Moreover, at the point of the hierarchical pyramid structure stood a charismatic mentor in life who guaranteed the realization of an "earthly paradise" through achieving *kosen-rufu*. And members could climb the rungs of this hierarchy by demonstrating their knowledge of Buddhism through a series of study examinations.

In effect, during this period of growth, one can observe several qualities that distinguish the Soka Gakkai from other new religions. First, whereas immediately following the war many of the other new religions grew rapidly as a result of the societal chaos and the reaffirmation of religious freedom in the new constitution, they had already begun to lose their initial momentum by the time the food shortage had ended and society had returned to a somewhat stable state. In contrast, the Soka Gakkai continued to increase its membership throughout the period of social stabilization and economic development. Second, while other religions accepted mutual coexistence as a premise, the Soka Gakkai's attitude was basically exclusive, attacking all other religions for propounding erroneous teachings.[10] It did not even recognize, for instance, the amalgamation of Shintoism and Buddhism seen in Japan in the last 400 years or so.[11] And, from this viewpoint, what determined the "value" of the believers within the Soka Gakkai was the extent to which they were successful in their propagation activities. Third, a point that is of particular importance with respect to the subject at hand, the other new religions tended to respond to personal insecurities and dissatisfactions with a philosophy of self-restraint and morals. Because of this inner-directed orientation, they showed an overt tendency to avoid involvement in social problems as much as possible. In contrast, the Soka Gakkai, by focusing on the link between benefits in this lifetime and victory over present circumstances, possessed the characteristics of a social movement from the very start. Judging from this analysis, it was hardly surprising that only four years after the Great Propagation Campaign was initiated, the Soka Gakkai began to make its move into local assembly politics.

Launch into Japanese Politics and *Obutsumyogo*

In 1955 the Soka Gakkai entered local assembly politics. Beginning with the election on April 24 of then general director, Takashi Koizumi, in the Tokyo metropolitan assembly elections, the Soka Gakkai succeeded in getting fifty-one of its fifty-two candidates elected in the April 30 unified local elections, mainly for the ward assemblies in Tokyo.[12] From this point on, the Soka Gakkai's

[10] In the case of the Soka Gakkai, vigorous doctrinal debates on Buddhism were held with other Nichiren schools (mainly the Minobu sect), which all claim Nichiren as the founder. This served to establish the Soka Gakkai's identity. In addition, the Soka Gakkai, which was founded as an organization of lay believers of the Nichiren Shoshu, has sometimes differed in opinion from the priesthood of the Nichiren Shoshu.

[11] During the Edo period (1600–1867) it was not unusual for Shinto gods and Buddhist gods or Buddhas to be worshipped side by side. Not only was it a custom to hold Shinto weddings and Buddhist funerals in the lives of ordinary people, the cases are too numerous to mention in which Shinto shrines and Buddhist temples exist within the same compound.

[12] With the new start of established local autonomy and local governance after World War II, the general rule has been to hold local elections throughout

involvement in local assembly politics increased rapidly, to the point where in 1967 the local assembly members numbered close to 2,000. Moreover, at the national level, three members were elected to the Upper House during the 1956 campaigns, and with each subsequent Upper House election, which took place every three years, the number of its elected representatives increased.[13] At first, these representatives belonged to the Komei Political League, a section within the Soka Gakkai itself. In 1964, however, Daisaku Ikeda, third president of the Soka Gakkai, suggested the institutional separation of the Soka Gakkai as a religious body and the League as a political body. Thus was formed the Komeito political party, built on the preexisting Political League. Finally, in 1967, the Soka Gakkai fielded thirty-two candidates for the Lower House elections, of which twenty-five were elected. When it succeeded in getting forty-seven members elected in 1969, it became the third largest party nationwide. In this way, albeit through the form of the Komeito, the Soka Gakkai launched itself with full force into national politics.

What, then, is the relative weight that the Komeito carries in present-day Japanese politics? Given current conditions, this is actually quite difficult to gauge. Ever since the collapse of the Liberal Democratic Party (LDP) administration in 1993, a far-reaching transformation occurred in the Japanese political party system. As of October 1998 the Komeito was not represented in the Lower House.[14] Nevertheless, one could attempt to measure

Japan (for heads of local government and for representatives at the local assembly levels) on the same day, a system known as the "unified local elections." This system has collapsed and is no longer applied uniformly, but unified local elections are still held.

[13] The Japanese Parliament or Diet consists of two houses: the House of Councilors (Upper House) and the House of Representatives (Lower House). The prime minister being elected by the Lower House, the latter is of central importance in national politics.

[14] In the overall momentum for realignment and repositioning of political parties after 1993 a new political party, the New Frontier Party, was formed in December 1994 from a merger of several parties and groups in opposition. Equally participating were all Lower House representatives from the Komeito as well as those councilors who faced new elections as their terms were

its general influence by examining the Upper House elections. In the Upper House elections held in July 1998, the votes garnered in the nationwide constituency (proportional representation) by the Komei political group (a derivative of the former Komeito) numbered approximately 7,748,000—about 14 percent of the total number of votes. In the previous election in 1995 the Upper House candidates ran as part of the newly formed New Frontier Party, with which the Komeito had merged, and thus the relative polling score cannot be ascertained. However, in the 1992 elections, while the Komeito garnered only about 6,415,000 votes, this is accounted for by a significantly low voter turnout. It still captured about 14 percent of the total number of votes. Since the transition to the current electoral system in 1983,[15] the Komeito's relative polling score has remained within the range of 11–16 percent, suggesting that the Komeito, and incidentally the Soka Gakkai, has secured a stable position in Japanese politics.[16]

Given the above, it would appear that the development of the Komeito mirrored the rate of progress in the Soka Gakkai's propagation activities. As for the rationale behind the Soka Gakkai's decision to participate in the realm of politics by running numerous candidates for the Diet and local assemblies, documents from the early period that would offer some clarification are unavailable. However, according to a statement made much later by Einosuke Akiya, fifth president of the Soka Gakkai, one of the motives for

ending. Those remaining with Komeito formed a political group, Komei. Later on, many of the representatives who had joined the New Frontier Party split off again to form the Shinto Heiwa (New Peace Party), only to merge with Komei in November 1998 to form anew the Komeito. See also the discussion in the next section in this chapter.

[15] Voters cast two ballots—one for their chosen party in a nationwide proportional representation system, and one for a specific individual in local constituencies.

[16] There are no examples in Japanese history, either before or after World War II, of religious organizations running their own political candidates except for the Soka Gakkai. Names of other religious groups do surface come election time, but this is because established politicians use religious groups as a reliable source of votes. Moreover, religious political parties of the type known in the West have never existed in Japan.

getting involved in politics was to "get politics into the hands of the common people."[17] In any case, the book *Current of Revolution: 45 Years' History of the Soka Gakkai*[18] records the bare facts: "In the year 1955, the Soka Gakkai was brimming with an ever-enthusiastic spirit as it made progress . . . and . . . the General Director at the time, Takashi Koizumi, announced his candidacy for the Tokyo Metropolitan Assembly elections. This marked the beginning of a Gakkai member's venture into politics." The ensuing passages state that "a fair number of members belonging to the Culture Division presented themselves as candidates in the unified local elections held this year," but offer no further explanation as to why it is that the members of the Soka Gakkai's culture division— formed in November of the preceding year and comprised mainly of academics, educators, and entrepreneurs—should enter politics. However, a closer examination of the passages that follow reveals references to "the unified local elections, which can be considered the inaugural campaign of cultural activities" or "beginning with religious revolution, a vast momentum of revolution was launched in the realms of politics, economy, education, and culture." This suggests that the Soka Gakkai's presence in politics was to be considered as one facet of "cultural activities." As in the propagation activities, the youth division members were to play a central role in the elections.

In this way, the Soka Gakkai's participation in politics progressed in cadence with its propagation activities—in discrete stages, yet with dramatic speed. One could say the basis for this action was indeed Nichiren's teachings. As mentioned above, the crux of Nichiren's teachings is to save the world in its present state, here and now. This position forms the underlying principle for the concepts *obutsumyogo*, or the "convergence of *oho* and *buppo*,"[19]

[17] Speech at the Japan Foreign Press Club, 1994.
[18] (Tokyo: Seikyo Shimbun Press, 1975). This book can be considered the official forty-five-year history of Soka Gakkai.
[19] Although it is hard to define the word *oho* in a succinct manner, in the case of Nichiren Buddhism, it can be considered to designate the principles of politics. If we limit ourselves to "politics," "convergence of *oho* and *buppo*" implies that the Buddhist philosophy of compassion and dignity of life serves

and "establishment of a national high sanctuary,"[20] which became passwords for the Soka Gakkai's entry into politics. *Obutsumyogo* is an idea in which both *oho* and *buppo* spiritually and morally concur to bring about a peaceful and tranquil country and society. The idea of establishing a national high sanctuary is, to use Nichiren's expression, an attempt to accomplish *kosen-rufu* by constructing a sanctuary upon official mandate by the country or with the acknowledgment of the emperor and of the Kamakura shogunate at that time.[21] Thus, the Soka Gakkai's entry into the political arena, far from being inconsistent with the Great Propagation Campaign, was an attempt to extend the realm of its activities in the quest for *kosen-rufu*.

However, incorporating *obutsumyogo* as a key component of the rationale for entering into politics was not without problems. In this day and age the concept of *obutsumyogo* in and of itself cannot designate concrete policies, as it may have done in the time of Nichiren. It goes without saying that, according to this concept, the present world, being in a state of chaos, suffering, and delusion, requires reforms and efforts to make it a better place. Yet as long as one advocates consistency of *oho* and *buppo*, such reforms preclude a complete rejection of the existing system and the institution of a regime based on divine right as an actualization of religious convictions.[22] Indeed, what the Soka Gakkai and its

as an underlying principle in politics and is manifested in the realm of politics through the actions of politicians. Thus, here, it would not be incorrect to consider *oho* to signify "politics."

[20] "Sanctuary" generally refers to a place where the ceremony to confer the Buddhist precepts is held—an ordination platform for the teaching of Buddhism.

[21] The idea of establishing a national high sanctuary involved an element that touches on Article 20 of the Japanese constitution regarding "freedom of religious beliefs", and thus provoked widespread debate in the public domain. Even within the Soka Gakkai there was no unanimous opinion on this issue, but after much reflection the Gakkai, in 1970, clearly abandoned its advocacy of establishing a national high sanctuary on the basis of its position of protecting democracy and the constitution.

[22] The concept of *obutsumyogo* was criticized as representing unity of state and religion, but these apprehensions turned out to be without cause. It is exactly as the Soka Gakkai asserts: "politics . . . based on *obutsumyogo* must

candidates called for during the early stages was not a complete overhaul of the existing system, but simply an end to the corrupt and degenerate state of Japanese politics, along with clean and fair elections.[23]

Thus, even though *obutsumyogo* may have been a principle underlying the Soka Gakkai's involvement in politics, one cannot posit that the Soka Gakkai has consistently sought to transpose its religious objectives to the political arena. Examined from the perspective of *oho* and *buppo*, it might be conceivable that the Buddhist virtues of compassion and dignity of life serve as standards for action in society, but Buddhism itself could never serve as an underlying principle that would translate into specific policies. Rather, it is here that *oho*, as a set of principles that prescribe the actions and behavior of the religious group in this present world, comes into play instead of *buppo*—serving to "rectify" the way politics should be. To put it bluntly, one could consider that the presence of Soka Gakkai members in the world of politics in itself represents the concept of *obutsumyogo*. Traditional religions in Japan have always tended to distance themselves from the real world, evolving toward form without substance, as rituals increasingly took on an importance of their own. This has encouraged the constant appearance of new religions that expound benefits in this world. This characteristic of new religions in Japan is common also to the Soka Gakkai. However, the Soka Gakkai differentiates itself from other new religions by its active involvement in the realities of the present world, based on the concept of seeking harmony between *oho* and *buppo*.

refuse and distance itself from authoritarianism" (*Seikyo Shimbun*, Jan. 8, 1967).

[23] The Japanese word "Komei" means clean, fair, and disinterested. Until the formation of the Komei Political Federation, the expression "Komei elections", or "clean elections", was used by the election administration commission at each level of government in a campaign to prevent election fraud. The fact that this campaign expression was used as the name for organizing a political party is indicative of the nature of the relationship between the Soka Gakkai and politics.

During the course of its phenomenal rise in political prominence, the Soka Gakkai developed a reformist image, as exemplified in the expression "humanistic socialism," and emphasized the abolition of the present state of affairs. Yet even during this stage the Soka Gakkai failed to elaborate fundamental solutions for changing the existing system, and such progressive stances receded rapidly as its influence grew. Although social welfare, peace, and freedom of religious beliefs remained part of its political goals, it could be said that the very fact that such goals were never explicitly developed as systematic policies meant that the objectives of the political movement ended up by being directed toward its own expansion, rather than toward the realization of some principle or ideal. It is no surprise that this logic or reasoning, based on the concept of consistency between *oho* and *buppo*, should give rise to competition for electoral seats when transposed to the field of politics, since the act of propagation also implies aims for extending influence as a goal unto itself. The race for electoral seats served to reaffirm its commitment to the democratic process, and thus, to win seats became a major objective of the Soka Gakkai's activities. Consequently, even investing a large part of its energy in that direction became simply a matter of course.

Once elected, the numerous representatives from the Soka Gakkai succeeded in presenting a layman's critique of politics, which was an expression of their impartial position based on a nonideological stance. One such Diet member professed, "Because I am not fully versed in the intricacies of politics, I will study seriously from now on." Such expressions of sincerity, untainted by stale, business-as-usual "professionalism," were completely incompatible with previous images of politicians in Japan. Indeed, the reality of Japanese politics is that everything is limited to a question of political manoeuvring, and the act of becoming a politician is in itself supposed to guarantee expertise and knowhow in politics. In fact, the job of a politician, far from requiring dedication or lofty ideals, is generally perceived simply as a job like any other, as long as it offers money, power, and prestige. Therefore, one cannot deny that this kind of sincere and serious attitude on the part of

Soka Gakkai-backed politicians shattered the way politics were conducted in Japan, serving as a catalyst for "cleaning up" the current situation. This layman's approach certainly made an impact on the debilitated state of postwar Japanese democracy, while having a positive effect on the development of the Soka Gakkai. However, because they voiced no fundamental criticisms against the existing system, representatives supported by the Soka Gakkai were faced with numerous dilemmas when they had to go beyond simple advocacy of clean politics to deliberating more concretely on various policy issues.

Founding and Development of the Komeito

Before evolving into a full-fledged political party, the Komei Political Federation was an organization internal to the Soka Gakkai, functioning as the political section of the culture division. As Daisaku Ikeda, then president of the Soka Gakkai, declared at the time, "We are not a political party . . . therefore, we are not making a move into the Lower House. We shall be backing various candidates only in those areas which are unrelated to party politics, such as the House of Councillors or local assemblies."[24] Thus, the Soka Gakkai had no intentions of seeking political power, and the function of the Komei Political League was merely to use the various assemblies as a forum through which to voice objections to the degenerate state of politics in the age of *mappo*. In 1964, however, the Soka Gakkai took the decisive step to enter the Lower House (although actual elections occurred only in 1967). Daisaku Ikeda explains, "Should [the members] consent, I think that the [Komei Political League] can, if need be, become a political party, or send [representatives to] the Lower House in order to realize *obutsumyogo*, as well as in response to the needs of our times and the demands of the people . . ."[25] By the end of that year the Komei Political League was reorganized to form the Komeito, as an independent political party outside the Soka Gakkai.

---

[24] *Seikyo Shimbun*, May 5, 1964.   [25] Ibid.

Furthermore, visions for forming a government were later elaborated, and the Komeito shifted its focus of activities to place more emphasis on the Lower House.

Although the formation of the Komeito and its entry into Lower House politics were generally seen as a watershed in the Soka Gakkai's political involvement, it seems this change of direction was considered to be a natural course of events by those within the Soka Gakkai. Hence the Komeito, despite its independent status, retained the image of being the political wing of the Soka Gakkai. Furthermore, the reformist, radical characteristic of the Komei Political League, not to mention its basic stance of raising political issues only when the situation could be said to demand it, remained unchanged. As outlined above, the Soka Gakkai is action-oriented. If it is true that this emphasis on concrete action is a guiding philosophy, then it inevitably follows that one of the goals for its activities in various fields must be to expand its influence as much as possible. Participation in politics was not only a means of broadening its influence, but also the manifestation of increased influence. As such, it seemed logical to start off by running candidates for the Upper House and local assemblies, where the chance of winning a seat was high, only to enter the Lower House later as its electoral base strengthened. Likewise it was natural that, when it was not a political party, it should compete for seats in assemblies where politics were less partisan, yet was compelled to become a political party in order to run for offices that were closely affiliated with party politics.[26]

In this way, the Komeito, which was launched as an independent organization distinct from the Soka Gakkai, successfully won twenty-five seats in the House of Representatives in 1967, and

---

[26] In the case of Japan, the great majority of representatives of the Lower House belong to a political party. However, until the 1970s this was not necessarily the case in the Upper House, which was considered to be relatively nonpartisan. Of course, in part as a consequence of change in the electoral system, at present the Upper House exhibits characteristics similar to the Lower House. As for local or regional assemblies, except for the major cities, one could say that there are more independent elected officials than not. The heads of local government are still mostly independent.

forty-seven seats in the late 1969 elections, rising immediately to become the third largest party.²⁷ At this point, however, one could say it had not fully succeeded in shedding its character as the political branch of the Soka Gakkai. This is evident in the party's fundamental principles and program, which echo Buddhist phrases used by the Soka Gakkai, such as "the great ideal of the fusion of *oho* and *buppo*" and "essence of life philosophy," while simultaneously promoting abstract ideals such as "global citizenship," "humanistic socialism," and "Buddhist democracy" that did not directly lend themselves to concrete policy elaboration. The usage of Buddhist terminology in the Komeito's program is significant for two reasons. First, it clearly served to steer believers' religious sentiments toward politics. Second, the above list of abstract "ideals" encompasses all major political ideologies present in modern society, with a certain doctrinal flourish. In other words, one could assert that, while the former served to channel the energies into action, the latter served as an eventual justification, should that become necessary, for the various positions it might have to take in response to changing circumstances.

In fact, the Komeito was to change its nature as an extension of the Soka Gakkai sooner than expected. In 1970, the year after it became the third largest political party in the House of Representatives, the so-called "freedom of press incident" occurred, exposing the close relationship that the Komeito enjoyed with the Soka Gakkai to public criticism. Komeito party officials allegedly tried to obstruct the publication of a book that was critical of the Soka Gakkai and the Komeito. The Komeito flatly denies the allegations, and the details of the case remain unsubstantiated. However, the incident prompted the Komeito to shed its religious identity and become an "open" party that enjoys more widespread support of the Japanese people. Serious steps were taken with a view to severing ties between politics and reli-

²⁷ The largest party at the time was the LDP, which constantly held the majority in the Lower House, thus forming a stable government. The second-ranking party was the Japan Socialist Party, the fourth, the Democratic Socialist Party, and the fifth, the Japan Communist Party.

gion, as proven in the amendment to the party's program and party regulations, and as reflected in the subsequent reorganization of party alliances and positions in the opposition. First, regarding the new party principles and program, all Buddhist doctrinal terminology, which abounded in the original version, disappeared. Policies were proposed in a more concrete form. For example, regarding the constitution, which is not even mentioned in the original document, the amended version declares, "Our party shall uphold the Japanese Constitution . . . and shall not only protect fundamental human rights, but also seek to secure fundamental social rights," clearly indicating its new orientation as a secular, non-religious party. Furthermore, Komeito's participation in the realignment of opposition party alliances became a serious option, hitherto impossible as long as it adhered to the religious tenets of the Soka Gakkai. As for the Gakkai, it officially renounced the idea of a national high sanctuary in 1970, which had been one of its religious themes. In its relationship with the Komeito, it decided upon clear guidelines not to appoint party representatives to leadership positions in the Soka Gakkai, and to dissociate itself completely from personnel affairs, candidacy decisions, finances, and management of the party.

After its new beginning the Komeito slipped to fourth position among political parties in 1972 with twenty-nine elected representatives, but regained its former ranking in the following elections in 1976 with fifty-six elected officials. Moreover, with fifty-eight seats in 1979, fifty-nine seats in 1983 (the best results ever reached since its formation), and fifty-seven seats in 1986, it is safe to say it remained secure as the third largest force in the Japanese Lower House. It is worth noting that the fifty-nine seats won in the 1983 elections were considered, by both the general observer and the Komeito, as reflecting the maximum extent of its appeal. That is to say, the incident in 1970 which had triggered the severance of ties between the Soka Gakkai and the Komeito had repercussions for the Soka Gakkai itself. In 1971 Soka Gakkai saw an end to its phenomenal growth, with only incremental increases in membership since that time. As a result, for the Komeito to continue its growth, it had no choice but to nurture support among electorates other than the Soka Gakkai members. Consequently, the party multiplied efforts to formulate more concrete and detailed policies, but it would seem that in the 1980s efforts to capture new electorates in this manner also had their limitations.[28]

Now let us turn to the actual policies and vision as elaborated by the Komeito after its break from the Soka Gakkai. The first point that should be raised concerns the Komeito's efforts to reestablish diplomatic relations between Japan and China. The Komeito delegation to China in June 1971 presented a five-point proposal for renewed diplomatic ties to Zhou Enlai and other top Chinese officials. This was accepted in a joint declaration whereby both parties expressed intentions to work together in that direction. The Komeito thus succeeded in setting the wheels in motion for normalization of bilateral relations. Furthermore, in May and July of 1972 the Komeito dispatched two more delegations to China, arriving at a basic accord on normalization of ties with that country. Finally, in September diplomatic ties were officially recognized between the two governments. It is not clear what exchanges took place between the Japanese government and the Komeito throughout this whole process. Be that as it may, one could appreciate this success as a result made possible only by the freedom enjoyed by a newly formed political party that upheld a "progressive centrist" position. By clearly indicating its political stance, the Komeito took a significant step toward asserting itself as a nonreligiously affiliated party.

After its major success on the diplomatic front, the Komeito turned its attention to domestic policy, announcing successive

---

[28] It is necessary here to look at the Soka Gakkai votes as a percentage of the total number of votes cast for Komeito candidates. Because actual statistics are unavailable, one is forced to rely on conjecture, but by calculating the number of obtained votes and the number of active Soka Gakkai members, we can surmise that approximately 90 percent in pre-1970 national elections came from Gakkai members. It would seem this percentage fell to 60–5 percent in the late 1970s and 1980s. Thus, one can conclude that the Komeito was successful in reaching voters outside of the Soka Gakkai, but even so, the level of non-Gakkai support probably does not exceed 40 percent.

measures centered on social welfare. However, with the LDP government's unchallenged majority in the Diet, and with each party emphasizing social welfare, one might say that the Komeito failed to get important results in this field. Yet, by the late 1970s the LDP's firm grip on the Diet began to slip, and by the 1980s it became a fairly common sight for the balance of power between the ruling party and opposition to be on equal footing. What is more, the Japan Socialist Party (JSP), which had consistently been the main opposition party during this period, failed to display interest in actively taking over the reins of power from the LDP. As a result, the Komeito, in order to fill the void, started playing a crucial role in the political landscape as a potential partner in a future coalition government. Although it had announced its vision for a coalition government of centrist and progressive parties as early as 1973 during the Eleventh Party Convention, it was not until the end of 1979 that it reached an agreement with the Democratic Socialist Party. By early summer 1980 the Komeito had also worked out an accord with the JSP on this matter.

The 1980s were thus a period of incubation for the Komeito, during which it continued to nurse its plans for a future coalition government. This coincided with the time in which it was becoming increasingly apparent that Japan's economy was entering the phase known as "the bubble economy." In contrast to the economy, politics was experiencing a form of impasse. During this period, the Komeito made successive proposals in the fields of social welfare, education, environment, and promotion of peace, but the LDP government largely ignored these. One should note that the Komeito's stance gradually showed signs of change prompted by experience with the realities of politics. For example, in its talks with other parties regarding possible coalition government agreements, the word "progressive" was dropped from the expression "progressive centrist," which had been mentioned in its party principles at the time of its founding. As for each set of policy measures, the interests of the *seikatsusha* (citizens at large) were gradually given more weight. Instead of its former position of advocating a more radical transformation of society, its calls for reforms, premised upon a basic acceptance of the present situation, were brought to the forefront.

Events in 1989 foreshadowed the turbulence of politics throughout the 1990s. First came the demise of the emperor Hirohito at the beginning of the year. This event aside, the political world was still reeling from the "Recruit affair" that had surfaced at the end of 1988.[29] Before the turbulence had subsided, the long-pending consumption tax went into effect on April 1, aggravating popular resentment. In addition, the convergence of such factors led to the LDP's crushing defeat in the Upper House elections held in July, thereby losing its long-held and uncontested majority, an event the significance of which was far from negligible to the political world. The LDP had, until then, been resting confidently and somewhat arrogantly on its absolute majority in both houses, a situation which allowed the LDP to avoid entering into serious policy negotiations with the opposition parties. With the upset of power, however, the LDP was forced to win over the opposition parties, at least in the Upper House, in order to get their policies enacted as law. It is thought that the Komeito used this situation to fullest advantage in getting its own policies passed.

In the Lower House elections in 1990 the Komeito suffered a setback, winning only forty-six seats, eleven fewer than in the previous elections, thus widening the gap with the second largest party, the JSP. Faced with these results, Komeito halted its discussions with other opposition parties regarding the establishment of a coalition government, which it had been pursing under various forms since 1973. Instead, it adopted the more realistic approach of a *rapprochement* with the LDP government in order to have at least some of its goals reflected in policymaking. This new strategy showed quick results. When the government decided on an addi-

[29] This corruption scandal involved Recruit, a joint-stock company, which distributed its shares to powerful politicians and other influential people before the public offering, allowing them to reap illegal profits. The politicians accused of having received such shares include former Prime Minister Nakasone, Minister of finance Miyazawa (later to become prime minister), Minister of Justice Hasegawa, and Secretary-General Abe of the LDP, the ruling party at the time.

tional $9 billion in support of the Gulf War in 1991, the Komeito, from its standpoint as a pacifist party, succeeded in having the government accept several of its conditions, such as limiting the aim of the aid package to nonmilitary use, reducing the defense budget to defray the costs of the aid package, and revising the budget; all in return for its support in voting the measure through. Similarly, in the following year, it actively supported the Peacekeeping Operations Cooperation Law from its fundamental position of promoting cooperation with the international community.

However, this was the extent of the constructive relations with the ruling party. As if to deal an additional blow to the LDP, already weakened from within by successive cases of corruption,[30] the recession in the economic market became obvious, and there was a general premonition of major upheavals to come in the political arena. With this major turn of events, the Komeito changed its strategy. It focused its energies on getting to the bottom of cases of corruption and, by resuming talks with other opposition parties, engaged in renewed activities for the eventual formation of a new coalition government in which it would play a pivotal role. By 1993 some party members split off from the LDP, adding further turmoil to the political arena. Finally, in June 1993 the joint motion by the JSP, the Komeito, and the Democratic Socialist Party for a vote of non-confidence in the government passed, resulting in the dissolution of the Lower House. Because the LDP fell far short of the majority in the July general elections, thirty-eight years of single party rule by the LDP came to a crashing end and gave birth, under Prime Minister Morihiro Hosokawa of the Japan New Party, to a cabinet made up of all the major opposition parties except the Communist Party. The Komeito garnered fifty-two seats in these elections, allowing it to maintain its position as

---

[30] The corruption scandal that came to light that year is known as the Sagawa Kyubin affair, in which the vice-president of the LDP at the time, Shin Kanamaru, admitted accepting illegal contributions of 500 million yen from the Sagawa Kyubin company. It is generally believed that the former prime minister, Noboru Takeshita, was also involved. Both were summoned to appear before the budget committee of the Lower House, but the facts were never fully exposed.

the third party in the coalition. Through active participation in this coalition government, Komeito secured four ministerial positions under the Hosokawa government, and six in the later Hata cabinet.

This non-LDP coalition government was to be short-lived, lasting only eleven months. The experience was useful, however, since the central role played by the Komeito revealed more clearly its true character. To be more precise, because of its relentless efforts to create a viable counterforce that could allow for a change in government, the Komeito, despite staying true to its founding principle, "Speak with the people, fight for the people, and live out your life among the people," and despite remaining constant in its pursuit of clean politics, was forced into one compromise after another in the face of real world politics. Its participation in the New Frontier Party, mentioned previously, is a prime example. Yet, if we take a realistic look at Japanese politics, it would seem that the mainstream political players did not follow suit. In this sense, the fact that ex-Komeito Lower House representatives were ultimately compelled to form a parliamentary group independent of the New Frontier Party, before regrouping as the Komeito in November 1998, is only indicative of the situation over the entire period.

The Komeito's basic direction since 1970 might be summarized as that of dissociating religious identity from itself as a party, while seeking to become a political party enjoying widespread support from the general Japanese public. However, at least with regard to the Lower House, it would seem that there were limits to the expansion of its support beyond a certain level. Reaching a high point of fifty-nine seats in the 1983 elections, the level has remained fairly constant since, hovering around fifty seats. Moreover, with the reform in the electoral system for the House of Representatives, maintaining its current number of seats may be difficult.[31] If that is the case, the future will inevitably present

---

[31] Lower House representative elections used to be multiple seat constituencies, with each constituency electing three to five representatives. Under the non-LDP coalition government, the electoral system was reformed so that

harsh realities for the newly regrouped Komeito. Soka Gakkai members will probably continue to vote for the Komeito, but its ability to capture additional votes from the general electorate and resume growth will depend on the kinds of concrete policies it elaborates as a new Komeito party.

Conclusion: The Komeito and the Soka Gakkai

As revealed in the above examination of its thirty-year history, the Komeito has made a conspicuous effort to distance itself from a narrow religious identity and establish itself as a party appealing to a broader popular base. And yet, one might say that there were inherent inconsistencies in this shift in orientation. First, considering the shift *away* from a religious identity, it remained a fact that the majority of the Komeito's representatives at various levels of government, numbering over 3,000, were members of the Soka Gakkai.[32] Indeed, one wonders what the departure from a religious identity could actually mean for a political party composed largely of members who practice one and the same religion. The steps undertaken to implement the "shift away from religious identity" consisted of an institutional separation of the Soka Gakkai and the Komeito, whereby one individual could not hold a position of responsibility in both. Insisting on a clear separation in matters of personnel, finance, and operational management

300 of the 500 Lower House members would be elected from single seat constituencies, with the remaining 200 elected by proportional representation from eleven blocs nationwide. This new system with single member districts works undoubtedly to the advantage of the large parties. Thus, when Komeito's representatives merged with the New Frontier Party, they must have had the new constituencies in mind. Only one election—that of 1996—has been held under the new system, when the JSP (which changed its name to the Social Democratic Party in 1996), which had continued to hold its second place ranking from 1955 until the fall of the LDP government in 1993, suffered a severe setback, barely winning fifteen seats.

[32] The Komeito has fielded non-Gakkai public figures and intellectuals as candidates in Upper House elections, but it seems this did not meet with much success. It is possible that communication between such candidates and party officials did not go as smoothly as they had hoped.

further reinforced the independence of each of these institutions. By these means, the separation of politics and religion was quite thorough. Nevertheless, from a religious standpoint, or rather a spiritual perspective, the Komeito is probably still heavily influenced by the Soka Gakkai. But of course, considering the process through which the Komeito was originally founded, this is not in the least bit surprising.

One might view the Komeito's shift *toward* becoming a political party enjoying a broad popular base of support as an attempt to become a "religious" political party in the sense of the Christian Democratic Union (CDU) in Germany, for instance. It is obvious that this was no easy task, since the contexts in which the Komeito and the CDU found themselves differed significantly. In a country such as Germany, where Christianity is universally accepted, a political party identifying itself as "Christian" in nature is likely to appeal to the society at large. Consequently, the CDU had little difficulty in becoming recognized as a political party representative of the people. In contrast, in Japan, with its legacy of religious syncretism, the Soka Gakkai religion built up a firm foundation of solidarity precisely because its beliefs diverged from those of other Buddhist schools and Shintoism. Moreover, try as it might to become institutionally independent of the Soka Gakkai, the support of the Soka Gakkai was probably indispensable to the growth, or at least to the electoral success, of the Komeito.[33] As such, in order for the Komeito to make a true transition to a political party enjoying wide popular support, it would probably be necessary for its members to leave the Soka Gakkai. However, if this were the case, it would mean the loss of its very *raison d'être* and, in all likelihood, would lead to the erosion of its position.

Despite the difficulties in the path of distancing itself from a religious image and of emphasizing its identity as a political party with a broad popular base, the Komeito persevered. However, the obstacles existed not only within the party and the Soka Gakkai, but also in the actual state of contemporary Japanese politics. As

[33] Regarding the percentage of Soka Gakkai members' votes in the total number of votes garnered by the Komeito, see n. 28.

the Komeito strove to establish itself as a widely based political party and entered the political stage with realistic policy proposals, it had to contend with the fact that several political parties already advocated basic programs and principles that differed only slightly from its own. True, these similarities in perspective formed a realistic base on which to build a coalition with the opposition parties. However, over a long period of time each of the four opposition parties had been centered on a clear-cut, firm ideological position (which one might even refer to as "religion"). As a result, one is forced to recognize that the risk of a political realignment turning into a political fission was constantly present. This threat did in fact play itself out, for the non-LDP coalition administration broke down in less than eleven months, so that, following a period of twists and turns, the Komeito eventually had no choice but to separate itself from the other opposition parties and to reassert an independent position.

Considering all of these points together, it appears that the Komeito and, consequently, the Soka Gakkai now find themselves at a critical juncture. The Komeito for a long time now has been unable to increase its numbers, at least at the Lower House level, and for the time being, the hope of reestablishing a ruling opposition coalition appears dim. Likewise, the period of rapid expansion in Soka Gakkai membership came to an end in the early 1970s, and the growth rate has remained minimal ever since. Viewed from a different angle, most of the Soka Gakkai's membership during its period of rapid growth came from the lower to lower-middle stratum of large urban centers, whereas the composition of the Soka Gakkai membership today closely mirrors the more diverse social class distribution of the population at large.[34] This reality surely holds great significance not only for the Soka Gakkai, but for the Komeito as well. It might be said that the Soka Gakkai no longer

---

[34] According to a general survey conducted at the beginning of the 1980s, close to 90 percent of the people consider themselves to belong to the middle class. Compared to the situation just prior to the high growth period, it seems that the class consciousness of the Japanese people has undergone major transformation, and this societal change is probably reflected in Soka Gakkai.

has a clear sector of the population on which to concentrate its propagation efforts. Meanwhile, the Komeito, which at one time had only to develop proposals with the interests of a specific social stratum in mind, now faces the challenge of developing concrete policies with the kind of diverse appeal that can win the support of the majority of the Soka Gakkai members.

When faced with outside criticism regarding its political activities, the Soka Gakkai and the Komeito have resolved the issues in a forthright manner. For example, when the "coal miners' union incident" occurred in conjunction with their initial venture into Upper House politics,[35] they countered the attacks by reaffirming the freedom of religion as guaranteed by the Japanese Constitution. In rebuttal of criticisms such as "unity of religion and politics" or "manipulation of politics by religion," which were voiced as they stepped into the Lower House political arena, the Soka Gakkai not only made a "declaration on the separation of religion and politics" but also took concrete measures to separate the Soka Gakkai and Komeito into two independent bodies. In yet another example, as the Komeito participated in the establishment of a coalition party and conducted campaign activities as part of the New Frontier Party following the downfall of the LDP administration, the Soka Gakkai's endorsement of the Komeito was criticized for being in violation of the principle of "separation of religion and politics." These criticisms were countered by the argument that even as a religious organization, the Soka Gakkai is guaranteed complete freedom by the constitution to voice its opinions in the political arena, and it is the given right of all Soka Gakkai members to lend support to any party. As these examples show, the separation of "politics" and "religion" is more or less complete in recent times—at least in the sense that political activities are placed in the hands of the Komeito, while religious activities are

[35] This affair evolved when the Soka Gakkai-backed candidate won more than 3,000 votes in the coal mining town of Yubari during the Upper House elections of 1956. The coal miners' union, fearful lest the close ranks and class unity be broken, tried to expel Soka Gakkai members from the union. Labor unions in Japan still insisted on "class consciousness" and "class unity" at the time.

left in the hands of the Soka Gakkai; the sole exception being that during the elections the Komeito can expect the full backing of the Soka Gakkai.

In conclusion, there are hardly any grounds to justify the criticisms directed toward the Komeito as a legitimate political party. As things stand today, one could even say that the Komeito has been able to establish itself as a "religious" political party in much the same way as the CDU, and it is possible that the party members agree to some extent with this impression. Of course, even if this were the case, one would have to admit that the question raised at the outset of this section remains unanswered: as long as both the Komeito and the Soka Gakkai are dissatisfied with simply maintaining the existing state of affairs, they will have to seek out new forums for action while continuing to preserve the separation of politics and religion. Although this may appear at first to be quite a challenge, closer examination reveals that their aims are compatible, since the Komeito places its emphasis on the implementation of its welfare policies, while the Soka Gakkai focuses its efforts on the realization of global peace. Thus, seen from another perspective, it suggests that if activities oriented to these two goals were to be conjointly effected by the Soka Gakkai and the Komeito at the societal level, it would open up new horizons for both sides in the future. After all, it is only natural that political parties should aggressively take part in social movements and, as can be seen in European countries, religious organizations play a critical role in resolving social issues.

5

The Changing Role of the Komeito in Japanese Politics in the 1990s

Daniel Metraux

THE decade of the 1990s has been a period of significant transition in Japanese politics. The stable "1955" system, consisting of continuous majority rule by the conservative Liberal Democratic Party (LDP) with significant opposition provided by the Japan Socialist Party (JSP), ceased functioning in the mid-1990s with the weakening of the LDP and the almost total collapse of the JSP. By late 1999 it became evident that no one political bloc could govern without forming a coalition with one or more other parties. The increased fluidity of Japanese politics has provided a unique opportunity for smaller political entities such as the Komeito, a party endorsed by the Soka Gakkai, to play an important role in the governance of Japan.

The Nichiren tradition in Japan has long featured a critical attitude toward Japan's ruling establishment. Nichiren himself criticized government officials of his day for their support of other Buddhist sects, which denied his assertion that the Lotus Sutra represented Japan's best chance to escape the severity of *mappo*.[1]

---

[1] The doctrine held that after the death of the Buddha, Buddhism would pass through three great ages: an age of the flourishing of the law, of its decline, and finally of its disappearance in the degenerate days of *mappo*. Medieval Japanese scholars of Buddhism believed that the inception of this age of evil would make it impossible for individuals to achieve Buddhist enlightenment by their own efforts. The individual would have no alternative but to throw himself on the saving grace of the Buddha. In contrast to this rather negative interpretation, however, the Lotus Sutra views *mappo* as the time when

The world view of Soka Gakkai today is also heavily influenced by a *mappo* perspective and has maintained the adversarial attitude toward the government.[2] The Komeito dissolved itself in 1994 when its members joined a new party, the Shinshinto (New Frontier Party). When Shinshinto collapsed in 1997–8, former Komeito members regrouped into a new party, the New Komeito. The Komeito itself has been an active opposition force since its inception in the 1960s.

By the late 1990s, however, the Soka Gakkai and the Komeito gradually developed a policy of greater accommodation with the ruling LDP and in October 1999 entered into a coalition government with the LDP and the Liberal Party (Jiyuto), another conservative party. The new coalition brought political stability to Japan before the Lower House election set for late 2000. The major incentive for this switch in strategy is that posts in the cabinet would give the party real power for the first time. Besides this, the LDP agreed to co-sponsor a number of important parts of the Komeito's legislative agenda.

Toshiko Hamayotsu,[3] deputy leader of the New Komeito, stressed in a November 1998 interview that one of the goals of Komeito has always been the creation of a progressive, "citizen-oriented" political alternative to the ruling "iron triangle" of LDP politicians, big business, and top bureaucrats. The progressive coalition, according to Hamayotsu, would better serve the needs

the essence of the Lotus Sutra will be propagated. A Chinese Buddhist scholar noted: "In the fifth five hundred years, the Mystic Law shall spread and benefit mankind far into the future."

[2] A Soka Gakkai official presents the following view of his movement's attitude towards the Japanese government: "Japanese governments have traditionally used religions to advance the interests of the state and manage society. Soka Gakkai is one of the few religious movements to have resisted this propensity. During World War II its cofounders, Tsunesaburo Makiguchi and Josei Toda, were imprisoned for their opposition to the religious statism imposed by the military government. Makiguchi died while in prison. SGI is not an anti-governmental movement *per se*, but encourages its members throughout the world to become citizens who make positive contributions to their societies."

[3] Hamayotsu has represented Tokyo in Japan's House of Councilors since 1992.

of ordinary Japanese by improving such areas as education and social welfare. Hamayotsu, however, endorsed the July 1999 accord with the LDP because the LDP had agreed to support much of her party's agenda.[4]

The recent history of the Komeito, and thus of the Soka Gakkai's involvement in politics, is a constant search for a workable "centrist alliance" that can challenge the LDP's dominance. The efforts bore fruit briefly in 1993 and 1994 when the Komeito played a leading role in two brief coalition governments and again in 1995–7 when the former Komeito merged with other opposition political parties to form the ill-fated Shinshinto. Komei forces regrouped in late 1998 to form the New Komeito with the hope of becoming a force that could wield actual power in a coalition against the LDP or in cooperation with a weakened and more permissive governing coalition.

The Soka Gakkai's Role in Politics

The Komeito was the first religious-based party in modern Japanese history. As a party with a strong religious base in Japan, the Komeito was difficult to classify in terms of the classical conservative–progressive division of Japanese politics. The Japanese media labeled the Komeito a "centrist" party in the early 1990s, which is different from the "progressive" label to which it was attached in earlier years.[5] Even so, few Komeito voters supported the party for ideological reasons. Rather, their support was based on the fact that the vast majority of them were members or supporters of Soka Gakkai, which strongly endorsed the party. Voter profile studies in Japan indicate that the vast majority of votes for Komeito candidates were cast by Soka Gakkai members, so the

[4] For further details on the coalition government, see Daniel Metraux, "Japanese Search for Political Stability," *Asian Survey*, 39/6 (Nov.–Dec. 1999), 926–9.

[5] Throughout the 1960s, 1970s, and early 1980s the Komeito worked closely with the Democratic Socialist Party and the JSP in their opposition to the pro-business and foreign policies of the "conservative" LDP.

platform of the candidates had little bearing on whether or not they were elected.[6]

Despite its strong ties with the Soka Gakkai, the Komeito was in fact an autonomous organization that ran its own day-to-day affairs. The Soka Gakkai is an active religious movement, the concerns of which are the needs of its members and the propagation of its doctrines.[7] The Komeito was a thoroughly political organization, the main interests of which were maintaining its seats in the Diet and influencing legislation. Both entities are broad-based organizations that must listen to a myriad of opinions among their millions of members before formulating policies. There are cases where individuals or groups of members will openly protest against decisions made by leaders,[8] and some members have on occasion stated their opposition to Komeito candidates.

There is frequent contact between the Soka Gakkai and the Komeito. Soka Gakkai and Komeito leaders often meet on a monthly basis to discuss issues, and the New Komeito has indicated intentions to hold meetings with Gakkai officials on an irregular basis when there are specific issues to discuss. It is important to note that, because it is a religious organization dealing with mainly religious matters *per se*, Gakkai leaders have not attempted to influence significantly the policy-formulating process of the party.[9]

   [6] Scholars of Japanese party politics have noted that, since Soka Gakkai members alone insured the continuance of the Komeito as a political party, it is natural that the Komeito was bound to protect the Soka Gakkai as a means of protecting itself.

   [7] There is a confluence in the ideology of the two organizations in that both proclaim a strong desire for world peace and passionate support for the United Nations and preservation of the environment. Nevertheless, the Soka Gakkai deals mainly with religious questions, while the Komeito is deeply involved with the major political issues of the day.

   [8] For example, during the early 1990s some youth members of Soka Gakkai openly criticized the Komeito's support for sending self-defense forces to Cambodia, and some Soka Gakkai members were angered when the Komeito was dissolved in 1994.

   [9] The Soka Gakkai has many "independent" affiliate organizations including its political groups, educational institutions such as Soka University, cultural organizations such as Min-On, etc. Although the Soka Gakkai initially created these bodies, they run their own day-to-day affairs with their own

The actual role of Soka Gakkai's spiritual leader, Daisaku Ikeda, has been a matter of some controversy in Japanese politics for several decades. As the self-proclaimed founder and avid supporter of the Komeito, he wields considerable potential influence in the political world. Some journalists and conservative politicians, as well as former Komeito president Yoshikatsu Takeiri,[10] have claimed that Ikeda plays an active role in Komeito affairs, *including* the selection of Gakkai-sponsored candidates for the Diet.[11] While it is difficult to determine his exact role, an examination of his daily itinerary would reveal that he would have very little time personally for political management and that most of the aging leader's time is devoted to religious affairs, traveling, and writing. Ikeda may well have influenced the Komeito in a macrosense, but in a

staffs. They are very "turf" conscious and would resent it greatly if leaders from Gakkai headquarters tried to force their will on them. The Komeito and its successors maintain close ties with the Gakkai hierarchy, but also take great pride in their autonomy. Komeito Deputy Leader Hamayotsu told me: "The Soka Gakkai became oversensitive to voices of criticism and maintained a somewhat distant stance from the Komeito" (interview, Tokyo, Nov. 27, 1998).

[10] Takeiri, president of the Komeito for twenty years until 1990, had been one of the closest aides to Daisaku Ikeda and played a key role in the normalization of relations between Japan and China in the early 1970s. When Takeiri retired in 1990, it became clear that his once close friendship with Ikeda had soured. Takeiri has accused Ikeda of autocratic leadership, noting that he at times behaves like the emperor. He claims that Ikeda played a role in the selection of Komeito candidates for the Diet and that he, Takeiri, and not Ikeda, was the most important Japanese person in the process that led to relations with China. Ikeda in turn has accused Takeiri of betraying the Soka Gakkai movement and of ingratitude for all of the help that the Gakkai gave him in his career. The Soka Gakkai, Komeito, and even some LDP members have criticized Takeiri for various "misleading statements" in his "memoir" published in the *Asahi Shimbun* including references he made that apparently enhance his educational background. Whatever the causes of the ongoing public feud between Ikeda and Takeiri, it is a clear indication that the Komeito and its successor parties have some degree of autonomy and that relations between them and the Gakkai have not always been smooth. See *Weekly Post*, Nov. 11–17, 1996, 1; ibid., Sept. 14–20, 1998, 4; *Asahi Shimbun*, Sept. 17, 1998, 7.

[11] According to Asahiko Mihara, a former LDP and later Sakigake Diet member: "The Komeito is a vertical party under the control of Ikeda. This is an anomaly in Japanese politics at a time when other parties are becoming more horizontal and democratic in nature" (Interview with the author, Diet, Apr. 28, 1994).

microsense he is clearly not involved. The Komeito and its successors have a life of their own; they are certainly not lifeless puppets ready to react to Ikeda's or to the Soka Gakkai's every whim. Thus, although the Komeito started out as the political arm of the Soka Gakkai and has always depended on it for its organizational muscle, it has "downplayed its religious ties [and] developed a pragmatic and flexible party orientation."[12] Furthermore, it has shown a willingness to deal openly with other political leaders and parties.

Since the 1970s the Komeito has worked closely with changing combinations of opposition centrist and progressive parties, and on occasion has made compromises and several tacit agreements with the ruling LDP. These tactics probably played at least an indirect role in persuading the Soka Gakkai to reduce its former exclusivistic stance and to become a more open and accommodative organization. The Soka Gakkai's bitter divorce with the dogmatic Nichiren Shoshu priesthood in the early 1990s freed the organization to open even more doors to the outside world. Soka Gakkai officials argue that their movement has retained its core religious values, which is probably true in a general sense, but the necessities of political compromise and pragmatism have had a profoundly mellowing effect on the organization.[13]

The Komeito embarked on an active campaign during the 1990s to secure a stronger place in Japan's rapidly changing political system. The slow decline of the LDP and the collapse of the JSP, long the major opposition party, led to the dream of forging

[12] Gerald Curtis, *The Japanese Way of Politics* (New York: Columbia University Press, 1988), 238–9.

[13] Ben Dorman, a Ph.D. candidate at Australia National University and a scholar on contemporary Japanese religious and political affairs, argues against the "accommodation" thesis. Instead, he suggests that the Soka Gakkai has always had a flexible system of adapting its teachings and policies to changing social conditions. A Soka Gakkai official reacted to this thesis by noting: "The separation from the Nichiren Shoshu priesthood did free the Soka Gakkai to be even more free to the outside world. This, however, does not mean that the Soka Gakkai has compromised its principles for political pragmatism. Moreover, a major reason why the Soka Gakkai has separated political affairs from its religious activities is that politics requires pragmatic compromise and tactics, which are not necessarily compatible with its religious beliefs and principles" (interview with Hiroshi Nishiguchi, Tokyo, July 21, 1998).

a new anti-LDP coalition, which was realized in 1993 when the LDP lost its majority in the Lower House and a "rainbow coalition" of opposition parties briefly took power. During this time Soka Gakkai members of the Komeito sat in the cabinet. The collapse of the Hosokawa and Hata cabinets and the inauguration of a new electoral system encouraged the Komeito to dissolve itself; its parliamentary members joined a new opposition party, the Shinshinto. However, the early demise of the Shinshinto in late 1997 obliged former Komeito members to rethink their political options. Should they reconstruct the Komeito and seek influence by becoming a potent alternative to the larger government and opposition conservative parties? To expand their influence, should they, at the risk of losing their identity, forge a new coalition with the Democratic Party of Japan (DPJ)? Or should they form a tacit working relationship with the governing, but increasingly vulnerable, LDP?

The July 1998 Upper House election may prove to have been a watershed indicating the increasingly rapid decline of the LDP. Japanese voters sharply rebuked the ruling LDP in the election, awarding it only forty-four of the 125 contested seats. The newly formed DPJ, led by Naoto Kan, made impressive gains, polling nearly as many votes as the LDP (12.2 million against 14.1 million), and the Japan Communist Party won enough seats to become the second largest opposition party in the Upper House. The Komei also gave a strong performance, receiving 7.74 million votes (14 percent of all votes cast), the highest recorded vote it has ever received in proportional representation races, and a clear indication that the Soka Gakkai, through its support of Komei, remains an important force in Japanese politics.

The Komeito's Ascent to Power

The Komeito, because of its ties to the Soka Gakkai, has strong local roots and a mass base of support across Japan. Because of the massive grassroots strength of the Soka Gakkai in some parts of Japan, the Komeito has many local headquarters, thousands of representatives and supporters sitting at every level of government, and a large group of Gakkai-member workers who, in addition to participating in various religious activities, volunteer many hours to support candidates who receive the organization's endorsement.[14] Because of its broad political and financial base, the Komeito, along with the Japan Communist Party, has the potential to become "the only mass political party in Japan" at the start of the new millennium.[15]

Events in the late 1980s and early 1990s clearly delineate the Komeito's irregular route in search of a political formula that could lead to a "centrist" political alignment to oppose the LDP. In 1989 the Komeito and three other moderate opposition parties—the Social Democrats, the Democratic Socialist Party (DSP), and the Shaminren (United Social Democratic Party)—met to discuss the possibility of cooperating in election campaigns. LDP losses and JSP gains in the Upper House election led some opposition leaders to contend that the LDP could be defeated. However, the talks failed when the JSP adopted an "arrogant" and "greedy" attitude following its electoral gains and demanded control over any potential opposition coalition movement.[16]

The noncooperative attitude of the JSP led the Komeito and the DSP to move away from the JSP in the early 1990s and seek a working relationship with elements of the LDP. Various Komeito leaders, according to one former LDP Diet member, had worked closely with the late Japanese prime minister Kakuei Tanaka and his large faction, so ties with the LDP were not difficult to build. According to Komeito Diet member Otohiko Endo, this move was necessary to insure orderly government in Japan:

The Socialist Party was always opposed to the LDP, no matter what. This obstructive behavior meant that there was always a chance that

[14] Before the Komeito's formal dissolution in 1994, the party had a strong base in the Diet with twenty-four seats in the Upper House, fifty-two seats in the Lower House, and about 3,000 elected representatives in local and prefectural assemblies.

[15] Interview with Dr Nathaniel Thayer, Washington, Feb. 25, 1995.

[16] Shigeru Ito, "Do or Die for the Socialists," *Japan Echo*, 20/1 (1993), 29.

government would come to a standstill. We agreed to cooperate with the LDP on some issues—we did *not* have a formal coalition[17]—with the hope that the Diet could operate in an efficient manner and the expectation that on occasion the LDP would consider our positions on issues in exchange for our support for their bills.[18]

The person who engineered this marriage of convenience was the LDP's former secretary-general Ichiro Ozawa. According to the JSP's Shigeru Ito:

Ozawa began to pursue a divide-and-conquer strategy immediately after the LDP's July 1989 setback, while we Socialists were still patting each other on the back. Soon Ozawa had formed a solid personal alliance with Komeito Secretary General Yuichi Ichikawa, and the two emerged as the pivotal figures in negotiations between the ruling and opposition parties.

The Ozawa–Ichikawa link led to an agreement for the LDP to support Komeito candidates in Tokyo, Fukuoka, and Hokkaido in the July 1992 Upper House elections in return for Komeito-backing of LDP candidates in some single-seat constituencies. Some have criticized this kind of mutual back scratching, but such is political reality: Co-operation between parties does not take place without tangible benefits to both sides. It is meaningless to discuss coalition plans with other parties unless we too are willing to cut deals like these. . . . The results of these key items on the country's political agenda . . . were decided by closed deliberations among the Komeito, LDP, and DSP.[19]

The alignment between Ozawa, the Komeito, and the DSP formed the basis of the incipient coalition groups after the July 1993 election. The successes of Hosokawa's Nihon Shinto (Japan New Party), the Shinseito (Japan Renewal Party), and the Shin Sakigake (New Harbinger Party) added fresh conservatives to the

---

[17] Endo said that the Komeito had a "cooperative relationship with the LDP and that the best situation for the Komeito would be for the LDP to be just short of a majority in the Diet so that Komeito votes could be used to tip the balance whenever necessary."

[18] Interview in Tokyo, July 9, 1992.

[19] Ito, "Do or Die," 30–1. A Soka Gakkai official challenges the accuracy of this statement, noting that the LDP did not support Komeito candidates in Tokyo, Fukuoka, or Hokkaido and that the LDP endorsed two of its own candidates in Tokyo in the July 1992 election.

coalition, while the weak showing of the JSP forced its few survivors to seek a working relationship with other opposition parties. The result was a rainbow-like coalition government that included the Komeito.[20]

The participation of the Komeito in the Hosokawa and Hata coalition governments met with criticism from some journalists, who speculated that Hosokawa himself was a Trojan horse for the real powers behind the coalition, Ichiro Ozawa and Daisaku Ikeda.[21] They charged that Ikeda and Ozawa had staged a marriage of convenience in order to seize control of the Japanese government. Both Ozawa and Ikeda allegedly felt that they would gain more in less time if they gambled on a partnership that could bring them power at the expense of the LDP and other opposition parties. Some scholars also alleged that the Soka Gakkai acted as Ozawa's chief source of funds and that Ikeda's chief claim to political power was his financial hold on Ozawa.[22]

The Political Revolution of 1994–1995

Two factors in the spring and summer of 1994 caused what then seemed to be a virtual revolution in Japanese politics. The first was

[20] The Komeito received four cabinet posts in the Hosokowa government and six posts in the Hata coalition.

[21] See Kamei Shizuka, Susumu Oda, and Iisaka Yoshiaki, "Shukyo to seiji: kingen fuhai yori kowai seikyooitchi" ("Religion and Politics: A Fear of the Unity of Church and State"), *Bungei Shunju*, 94/1 (1994), 174–6.

[22] According to Chalmers Johnson: "As of the end of 1993, Ozawa's chief source of funds was also an embarrassment to him. He is allied with Komeito, which is controlled by the militant, rich, and sometimes unscrupulous religious leader Ikeda Daisaku, head of the fundamentalist sect Soka Gakkai. The press refers to this alliance as the 'ichi-ichi line,' after the given names of Ozawa Ichiro and Ichikawa Yuichi, the leader of Komeito. Many liberals find this alliance deeply disturbing, and even faction leaders and power brokers within the LDP, some of whom might themselves want to ally with Ozawa, hold back from doing so because of this connection" (*Japan: Who Governs? The Rise of the Developmental State* (New York: W. W. Norton, 1995), 238). A Soka Gakkai official strongly denies speculation of a "marriage of convenience between Ikeda and Ozawa" and stresses that the "Soka Gakkai does not provide financial support to any party, including the Komeito" (interview with Hiroshi Nishiguchi, Tokyo, July 21, 1998).

the decision of the socialists (now the Social Democratic Party of Japan, SDPJ) not to join the Komeito and Ozawa's Shinseito in the formation in April of a coalition government under Tsutomu Hata. The SDPJ charged that the conservative Komeito and Shinseito were plotting to destroy the SDPJ while using their votes to maintain power. In June 1994 the SDPJ combined its votes with the LDP to oust Hata and form an LDP-dominated coalition led by socialist leader Tomiichi Murayama.

The second factor was the implementation of the election reform law passed in early 1994, which replaced the former 511 Lower House seats organized in multiseat constituencies with a combination of 300 single seat constituencies and 200 proportional representation seats. While the former multimember constituency system allowed even parties with minimal support in a region possibly to win a seat, the current system favors larger parties with a national organization and considerable funding.

The dilemma facing opposition parties was made clear in an election simulation survey conducted by the Kyodo News Service in late 1994. The results showed that the LDP would decimate a disorganized opposition, but win only a small majority against a united group. Opposition leaders, realizing the terrible price that they would have to pay for disunity, moved quickly to create what they hoped would become a stable united front.

The leaders of the Komeito, Shinseito, the DSP, and six other minority opposition groups announced plans to create a new opposition group—the Shinshinto—in late summer 1994. The formation of Shinshinto would enable opposition parties and politicians to present a united front in Diet debates and national elections. They felt that it was really a question of do or die; victory in national elections could only come if opposition groups pooled their resources and jointly selected candidates for national elections. The creation of a united opposition party, however, proved to be a difficult task. An immediate problem was the question of a united platform. Shinshinto had to develop a coherent program that clearly differentiated it from the LDP, but since Shinshinto's members came from a variety of ideological backgrounds and shared only a common desire to regain power, it proved to be virtually impossible to develop a cohesive platform that consisted of more than platitudes. A further problem was that each of the opposition parties had to disband in order to join Shinshinto. Dissolution was not such a difficult task for such recently formed parties as the Nihon Shinto, formed in 1992, and the Shinseito, formed in 1993. They were little more than parliamentary groups with no local roots or party organizations. It was much more difficult for older, established parties like the Komeito and the DSP, which had strong local organizations and a national following.

The decision to disband was especially difficult for Komeito leaders and followers. Soka Gakkai members had identified themselves with the Komeito for so long that the end of the party as a distinct entity meant a partial loss of identity. Their loyalty to Soka Gakkai also implied total loyalty to the party. Sceptics in the party said that the religious values and distinct character of the Komeito would disappear if it joined a new megaparty. Others complained that the party's strong stance in favor of welfare and peace would not find favor in the Shinshinto.[23]

Komeito reached a rather odd compromise at its national convention in Tokyo on November 5, 1994. The convention approved a plan to split the party into two groups, with all fifty-two Lower House members and thirteen of its Upper House members joining the Shinshinto. However, the eleven Upper House members not up for reelection in 1995 and all of the party's roughly 3,000 prefectural and municipal assembly workers would belong to a new entity called Komei, which would inherit the old Komeito's party organization, staffers, and daily newspaper.[24] In effect, the Komeito decided to have it both ways. The bulk of its national parliamentarians joined the Shinshinto and ran for reelection under its banner, but the national structure of the Komeito remained intact. Thus, the dissolution of the Komeito was more

[23] Mari Koseki, "Komeito Approves Plan to Divide into Two Parties", *Japan Times Weekly*, International Edition, Nov. 14–20, 1994, 6.
[24] Ibid.

fiction than fact.[25] The motivation to join the Shinshinto was apparently sincere, but the decision to retain a party structure that could easily be revived was a good insurance policy.

The Komeito's role in Shinshinto created as many problems as benefits for the stillborn party. The Soka Gakkai's massive organization and millions of voters gave the new party a potentially strong base, but a number of Soka Gakkai members were so angry about the organization's "abandonment" of the party that they refused to vote for the Shinshinto under any circumstances. There were also millions of Japanese who still distrusted Soka Gakkai and who therefore shied away from the new party as well. The Soka Gakkai also announced that it would broaden its political perspective, conceivably endorsing candidates across the political spectrum.[26] Soka Gakkai Vice-President Hiroshi Nishiguchi explained in a 1997 interview that the Soka Gakkai was more interested in helping elect quality candidates who were seriously interested in political and financial reform and who spoke out on social issues that affected citizens than in pushing a party of its own making.

The endorsement process indicates some degree of involvement by popular membership and decentralization in the Soka Gakkai's political decisionmaking process. This policy ran contrary to the critical view offered by some journalists that the Gakkai's candidate selection process was tightly held by Ikeda and a few henchmen. It also suggested that the Komeito and its successor parties had a much wider popular base than most of Japan's other political parties, which were often little more than rootless temporary groupings of Diet members.

[25] A Soka Gakkai official questions the use of the word "fiction." He notes: "Now that the New Komeito has been formed, this argument might sound acceptable as the result, but the primary reason for retaining the Komei structure was that Shinshinto could not afford to assume the structure in its entirety, including a number of full-time staff and the daily organ newspaper. That is why the megaparty agreed to keep the local structure separate from the national level. We do not necessarily disagree, however, that an 'insurance policy' might have been an additional motive" (interview with Hiroshi Nishiguchi, Tokyo, July 23, 1998).

[26] Mari Koseki, "Soka Gakkai Could Back LDP, SDPJ," *Japan Times Weekly*, International Edition, Nov. 21–7, 1994, 4.

The Soka Gakkai explains its candidate endorsement policy in the following manner:

Since the former Komeito's dissolution, Soka Gakkai's stated endorsement policy is to principally endorse individual candidates. However, in elections involving the proportional representation system, specific parties will be endorsed. (The Soka Gakkai endorsed the Shinshinto until its dissolution. . . .)

One national, 13 regional and 47 prefectural Councils on Social Affairs determine the Soka Gakkai's endorsements. The councils' decisions are communicated to the membership through Soka Gakkai publications as well as at meetings of the organization. Members are free not to vote, and to vote for whomever they wish, but they are encouraged to vote for the endorsed candidates and parties.

The policies of endorsed parties or individuals are the subject of considerable scrutiny by Soka Gakkai members who can express their opinions either through correspondence to the party organ, the *Komei Shimbun*, or through representative Soka Gakkai leaders who communicate such feedback to Komei executives.

The organization's recommendations are based on candidates' and parties' expressed and demonstrated commitment to core values consistent with the Soka Gakkai's ethical and religious beliefs. These include: the sanctity of life and the dignity of the human person; protection of human rights and fundamental freedoms, such as freedom of religion and conscience; the enhancement of the welfare of ordinary citizens; a commitment to creating a Japan that will be a respected and contributing member of international society, and working through regional and global multilateral frameworks to promote peace and development. In addition, each candidate's personal integrity-character is scrupulously evaluated.[27]

The Soka Gakkai implemented its new endorsement policy by urging support for the Shinshinto in the 1996 general election, but the party was dissolved in December 1997, partly because of poor election results, but also because of disagreements over policy and party management. Many Soka Gakkai and Komeito officials were disappointed with the whole episode. According to Nishiguchi,

---

[27] Statement issued at press conference in Tokyo, July 2, 1998.

141

The Shinshinto had great difficulty establishing internal consensus and failed to find common ground on key issues and policies. We learned from this experience. In certain electoral districts in the last Lower House election, Soka Gakkai members supported Shinshinto candidates, genuinely believing that Shinshinto would challenge the prolonged single party rule of the LDP. Hence, after the election when some of these candidates either left the party to form another party or returned to the LDP, voters in the Soka Gakkai felt betrayed and complained that the former Komeito party should be more responsible in the future in selecting partners.[28]

The dissolution of the Shinshinto created a genuine dilemma for the former Komeito members. The splitting of the Shinshinto demonstrated the difficulty of forming a united opposition party only for the sake of having a strong opposition. Policy and personality differences caused too much internal dissent. The immediate decision was to regroup and "wait and see" what would happen before and after the 1998 Upper House election. Many non-Soka Gakkai—Komeito Shinshinto members joined a new grouping of parties, designated as the Democratic Party of Japan (Minshuto, DPJ) and led by veteran charismatic and conservative politician Naoto Kan. Others joined a new group of politicians called the Liberal Party, led by Ichiro Ozawa. Thirty-eight of the former Komeito members in the Lower House who had joined the Shinshinto joined together to form the New Peace Party, while nine others joined the new Liberal Party, and one joined the Reformers' Network Party. Former Komeito members in the Upper House officially became members of the Komei party. The Soka Gakkai thus found itself, at least temporarily, the key endorser of two separate but closely allied political groups.[29]

[28] Press conference in Tokyo, July 2, 1998.
[29] When asked about the political future of the nine former Komei politicians who had joined Ozawa's Liberal party, a Soka Gakkai official responded: "When the Shinshinto disbanded, the former Komei politicians were free to choose their future path. We respect the choice of these nine members to go with Mr Ozawa. When they run for election, we are quite sure that the Soka Gakkai members will give their support to them. If Komei chooses to emerge as a third force in Japanese politics, most probably these members will join this third political force" (Statement delivered in response to a reporter's question, Soka Gakkai press conference, Tokyo, July 2, 1998).

Soka Gakkai–LDP Relations

The attainment of political power is the key issue among most conservative Japanese politicians, who seemingly have little concern with deep ideological stances. The result is a continual minuet, in which conservative politicians are continually changing partners and forming new alliances with the hope of building a new power base. Despite their clear allegiance to core Buddhist values, Komeito leaders, perhaps with the tacit support of the Soka Gakkai, have at times developed informal understandings with leaders within the LDP; at other times they have joined with other centrist and progressive groups to oppose the LDP.

The combination of the poison gas terrorist attack by the religious sect Aum Shinrikyo on Tokyo subway commuters in March 1995, and the initial success of the Shinshinto in the Upper House elections during the summer of 1995, provided the LDP with a chance to launch an attack on the Soka Gakkai, a key Shinshinto supporter. The LDP's apparent plan of attack was to use the Aum incident to legislate a revision of the Religious Corporation Law that would give the government greater powers to supervise and regulate religious organizations including the Soka Gakkai.

The LDP-controlled government announced in late 1995 that it intended to make important changes in the Religious Corporation Law. The government stated that this action came as a result of complaints that the provisions of the 1951 law made it difficult for public authorities to protect the public from religious organizations that worked against the public safety. It noted that although Aum Shinrikyo engaged in the production of dangerous weapons and materials and engaged in its murderous crime spree, it went largely unnoticed by the central government and the public. After the attack several American congressmen expressed shock at the lack of oversight, asserting that their own investigations had turned up Aum's plans for terrorist attacks in Japan and the USA. Japanese leaders were embarrassed by the revelations, and supporters of the new law said it would insure that such breaches would not happen again.

The revised law places religions with a financial base over 80 million yen under the jurisdiction of the ministry of education (Monbusho) rather than under prefectural governments. It permits the Monbusho to ask religious groups to submit detailed financial reports at its whim, allows any person adversely affected by members of religious corporation to request a review of financial or other documents, and gives courts the power to disband religious organizations.

These actions are of great concern to many Japanese who believe that they are counter to the basic idea of the freedom of religion and the separation of church and state. University of Virginia Professor David O'Brien, author of the 1996 monograph *To Dream of Dreams: Religious Freedom and Constitutional Politics in Postwar Japan*,[30] suggests that the growing power of cultural conservatives, the waning appeal of aging liberals, and the political indifference of Japan's younger generation imply that the conservative preference for tradition will predominate, while the liberal tenets and sentiments found in the postwar constitution fade. Critics of these more recent actions warn that they may well lead to a fundamental restructuring of the foundations of Japan's postwar democracy.

The Soka Gakkai bitterly opposed the new law, saying that the government's actions against Aum Shinrikyo were little more than a camouflage for an attack against the Gakkai. Since the Shinshinto did very well in the 1995 Upper House elections, the Gakkai argued that the real purpose of the law was to destroy or at least seriously weaken the nation's leading opposition party. LDP spokesman Shizuka Kamei confirmed this allegation when, in a television news program on October 22, 1995, he said, "The purpose of the Religious Corporation Law is to take measures against the Soka Gakkai."[31]

The LDP also stepped up its political attacks on the Soka Gakkai during this period. Before the 1996 election the LDP's publication *Jiyu Shinpo* gave considerable coverage to a civil court suit by a for-

---

[30] (Honolulu: University of Hawaii Press, 1996).
[31] *Mainichi Shimbun*, Oct. 24, 1995.

mer Soka Gakkai women's leader, Mrs Nobuhira, that Soka Gakkai leader Daisaku Ikeda had sexually assaulted her on several occasions in the past. The Soka Gakkai vehemently denied these charges, noting that the civil case was filed only after Mrs Nobuhira and her husband had been dismissed from the Soka Gakkai for having allegedly failed to repay massive loans made to them by Soka Gakkai members.[32] The LDP's attacks ended in a printed apology when a Tokyo court terminated the case in early 1998 because of a lack of evidence.[33] The LDP, however, began to adopt a far less antagonistic attitude toward the Soka Gakkai and its political allies in early 1998 after the demise of Shinshinto. The failure of the LDP to win an outright majority in the 1996 election meant that it had to rely on the votes of cooperative politicians to insure the passage of legislation. Komeito Diet member Otohiko Endo noted in May 1998 that since Shinshinto is no longer a threat to the LDP, the party no longer mentions the importance of the Religious Corporation Law and has dropped most criticism of the Soka Gakkai.[34] Even journals like the conservative tabloid *Shukan Bunshun* reduced their anti-Soka Gakkai rhetoric in 1998.

The reduction in LDP hostility and the apology, however, did little to appease Soka Gakkai leaders and their political supporters. One spokesman noted in July 1998:

We were not convinced or fully satisfied [with the apology]. During the 1996 election campaign LDP publications and political leaders repeatedly made outrageous allegations against us. The Soka Gakkai repeatedly

---

[32] According to the Soka Gakkai, Japanese courts have ordered the Nobuhiras to repay 53 million yen ($410,000) with a number of cases still outstanding. Some independent commentators have speculated that the Nobuhiras' charges were motivated by financial distress and resentment over their dismissal.

[33] The Tokyo District Court ruled that in all of Mrs Nobuhira's claims the statute of limitations had expired. The court also ruled that additional claims of harassment made by the plaintiffs were denied because the foundation of these claims differed from the original cause of claim. The Nobuhiras then appealed their case to the Tokyo High Court, where the case was still pending in early 1999.

[34] Interview with Otohiko Endo, Tokyo, May 21, 1998.

contacted the LDP demanding retractions and apologies, but there was no response until this recent incident [apology].

We saw this [apology] as a political move. With the Socialists and Sakigake both leaving the coalition, the LDP saw former Komei party members as possible coalition partners. It was strictly a political strategy to ease Soka Gakkai members' anti-LDP sentiment and to pull the thorn. At the same time the decision was based on legal advice, damage control before the upcoming [1998] election. Legal experts within the LDP, former prosecutors and attorneys, analyzed the content of the articles and advised that some form of action should be taken to settle this incident before Soka Gakkai took it to court. . . . We know that the LDP's attitude will change according to political circumstances. Soka Gakkai members feel that the apology has come far too late and that the damage has been done. The apology was not the result of some backroom deal between the Komei and LDP. . . . An LDP–Komei coalition is unthinkable.[35]

The Soka Gakkai did not rule out the possibility of endorsing individual LDP candidates whose views are "genuinely appealing," and it would not encourage an entirely obstructionist attitude against the LDP. A spokesman noted that it was the responsibility of all parties and politicians to put the interests of the nation first and to support worthwhile legislation. However, the Soka Gakkai emphatically ruled out any chance of a working agreement with the LDP in the immediate future.[36]

[35] Soka Gakkai press conference, Tokyo, July 2, 1998. Diet member Otohiko Endo confirmed the LDP's "chameleon-like" stance in a May 1998 interview. Endo, a former member of Komeito, feels that the LDP's attacks and professions of friendship are all politically motivated. The LDP, according to Endo, will attack the Soka Gakkai when it views it as a political threat, but will withdraw its attacks when it feels a need for Soka Gakkai cooperation.

[36] Soka Gakkai press conference, Tokyo, July 28, 1998. At the July 2, 1998 press conference a Soka Gakkai spokesman noted: "Komei's stance is to cooperate with parties, whether it be LDP or DPJ, if this is deemed necessary in order to realize certain important policies, usually concerning welfare. If it cannot agree on a certain LDP policy, it may join with other opposition parties to reject the policy. If it agrees with the policy, then it will vote with the LDP on that one measure."

The 1998 Upper House Election

The 1998 Upper House election campaign focused on the ongoing economic recession and the need for radical reform of government administration and finances coupled with structural change in the relationship between government and the private sector. The Hashimoto administration downplayed the current crisis and talked only about piecemeal reforms such as the promise of a tax cut. Hashimoto failed to present a coherent plan despite sharp criticisms from opposition politicians and the press.[37]

Only a few weeks before the election most newspaper surveys indicated that the LDP would retain most if not all of the sixty seats that were at stake, and some optimistic LDP leaders predicted that the LDP would capture as many as sixty-nine seats to give the party a majority of 127 seats in the Upper House. The reality was very different. The party regained only forty-five seats; it received only 26 percent of the popular support and won just fourteen of the fifty contested seats decided by proportional representation. An even more disturbing result was the LDP's showing in urban areas. The party failed to return a single candidate in the multiple seat constituencies of Tokyo, Kanagawa, Saitama, Aichi, Kyoto, Osaka, and Hyogo.[38]

During the campaign the Soka Gakkai endorsed the Komei for the proportional representation race. The Gakkai also endorsed Komei candidates in the Tokyo and Osaka electoral districts. The organization endorsed two independent candidates in Saitama and Fukuoka and recommended a candidate belonging to the DPJ in Kanagawa. When Prime Minister Hashimoto resigned after the election, Komei members supported the DPJ leader, Naoto Kan, for prime minister.

---

[37] Komeito Diet member Otohiko Endo likened Japan's situation to the Titanic: "The conservative leadership's shortsighted view of Japan sees only the finery and wealth of a beautiful ship and has no idea how rapidly the vessel is sinking" (interview with the author, Tokyo, May 21, 1998).

[38] Soeya Yoshihide, "Out with the Old, In with the New," *Look Japan*, 44/511 (Oct. 1998), 25.

The election results demonstrated the political strength of the Soka Gakkai. Two Komei candidates won handily in the Tokyo and Osaka districts, and seven candidates were successful in the proportional election component. The independent and DPJ candidates endorsed by the Gakkai were also successful. The nine new Komei members, combined with the remaining thirteen members, whose seats will be contested in 2001, gave the party twenty-two seats in the Upper House.

The Birth of New Komeito

The various elements of the former Komeito regrouped in November 1998 to form the New Komeito, becoming the second strongest opposition party in the Diet with a combined membership of sixty-six legislators. The new leaders included Takenori Kanzaki as party head and Toshiko Hamayotsu as deputy leader.

By opting to form a distinct party, Komeito leaders and their Soka Gakkai backers have chosen an independent path rather than trying to reorganize a new coalition of opposition parties. An immediate goal is for the New Komeito to become the "axis" of a new "centrist alliance" of parties that is "both anti-LDP and anti-Communist." The approach is, however, supposed to be far more gradual than was the case for the Shinshinto. According to Kanzaki:

The Shinshinto was over-hasty in trying to form a big united party. It should have been a looser alliance for a while, so that cultural differences among the parties could have been settled. We must create a small but tight core first, then expand little by little. Not only Soka Gakkai, but also other groups such as labor unions told me that they want to cooperate with the New Komeito. It must be a loose alliance first, but could be a big united centrist party in the future. We, who failed once, cannot fail again.[39]

It is apparent that Kanzaki has learned a valuable lesson. Soka Gakkai voters represent a large bloc of very dedicated and reliable

[39] *Nikkei Weekly*, Nov. 16, 1998.

voters. They will generally work hard and vote for clearly identified Komeito candidates, but interviews with several Soka Gakkai members in late spring 1997 indicated a general lack of enthusiasm for the Shinshinto. These Gakkai members openly criticized the dissolution of the former Komeito, suggesting that they would follow the endorsement of the Gakkai only if there were Komeito candidates to vote for.

The fluidity of Japan's political system in the late 1990s has given large mass movements with strong local organizations a unique opportunity to exert considerable influence in elections, but the Komeito's base is still too small to do well nationally. The new electoral system, with its emphasis on single member constituencies, makes it difficult for smaller parties like the Komeito to survive on their own. Komeito must, on the one hand, work to expand its base; on the other hand, it must seek cooperative alliances with other opposition parties such as the Minshuto. A formal alliance between the two parties could cause a withering of both their support bases, but a mutual cooperation pact might lead to a stabilization or even growth of their constituencies.[40]

Although it is far too early to begin comparing the old Komeito with the new, conversations with party leaders may provide some useful hints. Deputy Leader Toshiko Hamayotsu expressed the goals of the New Komeito thus:

Since the end of World War II, Japan has pursued the sole goal of economic prosperity, making people seek only materialistic values such as money and social status. This should be considered the fundamental cause of today's social malaise and chaos in Japanese society.

One important aim of the New Komeito is to bring about a fundamental shift in values, from a system that is overly materialistic to one which is more humanistic. The politics of humanism aims to establish various social programs (including government and economic systems) that will serve and benefit ordinary people rather than power holders. This shift should include national policies designed to tackle the "iron triangle"

[40] Kanzaki criticizes the Minshuto for its lack of a clear ideological base and speculates that it is successful because it is so new and attracts mainly protest votes (ibid.).

Daniel Metraux

of the political, bureaucratic, and business establishments. While superfluous government funds have been spent on public investment including construction, serving the interests of that particular industry, other areas such as social welfare, culture, or education have been underfinanced. To take the Kobe earthquake recovery effort as an example, vast sums were spent on important infrastructure reconstruction, but so very little was designated for the restoration of individuals' lives.

The New Komeito and its predecessor parties have proposed a number of policies to revive the Japanese economy including structural reform and deregulation to create more open markets, and various measures to create employment opportunities. New Komeito has suggested the national budget allocation be changed from the current overemphasis on construction to a more meaningful allocation in favor of such areas as telecommunication, environment, social welfare, and culture.[41]

Hamayotsu responds to questions concerning the Komeito's ability to attract critical non-Soka Gakkai followers:

The New Komeito hopes to seek an expanded support base to include groups or individuals that share common humanistic values, regardless of their religion or other background. Potential allies might include Christian groups that support humanistic policies or labor union leaders who sincerely serve the needs of workers. In addition, New Komeito may join forces with grassroots citizens' groups working in such areas as social welfare, environment, and education.

The negative perceptions about the New Komeito and its links with the Soka Gakkai are largely caused by misunderstanding and prejudice about the Buddhist organization. Some voters do not endorse the party because they do not like the Soka Gakkai. Such perceptions can only be changed through the party's actual policies and performance. Approximately 3,000 local assembly members of the party have accumulated an impressive list of achievements in such areas as social welfare and the environment, and these efforts have been helping expand the party's support base. On the national level as well, the party tries to respond positively to numerous lobbying requests from various groups as long as such requests meet the party's principles and policies.[42]

[41] Hamayotsu interview with the author, Tokyo Nov. 27, 1998.
[42] Ibid.

150

A public opinion poll gauging public support for Japanese political parties in November 1998 indicated that the New Komeito
would receive only between 3 and 4 percent of the total vote if
every adult in Japan were actually to vote. The fact that Komeito in
fact receives 10 or more percent of the total vote in major elections
is more a reflection of the loyalty of Soka Gakkai voters, who
almost always vote, than of broad support for the party. The message is thus clear: the Komeito remains very much a party of the
Soka Gakkai bloc. It must expand this bloc considerably if it is to
become a truly important actor in national politics.

By early 1999 the New Komeito and Soka Gakkai leaders were
in a compromising mood, so much so that they expressed immediate interest when Prime Minister Keizo Obuchi approached
them in May with a proposal for a coalition government.
According to New Komeito Diet member Otohiko Endo: "A
coalition government would bring greater stability to Japanese
politics and would permit the enactment of some of our legislative
proposals. Today we are in an era where no one party can gain a
majority in Japanese elections. Compromise and cooperation are
necessary for political stability."[43] Endo stresses that economic
reform is necessary to save Japan from financial collapse in the
future: "We have proposals for real reform, which the LDP might
listen to if we join the government."

The LDP's weakness in the Upper House provides the key for
its coalition strategy. Japanese scholars and journalists speculate
that it would take huge gains in the 2001 and 2004 Upper House
elections to enable the LDP to get a working majority in that body.
A coalition with the Komeito and Jiyuto, however, would give the
government 141 seats—a solid majority.

There are many plausible reasons why the Soka Gakkai and
Komeito favor such an alliance. Perhaps the greatest desire is access
to real power. Except for its participation in two short-lived cabinets in 1993 and 1994, Komeito politicians have remained as
members of the opposition since the Soka Gakkai began to field

---

[43] Endo interview with the author, Diet, Tokyo, July 23, 1999.

candidates in the mid-1950s. A legislative aide at the Japanese Diet overheard one Komeito legislator remark to another, "Now we don't have to remain in the political wilderness. People will no longer treat us as foreigners."

Upper House independent Diet member Takujiro Hamada speculates that the Soka Gakkai wants insurance that when its aging leader, Daisaku Ikeda, passes from the scene, the Gakkai will avoid heated attacks from the conservative establishment during its difficult transition to a new generation of younger leaders. Representative Endo suggests that the LDP's proposal to reduce the number of proportional representation seats from 200 to 150 would negatively impact smaller parties like the Komeito. Withdrawal of the LDP's proposal would be part of the price of a coalition with the Komeito. Akira Tsukamoto, a prominent Nippon Television newsman, thinks that LDP threats to get the Soka Gakkai to pay more taxes for its many secular activities is an added incentive for coalition politics.

A coalition with the LDP is not without risk for both parties. Can a party that advertises itself as a voice for the have-nots in society keep afloat by joining the establishment? The Komeito says that a position in the government gives these people true representation, but several Soka Gakkai members have told me that they might not support Komeito candidates in future elections if the alliance goes through. On the other hand, the Shigatsu-kai, a federation of pro-LDP religious groups opposed to the Soka Gakkai, had threatened to urge followers not to vote for the LDP if it keeps its ties with the Komeito. In any case, the LDP–Komeito alliance does promise to bring at least temporary stability to Japanese politics.

6

The Role of Women

Atsuko Usui

T HE issue of religion and women has gained increasing
importance in the field of religious studies, prompted by
both the rise of feminism in the late 1970s and the reex-
amination of feminist theology within Christianity. Studies of
feminist theology have indicated the existence of a "solidarity
among women" whose daily living experiences were brought to
life within religious movements, and have emphasized the contemporary significance of this solidarity. However, these studies
have also revealed a course of history in which many religious
denominations lost their initial advocacy of gender equality,
became assimilated into patriarchal social structures, and even created a system that supported gender discrimination. Through the
same process the role of women became more rigidly entrenched,
and women collectively contributed to the acceptance of a male-
dominated organizational structure and belief system. When
addressing the issue of religion and women, it is necessary to examine the ways in which women's experiences in a changing society
were brought to bear on the activities of a religious organization,
as well as the kinds of activities pursued by groups of women themselves. This kind of research is currently under lively debate as an
issue of gender history relevant not only to Christianity, but to all
religions.[1] This chapter, as part of this ongoing research, examines

[1] See e.g., Yvonne Yazbeck Haddad (ed.), *Women, Religion and Social
Change* (Albany: State University of New York Press, 1985); Mary Hope
Bacon, *Mothers of Feminism: The Story of Quaker Women in America* (San
Francisco: Harper & Row, 1986); Wendy E. Chmielewski, Louis J. Kern, and
Marlyn Klee-Hartzell (eds.), *Women in Spiritual and Communitarian Societies
in the United States* (Syracuse, NY: Syracuse University Press, 1993); Tessa J.
Bartholomeusz, *Women under the Bo Tree: Buddhist Nuns in Sri Lanka* (New

the history and characteristics of the women in the Soka Gakkai in Japan.

Although the exact ratio of women to men among the membership of the Soka Gakkai is not available, it is widely estimated within the organization itself to be roughly 6 : 4, with women comprising the larger portion of the membership. Beyond this simple numerical majority, however, the impact and functions of the female membership on the organization and its activities surpass those of the male members. Although the female membership of the Soka Gakkai is substantial and has been frequently targeted by the mass media, the topic at hand has been little studied by academics. The analysis of the activities of women in the Soka Gakkai and the goals for which they have striven through these activities holds major significance in study of religion and women.

The Early Period: The Days of Makiguchi and Toda

In order to develop a general picture of the concerns and activities of women within the Soka Gakkai, this chapter will concentrate primarily on the women's division, a group comprised of married women. Although the women's division does not include the entire female membership of the Soka Gakkai, given the division's significance within the organization, it is arguably representative of the general interests and trends within that membership. The history of the women's division dates back more than forty-five years. Since its inception, just as is the case with the Soka Gakkai organization, the women's division has undergone changes in response to social conditions. The following gives a broad

York: Cambridge University Press, 1994); Ann Carr and Mary Stewart van Leeuwen (eds.), *Religion, Feminism and the Family* (Louisville, Ky: Westminster John Knox Press, 1996); Elizabeth Puttick, *Women in New Religion: in Search of Community, Sexuality and Spiritual Power* (New York: St Martin's Press, 1997); Haleh Afshar, *Islam and Feminism: An Iranian Case Study* (London: Macmillan, 1998); Ursula King (ed.), *Women in the World's Religions, Past and Present* (New York: Dragon House, 1998).

overview of the spirit of the women's division members' activities within the context of Soka Gakkai's history.[2]

In 1940 the Soka Gakkai was reorganized, resulting in the formation of a women's division, alongside the youth division and a group consisting of elementary schoolchildren. Under the direction of Presidents Makiguchi and Toda, lectures were offered on subjects such as "the mission of the women's division," or "propagation and women's daily lives." Since many lectures also centered on Makiguchi's pedagogical theories, and education was integral to the purposes of the Soka Gakkai when it was initially founded, it is not surprising that many of the female members in the early days were educators. During this time the leadership of the women's division in the postwar period and the principles underlying its direction were developed.

During the war, of course, the Soka Gakkai was in a state of virtual dissolution. Soon after the war nine divisions, including the women's division, were formed.[3]

Establishment of the Women's Division

In April of 1951, shortly before Toda's inauguration but immediately after the introduction of this new organizational structure, the first women's division chapter leaders' meeting was held. At that time, Toda stated: "Among the people assembled here today,

[2] Reference materials include: Soka Gakkai women's division (ed.), *Shirayuri no uta* ("White Lily Poems") (Tokyo: Seikyo Shimbun Press, 1981); *Kakumei no taiga: Soka Gakkai yonjunenshi* ("Current of Revolution: The Forty-Year History of the Soka Gakkai") (Tokyo: Seikyo Shimbun Press, 1975); Toru Aoki, *Soka Gakkai no rinen to jissen* ("The Ideals and Actions of Soka Gakkai") (Tokyo: Daisan Bunmeisha, 1976); *Seikyo Shimbun*; and *Daibyakurenge*. In addition, interviews with numerous women's division members served as primary sources. Although it would have been desirable to include a survey on the members' perspectives and consciousness, this was not to be the case for this chapter, and remains a plan for future research.

[3] The other divisions formed along with the women's division consisted of the youth and children's department, the health and welfare department, the general affairs department, the study department, the information department, the planning department, the financial department, and the organizational department.

there are a variety of women, from fishmongers' wives to wives of businessmen. However, when you gather here at the headquarters, I hope that you will all participate with the awareness and magnanimity worthy of women who live for the Mystic Law, of leaders of a large number of women."

Upon hearing these words, one women's division chapter leader (in her mid-twenties at the time) reflected, "With [this] guidance, I realized that this was a practice that could open up my own karma, while helping others to become happy at the same time; I thus began to participate in activities with a renewed determination."[4]

On June 10, 1951 Toda told the fifty-two women's division members who gathered for a dinner meeting:

The power of women . . . is truly monumental . . . When observing the development of the Soka Gakkai, and also its activities, it seems that the women are always one step ahead of men in initiating progress . . . Now that the Soka Gakkai has made a new departure, we must further strengthen the organization necessary for future development toward our goals. In order to do this, the capacities of everyone assembled here today will be indispensable.[5]

Encouraged by the fact that the women's division was the first of such divisions to be formed, the participating women's division members were infused with a sense of mission to lead the *kosen-rufu* effort. The following words are certainly reflective of this feeling:

Having taken part in the inception of the Women's Division, it was as if I had truly been awakened . . . Although I do not have a clear idea of what would actually constitute *kosen-rufu*, nor when that would be, I made a firm determination to contribute to this undertaking of *kosen-rufu*, doing *shakubuku* alongside President Toda until the very end.[6]

---

[4] *Shirayuri no uta*, 20.

[5] Ibid. 21. At this time Toda dedicated a poem to the women's division. It is from this that the white lily came to be the flower symbolic of the women's division.

[6] Ibid.

President Toda said, "We will soon begin regional propagation activities, requiring you to travel throughout Japan, but I wonder — will the women assembled here today be able to do that?" As I raised my hand, I simultaneously sprung to my feet, and I found myself virtually shouting out, "Sensei, when that time comes, please let me go anywhere, whether it be Kyushu [the southern island of Japan] or Hokkaido [the northern island of Japan]". At that time, I was so excited I gave little thought to my family and our dire financial predicament.[7]

This day came to be recognized as the founding day of the women's division.

Why was it that the female members were assembled at such an early stage, and the women's division was the first to be formed? Toda's basic attitude toward the women's division was that "No philosophy or religious practice can ever be a force rooted among the people if it cannot first win the hearts of women and succeed in gaining their consent." His conviction had been shaped by the bitter experience of having witnessed all the directors, other than himself, leave the organization because of their wives' feelings of mistrust toward the Soka Kyoiku Gakkai when Toda and Makiguchi were sent to prison during the war. However, the women were the first to rush to Toda's side when he was released from prison and started the reconstruction of the Soka Gakkai. In any event, these experiences led to a deep belief that, whether it be the ideals of democracy or the unity of the organization, both rested on the full endorsement of the women, who were representative of ordinary citizens. Hence, he felt that to mobilize the women was critical. When Toda repeatedly spoke of "the women as the driving force of the Soka Gakkai," and "*kosen-rufu* achieved through the efforts of women," in his speeches, one could say this was because he realized just how vital a role women, who were the basis of support for all Gakkai activities, played in the achievement of *kosen-rufu*.

---

[7] Ibid. 22.

Propagation, Prayer, and Changing One's Karma

With Toda's inauguration as president of the Soka Gakkai, both men and women, the elderly and the young alike, dedicated themselves to propagation activities in unison. The energy and enthusiasm of the women in this endeavor were considerable, and their efforts were often featured in the *Seikyo Shimbun* and *Daibyakurenge* articles published around this time. One woman, who was then serving as a women's division vice chapter chief, said: "As it is also written in Nichiren Daishonin's Major Writings, 'There should be no discrimination among those who propagate the five characters of *Myoho-renge-kyo* in the Latter Day of the Law, be they men or women'.[8] As such, when it came to propagation, there was no distinction made between men and women."[9] Another women's division chapter leader reflected back on that period, saying:

In those days, we devoted ourselves to propagation every single day . . . For people who held jobs, had many children, had difficult mothers-in-law, it was a veritable challenge simply to participate in any activities at all; none the less, every day was filled with the joy and conviction that nothing could prevent us from sharing this practice with others.[10]

The concept of "changing one's karma" as propounded by the Soka Gakkai had special relevance for these women. Such notions kindled a sense of hope in life, revealed new possibilities, and empowered them with greater control over their lives. Based on his own spiritual experience, Toda explained that enlightenment actually means to realize one's own inherent Buddha nature (the unlimited potential within all life as held by Nichiren Buddhism). He thus encouraged the members that they should not give up in the face of hardships by regarding them as their inescapable destiny, but rather that everyone could overcome difficulties and open

[8] *Nichiren Daishonin gosho zenshu* ("Collected Writings of Nichiren Daishonin"), Soka Gakkai version, new edn. (Tokyo: Seikyo Shimbun Press, 1952), 1360; *The Major Writings of Nichiren Daishonin*, i (Tokyo: Nichiren Shoshu International Center, 1979), 93.
[9] *Hirayuri no uta*, 32.   [10] Ibid. 30.

up new horizons for the future by facing all such circumstances with the firm belief in one's inherent Buddha nature. A collection of the accounts of the motivations behind the pioneer female members' decision to join the Soka Gakkai, published under the title *Wattashi ga nyushin o kimeta hitokoto* ("The Key Word in my Decision to Practice this Buddhism"),[11] demonstrates how important were the notions of "changing one's karma" and "human revolution":

I had very poor health ever since I was young . . . For me, the only friends I had were the hospital and the wood grain pattern on the ceiling of my dim room. At a discussion meeting I attended, a Young Women's Division member asserted "with this practice, we can change our karma". The concept of "being able to change one's karma", of which she spoke, completely transformed the doubts I had about [the meaning of] my existence.[12]

With the prolonged illness in my family, I had given up hope, believing that it was part of my immutable karma. However, an acquaintance of mine who was a Gakkai member spoke to me with great conviction and spirit—"If you practice this Buddhism, your prayers will become reality. You can change your karma. You will definitely see results. And without a doubt, you can become happy." As I had always believed that destiny was something that could never be changed, no matter the amount of effort, her words struck me like a sudden thunderbolt.[13]

Why did these women embrace so easily the simple idea that "To become happy, there is no other way but to propagate and pray," and thus start practicing this Buddhism? In order to address this question, one should recognize that these women were confronted by numerous hardships, with no hope of reprieve. While there are of course variations in individual circumstances, in general, daily life was fraught with illness and financial destitution in the chaotic aftermath of World War II, and these problems fell heavily on the shoulders of women. There was not a single one among them who did not wish to free herself from this situation. For women who had resigned themselves to illness or family

---

[11] Ed. Tokiko Tada (Tokyo: Seikyo Shimbun Press, 1980).
[12] Ibid. 28.   [13] Ibid. 52.

disharmony, the realization that it was possible to use their potential to change the direction of their lives filled them with enthusiasm and vigor, and a desire to take control in transforming their own lives:

Having decided to divorce my husband, I was in a state of despair. Just then, [a friend of mine who was a Gakkai member] told me, "You possess limitless potential. Only this Buddhism can enable you to bring this forth. If you practice, who knows how truly happy you can be from now on". Sure enough, in that instant, the tragedy of my impending divorce took a completely different turn for the better.[14]

Another member recalls:

My husband had passed away, I myself had fallen ill, and with my children, I was at wit's end. It was at this time that my friend—who was a Gakkai member—shared the practice with me for the first time, saying, "You yourself must forge the path of your own life. With this *Gohonzon* [object of devotion], you can become happy".[15]

Many came to understand that the erroneous interpretations and practice of other forms of Buddhism were the root cause of their suffering:

After my conversion, as I began to practice exactly in the way I was encouraged to, my first deep realization was the frightening effects of the erroneous understanding of Buddhism that our family had hitherto embraced.[16]

The way to overcome such effects was to devote oneself fully to prayer and propagation of this Buddhism:

Having experienced firsthand these alarming consequences, I had a burning determination to devote myself to propagation activities and to offer deep prayers of contrition for my past misguided actions.[17]

[14] Ed. Tokiko Tada (Tokyo: Seikyo Shimbun Press, 1980).
[15] Ibid.
[16] Tsueko Tanaka (ed.), *Haha no kofusho: Fujinbu no taikendanshu* ("Mothers' *Kosen-rufu*: Collected Experiences of Women's Division Members") (Tokyo: Seikyo Shimbun Press, 1980).
[17] Ibid. 168.

To have unshakable conviction in one's life: I believe that this is the great benefit which can only be gained through prayer and taking action to share this Buddhism with others.[18]

The stronger the desire to free themselves from their immediate hardship, the more committed these women became to their propagation activities, and their new experience of prayer began to create a positive, steady rhythm of self-development. As one woman expressed it: "Over time, the oppressed feeling that haunted me somehow disappeared, and I was overcome with an inexpressible joy and exhilaration that pervaded my entire being. It was a state of life I had never actually experienced before, and it was only later that I learned from another member that this feeling was in fact the true benefit [of practice]."[19] In this way, propagation and prayer enabled the women of the Soka Gakkai to experience for themselves a whole new life.

In his study the sociologist Hiroshi Suzuki attributed the growth of the Soka Gakkai to its response to discontent with the *status quo*, the desire for social reform, the feelings of alienation and isolation from the community, and the sense of helplessness—all of which were experienced by the interregional migrants amid the social chaos after Japan's defeat in the war.[20] At the same time that Japanese society as a whole was confronting these fluctuating conditions, women were facing changes of their own.

After the war the legal status of Japanese women improved dramatically, so much so that it has been said that "of all the changes [in postwar society], nothing is as epochal as the liberation of women and the elevation of their social status."[21] With the institution of women's suffrage in 1947, the wider acceptance of women at universities and in workplaces, the proliferation of labor

[18] Ibid. 145. [19] Ibid. 133.

[20] Hiroshi Suzuki, *Toshiteki sekai* ("An Urban World") (Tokyo: Seishin Shobo Press, 1970).

[21] This is a set phrase. The Japanese women did not have the vote and were not eligible for election, and were regarded as incompetent in the civil law before the war. So, in a sense, this phrase may be right, but, as many point out, it seems clear that the equality of the sexes has not been accomplished yet in Japan.

movements, and the formation of numerous women's organizations, democracy inspired a sense of vitality in women. Those
women who had survived much adversity in the chaotic aftermath
of the war, not to mention during the war, steadily acquired the
attitude that they themselves had to forge their own paths. In contrast to the subservient and subordinate lifestyles of women in the
past, women might now shape their own lives. It was precisely
because these women, more so than the men, greatly anticipated
the dawning of a new age that they were drawn to the concept of
"changing one's karma."

James White, who conducted a study on the Soka Gakkai in the
late 1960s, believed that the organization at that time was composed primarily of housewives and the working class. He suggested that the typical Gakkai member was a woman in her thirties
or forties, a housewife living in an urban area, with a relatively low
educational background and low household income, who was
prompted to convert to Nichiren Buddhism because of either psychological or societal distress. This depiction of women is rather
schematic, but his observations convey both the significance of
women to the Soka Gakkai at that time and its impact on them.[22]

One should bear in mind that White typified the Soka Gakkai
leader, in contrast to his earlier description of the general Gakkai
member, as a man in his twenties with a higher level of education.
The kind of gender role differentiation indicated by White, with
men giving directions and women receiving them, was often seen
in the Soka Gakkai organization. Members of the men's division
took on the positions as chapter and district leaders. Even in an
organization that relied heavily on women, the conventional attitudes regarding male dominance prevailed—and this despite the
fact that the Soka Gakkai exhibited strong tendencies to censure
the conservative nature of traditional organizational structures.
Having said this, it remains a fact that in the early days, the Soka
Gakkai recognized the importance of passionate determination.

[22] James White, *The Soka Gakkai and Mass Society* (Stanford, Calif.:
Stanford University Press, 1970).

Consequently, it was not so uncommon to find female leaders even at the chapter level, not to mention at the smaller district and group levels. Moreover, these women played a central role in the discussion meetings and participated in large numbers in the nationwide propagation campaign initiated in 1954. Without a doubt, the activities of the women, who took on the mission of *kosen-rufu* as their own, were the foundation of the pioneering period of the Soka Gakkai.

From "the Mothers of *Kosen-rufu*" to "the Champions of Culture": The Women's Division during President Ikeda's Time

After Toda passed away, Daisaku Ikeda (1928–), who had formerly served as the youth division chief of staff, took office as senior board member. Announcing his intent to "respect the individuality of each division, and allow each to function to its utmost potential," Ikeda directed his efforts to strengthening the women's division. His inauguration as Soka Gakkai president in 1960 inspired the women's division into further action, and under the slogan "Together with President Ikeda," the women's division solidified their commitment to their mentor.

In examining the function fulfilled by the women's division in this new era, it is necessary to focus attention on Yasu Kashiwabara, who was appointed as the national women's division chief.[23] A graduate of the Saitama Teachers' College for Women, she began her career as an elementary schoolteacher. She was assigned to work at the same elementary school as Makiguchi and joined the Soka Kyoiku Gakkai in 1940. Although at first she apparently tried to avoid any discussion on religion, she was among the first to rush to Toda's side after his release from prison. She attended Toda's lectures on the Lotus Sutra and assiduously scoured war-ruined Tokyo in an effort to gather together former

[23] Kashiwabara has continued to hold the most important positions within the women's division. In the year 2000 she held the post of vice-chairman of the board of councillors.

members. She thus became a pillar in the Soka Gakkai reconstruction, serving both as one of the six directors of the new organization and as a professor of the study department.

Kashiwabara's enthusiasm was expressed most fully in her propagation efforts, which resulted in the emergence of the next generation of women's division leaders. As of 1953 she even assumed the leadership of the Suginami chapter, which had been ranked among the top in terms of membership growth and activity. Articles in which she encouraged members or gave directions for activities appeared in every issue of the organization's publications.

Kashiwabara's appeal lay in her accessibility, candor, and friendly interaction with women; rather than approaching them from a theoretical perspective, she nurtured their morale and inspired them actively to pursue propagation activities. Her words "Women should use their husbands as floor cushions,"[24] which she repeatedly used to encourage women around 1954, are probably an apt reflection of her attitude toward life. Indignant at the fact that women continued to be subjected to male dominance and that they still had not been accorded much social standing, she emphasized the need for women to become confident and capable counterparts to men in all spheres of social activity. At numerous meetings her declaration that "We should expect many women to become professors, presidents of companies, and politicians" was met with thunderous applause among the women.

Having been appointed as the new women's division chief at the same time as Ikeda took office as president, her capacity for able leadership left a deep impact on the organization during the early days of President Ikeda's tenure. In her inaugural address she stated:

The power of women is not limited to the household, but rather is so strong as to influence the community and even the entire society. Let's take an objective look at our negative tendencies as women to cause problems through prejudice or impulsiveness; let's cast aside feelings of jealousy and inclination to complain; let each one of us become the kind of

[24] An expression meaning "Instead of being used by the husband, women should have them work to support the wives."

woman who can strive toward the great goal of *kosen-rufu* with absolute confidence.

Soon after his inauguration Ikeda established an overseas affairs section within the headquarters, revealing his intent on propagating Nichiren Buddhism beyond Japan. He then set off, along with Kashiwabara and the five other directors, to encourage members in the United States. Awaiting them were the Japanese women who had married Americans and settled overseas with their husbands. Ikeda and Kashiwabara encouraged these women by saying: "Strive to be the foremost women in the United States," and "Become happy as American citizens, create a totally harmonious household, and develop the kind of good fortune whereby you can enjoy leisurely trips back to Japan." On receiving this encouragement, these women began to introduce their husbands and friends in their neighborhoods to the practice, eventually resulting in the formation of overseas districts and chapters. The women played a key role in the expansion of Soka Gakkai activities in different regions of the world, just as they had in Japan.

As the activities of the Soka Gakkai became more diversified in the 1960s, not only was Kashiwabara visible in every new endeavor, it was clear that her influence transcended the women's division itself. The fact that she wielded such significant influence over all aspects of the Soka Gakkai's activities may well have been due to her individual abilities, but it also reflects the pivotal role of the women's division within the Soka Gakkai. Under Kashiwabara's leadership, the women's division welcomed a new level of responsibility and solidified their underlying strength.

A Women's Division with a Sense of Social Responsibility: The Birth of the Young Married Women's Group

Following the establishment of the culture bureau in 1961, Soka Gakkai activities were promoted in various cultural arenas. The culture bureau initially consisted of the politics, business executives', education and writers' departments, with the academic and arts department being formed later on. This new structure was intended to strengthen the leadership of the Soka Gakkai, laying the groundwork for future involvement in politics. When six Soka Gakkai members ran for office in the 1956 Upper House elections, Kashiwabara garnered the highest number of votes in her successful bid for office in the Tokyo electoral district. At the time of the Komei Political League's founding in 1961, Kashiwabara, as the sole female representative among the eighteen party members of the central executive board, was appointed director of the Komeito's women's bureau.[25]

The scope of the Soka Gakkai women's division activities was then broadened to include cultural areas as well as politics. When the White Lily Chorus was formed in 1962, Ikeda stated:

Those who allow themselves to be driven by sheer force of habit generally tend to become prosaic, to be overwhelmed by life, and to turn bitter, harboring complaints and jealousy, and eventually cease to make true progress. Unfortunately, this has been a common trend among women until the present. I hope somehow that this chorus will be the driving force of the Women's Division, as it stands on the forefront of our cultural activities, taking the first major step in promoting these activities on a global scale.[26]

As a goal for the new era of the Soka Gakkai, Ikeda set forth what he termed "the third civilization," a movement whereby ordinary people would play the pivotal role in shaping culture. For this to happen, it was necessary for the women, who constituted the sector of society most vulnerable to the pressures of everyday life and least active in cultural pursuits, to take the initiative. The chorus activities were thus one way to infuse a new sense of identity and purpose among the women's division members, as standard-bearers of culture. Women were encouraged to become exemplary citizens and thus to show concrete results of the practice.

Within the women's division itself, guidelines emphasizing women's roles and standing in society were set forth in quick suc-

---

[25] Kashiwabara was not the only woman who ran for election at this time. A municipal assembly member emerged from the women's division as well.
[26] *Kakumei no taiga*, 318.

cession. For example: "The women of the Soka Gakkai should strive to be trusted and liked by people in society at large, not to mention in the Soka Gakkai itself."[27] As the membership rose to the level of 3 million households in 1962, the Soka Gakkai gradually turned its attention away from further growth and toward fostering a more profound understanding of Buddhism in individual members. Consequently, efforts were made to solidify each of the separate divisions from within, thus strengthening the organization as a whole. This shift in focus was an attempt to build the kind of Soka Gakkai that was trusted by society, while avoiding the social friction that had previously arisen from propagation activities.

Japanese society itself was at a major turning point. Having emerged from a postwar period of turmoil, Japan had entered a phase of rapid economic growth. Similarly, the women's division was also undergoing change, with a new organizational structure being laid out in 1968. The baton was passed from Kashiwabara to a younger generation, led by a new division chief who had received training in the young women's division during President Toda's time.

Striving to reconstruct the Soka Gakkai, Toda gave encouragement to the women's division, whose members, as discussed earlier, responded by pouring their efforts into propagation activities, hence helping to strengthen the movement. However, it was the youth division, comprised of young men and young women's divisions, to which Toda entrusted the future development of the Soka Gakkai. While Toda recognized the importance of the women's division, their contributions were seen mainly as laying the groundwork; there were thus greater expectations of the youth division, who were to shoulder a heavier share of responsibilities in the future. The metaphor of the family was often used in the early days: "the Soka Gakkai is one large family." As with the conventional role of the "mother" in Japanese society, whereby the mother would work in the spirit of giving herself entirely for the

---

[27] The "dedication to the women's division" was made public at a women's division leaders' meeting held on Feb. 12, 1963.

sake of her family and serve as the foundation on which the growth of her children could be assured, the women's division members were valued as the foundation of the Soka Gakkai. None the less, despite the recognition of the significance of its role, the women's division clearly played a secondary or supporting role to the youth division.[28]

Although the restructured women's division placed emphasis on a youthful spirit, upholding as their motto "youthfulness throughout one's life," this did not simply imply that the median age of the women's division was lower. These were women of modern times, distinct from the women's division members of the early days of the Soka Gakkai, who, as housewives fending for their families, had struggled to make ends meet during the chaotic aftermath of the war. Although they too had experienced harsh realities during that turbulent period, the new women's division members, unlike their predecessors, were not bound by the lifestyle of the older generation of women. On the contrary, having been educated in the postwar period of democracy, they tended to favor a lifestyle in which they played an active and principal role.[29] As former members of the young women's division, "a solidarity of women with a philosophical base," they had conducted various study presentations, discussions, and debates, hence keeping pace with the young men's division. As these young women's division members graduated to the women's division, they came to form the core of the young married women's group in 1974, a group

[28] In Toda's speech recorded in 1959 he performed the song "Tabaruzuka" (a song in memory of soldiers fighting the 1877 civil war in Japan, mourning the loss of young lives) and stated, "This is the song of the women's division. This is the song of all the women who sent their precious children off to war." Toda further encouraged them, saying, "Is everything all right at home? Housewives should take good care of their husbands and children" (*Seikyo Shimbun*, Jan. 23, 1959).

[29] Some young women even criticized attitudes of women's division members. In a 1954 issue of the *Seikyo Shimbun* young women's division members commented on an area of concern to them: "The words that pour forth from the mouths of women's division members are slanderous." They also gave this rather severe assessment: "In order for the women's division members to avoid lapsing into slander, it is important for them to develop their own strengths, to fully utilize and expand their existing assets."

that possessed a sense of social awareness as well as a certain cultural sensibility.

Therefore, "youthfulness," as upheld by the incoming generation of the women's division, was symbolic of their image as women possessing both the ability to take action and the kind of vision that inspired confidence in society. This not only represented a new direction for the Soka Gakkai as a whole, it also coincided with the ideal sought by Japanese women in general, living in a society of high economic growth. Having been young women's division members prior to marriage, these women had learned what it meant to contribute to the organization. Shortly after the new women's division initiated its activities, it published the *Fuyo Journal*, an organ of the division,[30] and in their members' quest to become "women who read, write, and engage in dialogue," they not only got involved in propagation activities, but also launched themselves into the fields of journalism and publishing.

As Wives and Mothers

Around this time women's roles within the family, as mothers and spouses, were being reasserted by the encouragement issued from the women's division. Throughout Japan child development theories were beginning to place greater emphasis on the mother's responsibility, and the Mother and Child Health Law passed in 1965 reflected this perspective. Although women in contemporary society have often been criticized for lacking a sense of maternal responsibility, one would have to note that this was in fact forced upon them as a result of the gradual erosion of communal ties. As the dysfunctions of family life, and educational problems such as school violence and truancy, became recognized as widespread social issues in the 1970s, increasing attention was given to the mother's expected roles and responsibilities. Theories claiming the

[30] This journal ceased publication after twenty months, but none the less left its mark by contributing significantly to the raising of capable people and by providing inspiring guidance. The *Soka Fujin Shimbun* and the *Soka Joshi Shimbun* were initiated in 1993, but these too have since ceased publication.

importance of a mother's involvement in the first three years of a child's life were also popularized around this time.[31]

In the midst of this social context, the slogan "A life of fortune, a solid household" was adopted by the women's division, and numerous events and meetings were developed along the themes of "equally fulfilling the responsibilities of the home and Soka Gakkai activities," "how to excel in raising children," and "the awareness befitting a mother." The ideology of women's liberation, emphasized in the early days of the Soka Gakkai, receded to the background as priority was placed on the family and raising of children. Consequently, to fulfil their roles as mothers and wives and to be a sunlike presence within the home became a central goal.[32] The commitment to develop a "solid household" has remained part of the spirit of the women's division to this day.

In this way, the two goals of working toward a Soka Gakkai trusted and valued by the local community and of constructing a stable household complemented each other. Increasing importance came to be placed on becoming an exemplary household within the community. Around this time there evolved the notion that "as long as the wife is wise and is strong in her faith, this will give a sense of reassurance to the husband, allowing him to exert himself to the utmost both at work and in society," thus specifying the function of a wise wife. Similar principles were applied with regard to the development of the child. The belief was that a child's ability to focus on his or her studies depended entirely on the wis-

[31] There is little support for working mothers in Japanese society. Child care is a primary obstacle that women who want to continue working, are forced to confront. Not only are child care facilities limited, but the fees are exorbitant, even if one were to have access to such a facility. Husbands cannot be depended upon for support, and society tends to judge these mothers harshly. Thus, it is common for women to temporarily forgo their jobs and devote themselves solely to child rearing, returning to the labor force only as their children grow up. As a result, the M-shaped distribution of female labour force participation by age is maintained.

[32] Daisaku Ikeda's message at the 1975 meeting on the theme "My Practice of Buddhism." Incidentally, the goals of the young mothers' group consisted of "the four ideals of motherhood: a wise mother, a cheerful mother, a healthy mother, and a mother of strong faith."

dom of the mother. Thus, both the husband's social success and the child's educational achievement—the main criteria for a "model" family—became the responsibility of the women as spouses and mothers. In this sense, women continued to serve as the foundation of the Soka Gakkai as before, but instead of playing a behind-the-scenes role, their function took on a significance that was equal to, or presumably greater than, that of men, in that it was essential in displaying concrete results in the community. What resulted was a system of gender role differentiation in which men focused on their work, and the women concentrated on household management and child rearing—a system that supported Japanese society in its period of economic growth.

Changes within the women's division were also related to the changes implemented in the Soka Gakkai organization as a whole. Starting in the early 1970s, in conjunction with the growth in membership and the Soka Gakkai's entry into politics, the hitherto vertical structure based on the relationship of sponsor–new member was reorganized into a localized organizational structure. Whereas before, new members joined the same districts or groups as their sponsors regardless of where they lived, the new "localized" system allowed the members to participate in activities in their own neighborhoods. The women's division members were the ones most affected by this transition, for this alleviated the burden of time commitments and travel expenses required by visiting members' homes. They thus readily welcomed this new system. While the workplace was the primary arena for the men to show concrete results of this practice, the local community was the natural locus of the daily lives of the women's division. Thus, as the local community became the forum for introducing Buddhism, it gave the women's division an opportunity to link their day-to-day efforts to the development of good relations in their neighborhoods through Soka Gakkai activities.

Striving to Become a Well-Rounded Person: The Diversification of the Women's Division

Nevertheless, it would be rather simplistic for us to infer from the above that the role of the women's division was restricted to functions within the home. Certainly, there exist many religious groups in Japanese society that would not think twice about relegating women to the home, and the Soka Gakkai may be said to show traces of a similarly conservative attitude. However, inconsistent as it may seem, the Soka Gakkai was not so parochial as to limit women's activities to home life, for within the movement the greatest importance was placed on individual self-determination and responsibility. Consequently, it mattered little whether someone was a housewife or had a job; the control and responsibility for one's actions applied to any endeavor, in any field. In 1968 the *Seikyo Shimbun* introduced the results of a survey regarding the views of the young women's division toward employment and careers. This revealed that 6 percent of the young women surveyed felt that "One should quit work when one gets married or when one has children," and 64 percent agreed with the statement "One should be prepared to commit a lifetime [to one's work]." An NHK (Japan Broadcasting Corporation) opinion poll asked similar questions of a sample of all Japanese women (not limited to the Soka Gakkai), and found 29 percent agreeing with the first statement, and 22 percent with the latter. It might be inferred from this observation alone that a life dedicated solely to household management and child rearing after marriage was not what young women's division members envisioned as the standard way of life for a member of the women's division.

There appears to be a pervasive view among those outside the Soka Gakkai that Gakkai women have traditionally been housewives seeking recognition as members of society, and thus have used organizational activities as a substitute for effective participation in society. Accordingly, there has been a tendency to depict the women's division members as women who could not express their autonomy. However, from numerous interviews with female members and examination of various materials a distinct impression emerges that the proportion of Soka Gakkai women who work is quite high. Of course, it would be necessary to undertake surveys and other studies in order to substantiate this point. Moreover, it may be difficult to make positive assertions, as there are likely to be some variations based on region of origin or age group. It is also possible that many women do not work because they choose to devote most of their time to Soka Gakkai activities. Nevertheless, as will be elaborated below, one could safely say that the proportion of working women in the Soka Gakkai is fairly demonstrative of a widespread and ingrained desire to express one's full potential in society, and of the explicit link between the desire to take action in society and to show concrete results of the Buddhist practice.

Since both working women and housewives alike were encouraged to develop friendly relations, disregarding any boundaries that may exist between the realm of the home and the rest of society, the women of the Soka Gakkai were naturally expected to extend their sphere of activity beyond the home. In fact, the ideal of the well-rounded person who can be effective in the home as well as in society was adopted as one of the goals of the women's division:

> In the coming age, I believe human beings will be expected not only to display creativity and individuality, but also to become a "well-rounded person" who can participate effectively in any field . . . We must become the kind of people who can successfully manage all things, including housework, careers, political and cultural involvement, and personal interests, and in doing so, give full play to our creative potential.[33]

Although we cannot say for a fact, it appears that the call to "manage successfully both work and household duties" or to "become a well-rounded person" have not been directed toward the male members of the Soka Gakkai. It can be inferred that men were expected to place their work and Soka Gakkai activities

---

[33] Words commemorating the 1969 first women's division general meeting.

outside the home as their utmost priority and were excused from household chores or neighborhood obligations, while women, even those holding jobs, were expected to fulfill both the responsibilities in the home as well as in the local community. Whether the dual commitments at work and in the home are regarded as "the responsibilities of a well-rounded person" or a "twofold obligation" is a matter of personal interpretation. It appears that the women in the Soka Gakkai perceived them as a rallying cry to which they readily responded. In any event, it was clear that Japan had entered an age in which women's roles and activities were expanding into a variety of spheres.

As the number of female members grew and their life experiences became more diversified, the women's division itself began to reorganize into smaller groups. Since the women's division consisted entirely of married women, its members ranged widely in age from those in their twenties to those in their eighties. As the transformations in society took place at an ever accelerating pace, the differences in experience and understanding arising from the generation gap grew even more apparent. The Soka Gakkai, which had always striven to be sensitive to the needs of its members, clearly could not ignore this issue. Thus, various generation-based groups evolved within the women's division, one of which was the aforementioned young married women's group. For the older generations, the guidance division, and later the treasures group, were formed.[34]

The general trend toward an increasing number of working women in Japanese society had a major impact on the activities of the women's division. Nevertheless, here, as always, the women's division was quick to respond, and by 1968 the Tokyo federation of housewives and the working women's group had already been formed.

The activities of the former group generally aspired to improve the social standing of housewives and promote their social aware-

---

[34] In 1994 representative members aged 60 and above instituted the college of treasures group. Lectures for the women's division and study meetings continue to be held, led by former leaders in the women's division. Shortly thereafter, similar lectures were also offered to the men's division.

ness. They included specific projects such as surveys that brought to light the demands of housewives as consumers. The statement of a vice headquarters women's division leader of the time clarifies this point:

In the past, women's organizations have initiated movements on various fronts, and have had considerable impact both on a social and a political level . . . However, the voices of housewives have yet to be reflected on a broad scale. This federation of housewives, being formed at this significant juncture, has a great mission to promote a widespread people's movement, and to serve as the mainstay of women of all social and economic classes.[35]

The members of the working women's group were further divided among separate subgroups according to occupation, but all shared in the objective of bringing working women together and pursuing better living conditions, as well as taking concrete action toward the realization of social welfare. These subgroups, formed in the early stages of the group, currently cover a diverse array of occupations, including nurses, beauticians, and artists.[36] By holding separate meetings for discussion and guidance, each division was able to address occupation-specific issues, and the members found encouragement that only colleagues, who had directly confronted these issues, could offer. The working women's group was instituted in 1976 to explore the possibility of holding activities such as discussion meetings in the evenings or on Sundays. Today, the working women's group has developed to the point where it is now able to sponsor meetings in order to share experiences.

[35] *Daibyakurenge* (Oct. 1968), 44.

[36] The subgroups formed when the working women's group was established, such as *nazuna* (proprietors, managers, and hostesses of restaurants and bars), *himawari* (dressmakers), *ayame* (insurance policy salespeople), and *tampopo* (people engaged in different kinds of piecework at home), are an indication of those times. Currently spanning the membership of the social division and the culture department, these subgroups have become even more diversified, reflecting women's advancement into various spheres of social activity.

The Women's Division and Election Campaigns

It is possible that the formation of the two aforementioned groups in 1968 was influenced by the circumstances surrounding the Komeito's chances in the approaching Upper House elections. This was expected to be the most closely contested election yet, and related articles were featured throughout the New Year's Day issue of the *Seikyo Shimbun*. Perhaps because of such election forecasts, the importance of women's votes appeared prominently in the discussions among the Komeito executive officers. Kashiwabara, the Komeito women's bureau director at the time, referred to the words of President Ikeda: "Women should be sensitive to the trends in society, not tolerating the injustices and evils in the world, and fight for the establishment of a happy and peaceful society." He further stated, "Right now, the women's division is determined to have women play the pivotal role in winning in the Upper House elections . . . In order to determine the future direction of the country, we must make a concerted effort to raise people's awareness, ensuring the just and effective use of each woman's vote."

Thus, it could be surmised that part of the motivation behind the formation of these two groups was to mobilize and direct women's votes. No matter what the reasons, the publications that appeared around this time reveal that the women enthusiastically welcomed the formation of the groups, and that there was a growing consciousness and desire among the women's division members to contribute to politics and promote social awareness, in whatever way their capacity and position allowed. Taxes were an issue of primary concern, and in the fall of that year, when the water utility rate increases were proposed, members petitioned the governor of Tokyo to voice their protest. Furthermore, the women's division held several meetings to debate various issues, such as inflation or national defense. In response to the campaign pledges made by the Komeito to work on social welfare, to clean up politics, and to promote international peace, a heightened sense of commitment developed among the women; they would advocate the concretization of such principles.

Those outside the Soka Gakkai, who observed the assiduous efforts of the women's division around election time, made frequent critical remarks, such as "The women's division is nothing but a vote-collecting machine" or "[The Soka Gakkai] simply treasures the women because they have a lot of free time." Belying some of these comments was the attitude that "Women, who have no understanding of politics, are being manipulated by religion," based on the assumption, of course, that women are politically ignorant. However, if one analyzes the voices emanating from within the women's division, there is no indication that the women were blindly following policies imposed upon them from male leaders.

It is indisputable that women, or their influence, are not readily visible in the Japanese political world, but this in no way implies that Japanese women are uninterested in politics. Ever since the national elections of 1968, voter turnout among women has consistently been higher than that of men. Furthermore, from 1963 onward, in all regional elections ranging from gubernatorial elections to municipal assembly elections, the average female voter turnout nationwide has surpassed that of men. Rather than considering the underrepresentation of female political candidates to be an indication of a low level of awareness among women, the main reason seems to be that men dominate the political world, preventing women from entering this field. Hence, despite the interest in politics by Soka Gakkai women, and their strong sense of awareness regarding social reform, the world of politics and political parties remains male-dominated. As such, it is not an easy task to estimate the extent to which the will of these women is reflected in politics.[37]

[37] According to surveys conducted by each party secretariat in June 1994, the Komeito, with 45 percent of its total membership consisting of women, has the greatest number of female party members. However, in terms of the numbers of women who serve as party executive officers, the Komeito lags behind the other parties, with only three women out of a total of thirty-five. Nevertheless, some women, such as Toshiko Hamayotsu (currently acting head of the Komeito), have served as the head of the Komeito, and there are an increasing number of female party members coming from the legal

Having established subdivisions such as the Tokyo federation of housewives and the working women's group, the women's division introduced the office of secretary-general to serve as part of the executive body, and a system was set up whereby planning management would occur through consultation and deliberation. A man was appointed to head the women's division for the first time in 1969 because it was thought that this personnel decision was made in order for the entire Soka Gakkai organization to express its support for the women's division. Likewise, there was even a time that the national young women's division chief was a man. These occasional personnel appointments could be regarded by those outside the movement as acquiescence to the gender boundaries set by the society at large, whereby leadership positions must unquestionably be assumed by men. The position of women's and young women's divisions leader has since then reverted to women.

As Mothers of Society

In the 1980s, as the women's division celebrated its thirtieth anniversary, there was great anticipation that it was about to embark on a new phase. There were now second and third generation practitioners, and as their general standard of living had risen, new directions for activities began to emerge. The women's division increasingly focused on the lives of women in their forties and fifties, who were no longer preoccupied with child rearing, and on their desire to lead a fulfilling life. In the period immediately following the war the average life expectancy of Japanese women was 50, and thoughts on life after child rearing seemed irrelevant. However, by 1980 their average life expectancy reached 80, and many women were relieved of their child-rearing duties by their late thirties. Because of this major change in lifecycle, women found that their identity could no longer be centered solely on their roles as mothers. Accordingly, the nature of the mother's role

profession. One hopes that the numbers of female party officers will continue to grow. See "Survey on the Status of Women's Participation in the policy-making Process," conducted by the councilors' office on internal affairs, cabinet secretariat (office of women's affairs).

expanded to such that it took on a societal, or even universal, characteristic, rather than simply being a function limited to the confines of the home.

Daniel Metraux, who built on the study by White as he conducted research on the Soka Gakkai in the mid-1980s, emphasized the fact that the constituent membership in the 1960s differed greatly from those of the 1980s. He observed that, as Japanese society enjoyed a period of economic boom, there were fewer members suffering from financial problems than in earlier days, and the overall level of educational attainment had also increased. Although a large proportion of the membership continued to be housewives and blue-collar workers, and there were still slightly more female members than male members, Metraux pointed out that it would be a grave mistake to consider the Soka Gakkai to be a female-centered organization.[38] This was not to imply that the power of women's division activities had weakened, but was probably an indication that along with the diversification of women's living circumstances and awareness, it was no longer possible to reduce the various aspects of the organization to one single image.

Leading the International Movement and Peace Activities

Given the growth of the organization overseas, the Soka Gakkai International (SGI) was founded in 1975, with Daisaku Ikeda at the helm. The women's division also launched its own international group in 1979, sending its first delegation to China, and formed the Soka Gakkai women's peace committee the following year. These events fell within the framework of a new sphere of activities to mark the thirtieth anniversary of the founding of the women's division. The objectives of the women's peace committee, originally composed of fewer than ten members, were as follows: to contribute to the realization of a lasting peace based on

---

[38] Daniel A. Metraux, *Ningen to heiwa no taiga—Soka Gakkai no rekishi to rinen* ("The History and Theology of the Soka Gakkai"), trans. Yasuo Endo (Tokyo: Horyusha Press, 1989).

the Buddhist philosophy of Nichiren; to share widely the ideals of respect for the dignity of life, and to pass such ideals on to the next generation; and to construct a peaceful society without war. After its inception the entire division began to carry out concrete action for peace.

It was not that activities to promote peace were unknown prior to this period, whether within the women's division or within the Soka Gakkai as a whole. As early as 1957 the Declaration of the Abolition of Nuclear Weapons by Josei Toda indicated concern for peace-related issues and is considered to be the starting point of the Soka Gakkai peace movement. The youth division was the first to spearhead the peace activities, and so far has initiated such projects as fund raising for various humanitarian causes and publication of books on antiwar themes.[39] The contributions of women to these peace activities have been recognized since the early stages of Soka Gakkai's development. However, both the women's division and the entire organization were initially more intent on propagation and on refuting the Buddhist doctrines of other Japanese religious denominations. Later, as greater emphasis came to be placed on dialogue with those in the local and international communities, activities for peace gained in prominence. Accordingly, the role of women in maintaining peace was reaffirmed.

History of the Peace Movement within the Women's Division

Although the women's division may have been off to a late start in comparison to the youth division, its commitment to peace activities was just as energetic. In early 1981 it launched a series of conferences given by various academics or peace activists on the theme "On Women and Peace." Four or five of these conferences have since been held throughout Japan each year, numbering a total of ninety-one to date. Furthermore, on Aug. 15, 1981, commemorating the end of World War II, the women's division published

---

[39] The Youth Peace Conference, first established in 1979, includes the Young Women's Conference for Peace and Culture.

the first volume of an antiwar series entitled With Hopes for Peace. This was an immense undertaking spanning ten years, with the twentieth volume appearing in 1991 under the title *Far from Home: Wartime Experiences of Japanese Women Overseas.* These books have been well received, for they provide intimate eyewitness accounts of wartime history, as recorded by younger generations that have never experienced war. In terms of historical research, this anthology of oral history is invaluable in that the experiences of women, and, consequently, female viewpoints of history, are rarely documented. Moreover, its attempt to go beyond simply portraying women as victims of war offers a perspective on this subject that is of great import even today, and lends further credibility to this work.[40] In addition, the fact that the project was undertaken not by specialists but by "ordinary mothers," who appear to have worked hard despite their lack of specific methodological training, makes this project even more significant.

Since 1983 the Soka Gakkai has instituted a series of speech forums called "Women's Division Advocacy of Peace,"[41] which apparently provide an opportunity for members to share their own grassroots activities for peace. These meetings, which have gained in momentum and diversity over the years, number over forty-one to date, but this topic will be examined further below.

Another noteworthy dimension of division activities consists of the various exhibitions it sponsors. Effectively utilizing photographs and illustrations to present problems faced by contemporary society in a viewer-friendly manner, these exhibitions raise awareness of these issues among a wide audience. Starting with the "Mothers, Children, and War" exhibition held in Fukuoka in 1984, the successful 1990 "Unicef and Children of the World," and the 1991 "What are Children's Rights?" exhibits have since

---

[40] *Kappogi no jyugo*, xvii: *Daisan Bunmeisha* (Tokyo: 1987). This addresses the history of the *Dai Nipponkoku Boei Fujinkai* (Greater Japan Women's Defense Association), which began with the dedication of one woman to her nation.

[41] The title of these meetings changed in 1996 to "Women's Plaza: Perspectives on Peace."

been touring the country, showing in approximately forty-one venues, many of which are ongoing. Recently, there has been growing concern among mothers about the everyday lives of children. Attention has been brought to this topic not only in the form of an exhibition, but also by conducting a large-scale survey in 1996 to investigate the general awareness of the Children's Rights Treaty in educational institutions within Japan, a project which is currently ongoing. Furthermore, in an effort to encourage people to think about the present state of the family and reflect on its future, an exhibit entitled "Members of the Global Family" was launched in 1994, the International Year of the Family, providing a perspective on the changing forms of the family unit in accord with the times and with the transformations in the social structure. A total of 1.5 million visitors are reported to have attended these exhibitions.

The general impression of the Soka Gakkai in society at large has changed to a certain extent as a result of these diverse women's peace committee activities. This has mainly arisen from the efforts on the part of its members to solicit and incorporate outside expertise and information, thereby promoting open dialogue with nonmembers and other organizations. Coincidentally, from the 1980s grassroots "network" participation in environmental preservation movements or other volunteer activities became more prevalent among Japanese women. Such activities also sought to reform society through the collective efforts of women, and, as such, had much in common with the activities of the Soka Gakkai women's division. Indeed, it was precisely because they shared a similar sense of mission and awareness toward contemporary society that these exhibits succeeded in prompting joint cooperation with groups outside the Soka Gakkai. Many nonmember academics, activists, and officials invited to these events have given positive feedback, such as "I am deeply impressed by the extent to which members of the women's division have been carrying out grassroots activities for the sake of peace," or "It is wonderful that as anonymous, ordinary citizens, women have such an acute awareness of social issues and are so active."

One woman shared with the author the following reason for joining the Soka Gakkai:

As a student, I was inducted into the student protest movement, debated Marx, sang antiwar songs to the strumming of the guitar, or participated in demonstrations . . . and considered myself to be a full-fledged activist. Upon graduation, however, my friends dropped out of these activities one by one, and I completely lost faith in human nature and became overwhelmed with a sense of powerlessness, that society could not be changed after all . . . At that time, however, I became aware of what the Soka Gakkai was doing, and was amazed. I saw ordinary men and women pray seriously, out of noble intentions, for people's happiness, the development of society, and world peace, acting assiduously, quietly, but earnestly, without pay. I was ashamed of myself because I had just been pursuing theoretical ideals, but at the same time was overjoyed at the thought that with that kind of solidarity, it was actually going to be possible to change society.[42]

It is worth noting the frequency and depth of engagement of Soka Gakkai members in issues that are rarely given much attention by the general public.

An Awareness of Peace among Women of Soka Gakkai

What sort of awareness toward peace exists among the women in the Soka Gakkai? Judging from the nature of activities carried out by the women's peace committee at the time of its inception, emphasis was placed on opposing both war and military action, and stimulating increased awareness about preserving peace. On the occasion of the fortieth anniversary of the Japanese constitution in 1987, the committee conducted a survey of 3,000 women over the age of 20 regarding their perceptions of peace and the Japanese constitution. The foreword to the final report reads:

Women were victims of war, and at the same time, its accomplices. This survey was conducted in the hope that it would serve as a modest but concrete step toward peace, so that this episode is never again repeated . . . We will continue to promote even further our grassroots peace movement,

[42] Interviews by the author.

whereby even in today's peaceful society, women will appreciate the significance of the constitution in situations close to home, and uphold the dignity of life.[43]

Thus, the underlying motivation for the survey was the feeling that women, as the ones responsible for raising children, were precisely those who needed to become more cognizant of the importance of peace and the Japanese constitution (which, in Article 9, renounces all acts of aggression). The survey revealed that, while there was a strong desire for peace and absence of war, there was limited knowledge and understanding of current events or political affairs. Perhaps alarmed at the thought that such people might be more susceptible to manipulation by misleading information and thereby repeat the mistakes of the past, the committee began to devote even more energy to its activities. In any case, the project was innovative in that women surveyed other women on their perceptions of peace and expressed the conviction of the committee that a peaceful society would materialize when the awareness among women was heightened.

Whereas this basic stance remains unchanged, the women's division's awareness of the importance of peace and the nature of their activities have none the less diversified. This is reflected, for instance, in the statements made during recent Women's Plaza meetings.[44] As suggested also by the title of the published collection of their reports and declarations for peace, *Heiwa no daichi* ["Advocates of Peace"], there is a widespread sense of mission among women, in whom it has been ingrained since the early days of the organization that the advocates of peace are none other than mothers who nurture new lives. Their activities, reports of which they share with others during these meetings, do not consist of

[43] Soka Gakkai Women's Peace Committee (ed.), *Heiwa to kempo ni kansuru fujin no ishiki chosa hokoku* ("Women's Awareness Survey Regarding Peace and the [Japanese] Constitution") (Tokyo: Soka Gakkai Women's Peace Committee, 1988).

[44] Yoko Takagi (ed.), *Women's Plaza: Heiwa no Daichi III : Soka Gakkai fujin heiwa shucho taikai shu* ("Advocates of Peace: A Record of the Convention on Perspectives of Peace Held by Soka Gakkai Women's Division") (Tokyo: Daisan Bunmeisha, 1998).

direct protest or action against war. Rather, they suggest that women are engaged in numerous social outreach programs as "builders of peace," by getting involved locally in volunteer activities, recycling efforts, improvement of agricultural methods, support for the handicapped, or international exchange. All these areas are linked to problematic issues that have yet to be solved by modern Japanese society, and, in this sense, these activities epitomize the course of action that needs to be taken in the future.

However multifaceted the range of activities become, the underlying stance remains unchanged—the written experiences in *Heiwa no daichi* are characterized by a sense of happiness in living life, as each member manages to transform her hardships into a springboard for overcoming obstacles. These reports clearly manifest their determination to lead lives fully rooted in their immediate surroundings, by making the best of what their local community has to offer. This attitude is reflected in such statements as the following:

With firm conviction that peace will be built not through hollow words but by concrete action, I will overcome any difficulty and do my best in the future.[45]

By expanding networks of friendship with other mothers [who also have children suffering from similar disabilities] in my local community, I will strive to realize a truly peaceful society where children can coexist and live together in harmony.[46]

I would like to continue in my efforts to revitalize the local community.[47]

What is more, these women's ability to organize and to take action is remarkable, whether in networking with other people in similar circumstances or in voicing their opinions to public authorities.

The experiences of such women are not only shared in these kinds of forums, but are also regularly reported in Soka Gakkai publications. Some women's division members have taken the initiative in caring for the elderly in communities suffering from an aging population or depopulation; others in the agriculture group have striven to improve cultivation methods or to restructure

[45] Ibid. 16.   [46] Ibid. 37.   [47] Ibid.

financially their agricultural business. While these are inconspicuous efforts, which require perseverance and may take a long time
to show results, the function these women fulfill in society is vital
for their respective communities.

These women share the conviction that interactions with others
contribute to the realization of world peace, and that life should
not be approached in a passive manner, preferring instead to live
life to the fullest and manifest their potential. This approach is consistent with the Buddhist view of life and the concept of "changing
one's karma," its validity manifested in society through the various
experiences of these women.

One of the long-standing guidelines for the women's division
has been that of a "stable family," and any references to "society"
usually implied the "local community." Although these tendencies
have not completely disappeared, SGI activities at an international
level, and especially the dialogues of Daisaku Ikeda and human
rights activists and academics the world over, have had an impact
on the members. They increasingly seem to consider themselves
within a wider context—that is to say in relationship with the rest
of the world—and consequently, they see the local and the international communities as being compatible, nonexclusive entities.

This perception is well expressed by Noriko Oguma, the present
chairperson of the women's peace committee:

Fundamentally, I believe that the underlying principle in all endeavors is
for every single person to respect one another and to gain each other's
trust.[48]

Whereas diplomacy, which rests on political leadership, may also be
important, I realized that we will eventually create a peaceful world when
we, as ordinary citizens, discuss culture with people from around the
world, based on mutual respect and consideration.[49]

Our peace movement begins when people, reflecting on their own lives,
transform themselves from within. Throughout this process, we hope to

[48] Ibid.
[49] Ibid. 1–2.

inspire each other, as friends, to develop a heightened awareness of the value of peace, thereby constructing a peaceful society. In our capacity as mothers, we will continue to promote a peace movement for a new era, starting with our own neighborhoods, and extending our reach to the greater society and the entire world.[50]

Of course, such statements are made by only a fraction of the many that make up the women's division, but they are not exceptional.

The vision of peace within the women's division has always been that "heart-to-heart, open dialogue cultivates peace," but recently it seems this is being stressed even further. Even the women's division meetings reflect this trend, placing greater emphasis on small-scale gatherings that allow for more direct dialogue. The annual event considered to be most important for the women's division is the women's division general meeting. At the outset, these meetings were an opportunity to bring representatives from the outlying areas together. However, the format has been gradually shifting toward that of small group meetings held on a local basis, so that the foremost priority today is to develop fully the groups in communities to which members feel closer attachment. Not only is the Soka Gakkai, as part of SGI, diversifying its activities on an increasingly global scale, it is concurrently reinforcing ties with the surrounding community—a move propelled, not surprisingly, by the women's division.

Perception of Women in the Soka Gakkai

So far, this chapter has traced the history of the women's division. Although it may seem that too much attention has been given to the early period of its development, this can be justified in that the Soka Gakkai's guiding principles appear to have been elaborated mostly during those years. Likewise, this has been necessary in order to emphasize that the movement has reacted with sensitivity to the changing times. The author's view is that the women's division activities, as well as the way these women lead their lives,

[50] Ibid.

reflect this dual aspect in the most striking manner. For this reason, this section seeks to summarize perceptions and views on women in general that underlie their Gakkai activities. Later, by considering various matters regarding women and gender within the organization, I hope to reveal the characteristics of the Soka Gakkai and the issues it must still address.

What attracted women to the Soka Gakkai was, on one hand, Josei Toda's ideas about how people could obtain benefits, which were based upon his view of life and, on the other, the theory of Nichiren Buddhism, which spoke of salvation of women on equal terms with men. The latter centered on treatises and letters compiled in the *Gosho* ("The Major Writings of Nichiren"), such as "Kanjin honzon sho" ("On the True Object of Worship"). Nichiren, in his "Shoho jissou sho" ("The True Entity of Life") wrote, "Exert yourself in the two ways of practice and study. Without practice and study, there can be no Buddhism,"[51] making it clear that study of Buddhist philosophy is a key component of the Buddhist practice. Great importance is placed above all on the study of these *Writings* by Nichiren. As stated in one guidance, "There is no doubt that those who imbue the *Writings* in the depths of their hearts, studying this work throughout their lives, will never fail to grow and develop. Whatever may happen, the *Writings* are the basis and the core [of our practice]. Everything else is secondary, and of minor importance."[52] For these reasons, through lectures given on a district level or by reading Soka Gakkai publications, female members study how women should lead their lives and what roles they should play in society. In this way, Nichiren's view on women is most influential.

While Nichiren had many female followers, he sent letters of encouragement, gratitude, or guidance to those women who were particularly strong in faith. These letters continue to be read and studied as timeless instruction for women (as well as men) who

---

[51] Nichiren, "Shoho jisso sho," in *Gosho*, 1361 ("The True Entity of Life," in *Major Writings*, i. 95).

[52] Daisaku Ikeda, speech given in 1968 on the occasion of the 17th young women's division general meeting.

have determined to carry out their faith in the Lotus Sutra. Nichiren expounded the nondiscriminatory nature of Buddhahood when he wrote, "In effect, then, both Shakyamuni and Manjushri, Devadatta and the dragon king's daughter, are all efficacies of the single seed of *Myoho-renge-kyo*, and hence all from the beginning have attained Buddhahood."[53] He further maintained that salvation is promised to them by the benefits acquired through practicing the Lotus Sutra, since "a woman who embraces this sutra not only excels all other women but also surpasses all men."[54]

The reason why the Lotus Sutra is considered, both in Nichiren Buddhism and in the Soka Gakkai, to be a teaching that allows women to attain enlightenment can be found in the Devadatta chapter. In this chapter of the Lotus Sutra an anecdote relates the tale of an 8-year-old daughter of the dragon king who attains enlightenment. The enlightenment of a female dragon, just as she is and not after death, is taken as proof that all women can achieve enlightenment in their lifetime, as they are in the here and now. Accordingly, Nichiren writes, "though the women of Japan may be condemned in all sutras other than the *Lotus Sutra* as incapable of attaining Buddhahood, as long as the *Lotus Sutra* guarantees their enlightenment, what reason have they to be downcast?"[55] and taught that there can be no enlightenment for women unless they believe in the Lotus Sutra.

Traditionally in Japanese society it has been said that women are envoys from hell, with the outward appearance of a bodhisattva, but with the heart of a demon. There has also been the view that they are destined to lead lives of triple subjugation, obeying first their parents as children, then their husbands as wives, and finally their sons once they become aged mothers. While these common perceptions do not exactly reflect the teachings of Shakyamuni,

---

[53] Nichiren, "Devadatta", in *Gosho*, 797.

[54] Nichiren, *Shijo kingo dono nyobo gohenji*," in *Gosho*, 1134 ("The Unity of Husband and Wife," *Major Writings*, v (1988), 157).

[55] "*Sennichiama gozen gohenji*," in *Gosho*, 1311 ("The Sutra of True Requital," *Major Writings*, vi (1990), 250).

there is little doubt that they were none the less widely circulated as religious statements serving to justify the subservience of women. The Soka Gakkai asserted that the cause for misfortune lay in women's dependence on religious beliefs that upheld misogynist teachings and that the only way for women to become happy in the Latter Day of the Law[56] was to chant *Nam-myoho-renge-kyo*.

It is not difficult to imagine that, in stark contrast to the thrust of prior Buddhist teachings, Nichiren's attitude toward and encouragement of the female believers of his day allowed women in the Soka Gakkai to regain their self-esteem and support their efforts in establishing their own identity. Nichiren Buddhism's theory concerning the enlightenment of women empowers them and is attractive to those who believe that a truly equitable age is at hand.[57]

At the same time the Soka Gakkai, in its early period, was also influenced by another entrenched perception that women harbor greed, jealousy, and complaint. During a study lecture Toda referred to a passage from Nichiren's writings: "those of the Dharma-realm [real world] who are marked by greed, anger, and foolishness are all dragon king's daughters."[58] However, Toda asserted that such traits could be overcome when they embrace the Lotus Sutra.[59] In yet another example, members declare in the *Fujinkun* ("Precepts for Women"), which documents the women's division spirit in the pioneering days: "We . . . are passive, narrow-minded, and complain extremely often . . . [but] let us recognize our own faults and, while struggling with our weaknesses, pray deeply to the *Gohonzon*."[60]

---

[56] A Buddhist view of the last of the three periods following Shakyamuni Buddha's death. The Lotus Sutra views the Latter Day as the time when the essence of the sutra will be propagated.

[57] Kazuhiko Yoshida, *"Ryunyo no jyobutsu"* ("The Enlightenment of the Dragon King's Daughter"), in Kazuo Osumi (ed.), *Women and Buddhism*, ii: *Salvation and Teachings* (Tokyo: Heibonsha, 1989).

[58] *Gosho*, 797.

[59] Josei Toda, quoted in the *Seikyo Shimbun* , Sept. 4, 1953.

[60] Shimako Inoue, women's division chief, as quoted in *Fujinkun* ("Precepts for Women") (May 1953).

While the notion that "women breed jealousy" is considered by some to be a construct of a feudalistic family system, there was a widespread belief that all women naturally displayed such characteristics. To overemphasize that the Lotus Sutra can save these "inferior" beings presupposes, if anything, that women in fact do compare unfavorably to men. Nevertheless, Toda's theory of attaining Buddhahood does not imply that women alone should be held in contempt, since both men and women, as common mortals, are prone to be as foolish as the next person. Yet it seems that women were more often the target of such analyses, and they in turn were amenable to criticism and repeatedly reflected on their own behavior.[61] This can be seen as another indication of their sincere piety, but it would seem there is a somewhat strong tendency to accept this "theory of inborn nature" as applicable to women in general.

The Soka Gakkai believes that each individual has a specific role in life that only he or she can fulfill. Some often quoted passages from the writings of Nichiren are: "Women support others and thereby cause others to support them,"[62] or "It is the power of the bow that determines the flight of the arrow, the might of the dragon that controls the movement of the clouds, and the strength of the wife that guides the actions of her husband."[63] Both teach the importance of wives fulfilling their role in assisting their husbands. Rather than blindly obeying them, wives are to support and encourage their husbands in a discreet manner. In other words, these passages explain that to let one's husband seem to take the lead, while actually being the true driving force, is the way a wife can live her life in the wisest possible manner, making the best use of her characteristics as a woman. Men may appear to be superior on the surface, but in reality "women are like the earth for men,

---

[61] One academic has labeled such a disposition "the earnest principle of self-reliance." See Tsutomu Shiobara, *Soshiki to undo no riron* ("The Theory of Organizations and Movements") (Tokyo: Shinyosha, 1976).

[62] Nichiren, "Kyodai sho," in *Gosho*, 1088 ("Letter to the Brothers," *Major Writings*, i. 146).

[63] Nichiren, "Tokiama gozen gohenji," in *Gosho*, 975 ("The Bow and Arrow," *Major Writings*, vii (1994), 125).

where they can find peace of mind."⁶⁴ This implies that women also largely determine the extent to which men can fully exert themselves to the best of their ability in society. As a result, it is understood that women in fact have greater influence than men. This idea actually reveals an undeniable aspect of Japanese society: "male superiority" is really only a professed principle, since both the society and the family unit depend entirely upon women to function. While it is a fact that women find themselves in a weaker social position, the reverse is often true in the privacy of their homes and relationships.

For women concerned with improving or maintaining marital relations, this Buddhist concept may provide spiritual and moral support. It should also be noted, however, that this approach is not new but rather reflects the traditional nature of relations between men and women in Japanese society, in which family units continue to revolve around a division of labor according to gender.

Relationships with Women's Liberation Movements

At a time when the pioneer women's division members were directing their energies toward propagating Buddhism with others, many women's organizations and movements were campaigning on various fronts to protect their livelihoods. Out of the sense of crisis surrounding Japan's renewed military buildup, especially after the outbreak of the Korean War in 1950, many women became peace activists, asserting the pacifist nature of the Japanese constitution.⁶⁵ Soka Gakkai documents from that period indicate that the women's division was conscious of the trends of such women's movements. In fact, a kind of rivalry prevailed: "However successful such movements may be, it is impossible for women to be saved without inner transformation through having faith in the Lotus Sutra," one article held. Their position was that the women's movements address only societal issues, failing to

⁶⁴ Daisaku Ikeda, *Watashi no zuihitsu shu* ("A Collection of my Essays") (Tokyo: Yomiuri Shimbun Sha, 1970).
⁶⁵ Art. 9 of the Japanese constitution prohibits the use of military forces except for self-defence.

shed light on the immediate issue of happiness in individual women. In addition, they point out that such action is often led by people holding the one-sided view that there should be parity between the sexes in all areas, and hence that the movements tend to be out of touch with the masses. Gakkai women, who revere inner salvation and attach importance to solidarity among the common people, found it difficult to agree with either of these two points.

The fact that the movements' demand for absolute parity between the sexes is seen as a "distorted" view indicates that ideas such as "femininity" or "the traditional roles of women" are still prevalent among the women within Soka Gakkai. There are two possible explanations why such social campaigns, including demonstrations and strikes led by women, have not obtained support from Gakkai women: first, the Soka Gakkai aims for spiritual salvation; and second, such actions have been traditionally deemed "inappropriate" for women.

What then is the understanding of "equal rights between men and women" within the Soka Gakkai? The editorial in the July 1, 1951 issue of the *Seikyo Shimbun* on the topic "What Exactly are Equal Rights? Cooperation in Working toward a Great Goal Gives Rise to Equality between the Sexes" declared as follows:

Men and women diverge in many ways, both spiritually and physically. This must be because their functions in their personal life and in society are different. The unique, absolute right, which both sexes deserve, comes about when men and women work in close unity throughout their lives toward achieving a great objective, in order to grasp true happiness for themselves. Only when they both share in the common effort necessary to reach a specific goal can we assert that men and women are equal, and that they enjoy equal rights.

In other words, equal rights become a reality when men and women make the most of their respective qualities and cooperate as one. When compared to the traditional misogynous societies where the presence and opinions of women were ignored, this cooperation between the sexes propounded by the Soka Gakkai lends comparatively greater weight to women as individuals.

To summarize the Soka Gakkai's views on women and married couples, one could say that "to be in full control over one's own life" implies establishing one's own existence as an individual while recognizing that identity exists in conjunction with her relation to her husband and children. The perception that their existences are intertwined with others is brought to the fore in their social and peace movements. From another perspective, however, this emphasis on interconnectedness might appear to some as an inability to break free from dependency on others. Furthermore, in such cases, one tends to define identity and individuality in relation to differentiated gender roles. Because these ideas are repeatedly mentioned, some feminists maintain that the Soka Gakkai position is nothing other than an assertion of the position of women as inferior to that of men, similar to the traditional Japanese opinion that wives should discreetly support their husbands. They criticize such teachings as simply providing comfort for women unable to become spiritually independent of their husbands or children.[66]

The debate poses an important question: Is the independence of individuals and emphasis on their relations with others mutually exclusive? In other words, are all relations repressive in nature? While relations that stress gender roles are certainly constraining, can we nevertheless relinquish entirely a way of life that attaches importance to our interrelated existence with others? This is a critical issue for the feminist movement. From the 1980s the Soka Gakkai women's division increasingly established closer ties with women outside the organization as they cooperated in peace and environmental protection movements, or in campaigns to assert the importance of women's points of view. A certain distance, however, remains on the part of women in the general public. It is clear that the Soka Gakkai's perspectives on women and on gender role differentiation—outlooks that were accepted by its female members— are precisely what prevents them from overcoming the discordance with their contemporaries, especially with those who seek to establish themselves as individuals unconstrained by gender.

[66] See e.g., Setsuko Inoue, *Shufu o misuru shinshukyo* ("The New Religious Movements have a Fascination for Housewives" (Tanizawa Shobo, 1988).

None the less is it not strange that only women are criticized? What does the other party concerned — the male members — think and say? The short answer to this question is that it would seem that male members rarely confess "what our shortcomings as men are." However, Ikeda has time and again addressed strict words to the male leadership. During a commemorative meeting for chapter leaders he said, "To say that men in general tend to be objective is a nice way of putting it. However, they experience difficulty putting something into action, even when they theoretically understand its value. In this respect, women tend to be much more courageous and action-oriented."[67] At another meeting he pointed out, "Can it not be said that the root cause for the greatest tragedy in past history is that the specific propensity of women for peace and construction has constantly been suppressed, trampled, and suffocated by the male logic of conflict and destruction, and thereby never given the chance to influence the era?"[68] Here again, the accent on gender role differentiation is there, but by the same token, leaders in society who are able to see through the unfair nature of male-dominated history are also few and far between in contemporary Japan. Ikeda equally remarks, "President Toda once said, 'It would be a grave mistake to assume that jealousy is a characteristic belonging to women alone. Men also can be jealous. . . . There is a male version of jealousy.' "[69] We can infer from these passages that Ikeda cherishes the ideal of an organization in which women's ability to take action and their realistic approach are put to best use, since he has witnessed how men's theoretical arguments, envy, and attachment to power have invited corruption and strife within the organization.

As a matter of fact, the women's division does not always "defer" to men by allowing them to appear as if they are in control; sometimes, the women's division makes strict demands of men's

[67] Speech given on July 29, 1989 at a chapter leaders' meeting commemorating the beginning of the 60th anniversary of the Soka Gakkai's founding.

[68] Speech given on Mar. 1, 1969 at the 1st women's division commemorative general meeting.

[69] Speech given on Feb. 16, 1989.

division leaders. It seems that the issue could be condensed into a question of the extent to which men's division leaders or general members seriously consider such criticism from their more senior leaders or from women to apply to themselves; and of whether they modify their attitude and behavior accordingly within the Soka Gakkai organization, their workplace, or in their homes. Under the present circumstances, as their opinions have yet to be heard, it is impossible to fathom whether or not male members are aware of their own gender issues. In other words, it is evident that a deeply entrenched problem exists among the men, and the time has come to reconsider the imbalanced level of awareness between men and women regarding the gender issue within the Soka Gakkai.

The Organization and Women

The women's division has extended its network of relationships beyond Japan to countries throughout the world. More than half of SGI members worldwide are women.[70] Since the beginning of the 1990s the SGI has been holding women's conferences, bringing together women's and young women's division members from each country. In 1996 the first World Women's Peace Conference was held on the theme "Women in Dialogue—Champions of Human Rights," with approximately 200 women's division and young women's division representatives from thirty-three countries in attendance. From these figures, it is obvious that the women's division constitutes a formidable force, not only because of its size, but also because of the extent of its involvement. As mentioned above, the Soka Gakkai women's division in Japan is composed of a substructure within the overall organization that can accommodate each member's individuality and different lifestyles, allowing for close attention and guidance in fostering capable individuals.

[70] From *Ningen kyowa no kachi sozo*, 21 ("Creating Values in the Twenty-first Century") (Tokyo: Seikyo Shinbun Press, 1996).

The formation of diverse women's groups within the organization that started in the 1970s occurred in the context of the changing and diversifying lifestyles of women, because of which it became problematic to group women together into a single, unified "women's division." However, despite the increasing diversification of women's activities, the women's division itself did not recede into the background, and neither was its *raison d'être* ever questioned. In fact, the more its members became active in all aspects of society, the more the women's division acted collectively and increased its overall impact. The underlying idea that "it is up to the mothers to save the earth" has served to further reinforce their solidarity.

This prompts us to consider the extent to which women participate in the overall decisionmaking organs of the entire Soka Gakkai. One point of contention raised by women outside the organization is that none of the numerous vice-presidents within the Soka Gakkai are women.[71] Moreover, while the number of women on the central committee, which is the principal decisionmaking body of Gakkai activities, has increased sharply, it has yet to reach 50 percent.[72] As for the highest deliberative body, the board of councilors, the number of female participants is reported to be around thirty. To make up for this disproportionate representation, three women leaders were appointed to the recently instituted office of the president, but these appointments only serve to reconfirm that the structure of the Soka Gakkai organization continues to function along gender lines.

Let us now consider the reactions of SGI members overseas to an organizational structure that maintains a system of traditional gender differentiation. The interviews with SGI-United Kingdom members conducted by Bryan Wilson and Karel Dobbelaere reveal

---

[71] Nanzan Institute for Religious and Culture (ed.), *Katorikku to Soka Gakkai: Shinko, seido, shakaiteki jisseni* ("The Catholic Church and the Soka Gakkai: Faith, Systems, and Social Activities") (Tokyo: Daisan Bunmeisha, 1996).

[72] Of 130 total members, forty-four were women's division, and five were young women's division as at Dec. 1998, according to an interview conducted with executive leaders of the women's division.

an antipathy toward dividing the organization along gender lines. One woman in her mid-twenties professed, "It was difficult to accept the separation between young Women's and young Men's Divisions. . . . I hated it, because it was sexual discrimination."[73] Another member, a male arts teacher, replied in his interview, "I do not agree with this classification into young Men's and young Women's divisions. . . . there are aspects that seem somewhat discriminatory."[74] The rationale for such antipathy on the part of quite a few members may lie, as the authors indeed point out, in the fact that the UK organization is mostly comprised of young and single members. Of course, since other believers have stated that their aversion gradually subsided as they started to support and help other members in the organization through their activities, it would be a biased approach to accentuate only the negative opinions. However, such honest reactions toward gender-based divisions within the organization are of considerable interest precisely because they are infrequent in Japan.[75]

In response to a criticism at a symposium that none of its vice-presidents were female, a Soka Gakkai representative stated, "Regarding the issue of female leadership,[76] we would like you to consider that the situation is different if one takes into account the SGI as a whole."[77] With the development of the SGI's organization around the world, the specificities of the Japanese organization emerge even more clearly. The top leaders in India and Canada are women, and in America women have been appointed as vice-general director or as head of the culture department. In Germany, also, the youth division leader is a woman.

In Japan marital status remains the distinguishing factor between membership in the women's and the young women's division. On pages featuring experiences of believers in the *Seikyo Shimbun*, portraits of happy families appear almost every day: to get married and have children continues to function as a model of

---

[73] Bryan Wilson and Karel Dobbelaere, *A Time to Chant: The Soka Gakkai Buddhists in Britain* (Oxford: Clarendon Press, 1994).
[74] Ibid.   [75] Ibid.   [76] This is also an issue in Japan.
[77] Nanzan Institute (ed.), *Katorikku to Soka Gakkai*, 139.

ideal happiness. But can marital status really be the primary factor in determining where women belong? Moreover, even if one admits the importance of family ties, could it not be said that the Soka Gakkai remains attached to a rigid, stereotyped image of families, in an age when the definition of what constitutes a family is in itself diversifying?[78] In the future the Soka Gakkai will most likely face the challenge of reconsidering its organizational structure as it falls under the scrutiny of the public eye.

Towards a Century of "Women's Rights"

Yoko Takayanagi, the present leader of the women's division, states:

The twentieth century has been a century of war, with men holding the dominant position. The world in which we live today—as we shudder at the threat of nuclear war, are pained by the spreading of global pollution—is the cold, harsh reality that is a far cry from peace . . . The solidarity and action of as many women as possible who are awakened [to this critical situation] hold the keys to breaking through the confusion of the new century.[79]

Quoting Daisaku Ikeda—"[Ranging from something as small as] the harmony and happiness of the family to [something as vast as] world peace, women are always pivotal in creating harmony"— Takayanagi called upon her fellow members "to bring forth the courage of women who cherish peace; to share the wisdom of women who are firmly rooted in the reality of their [everyday] lives; and to advance toward the era of women, in order to make the twenty-first century a century of humanism." In this way, she expressed the enthusiasm of the entire women's division as they enter the twenty-first century.[80] Since the 1994 lecture series on

---

[78] Gender as portrayed in the media is also likely to become a major issue in the future.

[79] Takagi (ed.), *Women's Plaza*, 1–2.

[80] "On Women's Division Activities," *Seikyo Shimbun*, Dec. 5, 1998.

peace, "Women and the Twenty-first Century" has been adopted as a new theme.[81]

Following its separation from the Nichiren Shoshu priesthood in 1991, the Soka Gakkai, in what it considers to be a "religious reformation of the Heisei era," has intensified its criticism against religious authoritarianism. The women's division, with its characteristic ability to take action, embarked on a nationwide campaign denouncing the state of the priesthood by "standing up resolutely against tyranny, inhumanity, and injustice,"[82] and has been designated as the driving force in repudiating the corruption of priesthood. In addition, the Tokyo Women's Division Day was instituted to commemorate the day the Soka Gakkai received the notice to disband from the clergy.[83] On that occasion, the motto for its 1995 general meetings was announced. This motto, "Together as mothers, let's protect peace and human rights," indicates that with the eruption of the priesthood issue, the idea of human rights has gained in prominence among the women's division.

The "spiritual authority" upheld by traditional Buddhist schools has indeed always been predicated on the exclusion of women. The monopoly and power of the clergy was conspicuous when performing funeral rites. After its separation from the priesthood the Soka Gakkai, compelled to conduct funerals that did not depend on priests, started to conduct funerals officiated by fellow members. This symbolized their independence from so-called "traditional" religions, but also represented a significant act toward independence for the women. This is because, despite minor variations from one Buddhist school to another, women have for all practical purposes never had a role in funeral ceremonies in traditional Buddhist schools. "Funerals conducted by fellow members"

---

[81] The women's division has instituted local "twenty-first century conferences" in various areas up to May 3, 2001. These meetings are aimed at developing key women's division members to take on responsibilities in the new era.

[82] Fujinbu Shogenshu Kanko Iinkai (ed.), *Renaissance of the Twenty-first Century* (Tokyo: Daisan Bunmeisha, 1993), 4.

[83] *Seikyo Shimbun*, Nov. 18, 1994.

hold great promise for reforming the firmly maintained sexual discrimination within the traditional religious community.

We may note that women have indeed been nominated as ministers of ceremonies who lead the funeral ceremonies or otherwise lend assistance. It is not rare for women to conduct the funerals, depending on the situation. While it seems that the function and roles of such posts have yet to be clearly defined,[84] we look forward to future developments in this field.

As mentioned above, "education for and of human rights" has become a prime concept for the present women's division, but to what degree do its members feel genuinely concerned about this issue? Needless to say, the human rights of individuals cannot exist in isolation, and human rights, be they of children or women, are all interrelated. However, there are some issues specific to women's human rights. While the Soka Gakkai women's division—especially the women's peace committee—has enthusiastically embraced the cause of children's rights, and despite its repeated assertions that the "twenty-first century is the age of women," we are left with an impression that the issue of women's human rights is not extensively discussed.[85] We could ask ourselves why this should be. As a religious organization that is sensitive to the salvation of women and to equality between the sexes, one hopes that the Soka Gakkai, by provoking debate and bringing aid, will further insist on its teachings regarding dignity of life when it comes to problems such as violence against women.

None the less, in the campaign for children's rights it is easier for women to function in their given roles as women and mothers, whereas advocating women's rights requires an overhaul of such gender roles themselves. In this sense, when broaching the matter of women's rights, the underlying principles that had long inspired the women's division will probably have to be reconsidered. Of

---

[84] Details provided by the office of public relations.
[85] Toshie Kurihara (ed.), *Josei no tame no ningengaku seminar* ("The Human Studies Seminar for Women") (Tokyo: Daisan Bumeisha, 1997). This is the only publication that addresses Soka Gakkai and women's human rights, suggesting that Soka Gakkai has only started to address this issue.

course, it would be difficult to posit that society already respects the decisions and existence of women or mothers as fully independent and worthy in themselves, so to voice opinions from their standpoint continues to be an effective strategy toward building a solidarity among women. In addition, since a single individual is often powerless in the formidable task of changing the society in which we live, everyday cases of discrimination tend to be overlooked in the Soka Gakkai as well: it would require the full mobilization of the entire organization and its influence to effect redress. Thus, it is essential that women empower themselves through mutual encouragement.

At the same time, however, to stress excessively the solidarity of women can have the undesired effect of minimizing the value of a woman's individuality. Especially in Japan, where differentiation by such factors as social class or ethnic origin is indistinct, collective grouping along gender lines tends to be accepted without much resistance. While it is obvious that to place women at the bottom of the social structure is a form of violence against women, it is also true that to glorify their nature when they are collectively organized is again another form of oppression of the individual woman. This is a matter that must be approached very carefully, and could be considered the most problematic issue facing researchers in feminist studies.[86]

Any enquiry into the state of women's rights is inextricably linked to the issue of whether traditional gender structures are repressive for both men and women. Besides considerations of sexuality, which inevitably enter into the debate, the question of life ethics from the standpoint of women themselves also becomes an area that requires urgent attention. It would seem that the women of the Soka Gakkai have so far failed to pursue these angles as topics of concern. We look forward to observing how the women's division or the women's peace committee will address these pressing issues in the future.

[86] See e.g., Marianne Hirsh and Evelyn Fox Keller (eds.), *Conflicts in Feminism* (New York: Routledge, 1990).

Conclusion

This chapter has examined the activities of the Soka Gakkai women's division from its inception to the present, and to determine its contribution toward the development of the religious organization. It is noteworthy that these women did not simply approach life in a passive manner, but reinforced solidarity among themselves by placing the highest value on asserting full control over their lives. At the same time, this study has revealed potentially problematic aspects associated with the perspective on women as reflected in the spirit of their activities in the past, as well as the possible implications that face the organization in the future. This chapter may be criticized for having taken a somewhat one-sided stance to these questions. However, being well aware that women's opinions and attitudes fluctuate with the times, and that opinions vary from one individual to another, there should be no cause for pessimism regarding future developments. As the women's division has continued to advance, it is reasonable to expect that it will tackle these gender-related issues in face of increasing globalization. In this respect the activities of the women in the Soka Gakkai provide a prime example, aside from the relevance of their past history or their present-day situation, for the future of research in the field of religion and women.

Many of the problem areas discussed in this chapter apply not to the Soka Gakkai alone, but to the entire social structure of Japan. Fifty years ago the Japanese started out from devastated remains at the end of the war to build the prosperity we know today. This success was carried by the family values and the system of gender-based division of labor. By accepting and conscientiously abiding by these rules, women played a large part in contributing to the prosperity of the Japanese society, just as they have to the growth of the Soka Gakkai. However, to bring about a society that allows all people to lead meaningful lives as we enter the twenty-first century, an evaluation of the "gender structure" that has long characterized organizations in Japan, whereby social functions were rigidly divided according to gender, is in order. For this reason, such issues should be examined not only by the Soka Gakkai and other religious groups, but by social institutions of all kinds in society. Should the Soka Gakkai choose to be a religious movement that seeks not only to relieve immediate suffering, but also to build a new ethical structure of value creation on a global scale, it is inevitable that it should elaborate ideals and engage in actions that take gender issues into consideration.

7

The Movement and the Japanese Media

Takesato Watanabe

MEDIA accountability—that is, the media's recognition of its social *raison d'être* and responsibility—may be defined by and differentiated into the following nine functions: (1) to provide accurate information; (2) to offer opinions and editorialize; (3) to serve as a forum for the exchange of views among citizens; (4) to educate; (5) to spearhead a broad array of campaigns on a society-wide basis; (6) to entertain; (7) to provide a medium for advertisement; (8) to promote social welfare; and (9) to report on natural and man-made disasters. The conclusion wrought by the amalgamation of these nine points is this: The principal social function of the media is to provide its audience—be they readers, listeners, or viewers—with information that serves as a basic tool to assist their judgment and actions in the construction of a better, and truly civic, society. Ultimately, then, the media must serve to protect the lives and possessions of its audience.[1]

There is a general deficiency of public service in Japan, however. Advertisements outnumber feature articles in newspapers, while more than half the prime time broadcasts on television are entertainment programs. News-gathering organizations routinely withhold coverage of criminal activity committed by members of Japan's elite political and business communities—crimes about which the people have a right to know—in spite of having learned of these crimes in advance of the police investigation. They may

---

[1] Takesato Watanabe, *Media Literacy* (Tokyo: Diamond Press, 1997).

devote copious reportage to a few individual cases, but they face obstacles in providing much information in the way of structural reforms to prevent future infractions.

To exacerbate matters, while media executives (who are summoned to the Diet after every fiasco) are visibly chastened in front of the members of the Diet and ministry of posts and telecommunications (MPT) and offer pledges to change the way they operate, there is almost never evidence of fundamental redress or reform. Rather than implement meaningful change, they seem content to wait out the storm. As a result, similar problems recur, causing public confidence in the media and journalism to wane. Seen from another perspective, the reason for so much entertainment-driven media content today[2] is that such programming is far less controversial and thought-provoking. As such, it fails to challenge the interests of the powerful—a situation the legislative and bureaucratic arms of government tacitly encourage. This is the stark reality of the social information environment in contemporary Japan.[3]

There are basically two kinds of media: the one-versus-many framework of the mass media and interactive communication—the conversations, telephone calls, and Internet exchanges people conduct as a matter of daily routine. In the vast majority of instances, however, information acquired from the former provides the basis for the latter. Japanese readers spend no more than an average of twenty minutes reading a newspaper per day, a figure that has essentially been static for the past ten years. In comparison, viewers spend an average of 3 hours 28 minutes a day watching television.[4] The predominant mass medium in modern Japan is television.

There are four principal factors underlying this media phenomenon: first, the dynamic of state control; second, commercialism, which favors the agendas of large corporate advertisers but evades

[2] According to my research, more than 70 percent of all television programs fall under the genre of entertainment.

[3] Takesato Watanabe, *Sociology of Media Fraud* (Kyoto: Sekaishisosha, 1995).

[4] NHK, *Kokumin seikatsu jikan chosa* ("How the Japanese Spend their Lives") (Tokyo: NHK Shuppan, 1995).

major social issues; third, management prioritization of profit and entertainment programming; and fourth, the abundance of journalists who are ill prepared to practice their trade, and the absence of a performance review system for the media. Moreover, these factors are just as applicable to the content generated by the Japanese media as it enters the much heralded age of multimedia; indeed, their influence is likely to grow even stronger over time.

The first factor is a dynamic instituted by the Japanese government. Networks must receive approval from the MPT in order to renew their broadcasting license every five years. And because all five national television broadcasters also belong to media conglomerates that own national newspapers (Asahi, Yomiuri, Mainichi, Nikkei, and Sankei) as their core businesses, the state, in effect, can dictate to Japan's largest newsgathering organizations.[5] Networks may be able to neglect the real needs of their viewers, but they neglect the whims of MPT regulators at their peril. The Japan Broadcasting Corporation (Nihon Hoso Kyokai, NHK), being a public network as well as a public corporation belonging to MPT, requires the legislative approval of the national Diet for its annual budget and senior personnel appointments, including the post of NHK chairman. It is thus under tighter rein than its privately owned counterparts.

The second factor is the medium's tendency to avoid criticizing large corporate sponsors in order to retain their sponsorship. Of the 5.9 trillion Japanese yen companies spent on advertising in the fiscal year 1997/8, 3.5 trillion yen went to the four mass media sectors—television, radio, books, and magazines. The largest single advertiser was Toyota Motor Corporation. The television prime time dramas that ran its advertisements almost never featured

---

[5] While MPT licenses keep the television networks at bay, the mainstream print media is also tethered to the government through the *keiretsu*, or network affiliates, and the *kisha kurabu*, or press club, system. Members of the system are privy to information and gossip by politicians and bureaucrats that is not offered to nonmembers, yet they must abide by a set of strict rules governing publication. Those who dare to break them face exclusion or expulsion; by which means the state is enabled to control the information it provides to the Japanese press.

traffic accidents or other incidents portraying the negative effects of automobiles. The protagonist is shown cruising in a model the sponsor wants to sell; the antagonist is seen fleeing in a rival manufacturer's car—a subtle attempt to impress upon younger viewers which car they should be driving in real life.

The third factor is the television media's willingness to exploit the baser interests of viewers by spicing content with sex, scandal, and sensationalism in order to attract higher ratings. These programs almost invariably contain speech and scenes that are offensive or demeaning to one societal minority or another. They routinely flaunt the human rights—particularly the right to privacy—of those they depict. And while such programming proliferates, other programs that deal with issues of real import to the Japanese, such as documentaries on an aging society, are relegated to late night time slots. The mandate to entertain rather than inform lies in stark contrast to the Broadcasting Law charter, which envisions the objective of the broadcast medium as assisting in "the achievement of a healthy democracy." And this disposition is rapidly spilling over into the print media through its corporate and synergistic relationship with television.

The fourth factor is the media's lack of understanding with regard to its role in society. The primary role of the press is to serve as a public sentinel over those in power. This concept has been validated over time through historical precedent—that is why democratic societies guarantee the freedoms of speech and expression; why journalists are allowed to exercise the right to interview on and investigate whatever issue they deem newsworthy. Yet an increasing number of people working in the media industry lack this most basic understanding and commitment. Nor does the dearth of scholars who adopt this perspective in their study and discussion of the Japanese media help the situation.

Yet the principal obstruction to the facilitation of meaningful change in Japanese media is the collusive and self-serving relationship of media management with the government and business elite. They not only dominate the debate over the media and its technologies, but also work to insure that they remain the chief

beneficiaries of them—a dysfunction abetted in part by a compla-
cent, often coopted, academia. As a result, discussion of reform
hardly ever surfaces to the level of public scrutiny. Nor is the *status
quo* seriously challenged by the array of major opposition political
parties and their complementary constituencies, including the 8
million member Rengo, the nation's largest labor confederation.

Media Coverage of Religion in Japan

My research on media theory and ethics revolves around three core
premises. The first is the media's obligation to propagate information, renewed on a daily basis, so that it functions as an educational
institution as vital to society as are schools. The second posits that,
in today's global society, effective exchange of information can no
longer be dependent on face-to-face communication. The optimal
governance of civil society in this day and age can be achieved only
through the exchange of news, ideas, and dialogue as provided by
a capable and properly functioning media. The third, however,
holds that the first two premises are largely ignored by Japan's
media institutions, and the information they provide is in frequent
contravention of these ideals.

This dysfunction clearly manifests itself in the media's approach
toward religions in Japan. Careful analysis of this coverage reveals
the following five characteristics:

1. As evident in the reportage of Iyesu no Hakobune—a home-
   grown Christian sect that encouraged young Japanese
   women to leave their homes and families for a communal life
   in the 1970s—and the 1995 alleged subway nerve gassing by
   the Aum Shinrikyo, *the media has long associated religion with
   anti-social behavior or, at times, with criminal tendencies, and
   tends to depict unorthodox religious activity in a sensationalist
   manner.*

2. Concurrent with such coverage, however, is the *deferential
   treatment accorded to traditional religious sects and their mani-
   fold rites.* Among the most common scenes are those of
   Shinto priests blessing newly constructed bridges, flocks of

young, kimono-attired children paying their respect to Shinto shrines and Buddhist temples on national holidays, and the invariable television broadcasts of the New Year pilgrimages made annually by millions of Japanese.

3. *Media deference is also extended to the architecture of traditional religious sects* as seen in the frequent footage of renovation and completion ceremonies of shrines and temples of the larger, established sects such as Nishi-Honganji.

4. The media has always taken *a favorable attitude toward demonstrations of foreign interest in Japanese culture and thought*. Articles on and interviews with foreigners who practice Zen meditation, or scenes of foreign tourists visiting shrines and temples in Kyoto, Kamakura, and Nikko, can be found in abundance.

5. At the time of the debate on the revision of the Religious Corporation Law, the Japanese media took *a critical stance against the tax exempt status of religious organizations*. Further, a similar stance was reflected in the media's reportage of religious organizations' involvement in political campaigns.

In stark contrast to this generic coverage of religion is the near total absence of media perspectives that deal with spirituality and the philosophical underpinnings of faith as seen through the eyes of an objective observer. In short, the Japanese media is bereft of insights into the fundamental values of humankind—what to believe in life and how to live it. Religion is merely sketched as one detail in the overall picture of Japanese life, and this superficial treatment fails to address the deeper issues, such as how religious belief inspires people to undertake activities to improve society or to make for a more peaceful world. Indeed, about the only religious activity that attracts much media attention—from the networks and national and regional newspapers to the tabloid dailies and major magazines—is when a prime minister, ministers of state, or members of parliament visit Yasukuni shrine, where the war dead are enshrined. But the issue here is less religious than constitutional—such officials are paying their respect as public servants.

Critical articles about the imperial family are virtually nonexistent in Japan. As limited as the coverage tends to be, imperial matters can still thoroughly dominate the Japanese media, as demonstrated by the blanket coverage devoted to Emperor Hirohito's death in 1989. While the event was indeed newsworthy, it clearly did not merit the excessive coverage which ensued (televisions did not air commercials during the long coverage of the mourning). Public sentiments toward the emperor and the imperial family are shaped by the media, which in turn influences the Japanese people's attitude to religion. As Kenji Hishiyama contends:

Religion in Japan has on numerous occasions been exploited as an instrument, either to rule the state or to preserve its authority. In return, religious sects have served their own interests by currying favor with or manipulating those in power in a particular era in order to secure economic stability or preferential treatment. Buddhism in ancient Japan was employed as a state religion; likewise, in the years after the Meiji Restoration, the government devised what was termed "state Shinto"—having fused Shintoism with the imperial system—as an ideological means to achieve national unity and maintain public order. The framework of control it established was familial in that the relationship between state and religion was like that of parent and child: all Japanese were equal as subjects before the emperor, the "living god." Since it determined who would rule and who would serve, it functioned as an ideology to conceal and suppress class conflict.[6]

This framework was kept intact even after the Japanese defeat in World War II, when the Allied Occupation—under the leadership of the US government—adopted a policy absolving Hirohito of his complicity in the war, so as to facilitate its control over the country. The decision established the preservation of the imperial system in post-war Japan—and with it, the system's deeply rooted influence over religion. That this connection remains viable can be

[6] Kenji Hishiyama, "Minshu shihai to shite no shukyo soshiki" ("Religious Organizations as an Instrument of State Power"), in Gendai to Henkaku Editing Committee (ed.), *Gendai Nihon no shihai shihai kozo* ("Ruling Power of Contemporary Japan") (Tokyo: Shinchiheisha, 1984), 193.

seen in a recent ministry of education directive ordering the singing of the national anthem, with its lyrics of adulation for the emperor, in all elementary and middle schools, a move hailed by the clergy of many of the established Buddhist sects.[7]

A modern democracy should not have any place for a hereditary absolute ruler. However, in Japan the emperor remains at the social pinnacle, while ordinary citizens, unable to scale its height through effort or ability, are forever barred from the exalted pedestal. There are also postwar Japanologists such as Shichihei Yamamoto, who justify the amorphous and equivocating notions of religion embraced by most Japanese—a construct forged from Meiji era nationalism and founded on the inviolability of the myth of racial homogeneity, the basis of *Nihon-kyo*, or "Japanism."[8] These scholars assert that this is a religious system of pacifist belief, unlike Christianity or Islam, which, in their view, explicitly separate deity from humanity, religion from religion. As a rule, however, the most devout adherents of *Nihon-kyo* also happen to be the most nationalistic. Most are conservative politicians and members of the business elite—individuals whose security and social privilege are inextricably linked to the sustenance of the imperial system, and who interpret the absolution of Hirohito's wartime complicity as their own absolution.[9]

All told, this matrix of influence and interests binding the media, state, and religion in Japan has impeded, within the Japanese press, the recognition that freedom of speech is the freedom to question and criticize those in the highest authority.

It also helps to explain why media coverage on the reality of the activities of the Soka Gakkai, Japan's largest religious organization with an estimated membership of 4 million households, is virtually

---

[7] On the social structure of this phenomenon, see Takesato Watanabe, "The Revisionist Fallacy in the Japanese Media", *Doshisha Social Sciences Review* (Mar. 1999), 1–45.

[8] Shichihei Yamamoto, *Nihon-kyo ni tsuite* ("On Japanism") (Tokyo: Bungei Shunju, 1972).

[9] R. N. Bellah, "Japan, Asia and Religion in Reports on Work in Progress," *Sociological Inquiry*, 39 (1969); Ian Buruma, *Wages of Guilt* (London: Random House, 1994).

nonexistent. What press coverage there is relating to this lay Buddhist group is primarily negative for the reasons cited below. The negative coverage is not limited to the domestic media, but is found in the foreign press as well, since the latter file stories that either are loosely based on the former's reports or actually quote them. Dependence on Japanese media sources by the foreign media, moreover, has been instrumental in fostering misconceptions about Japanese religion in other countries.

Media Coverage of the Soka Gakkai in Japan and its Causes

The distortions generated in the reportage of the Soka Gakkai, the largest religious organization in Japan, as well as its virtual dismissal by the Japanese mainstream media, are shaped by the following causes: (1) a power structure which derives legitimacy through the preservation of the imperial system; (2) the scope and scale of the Soka Gakkai's political influence; (3) its history of defiance and autonomy; (4) the Japanese media's dependence on large corporate advertisers; (5) the existence of media companies such as Bungei Shunju and Shinchosha, which maintain collusive ties to the state; (6) the uncompromising religious convictions of the Soka Gakkai and social disapproval of its initial period of aggressive proselytizing; (7) media coverage of Soka Gakkai's vast financial resources; (8) the framework of social intolerance in Japan; (9) the proliferation of media stereotypes; and (10) the inadequacy of media relations skills and training employed by the Soka Gakkai as a social entity. These ten factors will be examined to explain the ways in which they interact to produce the general sense of public antipathy that exists toward the Soka Gakkai.

The Web of Imperial Power and Influence

As discussed earlier, the Japanese power structure acquires its legitimacy through the imperial system. To better understand the politicoeconomic context through which the structure interacts with and influences religion, and the occasions on which it reveals its pro-imperial, extreme rightist notions of historical revisionism, let us examine two specific cases—first, the life of Ryuzou Sejima, perhaps one of Japan's more powerful postwar figures whose influence predates the war, and second, a recent NHK broadcast.

Sejima, born in Toyama prefecture in 1911, was a graduate of the imperial army's military academy and distinguished himself as a staff officer in the expeditionary forces occupying China. After the war Sejima was employed by trading conglomerate, C. Itoh Corporation, and quickly rose through its ranks, ultimately serving as its chairman. Corporate success also spelled growing political clout: he served on a number of high profile state commissions and gained considerable prominence for his *de facto* leadership of them. His wartime connections are believed to have played a major, albeit covert, role in the successful conclusion of Japan's negotiations with South Korea and Indonesia for war reparation. At present, he acts as a special advisor to C. Itoh and chairs the Inamori Foundation (founded by Kazuo Inamori, chief executive of Kyocera Corporation). Sejima also serves as the chief lay representative of Nishi-Hongan-ji Temple, one of Japan's oldest Buddhist sects. Interviewed by a newspaper in 1998, Sejima said of religion and patriotism, "For me, there isn't any contradiction between my religious beliefs and my duty as a citizen to execute war."[10]

The ties that link established religious schools to the Japanese power structure are abstruse—yet meaningful—and historical. Higashi-Hongan-ji, for instance, also subscribes to the Jodo Shinshu Buddhist sect, and therefore is closely affiliated in religious doctrine with Nishi-Hongan-ji, whose parish Sejima represents. The wife of Higashi-Hongan-ji's high priest is the younger sister of the late emperor Showa Hirohito. A further example is the Tendai sect—perhaps the earliest Buddhist school of thought to be imported to Japan. Because its priests were dispatched under imperial patronage to China to study Buddhism ten centuries ago, the sect has traditionally been among the staunchest supporters of

[10] *Kyoto Shimbun*, evening edn., July 21, 1998.

the imperial family. To this day the sect reports to the Imperial Household Agency whenever its disciples successfully undergo the most rigorous esoteric practice of the Tendai sect, and the agency in turn issues certificates recognizing their success.

There remains in Japan today an age-old social dynamic— that is, association with the imperial system consolidates one's standing in society. As do countless other Japanese institutions in search of recognition, the Inamori Foundation, which ranks among the largest of its kind, always invites a member of the imperial family for its annual endowment ceremony. The ritual is similarly repeated at every major public event worthy of note. The dynamic is equally conspicuous among students and the alumni of Gakushuin University—the prestigious center of education of the imperial family—and its affiliated schools.

Given this backdrop, the case of a recent NHK broadcast may be examined. Millions of Jews and other "non-Aryan" ethnic minorities were systematically killed by the Nazi regime over the course of World War II. History now recognizes that Chiune Sugihara, then deputy consul of the Japanese consulate in Lithuania, issued 2,500 individual and family transit visas between August and September 1940 to some 6,000 Polish Jews who sought refuge in Lithuania following the Nazi invasion of Poland, which Germany and the Soviet Union had secretly agreed to partition in 1939. Sugihara did so in spite of repeated demands by both the Soviets and the Japanese foreign minister Yosuke Matsuoka that he desist.[11]

Yet NHK's "Views and Opinions" program (transmitted on April 29, 1998), which featured Sophia University professor Shoichi Watanabe, not only disregarded the fact that the Japanese government was all too indifferent to the plight of foreign refugees during the war: it painted a highly revisionist assessment of

[11] In two separate telegraphs dispatched on Aug. 14 and 16, 1940 Matsuoka rejected Sugihara's request for formal ministry approval to issue the transit visas (Yukiko Sugihara, *Rokusen-nin no inochi no biza* ("Visas for Six Thousand Lives") (Tokyo: Asahi Sonorama, 1990); Hirrel Levin, *In Search of Sugihara* (New York: Free Press, 1996)).

historical truth. As fascinating as some of Watanabe's baseless allegations were—among them, that Japan had adopted the most humanitarian of policies toward the Jewish people at the time (unlike the United States and United Kingdom), that it had disavowed the practice of racial discrimination, and that Sugihara was merely acting under foreign ministry instruction in issuing the visas—none could compare with the remarkable timing of the broadcast, April 29, Hirohito's birthday.

During the war thousands of Jews in occupied Europe fled for their lives to Britain and the USA; Japan neither accepted them as refugees nor permitted them to naturalize. Although Sugihara himself only managed to issue transit visas to the refugees, he deserves the highest recognition for saving their lives: many of the Jews who could not leave Lithuania (which Stalin grabbed in the deal with Hitler, only to have it seized by Nazi Germany when it later invaded the Soviet Union) were killed. Watanabe's assertions about the humanitarianism of the Japanese government are clearly invalid, as evidenced not only by the colonial policies it enforced in Korea and China but also by its postwar reprimand and premature "retirement" of Sugihara for his purported insubordination. Indeed, his *de facto* firing was such an impediment to the restoration of diplomatic relations between Lithuania and Japan in 1992 that then prime minister, Kiichi Miyazawa, having been grilled before the Diet over the issue, hastily dispatched his deputy foreign minister to the Sugihara family to apologize for the ministry's misconduct.

Propaganda seeking to absolve Hirohito of his responsibility in the war and glorify militarist aggression is not uncommon. The distortions of historical fact aired on NHK can be seen in the cinema as well, due in large part to the network of influential revisionists that exists in Japan. The heroic protagonist of "Pride: The Moment of Destiny," a Japanese film that opened in theaters in the summer of 1998, is a class A war criminal, Hideki Tojo. The movie is the brainchild of the Sophia University professor Shoichi Watanabe and Hideaki Kase, the film's executive producer, both of whom maintain that the Nanjing massacre is a figment of Chinese exaggeration based on uncorroborated testimony. They believe the Japanese youths who died in the war sacrificed themselves in an attempt to liberate Asia from the white man's yoke, and think that those who see Japan as the aggressor nation subscribe to a "self-flagellating world view."

As the above-mentioned cases attest, the fabric of Japanese society is thus dominated by a tapestry of interwoven connections to the imperial system, its influence reaching out far beyond religion and the media. Those with "connections"—or who can afford to seek out connections—comprise the "respectable" elements of society. The Soka Gakkai, however, did not legitimate itself through such ties. Its history is one of tension with the established powers—and, by extension, the imperial system—beginning with its rejection of state Shintoism and its refusal to sanction the war effort in the 1940s. Further, in today's Japan, where nationalistic tendencies are starting to reemerge, the global perspective and activities of the Soka Gakkai may not be rightly appreciated.

Soka Gakkai's Powerful Political Presence

In the House of Councilors' elections held in July 1998 the Soka Gakkai-supported Komei Party garnered 7.75 million votes. The figure represented 14 percent of the total ballots cast nationwide, and of the 252 parliamentary seats up for reelection the Komei secured twenty-two. While the party and lay Buddhist organization are functionally and financially autonomous, analysts of other political parties, journalists, and political commentators essentially share the view that some 90 percent of the Komei's votes are generated by the Soka Gakkai.

The Soka Gakkai is exceptional in that no other large Japanese religious organization engages in both social and political issues—from the promotion of human rights to the protection of the environment and abolition of nuclear weapons—as actively as it does. Its political involvement predates the Komeito party, which it founded in 1964. It first successfully fielded candidates for the

Tokyo municipal assembly in 1955. While the Komeito itself has since undergone various transformations, including its merger with the now defunct Shinshinto (New Frontier Party) in 1995 and subsequent rebirth as the New Komeito in 1998, the Soka Gakkai has consistently remained its largest constituency and a force to contend with in Japan's political arena.

In the aftermath of the general elections of 1993 the Liberal Democratic Party (LDP) fell from power for the first time in thirty-eight years, the outcome of widespread public discontent and a desire to change Japanese politics. Its parliamentary majority was lost, as a group of dissidents left to form their own party. Although the LDP managed to reinstate its conservative rule by entering into a coalition government with the Social Democratic Party of Japan in 1995, it still viewed the opposition parties as posing a genuine threat to its grasp on power. The Communist Party was excluded from the list of potential rivals, primarily because the policies it advocated insured its political isolation. Since the Socialists had been coopted, the LDP saw the Komeito—as the second largest opposition party after the Socialists—and the direction it would take as its principal axis of competition.

In 1994 Komeito dissolved and joined with other opposition parties to form Shinshinto. The new coalition gained more votes than the LDP in the 1995 Upper House election. In an effort to keep power, the LDP began a smear campaign against the Soka Gakkai, which at that time was a key force in Shinshinto, attempting thereby to erode its non-Soka Gakkai support. These attacks were designed to take advantage of the wave of public revulsion against religion in general, coming in the wake of the Tokyo subway gas attacks allegedly committed by the Aum Shinrikyo. LDP officials made statements suggesting that Soka Gakkai's support of Shinshinto was "a plot to take over Japan and impose its belief as a state religion." In the closing days of the 1996 general election campaign, LDP public relations chief Shizuka Kamei stated, "There are only two religious groups which tried to control the nation; one is Aum Shinrikyo, and the other is the Soka Gakkai. Aum used sarin gas and automatic rifles to do so, and the Soka

Gakkai controls politics through elections."[12] Millions of campaign flyers were distributed, entitled "Emergency Report: More Dangerous than Aum, Soka Gakkai in Shinshinto's Clothing".

In the prevailing mood of panic and suspicion toward religion in general, the LDP succeeded in passing a revision of the Religious Corporation Act in 1995. During the debate on the revision of the act LDP officials made statements implying that passing the law would damage the Soka Gakkai and, in doing so, undermine the image of their political opponent Shinshinto.

These public attacks provoked little resistance from other large religious sects such as Kofuku no Kagaku, Reiyukai, and Seicho no Ie, which were openly hostile to the Soka Gakkai. Their antipathy to Soka Gakkai played neatly into the hands of conservative politicians who shared a common interest with these denominations.

Although the Soka Gakkai has not been involved in domestic politics for long, it has come to be recognized by most Japanese as an influential political force, as well as a religious one. This social perception may be responsible for a large degree of unease and hostility with which other religious sects regarded it. Religious participation in the political process is hardly unique in other democracies, though denominational constituencies abroad are rarely subject to the kind of social criticism that the Soka Gakkai has encountered through its support of the Komeito.

Religion has, for the most part, emerged as an expression of discontent and insecurity, be it material or spiritual, over the social conditions of the time. Though they may be reformist at the time of their advent, most religions eventually seek the patronage of the political *status quo*. The Soka Gakkai's political stance remains relatively progressive, making it a distinctly different creature from other Buddhist sects such as the Hongan-ji and Tendai schools, which are comprised of comparatively older believers with generally far more conservative political preferences.

---

[12] Shizuka Kamei's campaign speech in Hachioji, Oct. 2, 1996.

A History of Defiance and Autonomy

The Tepodong missile launched by the Democratic People's Republic of Korea in August 1998 caused uproar in Japan because it flew over the Japanese mainland on its way (according to Pyongyang) to orbit the earth as a satellite. The reaction in Japan stood in sharp relief to the relative calm that prevailed in neighboring China and South Korea. Just prior to this incident another clamor had erupted in Japan over the nuclear tests conducted by India and Pakistan, when a parade of government officials led by the then prime minister, Ryutaro Hashimoto, and the media condemned the move. They contended that Japan, being the only country ever to suffer a nuclear attack, was compelled to condemn the tests, reiterating its three principles of neither manufacturing, nor stockpiling, nor allowing nuclear arms on Japanese soil.

Still, while the political decisions taken in Pyongyang, Karachi, and New Delhi to pursue costly space programs or nuclear weapons development at a time of economic distress may not have been sound, Japan had little right to criticize their choice. The Japanese government is alleged to have tacitly accepted the deployment of nuclear weapons at US military installations in Japan for years, weapons ready to be used against North Korea—or any other country in East Asia or the Indian subcontinent should the need arise—on a twenty-four-hour basis.[13] It would not be surprising, then, if these threshold nations should have felt that Japan posed a greater threat to them than they did to it.

This latent hypocrisy in government policy is not well understood within the media; much less so by the Japanese people because of the misleading information supplied by the media. One of the principal causes behind this lack of understanding is the propensity not to question established notions, whether they are assertions based on fact or myths such as the homogeneity and uniqueness of the Japanese "race," or the superiority of Japanese-style management and business practices.

[13] Kei Wakaizumi , *Tasaku nakarishi-wo shimzemu to hossu* ("To Believe and Hope there was no Alternative") (Tokyo: Bunge Shunju, 1994).

The Soka Gakkai began as an association of educators who were critical of the Japanese educational system—at the time designed to foster unquestioning subjects of the state. Makiguchi interpreted Nichiren's Buddhism as a religious teaching that encouraged the practitioner's active engagement to promote social good, even if it led to defiance of state authority. Thus, the religious and social views of Makiguchi and his cofounder, Josei Toda, constituted a provocation to the militarist authorities of the time. The military government enacted various laws, including the Religious Organizations Law (1940), and began a crackdown on religious groups in order to unify all religions under state Shintoism. Makiguchi and Toda were consequently arrested in 1942 when they refused to accept a state-mandated Shinto talisman, and charged with violating the Public Security Preservation Law and with acts of *lèse majesté*—insubordination against the emperor.

In 1957 Toda called for a comprehensive ban on nuclear weapons. This declaration was later followed by series of grassroot antinuclear activities by the youth and women's groups of the Soka Gakkai. It could be said that the Soka Gakkai earned anew the enmity of the Japanese establishment by challenging its basic policy—that is, to subsume political autonomy in exchange for security provided under the US nuclear umbrella.

Advertising Dependency of the Japanese Media

As with most countries, commercial broadcasters in Japan are heavily dependent on advertising for revenues. The ruling LDP, although it receives public subsidies, also depends on financial contributions made by corporations to conduct election campaigns and sustain its power base. This dependency on corporate donations holds true for the individual conservatives who belong to the party as well. Party or politician, they in turn act to protect their donors' interests, with the largest of them granted preferential treatment, not only for the larger sums they contribute, but also for their *keiretsu* affiliation to a vast army of smaller firms. In a distinctly Japanese scheme to avoid mutual destruction through mutual benefit, the LDP warns the largest media groups when they seek renewal of their broadcasting licenses, and the latter refrain from publicizing the powerful exposés which could threaten the former's grasp on power. As evidence that the LDP places immense value on this conduit, it routinely assigns the highest levels of party leadership to service its relations with senior media executives.

Large advertising agencies such as Dentsu Incorporated and Hakuhodo Incorporated also play a significant role in maintaining the collusive ties that link the media to business and politics. It is in the interest of such large advertising agencies to give priority to big businesses. Together they attempt to manipulate public opinion and maintain the *status quo*. Thus they prefer that the public remain unaware and ignorant of this pro-establishment mechanism in the media. It is also hardly likely that the media will give coverage or advertisement space to religious organizations like the Soka Gakkai. The ostensible reason would be the "religious impartiality clauses" contained in the Broadcasting Law and Broadcasting ethical guidelines—that no one particular religious tenet should be given media coverage.

In the Service of the State: *Bungei Shunju and Shinchosha*

Up until now I have discussed the inherent conservatism of the media and how it functions within a political and socioeconomic framework to maintain the *status quo* in Japan. Yet, as pro-establishment as the media in general may be, it pales in comparison to two specific media companies, Bungei Shunju and Shinchosha, which clearly act as instruments of state power. Their publications and periodicals are frequent vehicles of distorted historical facts, and they routinely feature articles that treat political parties opposing the LDP and civil movements seeking social reform with ridicule and castigation.

When the February 1995 issue of *Marco Polo*, a news monthly published by Bungei Shunju, ran a cover story written by Masanori Nishioka denying the existence of Nazi gas chambers, the controversy it caused went beyond the confines of Japan. Too inept as an attempt to challenge a thoroughly substantiated incident in world history, the piece invited near unanimous censure. In the early stages of the furor, its publisher seemed unperturbed, content to parry criticism with a casual promise to give equal space to opposing views in the future and the usual counter that *Marco Polo* was free to express its opinions. Yet Bungei Shunju's nonchalance turned to alarm as world-renowned human rights organizations such as the Simon Wiesenthal Centre in the USA joined in the opprobrium. *Marco Polo* was discontinued soon thereafter, the two issues crucial to the understanding of the modern world that it posed—first, denial of the Holocaust, and second, the significance of the freedom of speech and expression and their applicability in interpreting history—having gone unanswered.

As a publisher, Bungei Shunju has had a history of collaboration with the government: in the years leading up to World War II it was among the most vocal advocates of a military thrust into the Asian mainland, and led the Pen Corps, a team of propagandists and coopted journalists banded together under the auspices of a Japanese military intelligence unit, in its foray through occupied China. In the postwar era its articles and books have consistently denied the Nanjing massacre as well as the existence of the so-called "comfort women"—Asian women exploited as sex slaves by the imperial army. As with the Japanese media in general, it is motivated by profit and also by its willingness to foment public opinion favorable to the *status quo*.

Bungei Shunju outwardly explains that *Marco Polo* had to be discontinued when its larger corporate sponsors, owned or partly owned by "Jewish capital," either withdrew advertisements or threatened to do so. While such pressure may have indeed contributed to the monthly's demise, the publisher offers another reason to its peers. In a speech delivered at a media conference on June 10, 1996 Bungei Shunju's senior managing editor, Mitsuyoshi Okazaki, noted that the *Marco Polo* article was indeed factual, and hinted the possible dangers of Jewish terrorism. He further asserted that the magazine "was not discontinued because the feature it carried was untrue" or because of the subsequent loss in advertising income. Instead, he claimed that the decision was a result of information obtained from a certain source that Japanese expatriates might be targeted for terrorist attacks outside Japan.[14]

The nature of Shinchosha's reportage is similar to that of Bungei Shunju. Both publishers remain unrepentant and unreformed. When Bungei Shunju was admonished by a Tokyo superior court in July 1998 for a series of articles that made uncorroborated claims against a murder suspect, its senior editorial advisor, Kengo Tanaka, made his views on journalism explicit: "It is in fact more dangerous when a journalist is imbued with a sense of justice. That's because justice can at times assume the work of the devil . . ."[15]

The weekly magazines of the above two publishers regularly target the Soka Gakkai. Streams of sensational articles have been written about the organization in the past, ranging from sexual and financial scandals to criminal allegations.

Soka Gakkai's Religious Adamance and Early Proselytizing

As outlined earlier, the Soka Gakkai—as well as its prewar predecessor, the Soka Kyoiku Gakkai—interpreted the concept of Buddhahood in Nichiren Buddhism as a theory of equality.[16] This conflicted with the supremacy of the emperor, on which the authority of the state and militarist regime rested, leading to the imprisonment of its cofounders. This fact eludes recognition among most Japanese to this day, and the failure to grasp its import is reflected in the way the media covers the Soka Gakkai. While the media tends to evade complex historical realities in any country—as the British press does when it comes to Northern

---

[14] Speech given on July 10, 1996, *I-Media* (Asashi Shimbun), 152 (1996), 43–5.

[15] *Kane* (Sowa Bank) 51 (1998), 20–3.

[16] Nichiren taught that the Lotus Sutra expounded the equality of all living beings in that each possessed an innate potential called Buddhahood. Hence, every common mortal is a Buddha.

Ireland,[17] the US about native Americans, or the Chinese over Mongolia—the neglect of Japan's unpardonable wartime behavior by the Japanese media should not be overlooked.

Adding to the complexities involved in the media bias against the Soka Gakkai is the stigma the movement began to incur shortly after the war's end, a period when the movement achieved phenomenal growth in membership through aggressive proselytization, branded other Buddhist sects as "heretical," and confiscated the altars and talismans in the homes of those who converted.[18] Many of its more overzealous members were convinced they were being faithful to the tenets of Nichiren Buddhism. Soka Gakkai's dramatic growth, together with the fact that its ranks were primarily composed of the infirm and impoverished, was not welcomed by the establishment of Japanese society. The Soka Gakkai was deliberately stigmatized as "a frightening religion," and "a gathering of the poor."

Media Coverage of Soka Gakkai's Vast financial Resources

Funding to support the vast range of activities which the Soka Gakkai conducts on a local, national, and international basis is primarily generated through donations made by members. As the largest religious organization in Japan the total amount is thought to be considerable, although the Soka Gakkai does not disclose actual figures.

The organization's finances generate widespread suspicion in the public, which becomes another factor used by competing religious and political groups to criticize the Soka Gakkai. Much of this suspicion is stirred up by speculative press reports.[19]

Other media stories further reinforce the public perception that Soka Gakkai is endowed with immense financial resources. Some

---

[17] B. Ralston and D. Miller, *War and Words: The Northern Ireland Media Reader* (Belfast: Beyond the Pale Publications, 1996).

[18] Today Soka Gakkai's proselytizing has become less aggressive, and public complaint has quieted down.

[19] Some articles go as far as to claim that up to 200bn. yen (nearly $2bn.) is coaxed or coerced out of members every day.

of the negative coverage includes its concerted donation drive to build a grand main sanctuary for the Nichiren Shoshu sect it once belonged to. Other stories include the discovery of a vault filled with cash left in the woods—owned, as it turns out, by an individual who not only worked for the organization's headquarters, but operated a lucrative vending business on the side.

Since the aggregate of these media reports essentially yields a negative impression in the minds of not only its audience but those who file them, the cycle of innuendo and falsehoods becomes self-sustaining. This in turn creates an issue that threatens all religious organizations in Japan, for it incites a public clamor about their tax-free privileges under the Religious Corporation Law.

Japan's Social Framework of Intolerance

Even the most progressive and democratic of societies, from the ancient Greek *polis* to modern liberal democracies, maintain specific frameworks of discrimination and prejudice. When a politicoeconomic establishment exploits such frameworks to preserve and promote its power base, this gives rise to a rigidly hierarchical society such as exists in Japan through its imperial system.

A hierarchical social system not only demarcates a stratum for people to venerate and obey; it enables them to see those belonging to lower strata as inferior. Under the Japanese feudal system, for instance, the *burakumin* (who dealt in the killing of livestock and were despised for it) were considered pariahs occupying the lowest social rung in a caste system led by the samurai. In such a society the system works to incite the lower classes—who are prevented from discerning the discrepancies inherent in the system—to labor harder for the upper classes, and thus sustain the latter's grip on power. Indeed, the establishment in all societies routinely use prejudice and discrimination as a psychological safety valve for the disempowered to vent feelings of frustration and discontent with the *status quo*.

In Japan this social psychology at times acts to segregate the Soka Gakkai and its members from the rest of society. As the Soka

Gakkai leadership readily acknowledges, in its early days the movement's explosive expansion in membership took place most noticeably among the lower classes. This fact, as mentioned earlier, has stigmatized the Soka Gakkai as a religious outlet for the destitute. Branded in this way, especially in the 1950s and 1960s, the Soka Gakkai was often portrayed as a gathering to be feared. The extremely organized way its members prepare for and participate in election campaigns also fanned public suspicion—and its opponents often made use of this fear through innuendo: "Soka Gakkai is a religious organization of the poor people. Who knows what they will do if they band together."

Yet this framework of intolerance is flawed for two reasons: first, monetary wealth is obviously never an adequate measure of an individual's true worth; and second, the demographics of Soka Gakkai today reflect the demographics of Japanese society. Such a framework of intolerance has prevented the people from developing an impartial view of the Soka Gakkai.

Proliferation of Media Stereotypes

Public opinion is formed by the information provided by the media; once formed, it tends to serve as the basis for perceiving and processing new information. The media is also influenced, since it tends to select and disseminate information that caters to the public perception that prevails at the time. In his 1922 classic *Public Opinion*,[20] Walter Lippmann described this tendency to disseminate and receive information along preconceived lines as a "stereotype"—an explanation that very much applies to the Japanese media's postwar coverage of the Soka Gakkai.

To illustrate this point, consider *Tax Woman: The Sequel*, a film directed by Juzo Itami. It portrays a married couple, the high priest and priestess of a fictional "new religion" in bubble era Japan. They live a life of indulgence involving sex and purchasing expensive fur coats from the money they make evicting tenants in order to sell the land they rent at a huge profit. Being incorrigible tax evaders as

[20] (New York: Macmillan).

well, they eventually fall under the scrutiny of the tax bureau and are arrested. The film thoroughly reinforces the stereotype most members of its audience have about new religions that spawned in great numbers in the early postwar period. Soka Gakkai is often categorized as a new religion and is generally stereotyped as one of them.[21]

Similar constructs can be found in the Western press as well. In 1995 the British Broadcasting Corporation (BBC) produced and transmitted a one-hour television feature on the Soka Gakkai, which was rebroadcast in March 1996 as part of its weeklong special programming on Japan across Asia. The program opened with footage of the Aum Shinrikyo and scenes of the sarin nerve gassing in the Tokyo subways, then cut to an interview by a BBC reporter with Soka Gakkai honorary president Daisaku Ikeda. To introduce a Japanese religion with opening footage of Aum Shinrikyo will clearly lead the audience to have a negative image of the organization.

Prior to the first BBC broadcast the *Sunday Telegraph* had published a story dated October 15, 1995 by Robert Guest, entitled "Japan's Religious Sect Bent on Worldly Power," which was highly critical of the Soka Gakkai and its involvement in politics, accusing it of seeking secular power through religious means. The BBC program, it appears, took up the same angle as the article.

Such coverage of Japanese religion seems to have catered to an audience imbued with latent anti-Japanese sentiments. More specifically, it represented the culmination of stereotypical notions about the "alien" nature of Japan and Japanese religion no doubt harbored since the earliest British encounters with them. Nor is this phenomenon unique to the UK. The international edition of *Time* magazine dated November 20, 1995 also published a cover story on the Soka Gakkai entitled "The Power of Soka Gakkai," following shortly after an earlier story it featured on Shoko Asahara, the Aum guru. Parallels were clearly drawn between the two articles. These pieces underscore the earlier contention that

[21] Soka Gakkai's religious tenets are founded on the teachings of the Lotus Sutra—as interpreted by 13th century Buddhist monk Nichiren.

stereotypes in the media are self-perpetuating and that the Japanese media influences the manner in which the foreign press perceives and reports on Japan.

Inadequacy of Soka Gakkai's Media Relations Skills and Training

Given the global scope of modern societies, information is not truly authenticated unless it is reported on and disseminated by the media. A group that recognizes this phenomenon, then, is likely to seek maximum advantage from the information it provides. One example of a group that has not done so—yet has been damaged by such leveraged information—is the Soka Gakkai.

Skillful management of the media entails an understanding of the role the media play in society and their freedom. This understanding allows the provider of information to disseminate its message accurately and effectively. A significant volume of the negative press directed toward the Soka Gakkai is in fact attributable to the organization's ineptitude in this discipline and lack of understanding of the importance of "media training."

An incident that epitomizes its media relations weakness and the organization's lack of understanding of the concept of press freedom in a democracy took place in 1969, when some Komeito members, led by the then Komeito chairman, Yoshikatsu Takeiri, tried to halt the publication of *I Denounce Soka Gakkai*[22]—a highly critical account of the organization and its senior leadership. Takeiri approached Kakuei Tanaka, at the time LDP secretary-general, who later became prime minister, to persuade the author and publisher to relent. Instead, their subterfuge backfired, and the matter erupted into a controversy that would embroil the Soka Gakkai and tarnish its public image for decades.[23]

This incident epitomized the Soka Gakkai's shallow understanding of the importance of press freedom, of the media, and the

[22] By Hirotatsu Fujiwara, trans. W. C. Grant (Tokyo: Nisshin-Hodo Press, 1969, 1970).

[23] "A Memoir of the 1955 Political Face-Off", *Asahi Shimbun*, Aug. 26, 1998.

role it plays in a democratic society. Moreover, Soka Gakkai's media relations competence remains fundamentally reactive in an age when proactive media strategies are essential, not only openly to counter widespread public antipathy, but to enhance its visibility and transparency as a social entity.

At the same time it is vital that the Japanese public develops the media literacy to distinguish fact from conjecture, and genuine journalism from hidden agendas. Unfortunately, surveys consistently show that a large number of Japanese tend to believe what is disseminated by the media.[24] It may be this lack of scepticism that continues to sustain many of the negative stereotypes of Soka Gakkai.

Conclusion

As a rule, human character is formed through our association with family, our knowledge deepened through schooling, and our view and vision of the world and society at large modeled through information imparted by the media. In essence, then, the media is an educational institution that is supposed to serve us throughout our adult lifetime—a critical, and constantly expanding, dependency as we strive to fulfill our duty as responsible members of a civic society. The Japanese politicoeconomic establishment not only realizes this dependence, it manipulates the media to insure that the Soka Gakkai may never develop beyond a point where it can threaten its own influence and power.

As for the Soka Gakkai, it has been preoccupied with internal solidarity rather than external relations, as seen in its lack of effort openly and publicly to debate these issues. The organization's closed attitude toward the media is in part to blame for consistent criticism for its lack of transparency.

Obviously, no gathering of individuals is ever free of problems, and hence above criticism. If the criticism is valid, the Soka Gakkai

[24] According to a *Yomiuri Shimbun* survey of June 12, 1996, approximately 80% of the respondents felt that information printed in newspapers can be trusted.

should hear it with open-mindedness and facilitate its redress. If the criticisms are unfounded, then the organization should publicly rebut any falsehoods. The media, too, should possess the journalistic commitment to provide the Soka Gakkai with a fair opportunity for rebuttal, or should disseminate information about the group founded on fact.

The media, of course, need not treat the Soka Gakkai with undue favor. Yet it should remain fair in its representation as a significant social entity, an organization comprised of nearly one-tenth of the Japanese population, and one that holds considerable political influence. The media has the responsibility to be fair and to inform its audience of the organization's past and present activities both at home and abroad, so that Japanese society is not kept in the dark about this sizable minority. The Japanese media's dismissal of the Soka Gakkai's civil activities—its peace education work, its efforts to raise public awareness about human rights and war history[25]—is at the cost of a healthy development of the Japanese society. The resulting ignorance, in turn, only exacerbates the strains of historical revisionism that prevail through the Japanese power structure, inducing a sense of historical amnesia among the Japanese, which has profound implications for the rest of the world.

[25] The Soka Gakkai has sponsored the first Holocaust exhibition in Japan. Soka Gakkai's women's peace committee has published more than 100 volumes of war testimonials as part of its peace education project.

8

Toward a Pillar Organization?

Karel Dobbelaere

"PILLARIZATION" is the translation of the Dutch term *verzuiling*, coined to designate a particular societal structure that was first described and analyzed by historians and sociologists in the 1950s in the Netherlands.[1] It refers to the process by which pillarized structures are erected. Such structures or organizational complexes striving toward autarky or self-sufficiency are called pillars since they are active, on a religious or ideological basis, in areas that are primarily defined as secular. The more services a pillar renders, the more self-sufficient it is. A very good example of such an autarkic organizational complex is the Catholic pillar in Belgium. It embraces schools (from kindergarten to university), hospitals, old people's homes, youth movements, cultural associations, sport clubs, newspapers, magazines, book clubs, and libraries. It also has banks, a health insurance fund, a trade union, and a political party—the Christian People's Party. Although, since 1945, this party has officially been nondenominational, it continues to play a central role in organized Catholicism. The Catholic pillar provides almost all possible services from the cradle to the grave. In comparison, the Belgian Socialist and Liberal pillars are less autarkic: they provide fewer services, they do not have their own schools, and only a few medical facilities, relying rather on state schools and state hospitals. However, they have their own mass media (newspapers and magazines), sports clubs,

---

[1] J. M. G. Thurlings, *De wankele zuil: Nederlandse katholieken tussen assimilatie en pluralisme* (Deventer: Van Loghum Slaterus, 1978), 1–17.

youth movements, cultural associations, health insurance funds, trade unions, and political parties. In contrast to social classes, which integrate people on a horizontal basis, pillars do it on a vertical basis. Consequently, pillarization may be typified as an example of segmented differentiation, and by promoting segmented integration they may produce exclusiveness and an in-group mentality.

From the second half of the 1960s on, political scientists—like Daalder, Lehbruch, Lijphart, Lorwin, Huyse, Rokkan, and Steininger—became interested in pillarization.[2] They were intrigued by the political stability of religiously and ideologically segmented societies like Austria, Belgium, the Netherlands, and Switzerland. Consequently, pillarization was no longer regarded as restricted to the Netherlands, where, apart from the Catholic pillar, there were Protestant and Socialist pillars, or Belgium. Catholic pillars were also to be found in Austria, Germany, Italy, and Switzerland,[3] and Socialist pillars in Austria and Switzerland. In comparison with such structures as those found in Western Europe, a first question may be asked: to what extent may we call the organizational complex that Soka Gakkai has erected a pillar?

If the answer to this first question is positive, then a second question may be asked: how is the emergence and the extension of the Soka Gakkai pillar to be explained? Analyzing the European pillars, historians and sociologists have put forward several theories: the emancipation theory,[4] the political mobilization theory,[5]

---

[2] H. Righart, *De katholieke zuil in Europa: Een vergelijkend onderzoek naar het ontstaan van verzuiling onder katholieken in Oostenrijk, Zwitserland, België en Nederland* (Meppel: Boom, 1986), 14–15.

[3] S. Hellemans, "De katholieke zuilen buiten België," in J. Billiet (ed.), *Tusschen bescherming en verovering: Sociologen en historici over zuilvorming* (Leuven: Universitaire Pers Leuven, 1988).

[4] W. Goddijn, *Katholieke minderheid en protestantse dominant: Sociologische nawerking van de historische relatie tussen katholieken en protestanten in Nederland en in het bijzonder in de provincie Friesland* (Assen: Van Gorcum, 1957).

[5] R. Steininger, *Polarisierung und Integration. Eine vergleichende Untersuchung der strukturellen Versäulung der Gesellschaft in dem Niederlanden und in Österreich* (Meisenheim am Glan: Hain, 1975).

and the preservation theory.[6] The *emancipation theory* suggests that the function of pillarization was the emancipation of minorities suffering discrimination, such as workers (the Socialist pillars), Catholics (in the Netherlands and Switzerland), and the neo-Calvinist lower classes in the Netherlands who fought against the dominant liberals and the Netherlands Reformed Church. They used the pillarized structures to obtain societal recognition and the granting of equal rights. It is clear that this theory has only a limited applicability; it cannot explain the emergence of the Catholic pillars in homogeneous Catholic countries like Austria and Belgium. According to the *political mobilization theory*, pillars were erected to link the members of its different constituent organizations to the political party that defended their rights and privileges. This theory suggests that the political parties were the pioneers of pillarization, and presupposes that the initial organization of the pillarized complex was a political party, which is historically incorrect.[7] A more generally applicable explanation of the emergence of religious pillars is offered by the *preservation theory*, which explains the emergence and extension of religiously pillarized organizational complexes as an attempt to insulate religious people from a secularized world. Although such a complex process as pillarization can certainly not be explained by one single factor, Righart's comparative study of the Catholic pillars in Austria, Belgium, the Netherlands, and Switzerland convincingly demonstrated that preservation theory is the most generally applicable explanation. In the last decades of the nineteenth and twentieth centuries, the lower clergy was very active in building up and developing Catholic pillars, which was partly also an adaptation of the Church to modern society. Righart concludes, "Protection through adaptation, this in a few words, is what pillarization was all about."[8]

In that case, pillarization was a radical reaction to the process of functional differentiation that accelerated in the second half of the nineteenth century and affected both Catholicism and

---

[6] J. Billiet, "Beschouwingen over het samengaan van secularisatie en verzuiling," *De Nieuwe Maand*, 19 (1976), 244–57.

[7] Righart, *De katholieke zuil in Europa*.   [8] Ibid. 274.

Protestantism alike. In the Catholic world pillarization was a reactive policy: the clergy and part of the religious elite started creating a world segregated from the secularized world. To check the impact of secularization and to preserve Church control over the Catholic part of the population, they reverted to an older process of differentiation: segmentary differentiation—that is, the duplication of services in those sectors that were functionally differentiated from the religious subsystem. If the state and the differentiated subsystems were no longer to be organized according to Catholic doctrine, then the new civic liberties provided the opportunity for the establishment of Catholic organizations to protect believers from a secular, areligious or anti-religious, ideology.

We may conclude, then, that the process of functional differentiation provoked Catholic pillarization. "Dikes" were built to prevent the "secularization" of the Church's flock. However, in the Netherlands and Switzerland the Catholic pillar also had an emancipatory function, and the same was true for the Protestant pillar in the Netherlands. The Socialist pillars were first and foremost emancipatory. Through the integration of their organizations in one complex they augmented their power, and the Socialist Party became the political expression of this organizational complex. In the Catholic world its own organizations were gradually organized into a more and more centralized pillar, of which the emerging Catholic Party was the political expression. Hence, in Rokkan's terms, we can speak about an institutionalized pillar, interlocking a corporate and a political channel.[9] The near omnipresence of Catholic pillars in Western Europe may be seen as a segmentary reduction of "omnia instaurare in Christo." The organizational force of the Catholic Church, staffed with a large number of priests and religious people, and its populism[10] allowed the Church to adapt its strategy to the modern world in order to protect its flock from secular influences. Do the preservation and emancipation

[9] S. Rokkan, "Towards a Generalized Concept of 'Verzuiling': A Preliminary Note," *Political Studies*, 25 (1986), 563–70.

[10] S. Hellemans, "De katholieke zuilen buiten België," 270–1.

hypotheses, which seem to be the most plausible explanations for the emergence of religious and ideological pillars in Western Europe, also explain the emergence of the Soka Gakkai pillar, and is this pillar institutionalized?

In order to answer these questions, we must first give a description of the organizational complex of Soka Gakkai. Subsequently, we must ask ourselves if this organizational complex may be called a pillar, and more specifically an institutionalized pillar.

Soka Gakkai's Organizational Complex

Since its creation the organizational complex of Soka Gakkai that has been developed has taken into account the growing number of members of the association and its goals. There is, first of all, the association's organizational structure and its social life.

Organization and Activities

The basic structure of the association on the local level is the *zadankai*, or the discussion group, composed of ten to twenty people from the same neighborhood. In these groups, which meet once or twice a month, the members support each other, exchange their experiences, and study together. New members are encouraged by more experienced members, who also welcome people from the neighborhood who have expressed interest in the association. Several discussion groups make up a district. Districts in turn are integrated in chapters, and all members participate at all the levels of the lower echelons up to the chapter level. Soka Gakkai is more like a network of groups, in which members associate easily and freely, than a hierarchical organization. However, between the leaders there is coordination on higher levels: the chapters make up centers, and these are coordinated in a general center or region. These general centers make up Soka Gakkai (International) (SGI) in a country.

Within this structure, transverse divisions also exist. Normally, from the age of 35 members belong to the men's or women's division. Before that they are affiliated with divisions for youth (young men, young women, male students, female students, girls and boys, etc.). There are also professional divisions—e.g. for educators, artists, medical doctors, lawyers, managers, and others—who discuss the application of Buddhist principles in their domain of endeavor. According to the country, other divisions may exist: in Great Britain, for example, there are ethnic and national divisions; in Italy, divisions for young mothers, and one for homosexuals; in other countries there are divisions in enterprises, in rural communities, in apartment blocks, and other social settings. The number of reunions and activities in which a member may be engaged are numerous.

The attendance of members in discussion groups varies, according to country, from 75 to 85 percent, which is a very high participation rate. It seems that the attendance rate is highest in those countries with a small number of adherents—which may be explained by a strong desire to feel the support of the group and to create a plausibility structure in an environment where there is only a small chance of meeting other members outside the association's social life.

The associational life of Soka Gakkai is at least as developed as the associational life in the European pillars where the same type of associations are found: youth and adult movements for men and for women; and also associations for workers, managers, entrepreneurs, rural people, students, etc. Consequently, we may conclude that the associational structure is akin to that of the pillar structure in Europe.

Soka Gakkai and its "Performances"

The Soka Gakkai defines itself as a religious organization aiming at the promotion of education and culture, and it is indeed involved in the educational, cultural, mass media, and political fields. Its leaders seem to have understood that in a functionally differentiated society the religious subsystem does not occupy a privileged position and must prove its societal functionality by providing effective services to the other subsystems—what Niklas Luhmann calls "performances."[11] This is true of all subsystems and not only of religion. For example, the influence of science cannot be limited to the development and dissemination of knowledge, but must be felt above all in its performances, particularly toward the economic subsystem.[12] In the case of religion, its societal functionality cannot be limited to the expressive socialization of individuals, nor even to the promotion of a "human revolution." It is expected to provide other subsystems with original resources that support and enhance them. This is what Soka Gakkai is doing in diverse fields— particularly in education, culture, politics, and the media.[13]

Education

The pedagogical philosophy of the Soka Gakkai educational system is inspired by Makiguchi's main idea that people are capable of creating value. Education is the key for the development of this potential when it stimulates critical thinking and helps people to make wise decisions and to appreciate life in all its diversity. To this end, the Soka Gakkai organizes forums of discussion, seminars, and intercultural exchanges, and it has founded several schools. In some countries, such as Brazil, the SGI organizes literacy courses for adults—a good example of a "performance".

The educational system of Soka Gakkai comprises institutions from kindergarten to university. Since the launching of the educational program in 1964, four kindergartens as well as two primary schools and two secondary schools have been established. In 1985 Soka Gakkai founded a Women's Junior College, which offers two

[11] Niklas Luhmann, *The Differentiation of Society* (New York: Columbia University Press, 1982), 238–42.

[12] K. Dobbelaere, "Relations ambiguës des religions à la société globale," *Social Compass,* 45 (1998), 92.

[13] This part of the chapter was originally published in K. Dobbelaere, *La Soka Gakkai: Un movimento di laici diventa una religione* (Leumann, Turin): ElleDiCi, 1998), 65–86, and is slightly adapted. I want to express my gratitude to Dr Olivier Urbain for the English translation of the original manuscript.

years of study in business administration and English. Situated in a suburb of Tokyo, Soka University opened its faculties of law, economics, and letters in 1971, its faculties of education and business administration in 1976, and its faculty of engineering in 1991. The faculty of letters comprises the departments of Japanese language and literature, English literature, and foreign languages (Chinese and Russian), as well as a department of sociology and a department of philosophy, history, and Western classical languages. The university has also developed a correspondence program in economics, law, and education. Intensive Japanese courses are offered to foreign students. There are also specialized research centers at the university, including an Institute of Life Science, an Institute of Peace Studies, and other centers studying problems such as the environment and intercultural relations. These institutes organize seminars and publish their research results. The university also has exchange programs with about sixty universities in forty countries.

Two major traits characterize this educational system. First higher education is especially geared toward public service, education, economics, management, and languages. The law department prepares students for the bar examination and for national examinations giving access to public service positions. The results obtained by the graduates who have taken these examinations seem very creditable for a private university. Moreover, 100 to 200 graduates from Soka University are hired in the field of education throughout Japan each year, and it appears that 35 percent of companies registered in Japan employ its alumni. Second, the educational system is no longer limited to Japan: it encompasses kindergartens in Southeast Asia, and satellite university centers in Europe and the USA.

It is worth examining the extent to which Soka University reflects its Buddhist origins. In a recent discussion one professor from that university underlined that it was not a Buddhist institution, meaning that it was not based on Buddhist principles, in that its structure reflected the standard structure of Japanese universities. Soka University seeks to be a good university, capable of promoting the respectability of its Buddhist inspiration through the results of its alumni. More thorough and comparative research concerning universities would perhaps reveal some correlation between their respective inspirations and their extracurricular activities. Twenty-two years after its foundation the 24,000-strong Association of Alumni (Soyukai) stimulates contacts and mutual support amongst alumni, and this represents important support for their alma mater. Their presence in the administration of the state, in diplomacy, and in the economic and judiciary worlds, moreover, confers considerable credibility on Soka Gakkai.

Foreign language teaching is one of the priorities of Soka University, and this can be seen as an expression of the openness of Soka Gakkai toward the whole world. If the departmental structure stresses the importance of English, Chinese, and Russian, the interest in languages can also be seen in the teachings of widely spoken languages including Arabic, Spanish, Hindi, and Swahili, or historically and economically important languages such as Korean, French, and Italian, and even of less influential ones such as Polish and Vietnamese. Soka University of America (SUA), founded in 1987, follows the same approach. Its master's degree program in second and foreign language education trains students in the teaching of English as a second or foreign language. Based on applied pedagogy, this program includes study of the various kinds of English according to social classes, ethnic groups, sexes, and regions, in addition to the more traditional linguistics classes. SUA also offers courses in Japanese, elementary courses in Russian, Chinese, Spanish, French, and English, and American culture courses for Japanese students. Established in 1985 at Verrières-le-Buisson (France), the Study Center for European Languages is another satellite institution.

In 2001 SUA will open a new campus with a curriculum in the tradition of "liberal arts education," focusing on Asia and the Pacific. All students will be required to study a foreign language and follow four classes making up the common core, namely "perspectives on the self"; "the roles that science, myth, and religion play in formulating how we view the world"; "complexities of human rights in a pluralist society"; and "the issues of war, peace, and non-violence." More than merely following the traditional structure of American universities, the common core clearly reflects the ideological outlook of the SGI.

True to the humanistic vision of SGI, SUA has already started promoting extracurricular activities such as conferences on human rights. It has also established the Pacific Basin Research Center, which was launched in 1991 at the John F. Kennedy School of Government (Harvard University). The center concentrates on selected policy experiences in the Pacific region in order to under-stand the procedures that lead to a positive outcome,[14] such as suc-cessful policies in the field of human rights in Asia and the Pacific Basin. The university also has a Botanical Research Center and Nursery devoted to the study of indigenous plants, their restora-tion, and the dissemination of information about them.

The Soka University Institute for the Study of the Natural Environment is another way in which Soka Gakkai voices its con-cern for the environment. This institute is aimed at the restoration of the tropical forest along the Amazon river in collaboration with the State Center in the Amazon (Brazil). The department of edu-cation of SGI Brazil has also launched a Projeto Makiguti. Children from the northeast of the country are taught the basics of gardening: collecting seeds, sowing, caring for plants, and grow-ing vegetables. In a country where school absenteeism runs high, such a teaching style encourages children to attend school. Volunteers from SGI Brazil—psychologists, pedagogues, and others—also work with teachers of sixteen schools in order to improve the pedagogy of arithmetic and geometry using origami, and to stimulate learning by using manual work. The parents are integrated into these educational projects to raise consciousness of their role in their children's education, which is not exclusively the school's responsibility.

[14] John D. Montgomery and Dennis A. Rondinelli (eds.), *Great Policies: Strategic Innovations in Asia and the Pacific Basin* (Westport, Conn.: Praeger, 1995).

In a totally different vein, the Institute of Oriental Philosophy (IOP), established in 1962, aims at clarifying the essence of Buddhism itself, in stripping from it the influences of local traditions and the cultures of different countries. This type of research appears clearly in the programs of seminars, colloquia, and national and international congresses organized by the institute, as well as in its publications of books and journals, such as the *Journal of Oriental Studies*. This research has besides been enriched by a comparative analysis with other religions. The institute also explores the relations between Buddhism and life sciences, peace, environment, education, science, economy, and modern society. A European Center was established in Taplow Court (Taplow, Berkshire, UK) in 1989, with satellites at Sceaux (France) and St Petersburg, and an Indian center in New Delhi in 1992. The European Center, with the aim of revealing the "wisdom of the East" in Europe, has a library open to the public and organizes conferences at Taplow Court, and also in France and Germany. University professors discuss Buddhist philosophy, its relationship with European thought, and the application of Buddhist principles to various world problems such as peace and ecology. More recently the institute has organized colloquia on inter-Buddhist and interreligious dialogue.

In 1995 Soka Gakkai established the Makiguchi Foundation for Education. In line with the Soka Gakkai's commitment to the promotion of education, its aims are, among others, to grant scholarships to Japanese university students, to stimulate international exchange programs, and to donate books and equipment to schools. These donations of school books had actually started long before the creation of this foundation. The Soka Gakkai has also donated books and manuscripts about Buddhism and Japanese culture to Western universities, and scientific books to Third World universities and nongovernmental organizations (NGOs).

The major characteristics of the educational policy of Soka Gakkai can therefore be summarized as follows: stimulation of teaching, promotion of intercultural exchange, deeper understanding of Buddhist thought, and analysis of present-day world problems—

peace, ecology, education, intercultural relations, and global economics—from a Buddhist perspective. The goal of interreligious dialogue is more recent. It became possible only after the break with the Nichiren Shoshu sect, since the monks refused any dialogue with what they called "false religions." However, discreet contacts with other religions had already taken place before the split. For instance, representatives of Soka Gakkai, SGI, Soka University, and the IOP participated in world congresses as early as the 1970s.

Culture

SGI has culture centers in Japan and throughout the world. In Europe there are centers at Taplow Court, Florence, and Bingen (Germany), among others. These diverse buildings, most often acquired in a state of terrible decay, have been restored by professionals and by the members, who freely put their various talents to the service of their organization and, in this way, also contributed to the rehabilitation of a common cultural heritage. These diverse centers welcome symposia and conferences. They organize open days, festivals, and exhibitions, often in collaboration with other cultural organizations and with official authorities. Since 1992 a yearly festival—the Taplow Court Festival of the Arts—has offered classical music, opera, and modern popular music shows, as well as theatrical performances and poetry recitals.

As the expression of human creativity, art is indeed considered by Soka Gakkai to be a manifestation of cultural differences, which can promote mutual respect and bring peoples together—a concept thus formulated by Ikeda in a brochure of the Tokyo Fuji Art Museum:

Until the peoples of the world develop a mutual understanding and respect for each other, there is no way we can expect to achieve a peaceful world. It is the creation of art and music, coming from the depths of our lives, which expresses the rich spirit of a people or an age and communicates itself directly to the hearts of all humankind. There is no need for words, nor for chasing after difficult logic, but simply a wonderful communication of soul speaking to soul.

Established in 1983, the Tokyo Fuji Art Museum houses an important collection of Western, Japanese, and Chinese art. Thanks to an international exchange program, it organizes thematic exhibitions, and the museum's own collection has been exhibited throughout the world. Another medium of exchange, music, has been well served by the creation in 1963 of the Min-On Concert Association. Since then, Min-On has realized exchanges with more than seventy-five nations. And about 1,500 concerts take place throughout Japan each year. Several large—notably European and American—companies, as well as dance and folk music groups, have been invited to perform in Japan, and Japanese artists have given concerts throughout the world. Min-On also organizes a Festival of Contemporary Music and the Tokyo International Musical Competition—a contest for orchestra conductors, chamber music ensembles, singers, and choreographers. In France the restored Château des Roches in Bièvres, now called Maison Littéraire Victor Hugo, houses a large collection of mementos, manuscripts, and books by Victor Hugo, whose works are taught in Japanese secondary schools. But the interest in artistic development does not stop there, and Soka Gakkai and SGI encourage their members to establish brass bands, orchestras, chamber music ensembles, vocal choruses, and ballet groups to develop their artistic potential.

Besides their specific artistic and cultural aims, these activities may also take on a political character. In 1995 an exhibition of 400 paintings and drawings dedicated to peace and friendship, selected from more than 100,000 children's drawings from 160 countries and regions, was organized in Tokyo in collaboration with Unesco. Since then this exhibition has toured the world. In April 1996, for example, 250 of the paintings and drawings were displayed at the Unesco headquarters in Paris, and in 1997 the exhibition visited three Caucasian republics, where it was enriched with drawings and paintings by children from these countries ("Children of Caucasus Draw for Peace and against Wars and Violence"). This example illustrates clearly that besides having a genuine interest in artistic and cultural development, Soka Gakkai sees in art a vehicle for its message of peace and friendship between peoples. That is why the exhibitions are accompanied by seminars about peace and cultural diversity. It is noteworthy that these cultural activities do not always originate in Japan. In 1994, for example, at the initiative of SGI-Germany, an exhibition called "Leben in Deutschland. Fremdheit, Identität, Begegnung" ("Life in Germany: Strangeness, Identity, Encounter") was held in Cologne, accompanied by artistic evenings and conferences devoted to this theme. This type of endeavor is sometimes also the result of collaboration with local public authorities, as in Bingen, and affords a welcome to artists who are outside the movement.

The influence of artists, numerous amongst the SGI members, is also expressed in performances organized by the members. A good example is *Alice*, a musical comedy based on Lewis Carroll's *Alice in Wonderland*, which was presented in London by SGI-UK. In this adapted version of the story, Alice is a punk adolescent who would like to see changes in the center of her city, which she considers a lost world. As a story about regaining hope, *Alice* expresses the ideology of the Soka Gakkai very well. Three thousand members worked for two years toward realizing this production, and in doing so contributed greatly to their own unity and also created an important public relations event, as echoed by the press. Members and local artists also organize national art and charity festivals. Since 1981 Soka Gakkai has in addition animated and supported periodic SGI international festivals. These festivals symbolize the engagement of the movement for peace and culture through cultural and musical shows performed by representatives from the whole world. In 1997 the SGI International Festival took place in Hong Kong and 1,600 people from 100 different nations participated in the program, of which one part, "A Gathering of Nations," was a pressing appeal for a century of peace.

It is clear that, through art, Soka Gakkai seeks to express the value of human creativity in different cultures and, at the same time, to stimulate dialogue characterized by mutual respect. The cultural manifestations and festivals are the apotheoses of long preparation, and are the result not only of the performances of the artists but also of all the work of those behind the scenes. This pattern of activity symbolizes the fact that social change and peace—so much desired—are the responsibility not only of actors on the political stage, but also presupposes the collaboration of the common people—of those who, in some way, are behind the scenes. The festivals are rites in which the values propounded by the organization are celebrated on an international level. These rites stimulate the engagement of members and unite them in common cause with all those who aspire to foster peace throughout the world. That is why the presence of representatives from the United Nations (UN) or the reading of their messages is considered to be very important. Let us finally add that a part of the profits produced by all these activities go to UN humanitarian causes, which also benefit from special collections during the events.

Politics

The various secular spheres of society in which Soka Gakkai is engaged can be neatly distinguished from an analytical standpoint. From what has already been said, however, it becomes clear that in reality these spheres impinge on each other. Indeed, the "political" goals appear in the fields of education and culture, expressed in such concerns as peace, ecology, intercultural activities, and humanitarian aid. Moreover, as we shall see, in Japan, Soka Gakkai is also engaged in politics in the strict sense of the word.

On the international level the political engagement of the Soka Gakkai is mainly accomplished within the framework of the UN and Unesco. Let us first mention humanitarian aid. Collections are organized to help refugees in Africa, Asia, and Europe through the intermediation of the UN High Commissioner for Refugees. Several million yen are thus transferred in the form of currency, food, clothing, and blankets. Medical teams are sent throughout the world to care for these refugees and also to help the populations of areas hit by natural disasters. During the Kobe earthquake (1995) the Soka Gakkai welcomed the victims into its buildings, and members volunteered to help clear away the rubble. This mobilization of members has also been manifest during ecological disasters, when, for example, beaches, or fauna and flora are threatened. The Soka Gakkai organized a conference at Taplow Court about environmental and developmental problems in order to prepare for the UN world summit on that theme in Rio de Janeiro in June 1992, in which Soka Gakkai participated as an NGO. Whereas many other preparatory conferences had focused on the political, economic, scientific, and technical methodologies envisioned as solutions to these problems, this particular conference centered on the development of an ecological conscience. The Taplow Court Declaration states: "the ethics of environmental concerns are at the heart of our common future and shall abide though political movements fade, economic systems change, and ideologies are eclipsed and forgotten."[15] The declaration also insists on the contribution of spiritual values and cultural exchange, interreligious dialogue, education for the development of an ecological ethic, and the important role that women and young people should play in it. In his introduction to this publication Daisaku Ikeda underlines the role of local populations in the implementation of environmental protection measures. All these recommendations are in perfect accord with the spirit of the "human revolution"—the major driving force behind social change according to Soka Gakkai ideology.

With the support of the UN, Soka Gakkai has organized several exhibitions highlighting the scourge of war. From 1982 to 1988 the exhibition "Nuclear Arms: Threat to our World" toured twenty-five large cities throughout the world and eight in Japan. From 1989 to 1994 the "War and Peace" exhibition visited thirteen large cities. It can be said that the members show a constant interest in peace. The youth division has thus far published fifty-six volumes of stories telling of the sufferings endured by Japanese people during the Pacific War. The first twenty-eight volumes were collectively published in English in 1978 as *Cries for Peace*; the second part, *Peace is our Duty*, was published in 1982. In the

---

[15] D. Hall *et al.*, *A Dialogue of Cultures for Sustainable Development* (London: Commonwealth Human Ecology Council, n.d.), 2.

same vein, the book *Women against War*, published in 1986, is a compilation of forty stories by women, gathered by the women's division of Soka Gakkai. The aim of these publications is to ensure that young people are conscious of the horrors of war, in the hope that they will never have to go through the same ordeal. Inaugurated in 1994 in Tokyo, the exhibition "The Courage to Remember: Anne Frank and the Holocaust", coorganized with the Simon Wiesenthal Center, has to date toured nineteen Japanese cities and has been seen by more than a million Japanese. In line with this preoccupation, one should also mention the numerous personal messages sent by Ikeda to spread his plea for peace throughout the world. These messages have been gathered and published in several languages, the English title being *A Lasting Peace* (2 vols., 1981 and 1987). Finally, the Soka Gakkai has also organized diverse youth festivals for peace throughout the world. The second one in Europe took place in Milan in 1994.[16]

Human rights are another theme that motivates and mobilizes the members. In commemoration of the adoption of these rights by the UN, Soka Gakkai is currently organizing the world tour of an exhibition entitled "Toward the Century of Humanity: An Overview of Human Rights in Today's World." This exhibition was first shown in the offices of the UN in Geneva in 1993. In Rome and Milan in 1996 it was viewed by more than 50,000 visitors including a large number of schoolchildren, and it was put on again in Naples and Venice in 1999. A special brochure entitled *I diritti umani nel mondo contemporaneo* ("Human Rights in the Contemporary World") was published, and the bimonthly review of SGI-Italy, *Duemilauno* ("2001"), devoted about forty pages to human rights to commemorate the occasion. Seminars and conferences were also organized, with the participation of scholars of national and international repute. In Brazil this exhibition received the support of the UN, the presidency, and the government of the country, a fact that naturally made an impression on the members. The public was highly interested and, after

---

[16] M. I. Macioti, *Il Buddha che è in noi: Germogli del Sutra del Loto* (Rome: Edizioni Seam, 1996), 159–62.

viewing the exhibition and attending seminars and conferences, numerous people became aware of their rights—some even decided to lodge complaints to the relevant authorities. The Spanish members were also very concerned with problems of human rights—an observation that may probably be explained by the recent history of their country. In 1994 the youth division of that country contributed to the organization of an international conference on human rights in daily life at the Universidad de la Laguna, at which 500 participants and speakers discussed these issues and exchanged their experiences.

The engagement of Soka Gakkai in peace and human rights activities is not limited to the organization of exhibitions and conferences and to the publication of books and manifestoes. It has also led to the creation of specific research centers. In 1993 the Boston Research Center for the 21st Century was inaugurated in the USA. This center seeks to promote dialogue between scholars, activists, and representatives of various cultural, philosophical, and religious traditions in order to establish a common philosophical basis from which people might prevent war and promote respect for life and the earth. The dialogues and research projects organized by the center focus on civil society, human rights, nonviolence, intercultural and interreligious understanding, common values, and the governance of the global society. In 1997, for example, the center organized a consultation meeting with other centers to discuss the preparation of an Earth Charter aimed at establishing the principles of a global ethical framework for the respect of human rights, peace, economic equity, environmental protection, and sustainable development. In the same year a series of conferences on the theme "Religion and Ecology" was geared toward the search for an ethical common ground that could be shared by different religious families. Moreover, SGI has established the Tokyo Toda Institute for Global Peace and Policy, which, since 1996, has stimulated dialogue and cooperation between those who study peace problems, policymakers, and all those who are active in civil society. This institute focuses its activities on security, human rights, social justice, and cultural identity in a global context, offering scholarships to pre- and postdoctoral and senior researchers who are interested in these problems.

In Japan Soka Gakkai is also involved in politics in the narrow sense of the word. Since 1955 it has presented candidates at the local elections, and in 1964 established and lent support to a political party, the Komeito. In 1994 this party merged with other parties such as the Democratic Socialist Party (Minshuto) to form the Shinshinto, the Party of the New Frontier, which sought to achieve a two party system to counterbalance the power of the Liberal Democratic Party (LDP). However, at the local level, the policies of Komeito continued to be pursued by the Komei party. Soka Gakkai publicly supported Shinshinto at the national level and, at the local level, candidates affiliated with Komei. In December 1997 the Shinshinto coalition broke up, and almost all former Komei members then formed the Heiwa-Kaikaku, the Party of Peace and Reform, in the House of Representatives; they continued to use the former name—Komei—in the Upper House. On 7 November 1998 Heiwa-Kaikaku and Komei merged to form the New Komeito. Consequently, on the national and local level there is still a party which is related to Soka Gakkai, a party which has pursued for thirty years policies characterized by its interest in peace, disarmament, citizen's well-being, and religious freedom.

The Media

The publication policies of the Soka Gakkai throughout the world have already been touched upon. The *Seikyo Shimbun*, a Japanese language newspaper with a circulation of several million copies, is one such publication. It provides information about the activities of the organization and the actions of its leaders, gives advice to members, and analyzes Japanese and world events from a Buddhist perspective. The current president of Soka Gakkai, Einosuke Akiya, was a former editor in chief, a fact that shows how important this newspaper is to the Soka Gakkai's leaders. SGI publishes the monthly *SGI*, and the *SGI Quarterly*. There are also national publications in various countries. In the USA, SGI members may subscribe to two English language publications: a weekly newspaper, the *World Tribune*, serving as a public relations device, and the magazine *Living Buddhism*, which publishes study materials for the members. In Italy *Duemilauno*, which is distributed to a large public, contains articles of general interest written by specialists, and discussions about Buddhist principles. *Il nuovo rinascimento* ("The New Renaissance"), on the other hand, is directed at members.[17] This last type of publication exists in all countries where the movement has a sufficient number of members. Thus, Spain saw in 1997 the birth of the monthly *Vision Global*. SGI-France, with its much larger number of members, publishes, besides a weekly newspaper and a monthly magazine, the discourses, dialogues, and guidance of President Ikeda. The publications destined for members generally contain articles about the national and international activities of the organization, the guidance of leaders—in particular of President Ikeda—testimonies by members, excerpts from the *Gosho*, articles about fundamental concepts of Nichiren Buddhism, and excerpts from the *New Human Revolution*, a serialized history of the organization written by Ikeda.

All the publications for members aim to provide them with a constant flow of guidance, but they also have the mission of teaching Nichiren Buddhism. Moreover, the international activities of the organization, the establishment of institutes and centers throughout the world, as well as President Ikeda's travels and meetings with world leaders serve to communicate to the members a feeling of the important role that their movement plays in the quest for peace and in the elaboration of ecological and humanitarian policies.

[17] M. I. Macioti, *Il Buddha che è in noi: Germogli del Sutra del Loto* (Rome: Edizioni Seam, 1996), 128–9; L. Ferrarotti, "Leggendo *Duemila uno*," *La Critica Sociologia*, 111–12 (1994–5), 228–33; E. Tedeschi, "Leggendo 'Il Nuovo Rinascimento'," *La Critica Sociologia*, 111–12 (1994–5), 234–50.

Soka Gakkai's Organizational Complex: An Institutionalized Pillar

Since the corporate channel (its organizational structure and asso-ciational life, its educational system, its cultural agencies and pro-grams, and its press) is linked, on the local and the global level, with political channels, we may call Soka Gakkai's organizational complex an institutionalized pillar.[18] However, compared with some of the European pillars, it is only a small one—an embryonic pillar. How can we explain its emergence and the type of secular institutions that have been erected?

The type of secular institutions that Soka Gakkai has established may be partly explained by its origin: it emerged as an association of educators, hence the interest in education and culture. However, its religious philosophy has also had an impact. The title of the hagiography of the movement, *The Human Revolution*, expresses the central idea of its ideology: the key toward an endur-ing peace and human happiness is first of all based on self-transformation and not solely on social or structural reforms. Peace and human happiness are the result of personal efforts with the help of its religious practice, *gongyo* and *daimoku*. To succeed, education and the support of the organization are most helpful.[19] However, since Soka Gakkai considered all other forms of Buddhism provisional and heretical, it had to create some secular agencies to insulate its members from other Buddhist teachings. In this way, the school system was instrumental for the youngsters, and the mass media for the adults. The school system has also had a latent function: it has allowed the second and third generations to climb the social ladder. In this way, new generations have been emancipated.

If the preservation and emancipation hypotheses, which explain the emergence of Christian and Socialist pillars in Europe, help to explain the type of secular institutions that were established by Soka Gakkai, they do not suffice to explain its involvement in the

[18] Rokkan, "Towards a Generalized Concept of 'Verzuiling.'"
[19] Dobbelaere, *La Sokka Gakkai*, 47–63.

secular world. Since the different Christian churches were already well established in nineteenth century Europe, conversion was not a manifest function for the construction of Christian pillars there. However, newly established Christian movements have used secular institutions to recruit new members—for example, the Seventh-Day Adventist Church, which was established last century in the USA. All newly established religious movements need to grow if they are to survive. In establishing secular institutions, movements offer services to nonmembers and, at the same time, gain respectability, which might attract nonmembers. In doing so they promote conversions. Consequently, conversions may be another manifest or latent function for creating secular institutions. What elements, then, may play a role in selecting the type of secular institutions to attract potential members?

In the last century, when health was a major problem and modern medicine was developing, the Seventh-Day Adventist Church created hospitals and health institutions. In more recent times, since they have involved themselves more and more in the inner cities, social welfare has been another domain in which they have provided services. However, the involvement of this denomination in the secular world was not pure opportunism. Medicine is part of the Christian diaconate: Christ healed the afflicted, and the deacons of the primitive Church were in charge of the poor, the widows, the old, and the sick. So there is an elective affinity between the services provided and the basic philosophy of the Seventh-Day Adventist Church. The same is true for Soka Gakkai's involvement in the secular world. Giving assurance to the anomic masses in postwar Japan after the country's defeat, offering them a practice that promised a change of their karma, and working toward enduring peace constituted a message and a goal that appealed to people. Here there is a fit with modern individualism and the philosophy of the movement, which was coined in the concept of "human revolution." It must be said that there is also clear congruity between the goals of the movement and its political agenda: peace, human rights, ecology, civil society, and globalization are topical issues and mobilize many people. In Soka Gakkai members may have the feeling that they are tackling these concerns by supporting their organization, and by working on these problems in their everyday lives. This may also be an explanation for the movement's steady growth in Europe in this so-called postmodern period. Consequently, it seems that the conversion perspective for young movements is important: they try to gain respectability by involving themselves in the secular world, attacking those problems typical of modern life that have an elective affinity with their own philosophy; consequently, their involvement in the secular world is not purely opportunistic.

Unlike the arrangements common to the European pillars, the corporate channel of the emerging pillars in the new movements is not always institutionalized by being linked to a political channel—except in the case of Soka Gakkai. The Seventh-Day Adventist Church, for example, emerged in the USA, where constitutionally there is a formal separation of church and state, where no political parties have been created on a religious basis, and where private initiative without political links is legion in the fields in which these religious movements are involved. This explanation for not linking a corporate to a political channel also fits Japan. Indeed, other Japanese new religious movements involved in secular fields by a corporate channel lack a political channel. Consequently, Soka Gakkai's involvement in party politics is atypical for Japan and must be explained as a unique case. A key may be found in the writings of the third president of Soka Gakkai, Daisaku Ikeda.[20] Again the explanation is related to the ideology of the movement and the perception of the situation. To legitimize the establishment of a political party, Ikeda referred first of all to the ideology of his movement by pointing to two concepts of Nichiren Buddhism: *rissho ankoku* (the establishment of true Buddhism must preserve the peace of the nation) and *obutsumyogo* (in which *butsu* refers to *rissho* and the *o* of *obutsu* to the sovereign people). Combining these two concepts, he came to the conclusion that sovereign people must establish peace on the basis of true

[20] D. M. Bethel, *Makiguchi, le créateur de valeurs* (Monaco: Éditions du Rocher, 1996), 102–8.

Buddhism. To do this, citizens must be enlightened and awakened. However, this was not enough. According to Ikeda, Japan also needed a new breed of politicians, since the military of the prewar period had been simply replaced by politicians who were eager for power—ministers were appointed on the basis of the importance of the different political factions in the party and not on the basis of personal competence (his reference was clearly to the LDP). Consequently, a new political party had to be created—Komeito—dedicated to the needs and the well-being of the citizens. More research on this topic might reveal other explanations.

Finally, I want to point out that the level of Soka Gakkai's involvement in politics is not solely national but is also international: Soka Gakkai is involved in global politics, working directly with the UN and Unesco. Globalization is also a typical feature of its approach. It fits the trends of the postmodern society very well: it is global and local, a typical example of "globalization."

II

International Appearances

9

Immigrant Buddhists in America

David Machacek and Kerry Mitchell

SOKA GAKKAI first arrived in the United States as the religion of some Japanese war brides. Although many American servicemen converted to the religion of their spouses in the early years, SGI-USA's initial recruitment efforts targeted other recent immigrants from Japan, who, because of American immigration laws at the time, were also mostly women married to American men. For these early members, involvement in Soka Gakkai offered an opportunity to socialize with others who spoke their language and shared their customs.

While new even in Japan, the Soka Gakkai Buddhist movement offered a link to these early members' ethnic heritage. Buddhism, Nichiren Buddhism in particular, has long been a presence in Japanese culture. Whether Buddhists by birth or converts to Buddhism from other traditions, Soka Gakkai offered a sense of identity and belonging to those who, recently arrived in the United States, were faced with a new and unfamiliar environment.

After an initial period of organizing, however, SGI-USA began recruiting new members from the general population—and, by most accounts, with notable success. As SGI-USA's recruitment goals shifted, many changes were made to accommodate the new non-Japanese American members. This process of Americaniza-tion is well documented.[1] Indeed, virtually all of the research on

---

[1] J. Hurst, "The Nichiren Shoshu Soka Gakkai in America: The Ethos of a New Religious Movement", Temple University Ph.D. diss., 1980; D. Snow, *Shakubuku: A Study of the Nichiren Shoshu Buddhist Movement in America, 1960–75* (New York: Garland, 1993); D. Metraux, *The History and Theology of*

Soka Gakkai in America has treated the religion as a competitive and evangelizing new religion. Thus, research to date on SGI-USA has focused mainly on describing a religion that is exotic from an American standpoint and explaining why people raised as Protestants, Catholics, or Jews convert to Soka Gakkai Buddhism.

There has been little acknowledgment, much less analysis, of the fact that, for many, membership in SGI-USA represents less of a break with tradition and more a means of maintaining a sense of connection with their Japanese heritage. If the story of SGI-USA in recent times is one of Americanization—both in terms of the demographics of its members and in terms of the organization itself—what of that sizable minority of Japanese members? They have received only passing mention in the literature on Soka Gakkai in the United States. This chapter seeks to remedy the neglect.

Data on the ethnically Japanese membership of SGI-USA show a population in transition from one composed primarily of house-wives and service workers to one composed of highly educated white-collar workers, from first generation immigrants to the children of immigrants, and from the founding generation of converts to the first generation to be raised as Soka Gakkai Buddhists. The bulk of this chapter discusses the impact of these changes on SGI-USA and attempts to elucidate the shift in meaning that accompanies them.

Data and Methods

Data from Hammond and Machacek's survey of SGI-USA members allow us to provide at least a cursory account of what is happening among the ethnically Japanese members of SGI-USA.[2] Because the sample was chosen randomly from the list of subscribers to the four main Soka Gakkai publications distributed in

Soka Gakkai: A Japanese New Religion (Lewiston, NY: Edwin Mellen Press, 1988); P. Hammond and D. Machacek, *Soka Gakkai in America: Accommodation and Conversion* (Oxford: Oxford University Press, 1999).

[2] *Soka Gakkai in America.*

the United States, two of which are Japanese language publications, it captured many Japanese American members.

Indeed, one of the initial findings of that survey was that Japanese Americans, while a minority, are more strongly represented in the membership of SGI-USA than either SGI's own estimates or previous research would have led one to believe. Out of the 401 respondents, eighty-eight (22 percent) are ethnically Japanese, and this estimate is probably low. We have reason to believe that Japanese-speaking members of SGI-USA are underrepresented in the sample. The reason, of course, is that the survey was conducted in English, and many SGI-USA members who speak English as a second language had difficulty filling out the questionnaire. A few of these people informed us that they had someone assist them in filling out the questionnaire, and one returned the questionnaire in Japanese. Others replied only to tell us that difficulty with the language prevented them from participating in the survey. It is safe to assume that this latter response was most common among those SGI-USA members least familiar with the English language. In other words, the number of ethnically Japanese members of SGI-USA is probably higher than 22 percent. How much higher, of course, is virtually impossible to say.

None the less, the eighty-eight people who did reply offer a decent sampling of SGI-USA members of Japanese descent. The responses given by these Japanese members constitute our primary source of data for this chapter. As Hammond and Machacek note in appendices A and B in their book *Soka Gakkai in America*, to whatever extent we misrepresent SGI-USA *now* based on these data, it probably represents the direction SGI-USA is going in the *future*.

The Demographics of Japanese Members

We mentioned earlier that Japanese housewives dominated the membership of SGI-USA in its early phase of development. Many of these founders remain active in SGI-USA and are, fortunately, represented in our sample. The data on Japanese members, how-ever, tell a story of dramatic demographic change in recent decades. Specifically, they demonstrate the rising presence of three new groups among the younger Japanese members: (1) the first generation to be raised as Soka Gakkai Buddhists, (2) highly edu-cated and professional Japanese immigrants, and (3) the children of Japanese immigrants—second generation Japanese Americans.

It was easy enough to divide the eighty-eight respondents into two cohorts using the median age (44 years) as the cutoff point. Comparing these two groups on standard demographic indicators shows the transformation vividly (Table 9.1). First generation immigrants dominate the older cohort by a wide margin (81 per-cent). Furthermore, the demographics of these immigrants strongly demonstrate the impact of restrictive immigration laws in place in the United States until 1965.

Before 1965 immigration from Japan was limited to depend-ents of American citizens—mostly the wives and children of American men. Consequently, virtually all members of the older cohort are women (91 percent). Few achieved more than a high school education, though an impressive number did complete high school (46 percent), and many went on to trade schools or

Table 9.1. Demographics of Japanese members (%)

Demographic	Older cohort (age 44 +)	Younger cohort (age 43–)	All
Born in Japan	81	48	64
Born in USA	12	48	31
Female	91	61	76
Hold bachelor's degrees	5	23	14
Hold graduate or professional degrees	2	14	8
Professional or managerial workers	11	33	23
Clerical or sales workers	22	36	30
Housewives	39	10	23

junior college (29 percent), which demonstrates that they are educated. This limited education is reflected in the occupations of the older cohort. As would be expected from the above discussion, the most common occupation among these older members is homemaker (39 percent), followed by clerical or sales (22 percent) and service occupations (17 percent). Professional and managerial workers are relatively few, as are white-collar workers in general.

This contrasts sharply with the demographics of the younger cohort. About half of the younger Japanese members were born in the United States and their gender distribution (61 percent female) resembles that of Soka Gakkai members in general (including converts, which Hammond and Machacek report as 68 percent female).[3] More significantly, the younger cohort is considerably more likely to have achieved a college education. Compared to only 5 percent of the older cohort, 23 percent of the younger cohort hold baccalaureate degrees. Fourteen percent have completed graduate or professional degrees compared to only 2 percent of the older cohort. Consequently, we find many more of the Japanese members in the younger cohort employed in professional or managerial occupations (33 percent compared to 11 percent), a frequency that approaches that of Soka Gakkai members as a whole (40 percent) and compares favorably with the American population in general (29 percent). Notably, members of the younger cohort are a fourth as likely to identify homemaking as their primary occupation (10 percent versus 39 percent).

Perhaps the most notable religious difference to be found between the older and younger cohorts is the number of members who were raised in Soka Gakkai. Only 15 percent of the older cohort was raised in Soka Gakkai or Nichiren Shoshu Buddhism. Most (53 percent) converted to Soka Gakkai from some other form of Buddhism (Table 9.2). Just over half of the younger members, on the other hand, were raised as Soka Gakkai Buddhists.

In brief, the consequence of less restrictive immigration laws after 1965 and the advent of second generation Japanese

---

[3] Ibid. 46.

Table 9.2. Questionnaire: "In what religion were you raised?"

Religion	Older cohort (age 44+)	Younger cohort (age 43–)	All
Soka Gakkai, Nichiren Shoshu	15	56	35
Other Buddhist	53	13	33
Shinto	8	3	5
Christian	10	18	14
None	13	10	11
Other	3	0	1

Americans was a startling shift in the modal demographic characteristics of Japanese members of SGI-USA. The modal member of the older cohort is an immigrant housewife with a high school education. The modal member of the younger cohort remains female, but is a white-collar professional with a college education. She is as likely as not to have been born in the United States. Indeed, in many ways the younger cohort has come to resemble their non-Japanese fellows in SGI-USA.

These shifts signal further changes among the Japanese members of SGI-USA that will have a profound impact on the organization itself. As these younger members move into positions of leadership in SGI-USA, their religious demands, in combination with those of non-Japanese American members, are likely to guide whatever direction the organization takes in the future. If the younger cohort of Japanese members is becoming more like their non-Japanese counterparts in ways that are not merely demographic, it suggests that the deliberate process of accommodation to the American social environment described elsewhere in this volume will be complemented by more subtle forms of Americanization.

Compounding these shifts is the rising number of Japanese members who were raised in Soka Gakkai Buddhism, a change that is likely to have consequences of its own.

First and Second Generation Members

The transition from the founders to following generations is widely recognized in sociological circles as one of the most challenging developmental hurdles that sectarian movements face. Unlike the founders, whose membership in the sect expresses both the rejection of other traditions and the acceptance of a new one, those members who were born into the sect have not made an active decision to join. Consequently, second generation members do not often share their forebears' zeal for the new sect. Sectarian movements, especially those of the world-rejecting variety, run the risk of losing steam in the transition from the generation of founders to the upcoming generations of members by birth.

In fact, the data on Japanese members suggest that just such a process is occurring. While the differences are not always dramatic, the Japanese American members who were raised in Soka Gakkai score consistently lower on several indicators of involvement. Following Hammond and Machacek's analysis, let us begin with indicators of the private dimension of involvement—that is, ways of being involved that may or may not occur in the presence of other members.

Chanting is foremost among the private devotional activities performed by SGI-USA members, and the majority of all SGI-USA members report chanting twice daily as prescribed. Compared with 84 percent of Japanese converts to SGI, however, only 54 percent of those who were raised Soka Gakkai Buddhists report chanting twice daily (Table 9.3). Hardly any of the currently active members have given up chanting entirely, but we do observe a clear (and statistically significant[4]) moderating effect among those who were raised Soka Gakkai Buddhists. Alone, these statistics do not mean much, for they allow the possibility that even those who do not chant every day are involved in SGI-

---

[4] The limited number of cases in our sample may disguise significant results, especially when there are a large number of possible response categories. For this reason, we accepted the results as significant if the probability that the findings are due to random variation was lower than 0.10.

Table 9.3. Frequency of chanting (%)

Frequency	Converts	Raised SGI	All
Never	2	0	1
< 7 times a week	8	25	14
7–13 times a week	6	21	11
Twice daily	84	54	73

Chi-squared = 10.532, df = 3, p < 0.05.

USA in other ways. However, the pattern is repeated on indicators of time spent reading SGI literature.

Study, which for our purpose means reading educational material published in SGI newspapers and magazines, is a key value of Soka Gakkai Buddhists and a major component of private devotional activity. It must be kept in mind that two of the publications on which we have data are published in Japanese, thus limiting the number of American members who spend time reading them. However, even when we examine time spent reading the English language publications only, which ought to be higher for those raised in Soka Gakkai if language were the issue, we find that Japanese members who were raised in SGI spend less time reading than converts. Although weak statistically (reading the *World Tribune* approaches significance at p = 0.107; reading *Living Buddhism* fails to achieve significance at p = 0.514), this finding is consistent with other indicators of involvement, and this suggests the presence of a cohort effect.

Data on attendance at SGI events do not achieve significance. This means that those raised in SGI probably attend as often as converts do. This does not invalidate what has already been said about declining zeal, however. Attendance at worship services is often motivated by factors other than personal conviction, such as loyalty to one's family or friends. While those raised in SGI Buddhism appear to attend as often as converts, therefore, in combination with the declining zeal evidenced by the other indicators, it is likely that some at least attend for reasons other than personal

Table 9.4. Time spent reading SGI publications (%)

Hours reading	Converts	Raised SGI
World Tribune		
Never	8	14
1 hour	51	68
2–3 hours	27	18
4+ hours	14	0
Living Buddhism		
Never	29	32
1 hour	42	50
2–3 hours	23	18
4+ hours	6	0

conviction. In other ways, they are less active in the social dimension of involvement.

Japanese members who were raised in Soka Gakkai are less likely than converts to spend time talking about their religion with others and attempting to recruit new members. Converts are twice as likely as those raised in SGI to say they spend two or more hours every week talking about their faith with acquaintances (36 percent versus 18 percent). This does not mean that members raised in Soka Gakkai never speak about Buddhism with others, but they do so less frequently than do converts, which may certainly be taken as evidence of declining zeal.

It is not surprising to find, therefore, that members raised in Soka Gakkai also report being less active in efforts to recruit new members (Table 9.6). Converts are nearly twice as likely as birth

Table 9.5. Attendance at SGI-USA gatherings (%)

Hours per week	Converts	Raised SGI	All
Never	10	18	13
1 hour	14	18	16
2–3 hours	35	32	34
4+ hours	41	32	38

Table 9.6. Introducing others to SGI (%)

Degree of activity	Converts	Raised SGI	All
Very active	54	29	45
Somewhat active	32	50	39
Not active	14	21	17

Chi-squared = 4.693, df = 2, p < 0.10.

members to describe themselves as "very active" in introducing others to the faith. Members raised in Soka Gakkai are more likely to describe themselves as somewhat or not at all active in recruitment efforts.

Two final measures sum up these results nicely. In their book *Soka Gakkai in America* Hammond and Machacek develop an index of involvement that combines the private and social dimensions discussed above into a single measure.[5] This index captures nicely the pattern we have described above (Table 9.7). While most members, both converts and nonconverts, fall into the category of "general" members, Japanese members who inherited their faith are nearly three times more likely to be only marginally involved. Among converts to Soka Gakkai Buddhism, the balance tips in the opposite direction, tending instead toward "core" involvement, which means they are very active in both private and social ways.

The declining zeal for Soka Gakkai Buddhism from the founding generation to the next is, finally, reflected in members' atti-

Table 9.7. Involvement index (%)

Involvement	Converts	Raised SGI	All
Marginal	10	29	17
General	56	61	58
Core	34	11	26

Chi-squared = 7.579, df = 2, p < 0.05.

[5] Hammond and Machacek, *Soka Gakkai in America*, 64–5.

tudes about their involvement. When asked how likely it is that they might drop out of SGI-USA someday, 78 percent of the converts said they were confident that they would never stop chanting or participating in SGI-USA meetings. By comparison, 59 percent of Japanese American members who inherited their religion gave this response—still a majority, but by a much lower margin. While none of those members raised in Soka Gakkai said they were considering dropping out, they were more than twice as likely to say that they might cut down on participation in SGI activities (26 percent versus 10 percent).

These data confirm the notion that the transition from the founding generation to the first generation of members to be raised in a new sect is a process that involves declining zeal for the religion. This process has long been discussed in sociological literature on new religions, but it has rarely been documented. The reason is that most studies capture religions either as brand new religions composed exclusively of converts—many of which do not survive beyond the founding generation—or as established religions, the founding generation of which has long since passed. While the findings reported here are not surprising, the data from this small sample of Japanese American members of SGI-USA are a real sociological treasure.

It is likely that the continuing presence of new converts, both those of Japanese descent and those who are not, acts to counterbalance the cohort effect described here. Enthusiasm tends to be infectious, as anyone who has ever attended a sports event or religious revival knows. As second generation members of Soka Gakkai become more prominent in the organization in the future, however, the declining zeal found among members who were raised as Soka Gakkai Buddhists is likely to be felt. The ability of SGI-USA to sustain the commitment of second generation members will depend on a change in the meaning of involvement. Put simply, if the commitment of converts to a new religion expresses a rejection of other, more established religions, the commitment of second generation members expresses a desire to maintain an inherited tradition. That transformation of meaning can be hazardous for new religions, especially those of the world-rejecting variety. Children of converts may not wish to reject the rewards of participation in the social world, and the new religion must either accommodate their desire or run the risk of losing second generation members. Soka Gakkai, however, is far from world-rejecting—less so, in fact, in the United States than in Japan. In Soka Gakkai's willingness to accommodate the social environment and, consequently, in the successful assimilation of its Japanese members into that environment lies the transformation of meaning that is likely to sustain the commitment of Japanese American members beyond the founding generation.

Assimilation and the Meaning of Involvement

It is not uncommon for the children of immigrants to the United States to desire to fit in with the surrounding cultural environment. In some cases, this can mean rejection of the religion of their parents, especially when that religion is closely identified with ethnic identity. More often, however, the process of cultural assimilation involves a transformation of the meaning of participation in the religion. This appears to be case among Japanese members of SGI-USA who were born in the United States. The data reviewed in this section indicate that while being born and raised in the United States does not have a decisive impact on commitment to SGI-USA, it does appear to have attenuated some of the stark sectarian impulses found among members born in Japan. It also appears to have weakened the sense of ethnic cohesion, which, at least partially, accounts for the high levels of involvement among first generation immigrants.

Despite the relatively younger age of members born in the United States (median of 38 versus 51 for those born in Japan), a factor we know to be related to involvement, there are no significant differences on the index of involvement according to birthplace. That is, those born in the USA are nearly as likely as those born in Japan to be "core" members (17 percent versus 32 percent, n.s.), and what differences exist are probably due to age rather than birthplace. Interesting findings emerge, however, when we examine the individual indicators that make up the involvement index.

American-born members chant less frequently than do Japanese-born members. Compared to 82 percent of members born in Japan, only 58 percent of those born in the United States chant twice daily as prescribed (p < 0.05). This does not mean that the members born in the USA are not chanting regularly, since an additional 23 percent say they chant at least once a day, and none of them said they had stopped chanting entirely. It does show, however, that American-born members are somewhat less assiduous in their practice. There also appears a telling difference in what members chant for. American-born members are more likely to say they chant for success in their career than Japanese-born members. While this finding is easily accounted for by the age and occupational status of the two groups, it none the less points to the fact that members born in the United States attach a meaning to their involvement different from that of members born in Japan.

The amount of time spent every week at SGI-USA gatherings also shows modest, but clear differences. Compared to 43 percent of members born in Japan who say they spend four or more hours every week at SGI-USA gatherings, only 27 percent of American-born members attend meetings this often. American-born members were more likely to indicate that they spent only one hour every week at SGI-USA gatherings (30 percent versus 6 percent of Japanese-born members).

While members of both groups were nearly unanimous in denying the possibility of dropping out of SGI entirely, American-born members were more likely to say they might cut down on attendance at meetings—a finding that reinforces those above. Nearly one-fourth of all the Japanese members born in the United States said they might cut down on their attendance at SGI-USA gatherings compared to only one in ten of those born in Japan. Furthermore, those born in Japan were far more likely to state their commitment in unequivocal terms—80 percent said they would "never" stop chanting or going to group meetings compared to 55 percent of those born in the USA.

Overall, then, both groups show significant levels of commitment to Soka Gakkai, at least in that there is scant evidence that any are seriously considering dropping out. There are, however, notable differences on two indicators of involvement, with those born in the United States tending toward lower levels of involvement than those born in Japan. Why? We turn to this question now.

Part of the answer appears to lie in the sectarian impulse found among those members born in Japan. Recall that in 1991 the Nichiren Shoshu priests excommunicated the Soka Gakkai. It might be expected that members born in Japan, more used to the priestly orientation of Japanese religion, would have perceived the split as more harmful to Soka Gakkai than members born in the United States, where a lay-oriented, congregational model of religion predominates, and where the Nichiren Shoshu priests never played a very large role in Soka Gakkai. In fact, just the opposite is the case.

When asked their feelings about the schism from Nichiren Shoshu, the majority of members in both groups responded that SGI is better off. However, Japanese-born members are more likely to give this response than American-born members (67 per cent versus 56 percent, respectively). More telling, however, are the numbers who said SGI was harmed by the split. Twenty-six percent of the American-born Japanese members said SGI was harmed by the schism, while only one (2 percent) of the Japanese-born members gave this response.

One also finds divergences between the two groups in responses to questions about the influence on SGI-USA of events occurring to SGI in Japan. Surprisingly, members born in Japan are more likely than members born in the USA to say that events in Japan do not influence SGI-USA at all (35 percent versus 13 percent, $p < 0.10$). Although tests for statistical significance for these data encourage caution, the finding is consistent with attitudes about the schism reported above. We can be reasonably confident, therefore, in this finding. In short, Japanese-born members of SGI-USA are more likely to discount any effect of events in Japan on the religion in the USA, and when they assert such an effect, they are more likely to view it in a positive way. On the contrary, members born in the USA are more concerned about how events in Japan influence SGI-USA and are more likely to perceive them as potentially harmful.

These data suggest stronger sectarian views among the Japanese-born members than are to be found among their American-born counterparts. The older Japanese-born members of SGI-USA experienced first-hand the social conditions that gave rise to Soka Gakkai as a sectarian, reform-oriented, religious movement in Japan. To those members born in the United States, the social and cultural conditions to which Japanese-born members were responding in their decision to join Soka Gakkai simply do not pertain. Indeed, in other ways the American-born members express less of a connection to the Japanese heritage.

As one might expect, American-born members are much less likely to read SGI's Japanese language publications (roughly 90 percent say they never read them). This is to be expected for those who have grown up in an English-speaking country. But, in combination with other indicators of ethnic identity, the finding suggests movement away from the Japanese cultural heritage and assimilation into mainstream American culture.

The strongest evidence of such movement comes from a question asking whether respondents feel closer to people of the same ethnicity. Seventy percent of those members born in Japan said yes. By contrast, only 41 percent of the American-born members feel such a connection. Among members born in Japan, this sense of ethnic identity is manifest in relatively concentrated social networks. Half of the Japanese-born members reported that "nearly all" or "most" of their closest personal friends know each other. By contrast, 74 percent of the American-born members indicated that "only a few" or "none" of their friends know each other, indicating rather diffuse social networks.

In sum, while there does not appear to be a serious decline in commitment to Soka Gakkai Buddhism among members born in the United States, there is evidence of a decline in the amount of involvement and that decline appears to be related to a shift in the meaning of membership in SGI-USA. Members born in Japan appear to be more sectarian than their American-born counterparts, a finding that is related to a stronger sense of ethnic identity. The sectarian feelings and ethnic ties that motivate involvement among Japanese-born members, however, are decaying among those born in the USA and this results in a certain amount of decline in involvement, although not a major decline.

Taken together with data on feelings about the schism and ethnic identity, the apparent decline in involvement can be interpreted as indicative, not of a decline in commitment, but as a shift in the meaning of membership in Soka Gakkai among American-born members—a shift that is related to upward social mobility.

The Impact of Upward Mobility

Perhaps the most notable demographic shift among the Japanese American members of SGI-USA is the movement toward higher occupational status in the younger cohort. While housewives and service workers dominate the older cohort, the younger cohort is composed predominately of "new class" white-collar workers. It is reasonable to expect that the advent of the white-collar worker among Japanese members of SGI-USA will have an impact on the organization, though what that impact will be is difficult to discover on the basis of these data. Surprisingly few differences appear in indicators of involvement or social attitudes, though the differences that do appear merit discussion.

One might expect to find lower levels of involvement in SGI-USA among those members employed in white-collar occupations. Simply put, a white-collar worker's responsibilities rarely cease at the end of the workday. Success in these careers usually requires a considerable amount of self-motivated effort and continuing education outside of the workplace. In addition, the dollar value of time spent in job-related efforts tends to be much greater for white-collar workers than for housewives and laborers. These forces tend to minimize the amount of time individuals employed in white-collar occupations are able or willing to spend in voluntary activities.

This does not appear to be the case among members of SGI-USA. White-collar workers—which for our purposes includes individuals employed in professional, managerial, sales, technical, and clerical occupations—are somewhat, but not significantly, more likely be marginally involved in SGI-USA (Table 9.8). This is probably because of other factors related to both occupation and involvement. We know, for instance, that age is related to involvement. Younger members tend to be less involved than older members. Chances are, the minor differences found in involvement reflect the younger average age of the white-collar workers in the sample.

Table 9.8. Occupational prestige and involvement (%)

Involvement	White-collar	All others
Marginal	22	9
General	59	63
Core	20	29

Chi-squared 2.853, df = 2, n.s.

Notable differences appear in only one of the four major indicators that make up the involvement index—the number of friends who are members of Soka Gakkai. White-collar workers report an average of 4.8 friends who are members of Soka Gakkai compared to 6 for other members. In all likelihood, this is a function of employment outside the home. Half of all those Japanese members who are not white-collar workers are full-time homemakers. Among full-time homemakers, the average number of friends who are Soka Gakkai members rises to 8.7. Clearly, employment outside of the home affords more opportunity to develop friendships outside of Soka Gakkai.

This finding suggests that, while white-collar workers do not differ in the *extent* of their involvement, they do differ in terms of the *meaning* of involvement. To put the matter bluntly, the white-collar workers appear to have a more diverse social network and a more diffuse sense of belonging than do others in the sample. Consequently, it can be surmised that the self-identity and sense of belonging of white-collar workers is less focused on involvement in SGI-USA. Compared to others, participation in SGI-USA is thus relatively more voluntary in that there are more opportunities for involvement in other kinds of voluntary associations.

Indeed, those who are employed in white-collar occupations demonstrate greater involvement in associations outside of family and religion, such as sports clubs (25 percent versus 11 percent), hobby clubs (20 percent versus 6 percent), literary, art, or study groups (26 percent versus 11 percent), and professional societies (28 per cent versus 14 percent). Consequently, their social networks are less concentrated. When asked how many of their friends know each other, for example, white-collar workers are less likely to say "nearly all" (5 per cent versus 19 percent), and more likely to say "none" (10 percent versus 3 percent).

Furthermore, there is some evidence that white-collar workers are more likely to view their involvement in terms of participation in efforts for world peace—in other words, as an altruistic endeavor. Because of the way it was worded only twenty Japanese SGI-USA members responded to the question asking members to describe the most attractive feature of SGI-USA.[6] The responses of those who did, however, are suggestive. The most popular responses among those who are not white-collar workers were the people and friendships (17 percent) and the benefits of chanting (33 percent). White-collar workers were more likely to mention SGI's activities and goals (21 percent) and philosophy (21 percent). Given the small number of cases, we would have to be

---

[6] This question appeared in a series of questions about the conversion process. The first part of the question asked, "Apart from the teachings, can you say what originally attracted you to SGI-USA (NSA)?" The second question was as follows: "Is the original attraction still the most significant aspect of SGI-USA for you? If no, what is now the most attractive feature of the organization?" Obviously, people who were raised in SGI would have difficulty answering these questions.

cautious about placing too much emphasis on this finding. However, two further indicators of concern for social issues bolster our interpretation. White-collar workers were more likely than others to approve of religious organizations speaking out on the issue of nuclear disarmament (93 percent versus 77 percent, $p < 0.10$). They were also more likely to say they "do what is right for the environment, even when it costs more money or takes up more time" (83 percent versus 69 percent, $p < 0.05$).

It is notable that increased voluntariness has not resulted in lower levels of involvement. White-collar workers are no less involved in SGI than others. SGI-USA has been able to sustain the commitment of those whose time and energy is in the greatest demand from competing social forces such as careers and other voluntary associations, and the reason seems to be the same for ethnically Japanese white-collar workers as for non-Japanese American converts. As was found to be the case among converts to Soka Gakkai in both the United States and Great Britain, SGI's efforts to promote world peace and environmental awareness serve to sustain commitment beyond its ability to satisfy more immediate personal needs and desires.[7]

Conclusion

Sectarian movements usually form as an attempt to restore a tradition that, according to the sectarians, has fallen into apostasy. Even the most world-rejecting or other-worldly-oriented religions have a tendency, over time, to become more at home in the present social world. It has been suggested that this process of "secularization"—or becoming at home in the world—is driven, at least partly, by the very transition described above. Those members born into a sectarian movement were not given the opportunity to choose for themselves whether the demands their religion makes upon them are reasonable, especially when it comes to forgoing

[7] Hammond and Machacek, *Soka Gakkai in America*; B. Wilson and K. Dobbelaere, *A Time to Chant: The Soka Gakkai Buddhists in Britain* (Oxford: Clarendon Press, 1994).

the rewards offered by participation in the mainstream social order. Lacking their parents' zeal, they will tend to exert pressure on the movement to reduce tension with the surrounding social environment, and thus be able to enjoy some of the rewards that life in the world provides.

Furthermore, the more successful movements will eventually attract members from the more respectable social classes. This benefits the movement by conferring on it an aura of respectability. However, the presence of such people tends to put further pressure on the movement to reduce tension with the surrounding social environment. The more highly educated, professional members tend to move more rapidly into positions of leadership in the movement and, already enjoying the rewards of success in the world, will exert pressure on the movement to adapt to the surrounding environment.[8]

Immigrant religions, additionally, find it necessary to adapt to conditions in the social environment as the children of immigrants become assimilated into the surrounding culture. In the United States the adoption of English as the language of worship and accommodation to the congregational model of religious organization that predominates in the USA are two of the classic ways that immigrant religions adapt to the American social environment, and this has been no less true for Soka Gakkai.

True, this developmental model has only limited applicability to Soka Gakkai. Soka Gakkai was never very world-rejecting in the sense that it required members to abstain from the rewards of mainstream social life. It did—and to some degree still does—identify itself in opposition to the political and religious establishment in Japan as a movement of the common people. It remains concerned about the modern evils of political conflict, nuclear weapons, and environmental damage. Accusations of apostasy against the Nichiren Shoshu priesthood did not emerge until after the 1991 schism, which seems to have had other causes.[9] Even so,

[8] R. Stark and W. S. Bainbridge, *The Future of Religion: Secularization, Revival, and Cult Formation* (Berkeley: University of California Press, 1985).
[9] Hammond and Machacek, *Soka Gakkai in America*, 20–3.

only concerns about world peace and the environment had a significant impact on the character of the movement in the United States, and that concern has typically been expressed through active engagement with the social world rather than rejection of it.

Indeed, it is this unique style of inner-worldly asceticism that seems to have carried SGI-USA through these transitions without losing much in the way of the commitment of its members. Soka Gakkai affirms participation in the social world and encourages members to think of their involvement in the world as an opportunity both to improve that world and to grow spiritually. Asceticism in Soka Gakkai drives members into the mainstream social world and this makes it easier for the religion to sustain commitment beyond that resulting from either sectarian zeal or ethnic attachments. Thus, while there is evidence of a certain decline in sectarian fervor associated with the transitions described above, this has had no recognizable impact on commitment to the religion and only a little impact on actual involvement.

Finally, the data reviewed here suggest that the process of Americanization that has been noted of the organization itself in terms of its accommodation of new non-Japanese American members is taking place as well among its ethnically Japanese members. While SGI-USA rightly celebrates its ability to accommodate the needs of an ethnically diverse membership, the more uniform the cultural outlook of its members, the easier it will be for the organization to respond to their demands.

In conclusion, the accommodating stance that SGI-USA has taken with regard to the American social environment has allowed it not only to pass smoothly in that environment as a new religious supplier, but also to negotiate successfully several of the developmental hurdles over which sectarian movements often stumble and fall.

10

Organizational Isomorphism in SGI-USA

David Machacek

IN April 1997 Japan's Liberal Democratic Party (LDP) publicly acknowledged that it had misrepresented the facts of a
case in which Soka Gakkai's former president and current
spiritual figurehead, Daisaku Ikeda, was accused of raping a former
Soka Gakkai member. Soka Gakkai has existed in some tension
with the LDP for many years—a situation that can be understood
in relation to a long history of religious exclusivism in Nichiren
sects and Soka Gakkai's own anti-establishment personality.[1] For
many years the LDP has engaged in efforts to suppress Soka
Gakkai's political involvement, alleging that such involvement vio-
lated the principle of religious disestablishment and insinuating
that Soka Gakkai was attempting to establish a theocratic government in Japan. The current case, the Soka Gakkai alleges, was but
the latest instance of the LDP using the news media to spread false
rumors in an attempt to discredit Soka Gakkai. The LDP's public
acknowledgment that the facts had been misrepresented was therefore received by Soka Gakkai as a major public victory.

Whether the LDP's acquiescence will serve to vindicate Soka
Gakkai in the eye of the Japanese public remains to be seen, of
course. This is but one in a long series of controversies that have
plagued Soka Gakkai in Japan since its founding. That history,
however, raises an interesting question about the story of SGI in
the United States: Why has a religious organization that has been

---

[1] J. Stone, "Rebuking the Enemies of the Lotus: Nichirenist Exclusivism in
Historical Perspective," *Japanese Journal of Religious Studies*, 21/2–3 (1994),
231–59.

treated as a major public threat in its home country sparked so little controversy in the United States?

Two possible answers are meritorious, but tell only part of the story. The first—that social changes in the United States made it easier for new religious "suppliers" to compete in a "deregulated religious market"[2]—should not have favored Soka Gakkai over other Eastern movements such as the Unification Church and Divine Light Mission, or, for that matter, over new homespun religions such as Scientology. These religions were perceived as a threat by many in the American public and frequently subject to sensational media accounts that called their legitimacy into question—much as was the experience of Soka Gakkai in Japan. In short, the freedom to compete in a newly opened religious market did nothing to insulate new religious suppliers from captious public opinions. True, Soka Gakkai benefited from the more liberal social environment that emerged in the United States after mid-century, but judging from the experiences of other Eastern religious imports that began proselytizing American youth in this period, we would have expected Soka Gakkai to draw more attention than it did. The second answer—that Soka Gakkai's philosophy of happiness and ethic of taking responsibility for one's own life speaks to the experience of people living in a consumer-oriented culture and meritocratic society[3]—is certainly true and explains the appeal of this Buddhism to young, middle-class Americans. However, it presses the imagination to think that this quality should have protected Soka Gakkai from controversy—especially in a public long dominated by the Protestant ethic, and one that has historically been suspicious of exotic religious philosophies. The new consumerism and radical individualism

---

[2] Phillip E. Hammond and David W. Machacek, *Soka Gakkai in America: Accommodation and Conversion* (Oxford: Oxford University Press, 1999); Roger Finke and Laurence Iannaccone, "Supply-Side Explanations for Religious Change," *Annals of the American Academy of Political and Social Science*, 527 (1993), 27–39.

[3] Hammond and Machacek, *Soka Gakkai in America*; Bryan Wilson and Karel Dobbelaere, *A Time to Chant: The Soka Gakkai Buddhists in Britain* (Oxford: Clarendon Press, 1994).

extolled by Soka Gakkai stand in direct contradiction to the ethic of self-denial and moral community characteristic of Protestant culture. And Soka Gakkai's sanction of happiness and success as the visible rewards of hard work in this world opposes the traditional Protestant conception of work as a calling dedicated to the glory of God, and rewarded not on earth but in heaven. More so than some of the other new religions, which were often more austere than even conservative Protestant sects, Soka Gakkai's religious philosophy posed a direct challenge to the dominant religious culture. Why, then, did this new religion spark so little controversy?

The reason for Soka Gakkai's rather tranquil experience in the United States, I argue, lies in SGI-USA's compliance with American social institutions and a history of reforms designed to make this Japanese religion look as American as possible. To adopt the language of historian Catherine Albanese,[4] Soka Gakkai promoted a set of *extraordinary* religious beliefs and rituals very different from those of Western Christianity and Judaism. But, in doing so, it was careful not to violate *ordinary* American religion—that is, the rules and assumptions governing everyday behavior that reinforce "the bonds between members of a society, that provides social 'glue' to make people cohere."[5] By adopting the conventions of everyday culture, Soka Gakkai was implicitly expressing its intent to comply with the widely accepted rules of behaviour that govern American social life. In doing so, it established its legitimacy as a supplier of religion to the American public, or at least avoided direct challenges to its legitimacy. Thus, while many of the new religions, including some American-born sectarian movements, fended off accusations of such un-American activities as brainwashing, coercion, and child abuse, Soka Gakkai went happily about its business of spreading Nichiren Buddhism in the American public and developing an American branch of the organization.

[4] Catherine Albanese, *America: Religions and Religion*, 2nd edn. (Belmont, Calif.: Wadsworth, 1992).
[5] Ibid. 7.

Isomorphism in Religious Organizations

Over the course of its history in the United States SGI-USA has transformed itself from an organization with distinctively Japanese features to one that increasingly resembles other religious organizations in America. This process is not unique to Soka Gakkai. In fact, much sociological research has been devoted to organizational "isomorphism," or the processes whereby organizations come to share certain key features.

There are a number of reasons for organizational isomorphism.[6] State regulations may require organizations to adopt certain procedures in order to operate legally (coercive isomorphism). To qualify for government contracts, for example, contractors may be required to adopt equal opportunity employment practices. Or, manufacturers may be required to comply with workplace safety standards. There is a tendency, as well, for organizations to imitate the practices of organizations that are perceived as successful (mimetic isomorphism). Upstart technology firms might thus imitate the research and development practices of Microsoft. Furthermore, within organizational fields, some practices are considered normative (normative isomorphism). Compliance with normative practices gives an organization an air of legitimacy. Organizations that do not conform to expectations risk appearing illegitimate and thus jeopardize their chances of success in the social environment.

Because of the nature of the services they provide, religious organizations are particularly susceptible to normative pressures and thus legitimacy issues. A manufacturer of computer equipment could probably get away with idiosyncratic practices as long as the product was of reasonably good quality. The legitimacy of organizations that supply conspicuous products is thus largely dependent on the quality of the thing being produced. The quality

---

[6] P. J. DiMaggio and W. W. Powell, "The Iron Cage Revisited: Institutional Isomorphism and Collective Rationality in Organizational Fields," in Powell and DiMaggio (eds.), *The New Institutionalism in Organizational Analysis* (Chicago: University of Chicago Press, 1991).

of services provided by a religious organization, however, is not as easy to evaluate as computer equipment. How is one to tell whether one religion's beliefs are more or less true than another's? Any new religion may be subject to labeling by religious zealots as "false" religions, but such imputations are relatively feeble in a contest of "my beliefs versus yours," especially under conditions of religious disestablishment. More robust are questions about the legitimacy of a religious organization's practices. Thus, the anticult movement commonly attempts to raise the public ire, not by exposing the exotic beliefs held by different groups, but by accusing such groups of engaging in practices that violate expectations of how religious organizations should behave. We commonly find accusations of child abuse, brainwashing, coercion, or financial dishonesty in the literature of the anti-cult movement. In the contest of religions it is easier to discredit an organization's practices than it is to discredit the beliefs its members profess, especially in a society that upholds religious freedom as a positive value. In other words, the legitimacy of the organization is less dependent on the quality of the product and more dependent on the way it is being produced. The less conspicuous the results of an organization's procedures, the more important it is to the organization's well-being that those procedures comply with widely accepted expectations and norms.

Considerations of legitimacy are particularly important to new religions. Barring a major public scandal, religious firms with an established reputation, such as the Methodist or Lutheran Churches, are unlikely to succumb to questions about the legitimacy of their practices. Indeed, some misguided soul who tried to portray one of these mainline denominations as a "dangerous cult" would probably be dismissed as mentally ill. To new religions, however, innuendoes and suspicions can be devastating. As the "new kid in town," even minor differences in appearance or behavior can cause the religion to be cast off as strange, odd, or threatening.

New religions can elude challenges to their legitimacy by simply adopting the formal structures and organizational practices of organizations that are already accepted as legitimate in the society. John Meyer and Brian Rowan express the effect of compliance eloquently:

> By designing a formal structure that adheres to the prescriptions of myths in the external institutional environment, an organization demonstrates that it is acting on collectively valued purposes in a proper and adequate manner . . . The incorporation of institutionalized elements provides an account . . . of activities that protects the organization from having its conduct questioned.[7]

Thus, it is not uncommon for import religions to develop a professional clergy and formal worship services where no such practices existed in the country of origin. Such remedial concessions as the adoption of English as the language of worship, Sunday worship services and Sunday schools, and a voluntary congregational form of organization have been recognized as some of the classic means by which religious imports adapt to the American social environment.[8] Similar changes are readily observed in SGI-USA.

Isomorphic Changes in SGI-USA

The first American chapters of Soka Gakkai were organized in 1960, following shortly upon the election of Daisaku Ikeda as the movement's third president. Inspired by the extraordinary growth of Soka Gakkai in Japan in the two decades following World War II, Ikeda envisioned the spread of Nichiren Buddhism throughout the world—mainly in the democratic societies of America and Western Europe. Masayasu Sadanaga, a recent immigrant to the United States from Japan, responded to the call for *kosen-rufu* (the spread of Nichiren Buddhism) in the United States and organized the few adherents of Soka Gakkai already present in the United

[7] J. Meyer and B. Rowan, "Institutionalized Organizations: Formal Structure as Myth and Ceremony," in Powell and DiMaggio (eds.), *The New Institutionalism in Organizational Analysis*, 50.

[8] R. S. Warner, "Work in Progress toward a New Paradigm for the Sociological Study of Religion in the United States," *American Journal of Sociology*, 98 (1993), 1044–93.

States into the first American chapters. Ikeda's visit to the United States later that year marked the foundation of the Nichiren Shoshu Academy (NSA), which, after several name changes, is now Soka Gakkai International-USA (or SGI-USA), in Santa Monica, California.

The history of Soka Gakkai in the United States is a dual one. Although it is primarily as a religion of converts from mainline American denominations that SGI-USA has been of interest to American scholars, it should be kept in mind that the story begins with Soka Gakkai as the religion practiced by some Japanese immigrants to the United States. Kerry Mitchell and I take up the story of Soka Gakkai as an immigrant religion in Chapter 9 of this volume, but it deserves mention here if only to illustrate how different the story of SGI-USA might have been had it taken a different developmental path.

The early members, mostly the Japanese wives of American military men, were recent immigrants to the United States, and relied heavily on the Japanese organization for both practical guidance and financial support. Under the leadership of Sadanaga, who had come to the United States to study at an American university, these founders built an organization with recognizably Japanese characteristics. The polity was hierarchical, with leaders being appointed to office on the basis of personal mentor–disciple relationships. It also maintained the patriarchal disposition of the organization in Japan, in which women are excluded from holding most offices and organizational activities are directed from above. Indeed, SGI-USA's activities during this period often pointed to the Japanese homeland. SGI-USA organized mass pilgrimages to Japan to visit the head Nichiren Shoshu temple and worship the *Dai-Gohonzon*—the ancient scroll inscribed by Nichiren—enshrined there. Until temples were built to attract Nichiren Shoshu priests to the United States, new converts either had to travel to Japan or wait until a priest visited the United States to receive their personal copy of the *Gohonzon*—in a ceremony by which converts become full members. For this reason—and despite its distinctive lay orientation—Soka Gakkai in this early phase of development endeavored to build temples in major American cities and recruited priests from Japan to serve its American members.

Within a few short years, however, the growing presence of non-Japanese American converts stimulated a series of reforms. According to one estimate, the proportion of Japanese members in the American organization dropped from 96 percent at the time of its founding in 1960 to about 30 percent in 1970.[9] As early as 1963 some local meetings were being conducted in English rather than Japanese in order to accommodate new American recruits and converts. Over time such Japanese customs as removing one's shoes before entering the gathering place, kneeling on the floor during worship, and sitting in sex-segregated groups gave way to the more American conventions of wearing shoes inside, mixed seating, and sitting in rows of folding chairs. Transliterations of the *gongyo*—the chant recited by believers in worship—were provided for English-speaking members along with explanations of the meaning of the various prayers. Even the organization's name (Nichiren Shoshu Academy at that time), noted Jane Hurst, provided "an easy to pronounce acronym, NSA, which sounds very American."[10] Indeed, the organization's leader, Masayasu Sadanaga, changed his own name to George Williams in 1972— the name being chosen because of the frequency with which these names appeared in the Los Angeles telephone directory. Although replicating the Japanese organization originally, then, the history of SGI-USA exposes an ongoing effort to Americanize its image.

In addition to practical changes needed to accommodate American converts, SGI-USA has effected several reforms aimed at reducing tension with the surrounding social environment. In 1975 the foundation of Soka Gakkai International, headquartered in Tokyo, provided not only a formal structure to coordinate overseas expansion, but also a means of distancing these overseas organizations from Soka Gakkai's political turmoil at home. The Komeito—

---

[9] G. Williams, *NSA Seminar Report 1968–71* (Santa Monica, Calif.: World Tribune Press, 1972).

[10] "The Nichiren Shoshu Soka Gakkai in America: The Ethos of a New Religious Movement", Temple University Ph.D. diss., 1980, 164.

a political party founded by Soka Gakkai in 1965—became the source of international scandal as allegations of despotic intentions on the part of the Soka Gakkai surfaced in the Japanese media. Although the nascent organization in the United States still relied heavily on guidance and, presumably, financial support from the organization in Japan, formal separation reduced the risk of tension being transferred from Japan to the overseas organizations. In addition to insulating the fledgling organization in the United States from media scandal, formal independence from the parent organization stimulated a sense of self-identity in SGI-USA. Symbolically at least, by the late 1970s SGI-USA had left the nest.

The cult controversy in the United States in the 1970s and 1980s provided further incentive to Americanize SGI-USA. Soka Gakkai leaders watched and learned from other religions of Eastern origin, whose practices were at odds with mainstream American culture. Sudden changes in the behavior of young Americans who converted to these religions seemed to invite suspicion of psychological malady among converts, or even worse, accusations that these religions were brainwashing recruits. SGI-USA leaders paid attention to the negative media many of the new religions were receiving. Alert to the destructive potential of such rumors and suspicions, whatever their foundation in fact, from the experience of Soka Gakkai in Japan, leaders in the American organization sought to avoid undue public attention.

One of the first reforms made in this regard was to cease high-visibility recruitment practices and adopt a more low-key style of recruitment. Nichiren himself had suggested that, while effective in societies where his brand of Buddhism competed with other Buddhist sects, the combative style of recruitment *shakubuku* might not be appropriate in societies where Buddhism was not well known.[11] For such situations, he prescribed a less assertive recruitment method called *shoju*. In the mid-1970s it was this less aggressive style of recruitment that SGI-USA adopted. In favor of approaching strangers during *shakubuku* campaigns on the street,

[11] Stone, "Rebuking the Enemies of the Lotus."

debating religion with them, and then coaxing them to attend a Soka Gakkai meeting, SGI-USA members were encouraged to share the benefits they were experiencing from their practice with family members and friends in the hope that they would take an interest in learning more.

Additionally, by the late 1970s SGI-USA had ceased high-visibility public relations practices such as sponsoring parades and national conventions. Previously, SGI-USA sponsored frequent parades celebrating Buddhist pride, and even maintained a standing marching band and drum corps that could be assembled on short notice to participate in high-profile events. Yearly national conventions drew thousands to celebrate the Buddhist spirit. Indeed, one of the last such events was held in conjunction with the American bicentennial celebrations in Boston, New York, and Philadelphia—the theme, "200 Years from Now," evidencing as well the attempt to Americanize SGI-USA's identity and image.[12] However, such practices were stopped by the end of the 1970s.

In favor of high-profile events, SGI-USA invested its energy in endeavors less likely to attract public scrutiny. While marching and concert bands were maintained as part of SGI-USA's culture division, from the 1980s to the present they have been more likely to perform for private audiences in SGI-USA sponsored venues. The foundation of the Boston Research Center for the 21st Century, the Florida Culture Center, and Soka University of America in the 1990s gave SGI-USA a means of being involved in American public life, and thus to spread the message of happiness and peace through devotion to the Lotus Sutra, but through activities that resemble those of American mainline denominations.

Internally, as well, reforms in the organization's structure and the makeup of leadership reflect SGI-USA's ongoing effort to fit into the American social environment. In the 1980s SGI-USA ceased the more traditional practice of appointing leadership

---

[12] Hurst, "Nichiren Shoshu Soka Gakkai," 164.

positions on the basis of personal mentor–disciple relationships. Leaders were instead selected on the basis of demonstrated commitment to the religion and specific skills and abilities—a move, in other words, toward the rational bureaucratic model that predominates in American organizations, including most denominational hierarchies. In accordance with changing American gender roles, SGI-USA opened leadership positions to women. Additionally, there was a shift in organizational focus away from the national hierarchy and toward local groups and community centers. Instead of activities being directed from above, local groups were given greater autonomy to decide on activities according to the specific needs and interests of members. This change in focus from the national organization to the local group suggests movement toward the congregational model that characterizes most American religious organizations.

The process has been ongoing, but SGI-USA members see President Ikeda's visit to the United States in 1990 as a major milestone in this shift toward congregationalism. Although in close temporal proximity with the schism between Soka Gakkai and the Nichiren Shoshu priests, Ikeda's visit seems to have been prompted primarily by tensions that had emerged between members and some SGI-USA leaders. For some time SGI-USA's official policy had been to give local organizations maximum autonomy. But this was not always the case in practice. Some leaders feared that, without direction from above, autonomous local groups risked contamination by other religious ideologies, particularly those of the "New Age" variety. According to some, a stronger hand in leadership was therefore required to keep meetings focused on the teachings of Nichiren. Some members objected, however. Their objection was not to the desire to promote Nichiren Buddhism exclusive of other religious beliefs. Instead, these members objected to the way leadership was being exercised in SGI-USA. Strict direction from a religious hierarchy offended the sensibilities of American members accustomed to congregationalism, which gives rank and file members considerable influence in the way things are done in the local organizations.[13] In response, President Ikeda came to the United States and, in a televised broadcast to SGI-USA members, reiterated SGI-USA's independence from the organization in Japan and the importance of the Americanization process.

Among his major themes was that "all members are equal in front of the *Gohonzon*."[14] He was implying that the SGI-USA organization must become more democratic. He stated that the organization had become rigid and authoritarian: "A true leader is someone who protects his members, praising them and being tolerant toward them. In contrast, leaders who exploit their positions in the organization, rebuking people and acting in a high-handed manner, not only cause the Buddha's children to suffer, but make causes for their own suffering in the future as well."[15] He urged change to a more participatory organization. He wanted to open the group to society, so that there no longer should be any discrimination between members and non-members. In this way the leadership would be free to respond to the needs of members and the needs of society. One leader told Jane Hurst that "as the walls came down we could re-define SGI-USA as an organization and our place in American society." In any case the reformation of SGI was begun before the split occurred.[16]

It is not clear whether this opening up of SGI was a cause of the split with the priesthood almost a year later or an effect of already increasing tensions. Certainly, President Ikeda's decision to follow through on his push for a more democratic SGI would have sent a clear message to the priesthood that hierarchical authority was not something SGI would accept. Whatever the case, the 1991 schism further liberated SGI-USA from its Japanese heritage and fuelled the Americanization process. The priesthood never played a large

[13] This interpretation is based on telephone interviews with SGI-USA members, conducted as a follow-up to the 1997 survey by Phillip Hammond and myself.

[14] Daisaku Ikeda, "Become a Model for the Rest of the World," *Seikyo Times*, 344 (Mar. 1990), 7.

[15] Ibid.

[16] For the information about Ikeda's visit to the USA in 1990, I am indebted to Jane Hurst.

role in SGI-USA apart from formal ceremonial observances, but the obligation to support the temples and dependence on priests— trained exclusively in Japan—for such services as receiving the *Gohonzon*, weddings, and funerals amounted to an umbilical cord that tied SGI-USA to Japan. With that cord severed, and with the sanction of the international leadership, SGI-USA was freer to develop autonomously. The SGI charter adopted shortly thereafter in 1995 formalized the policy of decentralization. Article 6 reads, "SGI shall respect the independence and autonomy of its constituent organizations in accordance with the conditions prevailing in each country."[17]

Finally, the changing demographics of SGI-USA leadership foreshadow the direction of any future reforms. It can be assumed that, at the beginning, the leadership of SGI-USA was almost exclusively Japanese, as was the membership. Based on the 1997 survey, which includes a large number of people who hold leadership positions, nearly half of the national leaders today are non-Japanese. While Japanese members were more likely to indicate that they have held such positions in the past, the non-Japanese members in the sample expressed greater willingness to accept these leadership positions if given the opportunity in the future. This suggests that those Japanese American members most likely to hold national leadership positions have already done so, and thus that American converts are likely to dominate SGI-USA leadership in the future. Given the growing presence of both non-Japanese converts and second generation Japanese American members in positions of leadership, it is very likely that the Americanization process will continue unabated.

Already some changes that indicate a further shift toward congregationalism are taking place. At this time voluntary "ministers of ceremony" fill the roles formerly played by the priests in the conduct of weddings, funerals, and the conferring of *Gohonzons*. Given the emphasis on individual growth through personal practice and

[17] R. Eppsteiner, *The Soka Gakkai International: Religious Roots, Early History, and Contemporary Development* (Cambridge, Mass.: Soka Gakkai International-USA, 1997), 22.

study, which reduces the need for a specially trained clergy, such volunteers fill the gap in ceremonial leadership left by the schism, at least temporarily. It is unlikely, however, that this will be a permanent solution. The membership of SGI-USA is composed overwhelmingly of middle-class professionals with, presumably, only a limited amount of time available to spend in voluntary activities. Although the pool of potential volunteers is broadened by the fact that SGI-USA is now open to the possibility of women filling ceremonial roles, most of these women, as discovered in our 1997 survey of members, are also employed in full-time occupations. With the exception of some national full-time offices, SGI-USA relies exclusively on volunteer leaders. The need to fill ceremonial in addition to administrative roles with volunteers thus places an additional burden upon members, who, judging from their occupational profile and involvement in voluntary activities outside of SGI-USA, are already very busy. It is impossible to predict how long such voluntary leaders will be able or willing to respond to the demand for services, but it seems inevitable that this demand will eventually overwhelm the availability of volunteers to provide them, especially if the organization experiences future spurts of growth. Coordinating the activities of a religious congregation and providing religious services to its constituent members requires a considerable amount of time, specialized skill, and knowledge. Most religious organizations—including those that make no formal distinction between laity and clergy—eventually find it necessary to employ full-time leaders. It is likely, therefore, that the current voluntary ministers of ceremony represent a step toward the development of a professional clergy, and thus a further move in the direction of congregationalism.[18]

---

[18] In conversations with me, SGI-USA leaders have indicated strong resistance to the idea of a professional clergy in SGI-USA and to the notion that the current "ministers of ceremony" represent a step in this direction. That objection is based both on recent experiences with what SGI perceives as a corrupt priesthood and on ideological reasons that amount to a "priesthood of believers." My position is not that SGI-USA *should* develop a professional clergy, but that this may become a sociological necessity for the reasons cited above.

This brief account of the organizational change in SGI-USA illustrates a clear and ongoing process of isomorphic change. Founded originally by Japanese members present in the United States, it is understandable that SGI-USA would originally replicate the Japanese model. Over time, however, the organization has changed in ways that make it look more American. In addition to the growing presence of American converts, who now constitute about 75 percent of all members in the United States, the organization itself—its practices and structure—has changed, assimilating American cultural institutions in order to reduce tension with the surrounding social environment.

The Consequences of Isomorphism in SGI-USA

SGI-USA has not been immune to legitimacy challenges, but compared to some other new religions of Eastern origin in the United States SGI-USA's experience of legitimacy problems has been minimal. Most of these challenges have come from disgruntled ex-members who criticize the way authority is exercised and finances directed in the organization—concerns echoed by some currently active members in the 1997 survey. This suggests at least some internal pressure by American converts for greater control by local members, and thus for conformity with the congregational form that dominates American religious organizations.

Media coverage of the religion's activity has been sparse. There was some controversy in the 1980s about SGI's decision to build an American branch of Soka University in Los Angeles, but it was short-lived, and the university was built. Only one of the several manuscripts produced by American scholars entertained the possibility that Soka Gakkai was a potentially dangerous religion, and that book—James White's *Soka Gakkai and Mass Society*[19]—was about Soka Gakkai in Japan during the period when the religion's aggressive recruitment practices and involvement in politics caused considerable controversy among the Japanese public. SGI-USA

---

[19] (Stanford, Calif.: Stanford University Press, 1970).

has been typically open to scholarly inquiry and even receptive to the kinds of criticism that have been raised in these treatments. Indeed, SGI leaders pay close attention to what scholars have written about the religion and use these academic sources as a mirror to assess the religion's appearance to outsiders, making adjustments as necessary to avoid undue suspicion.

Even in the anti-cult movement literature SGI-USA has been largely ignored as a potentially dangerous "cult." This is probably because the people most likely to raise concerns—the family and friends of those who convert to Soka Gakkai Buddhism—have generally not done so. While most converts to SGI-USA say that family members or friends were skeptical about their decision to join Soka Gakkai at first, most of them also say that the skepticism passed quickly. Some even report that people who at first raised concerns that the converts had joined a "cult" eventually tried chanting themselves. Conversion to Soka Gakkai did not require dramatic or sudden changes in the behavior of American converts. With the exception of a daily regimen of chanting, which is usually done privately, converts went about their daily lives as usual, only perhaps with a greater sense of self-confidence and optimism. In brief, there was nothing about the conversion process that would have indicated to people close to the converts that anything untoward was happening.

One consequence of isomorphism, therefore, was that SGI-USA has been relatively immune to the kinds of prejudices that often plague new religions. Despite its exotic philosophy and ritual, SGI-USA adopted organizational practices that give the religion a very American appearance. And outward appearance is everything to organizations that supply such an inconspicuous product as religious faith. By Americanizing its image and adopting a low-profile public relations policy, SGI-USA was able to limit public exposure and thus to exert greater control over what the public saw and heard of the religion. This meant that if non-members learned anything about the religion, it was probably through friendly sources such as an SGI-USA member, an event sponsored by SGI-USA, or one of SGI-USA's own publications.

David Machacek

Limited exposure in the public media, combined with easily accessible sources of information provided by SGI-USA itself, has given the appearance of openness to examination, while at the same time maintaining considerable control over what the public sees. Thus has SGI avoided challenges to its legitimacy as a competitor in the American religious market.

A second consequence, related to the first, has been SGI-USA's ability to recruit new members from America's middle class. As SGI-USA Americanized its image, the somewhat marginal converts observed by David Snow in the late 1960s and early 1970s[20] gave way to the predominately well-educated and professional middle-class converts discovered in our 1997 survey of members.[21] In 1997, 43 percent of converts to SGI-USA had achieved at least a bachelor's degree, compared to 26 percent of the American public. Converts to SGI-USA were twice as likely as the public at large to have completed a graduate or professional degree (19 percent versus 9 percent, respectively). Their occupational profile mirrors educational achievement. Forty-five percent of SGI-USA converts are employed in professional, managerial, or administrative occupations compared to 29 percent of the American public. Compared to 24 percent of the American public, only 7 percent of converts to SGI-USA are employed in blue-collar occupations.

The potential cost of deviance can be very high for people employed in competitive occupations. The requirements of some new religions to wear distinctive clothing, live communally, maintain a regimented diet, evangelize co-workers, or forgo mainstream employment altogether can raise the cost of joining a religion so high as to be prohibitive to people with an investment in the mainstream social order. But nothing about the behavior or appearance of Soka Gakkai members would cue onlookers to deviance from the mainstream culture. Instead of rejecting American culture and social life as a potential threat to members'

[20] D. Snow, *Shakubuku: A Study of the Nichiren Shoshu Buddhist Movement in America, 1960–75* (New York: Garland, 1993).
[21] Hammond and Machacek, *Soka Gakkai in America*.

faith, Soka Gakkai's philosophy of personal empowerment and happiness encourages members to be successful, even exemplary, in their careers and interpersonal relationships. Whether the practice "works" in terms of helping members to be more successful in achieving their relationship and career goals—as the religion advertises—is beyond our capacity to judge. It is certain, however, that by accommodating ordinary American culture, SGI-USA minimized the cost of conversion and thus became a reasonable alternative for middle-class Americans with potential for upward social mobility.

This approach to mainstream social life not only makes conversion to Soka Gakkai a reasonable alternative for middle-class Americans, it no doubt also helps to explain the religion's appeal. That is, instead of rejecting the surrounding the social world, Soka Gakkai embraces it and even endorses its practice as a means of being happy and successful in this world. Thus, as has been pointed out elsewhere, Soka Gakkai confers religious meaning and moral sanction on the ethic of success and the spirit of consumerism experienced by members of both the American and British middle classes.[22]

Conclusion

Clearly some isomorphic changes, such as reforms in the organization's structure and means of ascent to leadership, may be mostly cosmetic—more a ceremonial performance expressing compliance with social expectations than a change in the way things actually get done. Other changes, such as SGI-USA's method of recruitment and changes in the conduct of worship services, represent real reforms in practice. In either case, the consequence of these reforms is to give SGI-USA an appearance of legitimacy and respectability, which reduces the likelihood that this new religion will be subject to scrutiny by potentially antagonistic or hostile agents. By complying with institutionalized norms of organized

---

[22] Ibid.; Wilson and Dobbelaere, *A Time to Chant*.

religious practice, SGI-USA established itself as having a rightful place in American society. Isomorphic change insured the success of SGI-USA, at least in the sense that it came to be accepted as a legitimate competitor in the religious market. Indeed, the organization's respectable image partially accounts for this new religion's ability to attract and retain decidedly middle-class American converts.

Two factors—the schism from the Nichiren Shoshu priesthood and the growing presence of non-Japanese converts and second generation children of Japanese immigrants—foretell the further Americanization of SGI-USA. Although SGI-USA remains tied to the international headquarters in Tokyo, the headquarters serves primarily as a communications center, exercising little influence over operations in the various national organizations. The severance of relations with the priesthood, therefore, had the effect of furthering the autonomy of SGI-USA. This, combined with the growing presence of members not born in Japan in positions of leadership, suggests that the isomorphic processes described in this chapter will continue, though it is difficult to forecast what specific changes might yet come.

11

Socially Inclusive Buddhists in America

David W. Chappell

I N the last twenty years Soka Gakkai has become the largest and most racially diverse Buddhist organization in North America.[1] While various studies have focused on its national policies and activities, none has examined the details of how this growth took place in individual regions. To fill in the picture, this chapter reviews the different trajectories taken by Soka Gakkai in three major centers: Los Angeles, where Soka Gakkai first began conducting meetings in English; Chicago, where African Americans first embraced Soka Gakkai in large numbers; and Miami, where Hispanics have recently emerged as a dominant force.[2]

In October 1960 the third Soka Gakkai president, Daisaku Ikeda, first visited America and appointed local leaders in major cities. George Williams (also known as Masayasu Sadanaga), who had arrived in America in 1958 and accompanied Ikeda on his tour, was confirmed as national director in 1963. While Ikeda administered the overall organization from Japan, under the dynamic leadership of Williams, in America Soka Gakkai attracted a diverse membership, which persists to this day. During this growth Ikeda reshaped the meaning of *kosen-rufu* from simply

---

[1] There may be many more Americans who have been influenced by and identify with Zen or Vipassana Buddhism, but there is no other Buddhist organization in America with as many active members as Soka Gakkai (presently called Soka Gakkai International-USA, or SGI-USA).

[2] For the methodological details and background for this research, see my article "Racial Diversity in the Soka Gakkai," in Christopher Queen (ed.), *Engaged Buddhism in the West* (Boston: Wisdom, 2000), 184–217.

propagating traditional Buddhism[3] to achieving world peace through global outreach in education, culture, religion, and diplomacy. By the mid-1990s Soka Gakkai had split from the exclusivistic priesthood of the Nichiren Shoshu sect and established more participatory lay leadership methods that changed Soka Gakkai from the model of a charismatic cult to a denomination (SGI-USA). While many other Buddhist groups also have organized local leadership, national evangelism, a global vision, and inclusive leadership methods, none have recruited a membership as diverse or as large as Soka Gakkai. The local histories examined here demonstrate that one of the key strengths of SGI-USA is its ability to organize individuals from a wide variety of ethnic and cultural backgrounds into an organic whole.

The American Experience

To understand the achievements of Soka Gakkai in America, it is helpful to place it within its cultural context. Until thirty-five years ago most American Buddhists were of Asian ancestry and most of these were Japanese.[4] The two largest Buddhist groups today are the Buddhist Churches of America (BCA), based on Jodo Shinshu, and Soka Gakkai. Although both groups originated in Japan, the BCA remains at least 90 percent ethnic Japanese,[5] whereas SGI-

[3] *Kosen-rufu* literally means to "widely teach and spread" Buddhism.

[4] Based on United States Census data, the US population of those with Japanese ancestry increased dramatically after 1900. In 1930 the majority of Japanese ancestry in America were still foreign-born (70,477 to 68,357), but by 1940 most were born in the USA (47,305 were foreign-born and 79,642 were born in the USA).

[5] The largest Buddhist organization in America outside of SGI-USA is the Jodo Shinshu (Buddhist Churches of America), but after a century in America it remains almost entirely Japanese (Kenneth Tanaka, "Issues of Ethnicity in the Buddhist Church of America," in Queen (ed.), *Engaged Buddhism in the West*).

[6] Although most immigrant Buddhist groups in the United States have remained cultural enclaves tied to their country of origin—whether China, Japan, Korea, Vietnam, Laos, Sri Lanka, or Thailand—Zen and Tibetan Buddhism have been exceptions. While the leadership of these two latter groups are often Japanese and Tibetan respectively, their membership largely

USA is the only American Buddhist group with a large number of African Americans and Hispanics (who represent over 30 percent of local leadership).[6] Since the 1960s Buddhism in America has also evolved among European Americans, especially Zen, Vipassana, and Tibetan Buddhism.[7] Jan Nattier recently outlined three kinds of American Buddhists: ethnic, evangelical, and elite.[8] She described Soka Gakkai as the major example of evangelical Buddhism, while noting that

The smallest degree of change between the form of Buddhism practiced in the homeland and in North America is observed in Evangelical Buddhism, perhaps because the only real representative of this category, the Soka Gakkai, has been subject to the tightest control by its missionary-oriented Japanese headquarters. In this group, adjustments seem to be taking place only on the most superficial level, as American songs and images drawn from American history are mobilized to serve quite unaltered religious ends.[9]

Whether or not this claim is justified will require more detailed study. It is clear, however, that there is one way in which SGI-USA

consists of educated middle-class European Americans. There are virtually no African Americans, Latin Americans, or Asian Americans from other parts of Asia to be found in these groups. For data on the number of African American and Hispanic local leaders in SGI-USA, see my forthcoming article "Racial Diversity in the Soka Gakkai," in which I analyze the ethnic identity of 2,449 local SGI-USA district leaders in eight cities and found 654 African Americans (26.7%) and 139 Hispanics (5.7%).

[7] The history by Rick Fields *How the Swans Came to the Lake: A Narrative History of Buddhism in America* (Boston: Shambala, 1981, 3rd edn. 1992) omits the story of the arrival and history of Jodo Shinshu in America, even though at that time it was the largest Buddhist group in the United States. The book compiled and edited by Don Morreale *The Complete Guide to Buddhist America*, 2nd edn. (Boston: Shambala, 1998) also deliberately chose to ignore Jodo Shinshu and SGI. Both authors have made marvelous contributions by collecting many obscure fragments from different parts of the country and showing how American Buddhism is not centrally organized or coordinated, so that Buddhists of one type can easily be isolated from others.

[8] Jan Nattier, "Who is a Buddhist? Charting the Landscape of Buddhist America," in Charles S. Prebish and Kenneth K. Tanaka (ed.), *The Faces of Buddhism in America* (Berkeley: University of California Press, 1998). I am indebted to Jan Nattier and Paul David Numrich for reading an earlier draft of this chapter and making several important suggestions for improvement.

[9] Nattier, "Who is a Buddhist?", 193.

is not like Soka Gakkai in Japan, nor like any other form of American Buddhism—namely, SGI-USA membership is more culturally diverse and multiracial than any other form of Buddhism either in Japan or in America.

Most studies of SGI-USA focus on how individuals converted. Each member can tell with enthusiasm the exact day when he or she received the *Gohonzon* and formally began his/her practice. Most members have a vivid story of how their practice started, often involving transformation in their personal lives through chanting and the personal encouragement of their sponsors. Both were crucial: the chanting and the human guidance. To understand any of the 45,000 active SGI members in America, one has to begin with their personal experience of transformation.

Soka Gakkai meetings and literature are filled with the sharing of personal experiences. Of course, there are miracles. And members thrill each other in exchanging stories about sudden reversals and unexpected windfalls as soon as they began their practice. But more pervasive and more constant is the daily miracle of transforming their "stumbling blocks into stepping stones." At the heart of this transformation are things to do (daily chanting) and a place to do it (before the *Gohonzon*), both of which are tangible embodiments of teachings about the interpenetration of all things and the accessibility of true reality (*ichinen sanzen*) in the act of chanting and grappling with life's difficulties.

The teachings of Chinese Tiantai affirm the idea that in one's problems can be found their resolution. The chanting of unintelligible syllables from a foreign language may seem mechanical, but it is not done mindlessly. One's problems are brought into the chanting, and with chanting comes the requirement to take ownership of problems as one's own karma. While seeing problems as one's own karma—a self-created hell—Soka Gakkai asserts that if one had the power to create this hell, then one also has the power to transform it. As a result, problems can point to potential benefits and become an occasion to find enlightenment. This transformation takes effort and a change of perspective, however, so guidance is needed and received through daily support from caring

SGI sponsors. In sum, the four ingredients for this alchemical transformation are a problem, a realistic but positive philosophy, personal guidance from other members, and focused but energizing practice.

In common with other religions in Japan that pray for practical benefits (*genze riyaku*), Soka Gakkai also teaches that practice will bring benefits (*kudoku*). This does not mean simply to make problems go away, but to enable people to develop their own faith and ability to change their life condition. Since a person is the cause of his/her karma, a person also has the power to change it. Those SGI members who give guidance[10] remember that they cannot solve the problems of other members and do not try to do so. Instead, they give practitioners encouragement to keep striving with their problems and to see their problems both as their karma and as a gift to bring about a practical benefit (*kudoku*). The secret at the heart of Soka Gakkai is the discovery that, through practice, individuals participate in a universal reality that unleashes their personal creativity to transform life's problems into blessings, to "change poison into medicine" (*hendoku iyaku*). This is the fuel that feeds the life of Soka Gakkai.

The personal support given to new members is part of the organizational genius of Soka Gakkai. Each is assigned to a group of five or six people who are responsible for almost daily contact, encouragement, and guidance. Several groups are organized into a district of twenty to forty people who meet monthly in someone's living room and include up to five leaders working as a team: a men's chief, women's chief, young men's chief, young women's chief, and a guidance leader. One of these serves as the district leader, often the men's chief, but the whole team provides mutual support and continuity as leaders change and vacancies arise. Although the group and district are the centers of personal practice, several districts are organized into a larger unit called a chapter. During Ikeda's first trip to the United States, he organized

---

[10] For practical illustrations of the kind of guidance that SGI leaders give, see Satoru Izumi, *Guidelines of Faith* (Tokyo: Nichiren Shoshu International Center, 1980).

several districts and one chapter (in Los Angeles) by appointing leaders who were to be responsible for recruiting and organizing members. As membership grows, several chapters are then organized into larger and larger units to form a pyramid topped by the national headquarters in Santa Monica, California.[11]

SGI-USA's earliest and fastest development took place in areas with the largest number of people with Japanese ancestry—namely, Hawaii and California. In 1997 the total number of district leaders in San Francisco (599), Los Angeles (458), and Hawaii (386) was 1,443. If, as there is good reason to believe, there is one district leader for every twelve to thirteen members, then this number represents about 18,000 active members.[12] By contrast, major urban centers such as Chicago (160), Boston (180), Atlanta (67), Philadelphia (120), and Miami (64) had a smaller number of district leaders. The exceptions to the pattern of SGI growth following Japanese immigration are the large number of district leaders in New York (465) and Washington, DC (336).

Los Angeles[13]

Many Japanese moved to California as laborers in the early part of the century and established themselves in farming or business, but

[11] Administration above the chapter level has fluctuated as membership has grown. In 1997 several chapters constituted a headquarters, several headquarters made up a territory, and two or more territories became a joint territory. In 1998 the level of headquarters was eliminated, the territory was renamed an area, and the joint territory was renamed a region. For example, New York and Los Angeles each have four regions, the former with 465 district leaders and the latter with 458 district leaders.

[12] Active membership is very difficult to determine in religious organizations unless a very strict accounting is made of members. There were only two cases in which I could compare the total number of members in local districts with the number of district leaders. One was in the report from New York, which gave a ratio of one district leader for every thirteen members in 1997. The other was the data collected by Stephen Bonnell from south Florida, which indicated one district leader for every twelve members. Consequently, I have used the figure of 12.5 members for each district leader.

[13] It is difficult to give sufficient thanks to the many hours of staff time and thoughtful assistance given to me during my various visits to the Santa Monica headquarters. I am indebted to General Director Fred Zaitsu and General

lost everything because of internment during World War II. In the 1950s *nisei* (second generation Japanese Americans) gradually rebuilt their lives in cities like Los Angeles and San Francisco, where they met Japanese Soka Gakkai members who were often wives of American servicemen. Several *nisei* had also joined the American armed forces during the late 1940s and 1950s and went to Japan, where they married Japanese wives who were Soka Gakkai members. Some of these *nisei* then became interpreters between Japanese-speaking practitioners and English-speaking Americans, and greatly assisted in the spread of Soka Gakkai in America.

The number of Japanese leaders in SGI, both first generation and *nisei* combined, is larger in California than in the other above-mentioned mainland cities. In Los Angeles 31 percent of district leaders were Japanese in 1997. By comparison, the cities with the next highest number of Japanese leaders were San Francisco (21 percent), Washington, DC (20 percent), and New York (12 percent). Since Los Angeles also had the national headquarters in Santa Monica, which is still dominated by Japanese leaders, the Japanese influence in Los Angeles was heaviest. Although Ikeda formed districts in the other cities he visited, he organized the members of Los Angeles into a higher administrative unit (a chapter) because, as he said, "Los Angeles is an important region that

Director Emeritus George Williams for their time and gracious support, along with other senior vice general directors at the headquarters—James Kato, Richard Sasaki, and Danny Nakashima. For bearing the daily burden of attending to my needs, I am grateful to Al Albergate, Carrie Rogers, and Nancy Simms of the public relations department, to Greg Martin of the organization department for preparing the various centers for my visit, to Gerry Hall of the culture department, Margie Hall, editor of *Living Buddhism*, Ted Marino of the study department, Eric Hauber and Jay Heffron of Soka University of America, Ian McIlraith of the youth division, and Matilda Buck, vice general director, Linda Johnson of the women's division, and Paul Oike of Rainbow district for their help. Special thanks go to Ann Miks of the organization department and archives, however, since she constantly shepherded me with patience, warmth, and wisdom into the history of the heart of Soka Gakkai in America and provided me with key sources.

will become the center of the *kosen-rufu* movement in America."[14] By 1997 the national average among the 2,449 district leaders of mainland USA cities, including Los Angeles and San Francisco, was 18 percent Japanese ancestry.

In Japan a *gaijin* (foreigner) group was formed about 1955 consisting largely of Americans. Haruo Kuwahara (now called Edward Clark) remembers those early days. He joined Soka Gakkai in Japan at the age of 14 on April 20, 1954. However, he wanted to come to the United States "to find out the difference between Japan and the United States," since he had seen America only in the movies. His main motive was to discover "why people in the United States enjoyed prosperity and democracy," even though "they had no *Gohonzon*, and where I came from was war devastation."[15] He recalls that "as soon as I got here, the first thing I did was to reach out to some members, especially Mr. Sadanaga" (George Williams). Sadanaga had arrived in Los Angeles in May 1957, but had then moved to Washington, DC, in the summer of 1958 with his sister and her husband, Roy Nishida, who was a *nisei*. Soon Clark met other *nisei* in the Los Angeles area, such as Ted Fujioka and Mike Kikumura, who had been introduced to Soka Gakkai through their wives and who played a pivotal role in communicating between cultures because they were bilingual. This process began very early.

Husbands who drove their wives to meet Ikeda when he first visited Los Angeles, such as Ted Fujioka and Tetsuji Baba, became friends while waiting at their cars for their wives. After joining Soka Gakkai, Fujioka assisted in the first English meetings, later to become a national vice general director. Baba could speak Chinese, having been stationed in northern China with the Japanese mili-

---

[14] Daisaku Ikeda, writing in his fictionalized account of his visit in *The New Human Revolution*, i (Santa Monica, Calif.: SGI-USA, 1995), 274 ff. Within the Los Angeles chapter six districts were immediately formed: St Louis, Olympic, First, West, Long Beach, and San Diego.

[15] Before Clark came to America in early 1960, he once met Ikeda and asked him how to realize his dream. Clark remembers that Ikeda "was young and dynamic and said I should ask my *Gohonzon*, so I did, and two months later I was on my way. Because I had no money, someone paid a one-way ticket, and I entered UCLA" (written questionnaire, 1997).

tary during the war. After becoming a member in Los Angeles, he spread Soka Gakkai to the Chinese in Monterey Park along with Chinese Soka Gakkai members who had arrived from Hong Kong and Taiwan.

Another *nisei*, Mike Kikumura, one of the first male district leaders in 1961, rose to be a national vice general director (the second in command) by 1980. Born in America in 1927, he grew up speaking English. However, he was sent to an internment camp at age 13 because of his Japanese ancestry, a bond of suffering shared by many Japanese Americans. Later he served in the Korean War, then returned to Los Angeles, where his wife introduced him to Soka Gakkai when he drove her to meetings. While it took him several years of listening to Japanese at Soka Gakkai meetings before he was fluent, he excelled at explaining Buddhism in colorful analogies to new American members.[16]

Ann Miks remembers an early Soka Gakkai meeting in 1961 when a neighbor took her mother there. Only 11 years old at the time, Ann went with her mother because she was afraid that her mother would be exploited by this new group. She recalls that the meeting was held in Japanese, and all those attending were women, with one exception, Mike Kikumura. Ann's mother was from Hawaii and joined immediately, but Ann remembers not liking the meeting because it was filled with so many crying babies and people who were sick and poor.[17]

[16] Many other *nisei* played important roles. For example, Jimmy Inaba was a *nisei* pioneer who helped translate Japanese Buddhist practice for young Americans. Although he was born in California, he grew up in Japan and did not return to California until 1958, when he began work as a gardener. He joined NSA in Feb. 1962 and eventually replaced Kikumura as Los Angeles chapter chief. In Jan. 1972 he became the caretaker of the SGI-USA Malibu training center.

[17] Ann's father, Mr Grayson Hagihara, was a *nisei* who had been born and raised in Hawaii, had served in the military in World War II, and then attended university in Hawaii and Denver before moving to Los Angeles in 1954. Although Ann and her father attended church, and her father, with a Bible in his hand, at first argued with Soka Gakkai members, he later attended meetings and helped as an interpreter from Japanese to English. He also joined eventually and continued to serve as an interpreter. Later he became a district chief (personal interview).

In January 1963 the Los Angeles Soka Gakkai bought and renovated an old post office to serve as the Los Angeles community center. Already by 1963 there was a Caucasian member from Santa Barbara who helped fix the plumbing. Edward Clark remembers that on July 3, 1963 the first discussion group in English was held at the Los Angeles community center. Since it was the night before Independence Day, using English was a way to celebrate Independence Day and to help a few of the English-speaking husbands of Japanese members who "wanted to know about Soka Gakkai" but had no study background. Various meetings in English started after that, and Edward Clark "was one of those recruited to attend meetings here and there" to explain Soka Gakkai. Usually these English discussion groups were organized in member's homes, as were regular district meetings. Bilingual leaders such as Edward Clark, Ted Fujioka, and Mike Kikumura were at the forefront in the early 1960s, but they were supported by many other bilingual *nisei*[18] who were active and contributed articles to the *World Tribune*.

Perhaps the California *nisei* who had the widest national influence on diversifying Soka Gakkai was Ted Osaki, who joined in the summer of 1964 in St Louis after his Japanese wife had joined. Born in Sacramento, Osaki returned to California as a member of the military to study at the University of California at Berkeley, and became very active in promoting Soka Gakkai in the San Francisco area in the mid-1960s. After graduating in May 1966, he was shipped to Libya, where he stayed until February 1968. He was then assigned to Washington, DC. Shortly after he arrived in the nation's capital, members began to recruit hippies in the

---

[18] Another bilingual *nisei* who joined George Williams, Ted Fujioka, and Mike Kikumura in the 1963–4 period was Richard Sonoda. Born in Hawaii, Richard Sonoda was introduced by a fellow employee in a department store in Los Angeles in Nov. 1963. He later joined in the Boyle Heights area of east Los Angeles in Jan. 1964 at a meeting in which the members were all Japanese except for one Caucasian and one Hispanic American. He was most impressed by the sincerity of the people who encouraged him to join, and by Williams, who gave him a dream and a practice whereby "the dream could be fulfilled" (taped interview in Santa Monica SGI-USA headquarters, May 20, 1997, and an individual history survey form).

Washington area, and these confused and alienated youths found in Osaki the friend, father figure, and leader that they needed. After becoming the youngest Asian American to be offered a promotion to lieutenant colonel, he resigned from the air force to avoid being posted to Europe. Instead he chose to work full time for Soka Gakkai and went to Chicago as the eastern territory chief just before the opening of the new Chicago community center on August 15, 1972, when African American membership was mush-rooming. Later, in August 1981, he was promoted to be national vice general director in Santa Monica. Thus, Osaki played an important role in San Francisco, Washington, DC, Chicago, and Los Angeles.

A turning point came in 1964 when a young American named Charles Parker appeared at a discussion meeting in Long Beach, California. Later, Ikeda would describe him as follows:

His hair and beard grew unattended. He wore dirty jeans and a wrinkled shirt, and was very skinny. He had no vitality. The look in his eyes seemed to say he had given up. He belonged to the generation just before hippies, called "beatniks". Since Japanese women were the only other people attending the meeting, his unusual appearance became a topic of conversation.[19]

Charles Parker was to begin a cultural revolution for Soka Gakkai that was celebrated in a promotional video called "From Hippie to Happy," which told how a generation of lost youth wandering the streets of America became transformed when they began chanting.

Charles Parker had been born in a small town in Oklahoma City, where his father led a jazz band that later moved to Los Angeles. After Charles graduated from high school in Santa Monica, he worked at various jobs until he dropped out, turned on to drugs, and wandered along the West Coast. After exploring various countercultural ideas, including Zen Buddhism, he was impressed by the new happiness in a friend who had recently joined Soka Gakkai. As a result, he attended a meeting in Long

[19] Daisaku Ikeda, "Charles Parker—'Hippie to Happy' Pioneer of Santa Monica," *World Tribune*, 29 June 1981, 6.

Beach, began chanting *nam-myoho-renge-kyo*, and joined. The next day he shaved his beard, cut his hair, and began spreading the good news. Charles Parker became the first European American to be appointed as a chapter chief, finally rising to become a headquarters chief in San Diego. Later he married another member, and his wife, Barbara, became the first European American young women's division leader.

Early in their practice a few teenagers from Beverly Hills came to a meeting out of curiosity. These were the first wave of young members who were to make Soka Gakkai racially diverse. One of the youths from Beverly Hills was Larry Shaw, who describes himself today as a "Jew-Bu." Over thirty years later he recalls that "in 1965, from a sociological point of view, there was an amazing phenomenon of tens of thousands of youth walking the streets" looking for some answers to life. A number of these began attending Soka Gakkai meetings in Los Angeles, which were still being held in Japanese. These early American members were often called *gaijin*, "foreigners," since most members were Japanese. Shaw recalls:

The leader, Mr. Sadanaga, usually spoke Japanese and just a few members spoke English. . . . We were a small group, a *han*, meeting within that Chapter. We used to hold meetings in the home of Mr. Kikumura on Bronson Street, near Vermont, off Crenshaw Boulevard. . . three or four of us went to Beverly Hills High School, and we went down to Crenshaw to seek for the truth.[20]

The period of being an isolated hippie at a Japanese meeting did not last long. Dave Baldschun was 19 years old when he attended his first meeting in Santa Monica in July 1966, and the earliest groups he remembers consisted of many young Caucasians with Japanese leaders. In those days Dave was a surfer and had very liberal parents who accepted discussion meetings in his home. Larry Shaw remembers that in 1965 all chapters in the Los Angeles area were 95 percent Japanese, but "by 1967 the chapter with the

[20] Taped interview in Santa Monica SGI-USA headquarters, (May 20, 1997).

310

largest and fastest growth was Santa Monica, which broke into three chapters—all American, ninety-five percent white and five percent African American. The other original chapters remained for the most part Japanese."[21]

The advent of African American members actually started in Japan. Some servicemen, like Herbert Mitchell, encountered Soka Gakkai as early as 1955. In Los Angeles other African Americans like Kenneth Levy and his friends spoke about "improving our lots," and joined as a way of dealing with anger and unhappiness. After the Watts riots in 1965 Levy found that chanting before the *Gohonzon* could help solve problems:

When I joined, I was an angry, confused, frustrated, 27 year-old African American, who thought the American Dream had eluded me, mainly because I was not able to achieve anything that would lead me toward a positive existence.

The leaders in SGI taught me many things. They talked about World Peace and gave me hope and courage for the future. I was taught responsibility by consistently calling members and reminding them of meetings, facilitating study meetings, giving personal experiences. Through my efforts, I became a reliable person.[22]

Even though their numbers do not match the general population, Latino leaders have also been part of Soka Gakkai for a long time in the United States, and Latin America is a vital part of SGI worldwide. However, growth has been slow. In Los Angeles Linda Delmar, who joined in the 1960s, found that she and her family were the only Latin members that she knew of "for a long time"; her district was mostly Japanese, African American, white, and Pacific Islander. However, she was attracted by the supportive environment:

People really took time to take care of you. I know that is what I felt as a young kid—taken care of and embraced. NSA was the only place that I

[21] An individual history survey form and taped interviews with Larry Shaw (May 20, 1997) and an untaped interview and an individual history survey form with Dave Baldschun (May 20, 1997).

[22] Taped interview in Santa Monica SGI-USA headquarters (May 20, 1997), plus an individual history survey and a typed statement.

really felt I belonged. The group was growing, and there was a great influx of different people. I saw everyone caring for everyone else. The organization was very inclusive, everyone was important.

In addition to personal changes brought about through chanting, Linda benefited from having responsibility in the organization: "I learned so much that I have been able to transfer to my personal and career life. Nowhere else did I get the training but SGI—not school, not at home. Working with people of all backgrounds in the organization has given me the confidence in the things I do in my daily life." Although there are occasionally problems in the organization, after thirty years Linda says, "when it comes down to it, there is always some one to listen and chant with you. That has not changed. I think this is the foundation—heart to heart relationships."[23]

Others, such as Lea Shadburn, found there were already Latin leaders when she began her practice in 1971, at the age of 13:

Because some of the leaders were also Latin, I felt I could reach out. Here were people of my own ethnicity practicing Buddhism. It made me pay attention. These early Latin leaders had such a genuine concern for all people and extended themselves to everyone, they had such a warm and encouraging spirit for everyone. I was not used to seeing this kind of behavior.[24]

Besides enjoying the diversity in SGI, a recurring theme in these written reports is the role that SGI played in helping minority members to develop their skills and build their confidence. Ken Levy affirms:

The SGI organization was like my parent. I learned a lot. I learned about determination and how to have a dream. I learned consistency, and I learned how to listen. But more importantly how to make my dreams come true based on my own effort and courage. I even learned how to

[23] Taped interview in Santa Monica SGI-USA headquarters (May 20, 1997), plus an individual history survey and a typed statement.
[24] Taped interview in Santa Monica SGI-USA headquarters (May 20, 1997), plus an individual history survey.

study and also about true friendship. . . . Each day I continue to apply all that I have learned and am learning in order to help all people.[25]

Another recurring theme is the ancient Buddhist lesson that our happiness is often determined by our understanding and attitude, rather than by external circumstances. However, SGI also emphasizes messages not found in early Buddhism—namely, not only that we are connected to our environment, but that we can change our environment; our happiness is connected to the happiness of others. A Chinese member in Los Angeles, who has practiced for over thirty years, wrote: "The truth is that happiness lies within us; and that the environment and us are one, so we need to make efforts to help others to become happy, too."[26]

Chicago

Like Los Angeles, Soka Gakkai in Chicago has lines of continuity from its earliest times.[27] Pioneers such as Tsuyako Liebmann (Japanese, joined in 1960) and Malvin Wright (African American, joined in 1965) still live and practice in the Chicago area. Although the first English discussion meeting in America dates from July 3, 1963,[28] by the fall of 1964 a letter from one Andrew L. Joshua— an English-speaking African American group leader—had

[25] Based on a taped interview in Santa Monica SGI-USA headquarters (May 20, 1997) with Ken Levy, plus an individual history survey and a typed statement from which this quote is taken.
[26] Taped interview in Santa Monica SGI-USA headquarters (May 20, 1997), plus an individual history survey and a typed statement by Judy Chow.
[27] I especially wish to thank the staff and members of the Chicago-SGI who hosted me during my visit, such as Edward Hamada and Daniel Aoki of the Chicago Culture Center, Charles Kelly, JoAnn Brewster, Doris North-Schulte of the Chicago Historical Society, Darnell Polphus and Mal Wright, Bud and Yonae Haynes, and of course, Guy McCloskey, senior vice general director. Guy has been leader of the Atlanta and Washington SGIs, and I have been fortunate to work with him as SGI developed relations with the Society for Buddhist–Christian Studies and supported the 1996 conference in Chicago.
[28] Stated by Edward Clark in Los Angeles on May 20, 1997, and also Jane Hurst, *Nichiren Shoshu Buddhism and the Soka Gakkai in America: The Ethos of a New Religious Movement* (New York: Garland, 1992), 142.

appeared in the *Seikyo News* encouraging more black members.[29] Malvin Wright had spent over five years in Japan and was familiar with chanting, but remembers only a few other black members at meetings in Chicago in the mid-1960s.[30]

Jesse Henderson recalls that the big upsurge in African American membership took place in early 1971, when many large meetings were held in the Liebmann home to chant in preparation for attending the general meeting in Seattle in July 1971. Phyllis Goodson joined later in 1971 after graduating from Northern Illinois University, which itself had only a small group of about fifty African Americans. During college she quit Christianity after being ostracized—no white members would sit in the same pew with her. In contrast, in the crowded Soka Gakkai meetings in the Liebmann home, people of various races were sitting almost on top of each other, as upwards of a hundred people tried to squeeze in. So many people came that neighbors complained to the local city alderman because of parking problems and noise from the two-hour meetings. Congestion was partially relieved beginning in 1972, when Chicago established its first community center.

It is startling to see the names of the leaders who attended the official opening of the Chicago community center by Ikeda in January 1975. One notices right away that, among the central leaders, Ted Osaki (the executive director) had adopted the name Ted Jackson, and Richard Sasaki (the vice area director) had adopted the name Richard Warren in an effort to Americanize. On further examination, the large percentage of African American leaders is impressive.

Phyllis Goodson remembers that in the initial invitation list there were no members from the Illinois territory, which was heav-

[29] Andrew L. Joshua, "American Negroes should be More Active in Faith," *Seikyo News*, 13 Oct. 1964, 3. Andrew was a karate teacher married to a Japanese wife and Soka Gakkai member, Joshua Tamiko.

[30] See the remembrances of President Ikeda for Mrs Liebmann and Mr Wright entitled "Tsuyako Liebmann—The First Chicago Chapter Chief," "My Friends of NSA (8)," *World Tribune*, 23 Feb. 1981, 6, 8; and "Malvin Wright—A Man Dedicated to Faith," "My Friends of NSA (10)," *World Tribune*, 9 Mar. 1981, 6, 8.

ily African American, so blacks felt hurt and spoke up. As a result, the final list had representation from outlying areas and from all races. The organizational structure of Soka Gakkai in 1974–5 had five levels from top to bottom: territories, communities, chapters, districts, and groups. In the 1975 name list small groups in the Illinois and Chicago East communities (with a heavy concentration of African Americans) were very numerous and out of proportion to the number of districts and chapters, probably because of a recent, rapid expansion at the grassroots level. Totaling all leaders from the 1975 list without separating them into levels, there are 122 blacks, 86 whites, 40 Japanese, 4 Hispanic, and 1 Korean. Several conclusions can be drawn. First, black leaders were more numerous than any other race. Second, all of the black leaders were found in only two communities—Illinois and Chicago East—which reflects the fact that Chicago is one of the most residentially segregated cities in the United States. Third, black leaders were found at every level except at the highest—territory level. Fourth, Japanese constituted a majority only in the Lincoln community. And finally, Hispanics were underrepresented in relation to their population ratio in Chicago.

The implication is that as early as 1975 Soka Gakkai in Chicago was becoming indigenized. Even though six of the seven top leaders were Japanese, at the next highest level Japanese leaders were a minority—with only six out of twenty-one leaders being Japanese; nine were white, and six black. The racial diversity of its leadership at this time represents a remarkable achievement by Soka Gakkai after only fifteen years of activity.

In 1997, based only on the 160 district leaders, the racial ratios are remarkably similar: 75 black (47 percent), 56 white (35 percent), and 26 Japanese (16 percent). This amazing constancy of ratios indicates that by 1975 the basic pattern of the Chicago Soka Gakkai community had stabilized and reflected the relative population ratios of the metropolitan Chicago area for whites and blacks. The only unusual features are the overrepresentation of Japanese, while Hispanics are underrepresented. Based on Chicago's population figures in the 1990s, Hispanics (mostly

Mexican Americans) represent over 20 percent of the population. Only about 2 percent of SGI members there, however, were Hispanic. Perhaps the reason is that most Mexicans came to Chicago in recent decades after the immigration laws changed in 1965,[31] just missing the major *shakubuku* campaigns of the 1960s and early 1970s.

The residential segregation of blacks from whites in Chicago is reflected in these statistics. In the 1940s, 1950s, and 1960s the north side of Chicago was white and Jewish, and the south side was mostly black. In the early history of Soka Gakkai in Chicago members were integrated through a shared community center, but in 1983 a south side community center was opened that largely served black members. On October 12, 1984 the Chicago Culture Center opened in north Chicago to serve everyone else. Since these two centers split the members racially, members built one larger, integrated center. In 1997 members showed me with great pride their new Chicago Culture Center at 1455 South Wabash Avenue—the location where Malcolm X gave his last address in Chicago.[32]

By the 1990s whites and Jews had moved to the suburbs, while many blacks had moved to north Chicago along with many new immigrants from Asia. For example, a Waukegan district meeting that I attended in a north Chicago suburb on June 1, 1997 had about eight white, eight black, two Chinese, two Japanese, and three Hispanic members. Since the Chicago SGI community is large, there are also monthly meetings held in five languages— English, Japanese, Spanish, Korean, and Chinese—as in other metropolitan areas.

The Chicago SGI is also active in sponsoring cultural festivals seeking to increase appreciation and understanding across racial lines. The Day of Chicago is an annual SGI event to celebrate the

[31] Cynthia Linton (ed.), *The Ethnic Handbook: A Guide to the Cultures and Traditions of Chicago's Diverse Communities* (Chicago: Illinois Ethnic Coalition, 1996), 13–18, 141–6.
[32] Information from Charles (Chuck) Kelly, Chicago district leaders' meeting videotape, May 31, 1997, at the Chicago Culture Center.

diversity of the community. Special features include an interracial African drumming unit that calls itself the World Peace Rhythm project. In addition, SGI has a special Korea Day in Chicago.[33] In 1997 diversity workshops were being conducted using materials from a national SGI workshop in Florida and other materials from the Chicago school system, where several members of the SGI culture department are teachers. While the national headquarters had also organized a diversity committee, the Chicago activities were based on local initiatives without the knowledge of national leaders.

In the summer of 1996 the Chicago SGI cosponsored an international interfaith conference at DePaul University entitled "Socially Engaged Buddhism and Christianity," which included the Dalai Lama. Another Buddhist–Christian project involved seven or eight interfaith meetings sponsored by the SGI culture department in 1996–7 and led by Libby Furman and Mandy Rivera. These local initiatives clearly demonstrate how, by the mid-1990s, SGI has become involved in interfaith dialogue and cooperation—a striking contrast to the exclusivistic policies of *shakubuku* evangelism and Nichiren Shoshu dogma.

Miami

The 1997 baseball World Series was won by the Florida Marlins. The winning hit was delivered by Edgar Renteria, a Hispanic ball player from Colombia, and the Most Valuable Player of the series, Livan Hernandez, was a Hispanic pitcher from Cuba. The 1997 season ended with sports commentators noting that the 1997 World Series marked the ascendancy of Hispanic ball players in the

---

[33] In contrast to most Koreans, who keep their distance from Japanese because they were invaded by Japan earlier in this century, there are many Korean members of SGI. Because Soka Gakkai was the only Japanese Buddhist group that opposed the war, it serves as a natural ally with Korea against Japanese militarism. Presently there are 220 community centers in Korea, in contrast to 64 in USA (*SGI Quarterly*, 14 Oct. 1998, 10–11).

major leagues.[34] But 1997 also marked the ascendancy of a Miami baseball team to world champion after only five years in major league competition. The rise to national prominence of Hispanic baseball players reflects the growing economic and ethnic presence of Hispanics in US society, but the sudden emergence of a Miami baseball team reflects the even more astounding rise of Miami as a major city in the last decade.

Florida has several distinct areas. This study looks only at the greater Miami region, including the five counties in the southeastern tip of Florida—mainly Palm Beach County, Broward County, Dade County, Martin County, and Monroe County. In Los Angeles and Chicago, analysis was limited to a review of the racial backgrounds of the district leaders. However, in south Florida much greater detail is available because of the research of Stephen Bonnell, SGI men's division leader of Miami #1 territory, who collected data on all 795 active members from every chapter in the Miami joint territory. This is a major achievement and the first time such a detailed report has been crafted. His figures are doubly important since they provide the main check on the assumption that the district leaders generally reflect the ethnicity of the members.[35]

Palm Beach territory has about 120 active members spread thinly over three counties: Martin County, Palm Beach County, and the part of Broward County that includes Pompano Beach. In the West Palm Beach district most leaders are white and only

[34] It is interesting that the 1997 baseball season also experienced the retirement by the Major Baseball Leagues of uniform number 42 in commemoration of the fiftieth anniversary of Jackie Robinson's entrance into the major leagues as the first black baseball player—the first time that a number has ever been retired by the whole major baseball league.

[35] I am indebted to Al Albergate, national director of community relations, who accompanied me throughout my visit to Florida. Also, invaluable help was provided by Tony Sugano (Florida joint territory chief) and his wife, Beverly, who hosted me in Florida, plus the staff of the Florida Nature and Culture Center (Harry, Cliff, Stefanie, Richard, and John), as well as to Monica Lema, who leads the Spanish language committee. A unique contribution was made by Stephen Bonnell, however, in undertaking the difficult job of tabulating the ethnicity of all the members throughout south Florida.

English is spoken, according to Shoko Braddock. The almost total absence of any Hispanic population in this region is reflected in the membership of the Palm Beach chapter (Stuart district and West Palm Beach district), where 50 percent of members are white, 20 percent Japanese, with only 5 percent African American, 2 percent Hispanic, and 23 percent mixed ethnicity. Southward, in Pompano Beach in Broward County, there is a larger representation of Hispanics (11 percent) and fewer Japanese (6 percent). Moving closer to Miami in the south, the Fort Lauderdale chapter had about 100 active members, who are almost evenly balanced between Anglo whites (40 percent) and Hispanics (35 percent), with only 10 percent African Americans, 5 percent Japanese, and 10 percent mixed.

Hispanic members finally emerge as a major presence in the city of Miami, however. In the north Miami chapter (one of the most diverse chapters in the country), Hispanics are dominant, representing 30 percent of the 125 members. The remaining membership is composed of African Americans (15 percent), Anglo whites (10 percent), Japanese (6 percent), Korean (5 percent), Caribbean (5 percent), Brazilian (5 percent), Chinese (4 percent), Indian (4 percent), Italian (2 percent), and others (14 percent).

The three chapters in the Miami #1 territory have 450 active members centered in Dade County. The central Miami chapter has an even balance of whites (35 percent) and Hispanics (35 percent), with Japanese, Italian, African Americans, and others constituting minorities. In contrast, the Kendall chapter was heavily Hispanic (45 percent), with only 20 percent of members being white and only small numbers of Caribbean, Japanese, and African Americans. The south Miami chapter's 145 active members were heavily African American (43 percent).

From these statistics, very different profiles emerge for different areas of south Florida. Although Hispanics were almost half of the Kendall chapter in the heart of Miami (86 out of 190 members), in the wealthy Palm Beach chapter to the north and the south Miami chapter to the far south, there were almost no Hispanics (only 2 out of 205 members). In the middle of these extremes, on the boundary between Broward and Dade Counties, the county line district contained thirty-four nationalities.[36] While Hispanics represent a growing segment of the American population, it is important to remember that they are also strongly linked to cultural regions in other nations. The Latin American committee of Miami SGI had representatives from nineteen different countries in 1995.[37]

The recent growth of Miami into a major US city (ranked eleventh in size in 1990) is based in large measure on the wave of Hispanic migration from the Caribbean and Latin America during the last forty years. The Miami population doubled during the 1950s from 495,000 in 1950 to 935,000 in 1960—a by-product of the Cuban revolution—and doubled again over the next thirty years to 1,937,000 in 1990. During this forty-year period non-Hispanic whites increased from 410,000 to a high of 776,000 in 1980 and then declined to 586,000 by 1990. The increase of blacks was much greater, beginning with 13 percent growth rate and moving up to a 20 percent growth rate during the 1980s, when the white population was declining at a rate of 25 percent. These groups pale in comparison to the Hispanic growth, however, which grew from a mere 50,000 in 1960, to 299,000 in 1970, to 581,000 in 1980, and reached 953,000 in 1990.[38]

What happened to SGI during these same years? Natsuko Montgomery recalls that from 1962 to 1965 there were no Hispanic members in the Miami area. By the early 1970s a few Spanish-speaking members participated—some who joined in south Florida and others who had become members in New York and then moved south.

[36] Monica Lema is the Spanish language coordinator for SGI in south Florida. She mentioned this statistic to me in an interview on Saturday June 7, 1997.

[37] Based on a copy of a May 25, 1995 fax, which lists the names and phone numbers of representatives from nineteen Latin American countries.

[38] See table 8 in Alejandro Portes and Alex Stepick, *City on the Edge: The Transformation of Miami* (Berkeley: University of California Press, 1993), 211.

Michael Uruncinitz, an immigrant from Eastern Europe, recalls a district meeting in Miami in early 1976, when someone noticed how diverse everyone was and proposed that the group "Stop right now and let's see where everyone came from." Sixteen countries were represented, mostly from Latin America and Europe. There were whites and blacks who could speak English, Spanish, Italian, and German. So the decade from 1966 to 1976 saw Soka Gakkai move from a Japanese religious group to the cosmopolitan mix that is typical today. Although there were only three black leaders in 1985, there were many black members active as early as 1975. Accordingly, the turning point in achieving racial diversity in south Florida SGI took place in the mid-1970s.

Table 11.1 reports the ethnicity of members and leaders from south Florida.[39] The biggest discrepancy between the membership and district leaders was the high proportion of Hispanic leaders compared to their representation in the membership at large. This ratio contrasts with the national leadership, which has been dominated by Japanese and white leaders without reflecting the growing black and Hispanic general membership. Although the profile of national leaders in the 1990s still reflects the earliest period of Soka Gakkai, recent appointments have started to reflect the more diverse constituency of the 1990s.[40]

Analysis

Less than forty years after the first Soka Gakkai groups were established in North America, Soka Gakkai has become the largest and most racially diverse Buddhist organization in North America. This rapid growth and indigenization was not a uniform process, however. Each urban center had unique dynamics, not just

[39] These data are from the report compiled by Stephen Bonnell, who was kind enough to share them with me.

[40] In 1997 an African American from New York, Shielah Edwards, was appointed as a national vice general director, and in 1998 Ronnie Smith, an African American from Washington, DC, was the only new appointment as a national vice general director.

Table 11.1. Ethnic composition of SGI in south Florida (%)

Ethnicity	Members	District leaders
White	29	33
Black	14	11
Japanese	7	11
Hispanic	26	37
Other	23	8
N	795	64

because of the different personalities of local leaders but also because of varying immigration patterns, racial mixtures, and social stability in the respective regions. Soka Gakkai members have crossed cultural boundaries—a distinct contrast to the more limited outreach of ethnic (Asian) and elite (European American) Buddhists.

Although I have highlighted the African American and Hispanic populations in Chicago and Miami, this accounting is partial, since other cities played major national roles. While Chicago and Miami are major centers of SGI growth in the United States, other cities have much larger memberships. Even Los Angeles has fewer district leaders (which, as indicated before, is a good indicator of the size of the membership) than New York and San Francisco. New York, in fact, has a very large African American and Hispanic membership. Accordingly, the three cities examined here should not be taken as representative of Soka Gakkai in America. Rather, they were chosen to recount local developments and to give important new data in these three major areas. But the full story involves other areas and other issues than those addressed here. For example, New York's story reflects not just local dynamics, but also the organizational conflict between the lay Soka Gakkai movement and the Nichiren Shoshu priesthood, which dramatically affected membership.

Being a mecca of artistic talent, furthermore, New York Soka Gakkai staged many cultural festivals and musical performances that attracted large audiences. When America was celebrating its bicentennial in 1976, over 10,000 members from around the country came to New York and enjoyed a range of performances, which included the nighttime "Toward the Dawn of World Peace" parade followed by fireworks on July 3, a culture festival on Wall Street on July 4, the "Spirit of '76" show at Shea Stadium between baseball games in a double-header, the 13th General Meeting at the Louis Armstrong Stadium, an International Show, and a fireworks display.[41] However, this enormous public outreach declined dramatically, and active propagation ended completely in the late 1970s when tensions with the priesthood led to Ikeda's resignation as president of the Soka Gakkai.

In the midst of the struggles with the Nichiren Shoshu priesthood, Ikeda began to regroup Soka Gakkai outside of Japan under a global banner, but Ikeda's star was dim in New York. When he visited the New York area in June 1981, only 200 people came to meet with him. Soka Gakkai membership in New York had almost disappeared by 1980. It took a decade of strenuous propagation activities in New York before Soka Gakkai recovered there, and today the New York SGI membership is about 6,000.

Among all Buddhist groups in America, Soka Gakkai excels in its organizational capacities. The social solidarity in Soka Gakkai is not an accidental feature or a byproduct of its teaching, but is at the core of its understanding and practice. One of the reasons why Soka Gakkai was attractive to those without social stability in the 1960s and 1970s was its capacity to welcome them into the organization and to develop their abilities. Homeless youth in the drug culture in the 1960s discovered that Soka Gakkai did not discriminate against them. The Japanese women who invited African Americans to meetings in the 1970s were also blind to racial differences. Everyone was accepted and encouraged to chant for whatever they wanted, lofty or mundane—for world peace or for money, drugs, and sex.

---

[41] Hurst, *Nichiren Shoshu Buddhism and the Soka Gakkai in America*, 268–9.

But those who began to practice Soka Gakkai soon underwent a transformation. They received constant personal support, which led to accepting responsibility for themselves and finally to accepting responsibility for others, which implied that they had to become organized, both in their personal habits and in their social relations. Soka Gakkai public events and musical performances were practical exercises of these skills. This social development is not a major part of Zen, or Tibetan Buddhism, or Vipassana, but it is at the heart of Soka Gakkai, which is not just socially active, but is socially transforming at the very core.

It has been said that there are no solitary Christians. A similar remark could be made about the bodhisattva career. In contrast to American elite Buddhism of Zen and Vipassana, which can easily be solitary and individual, Soka Gakkai emphasizes a global vision and social responsibility, both to other Soka Gakkai members and to all living beings.

The cultural festivals that celebrate the ethnic diversity of immigrants in urban SGI groups are not trivial, as seen also by the follow-up in workshops designed to appreciate diversity. What Buddhist group has a national diversity committee to sensitize its leadership to gays, minorities, and other marginalized groups? What other Buddhist organization publishes national newsletters in Chinese, Japanese, Korean, and Spanish? Only three other Buddhist groups have representation at the United Nations and sponsor local United Nations associations.[42] No other Buddhist group is planning a major university that incorporates peace studies and study abroad as a required part of their undergraduate curriculum. In the mid-1990s local districts in SGI-USA were reorganized so that membership would be based not on friendships and former connections, but on geographical proximity. The

---

[42] The other Buddhist groups registered at the United Nations were the Won Buddhists, Rissho Kosei-kai, and the Association of American Buddhists (based on a report by the committee of religious NGOs at the United Nations entitled *Survey of Activities of Religious NGOs at the United Nations 1995–1996*, kindly provided to me by its president, Revd Chung Ok Lee of Won Buddhism).

idea was not just to cut down on travel time, but also to promote local networks and local responsibility.

In sum, I would suggest that the organizational strength of Soka Gakkai is not a method to control membership as critics might claim, but an expression of social connectedness and social responsibility, which Soka Gakkai regards as the life of a bodhisattva and as their highest mission. So with thanks and apologies to Jan Nattier, I propose that in America there are three general categories of Buddhists: ethnic, elite, and *socially inclusive*. Based on its growth in three major cities, I would suggest that Soka Gakkai is the single, most prominent example of socially inclusive Buddhism.

12

Buddhist Humanism and Catholic Culture in Brazil

Peter Clarke

SOKA GAKKAI INTERNATIONAL, BRAZIL (BSGI) has an estimated membership of 150,000, over 80 percent of whom are of non-Japanese origin.[1] From a global perspective, this is the largest Soka Gakkai following, not only in Latin America but anywhere outside Japan. Greater success might have been expected in the more secular and pluralist contexts of Western Europe and North America than in Brazil, which, despite the "explosion" of Protestantism there since the 1960s,[2] remains a predominantly Catholic country.[3] There are signs, moreover, that this sudden explosion of evangelical Protestantism is now meeting with resistance from a "new" style of happy, healthy, vocational Catholicism inspired by the media-friendly "pop-star priests" or "stars of the altar," as the young priests who lead the revival are widely known, whose main pulpit is television, radio, and CDs.[4]

There are no obvious reasons why BSGI should continue to make steady progress in this highly charged, dynamic context of a revived and renewed Catholicism, which is reaching out to millions from many different religious traditions and particularly those in the neo-Pentecostalist churches with which it is in strong competition. Moreover, there appears to be considerable disconti-

---

[1] Interview, BSGI headquarters, São Paulo, Dec. 1998.

[2] D. Martin, *Tongues of Fire: The Explosion of Pentecostalism in Latin America* (Oxford: Blackwell, 1990).

[3] IX Recensemento Geral do Brasil, 1980, Fundação IBGE.

[4] Peter Clarke, " 'Pop-Star Priests' and the Catholic Response to the 'Explosion' of Evangelical Protestantism in Brazil: The Beginning of the End of the 'Walkout'?", *Journal of Contemporary Religion*, 14/2 (1999), 203–16.

nuity between BSGI's teachings and practices and the religious culture of Brazil, and this should prove to be a considerable setback to BSGI's development.[5] BSGI has no place for belief in a personal God, Jesus as Savior, faith healing, veneration of Mary the Mother of Jesus, pilgrimages to her many shrines, and belief in miracles — all of which are integral features of Brazilian religious culture, syncretized with Amerindian, African Brazilian, Spiritist, and Spiritualist beliefs.

BSGI appears to stand apart from this religious syncretism and, further, offers potential members none of the rituals, not even a healing ritual, associated with religious success in Brazil. It has acquired a reputation for strictness and single-mindedness in its teachings and practices. In its ceremonies there is no trace of anything Catholic in the form of prayers, rituals, beliefs, icons, or images. This exclusivist approach contrasts not only with that of folk Catholicism but also with the syncretist strategy of several of the more successful Japanese new religions in Brazil. These include Seicho no Ie (House of Growth), whose following is estimated at over 2 million, and Sekai Kyusei Kyo (the Church of World Messianity; henceforth simply, Messianity), which has over 320,000 devotees.[6]

Both of these new religions are unhesitatingly pragmatic in their approach to syncretism, incorporating, when it is thought to be necessary, Catholic beliefs, prayers, and rituals into their services and speaking continuously of God in personal terms, of his power and wisdom, and of the fundamental significance of the lives of Jesus and Mary. As one experienced and somewhat envious Japanese pastor of the Church of Perfect Liberty Kyodan in São Paulo commented: "They [Seicho no Ie and Messianity] have correctly understood that there can be no religion in Brazil without

---

[5] Rodney Stark, "Why Religious Movements Succeed or Fail: A Revised General Model," *Journal of Contemporary Religion,* 11/2 (1996), 133–47.

[6] Peter Clarke, "Modern Japanese Millenarian Movements: Their Changing Perception of Japan's Global Mission with Special Reference to the Church of World Messianity in Brazil," in P. Clarke (ed.), *Japanese New Religions in Global Perspective* (London: Curzon Press, 2000).

Jesus and Mary."[7] Even the Japanese Shingonshu temple—the largest Buddhist temple in Latin America, situated in the mainly Japanese town of Suzano forty miles to the east of São Paulo—has installed an image of the patroness of Brazil, Nossa Senhora de Aparecida (Our Lady of Aparecida), in the inner sanctuary to the left of the central figure of Fudo-myo-o and organizes a pilgrimage to her shrine at Aparecida in the state of São Paulo three times a year.

While the principal focus of this account is on the adaptive strategy of BSGI in the cities of São Paulo, in the south of Brazil, and Salvador, capital of the state of Bahia in the north-eastern region of this vast and culturally diverse country, comparisons and contrasts are made with the "strategic syncretism" of Seicho no Ie and Messianity. While others prefer the term neo- or self-conscious syncretism to describe the general approach of Japanese new religions, "strategic syncretism" seems more appropriate in the Brazilian situation. In this context, Seicho no Ie and Messianity reduce what might be termed their Catholic dimension during periods of success—for example, the recitation of the Our Father in one case has, with growth, become much less frequent and occupies a more marginal place in the services than previously—and emphasize it during times of stagnation and decline.

Carpenter and Roof have discussed the transplantation of Seicho no Ie to Brazil.[8] Earlier Derrett researched the effectiveness of the adaptive strategy of Messianity in Brazil and Thailand, focusing on the movement's activities in Brasilia and paying particular attention to such crucial concepts as the notion of God.[9] As will be seen, BSGI attempts to relate to Catholic culture by devel-

[7] Interview with Perfect Liberty Kyodan member, São Paulo, Sept. 1995.

[8] Robert Carpenter and Wade Clark Roof, "The Transplanting of Seicho no Ie from Japan to Brazil: Moving beyond the Ethnic Enclave," *Journal of Contemporary Religion*, 10/1 (1995), 41–55.

[9] E. Derrett, "The Universalistic Features of the Belief System of Sekkai Kyusei Kyo and the Group's International Expansion", Paper presented at King's College, London (1986); E. Derrett, "Signs along a Better Way: The Methods of Evangelization of a Japanese New Religion in Brazil and Thailand," in P. Clarke (ed.), *The New Evangelists* (London: Ethnographica, 1987).

oping what it refers to as a "Buddhist notion" of God. This endeavor to engage with Catholic belief notwithstanding, BSGI has historically been one of the few exceptions among Japanese new religions in the Brazilian context in its forthright opposition to theological and liturgical syncretism. Although in more recent times it has become more tolerant of multiple membership, it continues to insist on exclusively Nichiren Buddhist practices in its ceremonies.

Carpenter and Roof attribute Seicho no Ie's success in Brazil principally to what they term its "philosophy of ambiguity":

> The movement's continued success has been in large measure attributable to its ability to present itself to the Brazilian public as a philosophy rather than as a religion. What this has done is to cater to the spirit of religious tolerance that pervades the Brazilian psyche, while at the same time preserving a certain margin for manoeuvre in its relationship to those religious traditions of longer standing in Brazil, particularly the Catholic church.[10]

By identifying itself as a religious philosophy, Seicho no Ie has greatly simplified the process of adaptation to the Brazilian context, although elsewhere, including Europe and the United States, it has not achieved anything like the same success.[11]

It cannot be disputed that Seicho no Ie's success in Brazil has been due to more than its "advantageous ambiguity." As a movement, it has responded imaginatively and constructively to the changing demographic, political, and economic circumstances of Brazil. Not only did its own fortunes begin to improve dramatically from the mid-1960s, but so also did those of Messianity and Perfect Liberty Kyodan.[12] In all three cases, this improvement had much to do with the large-scale demand for healing, which they strove to meet, as well as their determination to reach out beyond

[10] Carpenter and Roof, "Transplanting Seicho no Ie," 49.
[11] Peter Clarke, "Accounting for the Success and Failure of Japanese New Religions Abroad," in Clarke (ed.), *Japanese New Religions in Global Perspective*.
[12] Peter Clarke, "The Cultural Impact of New Religions in Latin and Central America with Special Reference to Japanese New Religions," *Journal of Latin American Studies*, 4/1 (1995), 117–26.

the Japanese immigrant communities to the rest of Brazilian society. Translations of the services and "scriptures," or treatises of the founders, assisted this process, although in isolated cases they worked against it where no effort was made to insure that their content was appropriate. Fujikura, for example, illustrates the negative consequences for recruitment in São Paulo that resulted from a Perfect Liberty Kyodan translation of one of its booklets from Japanese to Portuguese intended for the guidance of women members. In a changing world, where feminist ideas were beginning to influence the thinking of younger women in particular, the text held up to them the *okusan*—or traditional Japanese housewife, who, unconcerned with career, devoted herself to the home and her husband's and children's needs—as their ideal.[13]

But more often the endeavor to present teachings in Portuguese and hold services in both Portuguese and Japanese demonstrated to the non-Japanese population that these Japanese new religions had both the desire and the capacity to relate to the cultural and religious peculiarities of the Brazilian situation. Moreover, as Brazil was experiencing rapid urbanization and modernization, the ethic and ethos of the Japanese new religions resonated with the demands made on many individuals who were directly affected by these processes.

Furthermore, while, as is widely understood, *virtus* alone does not make for growth, the evidence is clear that leadership of a charismatic kind has been integral to the success of Seicho no Ie and Messianity, and has also been important in the solid progress made by BSGI. In the case of Seicho no Ie, as Carpenter and Roof show, the counsel of its vice-president, Katsumi Tokuhisa, was decisive for its expansion in Brazil, particularly his insistence that the movement's focus and mission should be the non-Japanese Brazilian population.[14] The activities and philosophy of Messianity's vice-president and the present leader of its operations

---

[13] Y. Fujikura, "Alguns aspectos de Inculturação no trabalho missionario da Perfect Liberty Kyodan no Brasil," Pontificia Universidade Catolica de São Paulo MA diss., 1992.

[14] "Transplanting Seicho no Ie," 49.

in Brazil, Revd Tetsuo Watanabe, were equally decisive for that movement's impressive transformation from a small, ethnic Japanese movement in the mid-1960s to an overwhelmingly all Brazilian movement by the mid-1980s.[15] On arrival in Brazil in the early 1960s Watanabe made for Rio de Janeiro, which had a much smaller Japanese population than São Paulo, and through the daily administration of *johrei* (spiritual healing) became known there as the Japanese healer.[16] Among his converts were two high-profile Brazilian international soccer stars, whose subsequent impact on the growth of the movement in Rio, and further north in Bahia, has been considerable.

Teachings and rituals have also appealed. Those of Seicho no Ie have stressed the importance of gratitude to the ancestors as the principal means of sustaining the family and relationships generally, the necessity to develop a spiritual motivation for action, the power of the mind to heal, and the cultivation of the mind and soul through art and beauty. Messianity has focused on *johrei*, *shizen noho* (natural farming), the sacred essence of nature, and has pursued with vigor the implementation of its millenarian dream by constructing a model of Paradise on Earth at Guarapiranga on the outskirts of São Paulo. It is in the process of planning the construction of a new age city in the south of Brazil, to be completed during the next ten years. This ideal urban complex will be founded on the principal of the Law of Nature, or Universal Law, which consists essentially of preventing the destruction of the planet by outlawing (by democratic means, it is stressed) the use of all artificial means of healing and food production.[17] The role of Brazil in Messianity's global mission strategy is that of a "catalytic converter." That is, once the rest of the world becomes aware of the invaluable benefits to human living enjoyed by the inhabitants of this model city, they will feel compelled to demand an environmentally friendly style of life that recognizes and respects the sacred character of nature from their own governments.[18]

---

[15] Clarke, "Cultural Impact of New Religions," 123.
[16] Interview with pioneer Messianity missionaries, São Paulo, Dec. 1998.
[17] Clarke, "Modern Japanese Millenarian Movements."   [18] Ibid.

Returning to the appeal of "philosophical ambiguity," it is worth pointing out that age is a factor in determining the extent to which this exercises a positive influence on potential recruits. I have found that it is generally those members over the age of 35 who feel most comfortable with this ambiguity, principally for the reason that it allows them to continue to define themselves as Catholic and to practice their Catholicism if they so wish. Seventy-nine percent (of an admittedly limited and unrepresentative sample) of Seicho no Ie members responded in the affirmative when asked if they still felt they belonged to their former religion, which for a majority was Catholicism. Many replies were but variations on the following, given by a Brazilian woman in middle age: "Seicho no Ie is a philosophy of life by means of which we come to understand our religion of origin better." The metaphor of Seicho no Ie as the midwife that assists in the process of spiritual enlightenment is frequently used by members to describe how they come to a new and deeper understanding of Jesus and Christianity as their knowledge of the movement's teachings deepens — in particular as they absorb the truths of Masaharu Taniguchi's commentary on the gospel of St John.[19] The younger age groups (20–9 and 29–35) were less concerned with this kind of theological continuity. When a Japanese new religion does become a member's religion, it is in a personal, private, and individualistic sense. In the words of one informant, "Seicho no Ie is a religion for me. Religion is that which connects man to God. It is something you live out in your daily life and follow its principles. I do that with Seicho no Ie."[20]

When Messianity's and Perfect Liberty Kyodan's membership size are compared with that of Seicho no Ie, it provides further evidence that, in the Brazilian context, a Japanese movement's membership decreases as the percentage of those who declare they no longer belong to their former religion increases, especially if this was Catholicism. As we have seen, 79 percent of Seicho no Ie members continue to define themselves as Catholics, and the estimated membership is 2 million. This compares with 25 percent of

[19] Seicho no Ie interviews, São Paulo, Sept. 1995.   [20] Ibid.

Messianity members and 16 percent for members of Perfect Liberty Kyodan who continue to identify themselves by their previous faith. Their estimated size of membership is 320,000 and 130,000, respectively.[21] However, BSGI, where the membership, as previously pointed out, is estimated at 150,000, seems to be an exception. In this case, the percentage of those who continue to identify themselves as Catholics appears to be considerably less even than that of Perfect Liberty Kyodan.

Soka Gakkai has consigned a crucial role to Brazil in its global mission, which is to spread *kosen-rufu* to the rest of the world, and this boundless confidence and faith in Brazil as the vehicle for global renewal is perhaps more surprising than in the case of Messianity cited above. Ikeda was clearly aware, when he launched the Brazilian district of Soka Gakkai, that the theological and cultural distance between Nichiren Buddhism and Latin-based Catholic Christianity was a potential obstacle to his movement's development in Brazil. He likened his pioneering journey to Brazil in October 1960 to that of the first Catholic missionaries to Japan in the sixteenth century: as a voyage into unknown territory, without any knowledge of the culture, customs, and language of the people he was seeking to convert.[22]

This chapter will now examine how this Japanese new religion, considered to be rigidly orthodox and exclusivist, has responded to the predominantly Catholic, albeit highly eclectic and syncretistic, religious culture of Brazil. I will first of all consider the movement's progress to date in São Paulo, then discuss its development in Salvador, Bahia, north-eastern Brazil, where there is far less knowledge of or contact with Japanese religion and culture.

Historical Overview of BSGI

The first district of Soka Gakkai International (SGI) to be established outside Japan was inaugurated in São Paulo on October 20,

---

[21] Ibid.
[22] Daisaku Ikeda, *Nova revolução humana* (São Paulo: Editora Brasil Seikyo, 1994), 181.

1960. On that occasion President Daisaku Ikeda told the hundred or so Japanese settlers who had gathered for the ceremony at the Cha Flor Hall, situated in the largely oriental suburb of Liberdade, that Brazil had been entrusted with the mission of proclaiming Nichiren Buddhism not only throughout Latin America but throughout the world.[23] His optimism was doubtless inspired by an element of romanticism. The vastness, variety, and beauty of that country had captivated Ikeda.

Brazil was not entirely unknown territory, for Soka Gakkai already had a small foothold in both the south and the north of the country. There were a number of Soka Gakkai families in the city of São Paulo; others were scattered across the interior of the state of São Paulo, Paraná to the south of São Paulo, further west in the state of Mato Grosso do Sul, and the northeastern states of Bahia and Para. Few of these families knew each other, and most were to meet for the first time on the occasion of the launching of the Brazil district. Ikeda's visit and his intentions were made known ahead of his arrival by word of mouth and by advertisements in the Japanese newspapers in circulation in Brazil. But, even then, not all of those who eventually gathered for the launching of BSGI were well informed, even about major changes in the movement. Several were surprised to learn, for example, that Ikeda was the actual president of Soka Gakkai, unaware of the death two years earlier of his predecessor, Josei Toda (1900–58).

Most of the pioneer members of BSGI, it is important to remember, were post-World War II immigrants and—unlike a majority of the pre-World War II Japanese settlers, who always intended to return to Japan—saw Brazil as their permanent home. The first Japanese immigrants—*issei*, who began to enter Brazil in 1908 mostly to farm and work on the coffee plantations of São Paulo[24]—were constantly moving between two worlds emotionally, psychologically, and spiritually. One of the clearest expres-

[23] Daisaku Ikeda, *Nova revolução humana* (São Paulo: Editora Brasil Seikyo, 1994), 191.
[24] T. Suzuki, *The Japanese Immigrant in Brazil*, ii (Tokyo: Tokyo University Press, 1969).

sions of this emotional ambivalence was the reference to the death of a family member or Japanese acquaintance as "death in a foreign land." It was believed that the soul of the deceased would return of its own accord to Japan. Few were qualified to read the appropriate sutras for the departed, and the memorial tablets, which should have been erected in a graveyard or its equivalent and cared for, were left to gather dust in the bedroom of the head of the family. There was little by way of religious activities, as Handa's account of the Japanese *colônia* in Brazil shows.[25] In the Japanese school the Imperial Rescript on Education of 1890 was given a prominent place, as was the portrait of the emperor, and this kind of civil religion abroad was designed to insure the formation of loyal Japanese citizens. This is what the early settlers sought, and they were often aggrieved that their government in Japan did not display greater concern for their well-being.

The post-World War II immigrants were not only committed to settling permanently in Brazil, they were also determined to preserve their Japanese culture and inheritance, and displayed no willingness for Brazilianization. Thus BSGI, in deciding on its mode of insertion into Brazilian society with a view to fulfilling the ambitious targets it had set itself for Brazil as the dynamo of global *kosen-rufu*, would have to clear a pathway between catering to the spiritual needs of a small ethnic Japanese minority and embarking on a program of rapid Brazilianization. Either course on its own would have seriously affected the movement's early progress. The former would have risked alienating Brazilians of non-Japanese origin; the latter, the existing Japanese membership, whose pioneering qualities and commitment to *shakubuku*, or vigorous evangelism, were essential.

BSGI: Success without Healing and Syncretism

The importance of both healing and syncretism has been highlighted above in the early success of Seicho no Ie, Messianity, and

---

[25] T. Handa, *Memórias de um immigrante Japones no Brasil* (São Paulo: Editora T. A. Queiroz/Centro de Estudos Nipo-Brasileiros, 1980).

Perfect Liberty. Healing, in particular, was decisive in the early stages of Mahikari's takeoff in Brazil, and continues to be pivotal to that movement's appeal there. In every case, with the exception of Messianity, the emphasis is less now than at the beginning on physical healing and more on spiritual and psychological well-being, or self-discovery. One Brazilian female adept of twenty years' standing in Mahikari replied unhesitatingly when asked what participation in the movement had meant for her: "In coming to Mahikari I met myself for the first time."[26]

While BSGI offers no healing ritual as such and does not "permit" syncretism in the form of incorporating Christian teachings, rituals, and images into its services, it has nevertheless accepted Brazilianized procedures and arrangements at discussion groups and meetings, and local preferences regarding the position for chanting, which is to sit on a chair—an innovation that gave rise to considerable controversy in the United States in the late 1960s.[27] Moreover, unofficially, healing rituals have been important to BSGI's appeal. Ordinary members speak of using chanting as a means of healing, and some are self-proclaimed spiritual healers who attract substantial numbers of clients. Included among these is the 85-year-old member who arrived in Brazil from Hiroshima in the early 1950s and practices "solar healing" in the town of Suzano, close to São Paulo. This involves transmitting the energy he receives early each morning from the sun to his clients through a ritual process devised by himself.[28]

The importance of solar healing and chanting as healing rituals notwithstanding, BSGI's ideology, in particular its interpretation of karma and its notion of a Third Civilization, has been both highly effective in motivating the membership and in reinforcing their sense of vocation. The interpretation of karma, to those who heard it expounded by President Ikeda in São Paulo at the inaugural meeting of the Brazilian district in October 1960, was felt to be both highly relevant and liberating. In response to a question

[26] Seicho no Ie interviews.
[27] Clarke, "Success and Failure of Japanese new religions."
[28] Seicho no Ie interviews.

from a female member—aged 35, mother of three children whose husband had recently died, and who described herself as "disoriented"—Ikeda "revealed for the first time," according to those present, the true meaning of karma. Informed by other Buddhist teachers that her misfortunes were the result of the karma of previous lives, Ikeda explained instead that this member's sufferings, and those of any other member present at the ceremony, were preparation for a noble mission. He dismissed any explanation of them as negative conditions.[29]

Expounding Nichiren Buddhist teachings, the President of Soka Gakkai reportedly emphasized that the true, authentic law of cause and effect was contained in the principle of *ganken ogo*, according to which loss, deprivation, suffering, and all misfortune are potentially positive conditions in so far as they enable those afflicted to transform their lives. Through the practice of Buddhism, adversity becomes a symbol of hope and achievement. The questioner, if she dedicated herself to rearing and educating her children in a land where she spoke no more than a few words of the language, "would become a mirror for all other widows."[30] She had been born, as had the others present, Ikeda explained to her, to become a "Boddhisattva da Terra" (Savior of the Land), to carry out *kosen-rufu* there, and to build a land of eternal peace and tranquility.[31]

Interpreted thus, the notion of karma was not only inspirational but also imposed a commitment to fulfill one's vocation or calling. There could be no personal well-being or success without evangelism, as these were inextricably linked with *kosen-rufu*. That is, a positive outcome—in terms of relationships, health, and material prosperity—was predicated on the spreading of Nichiren Buddhism, or Buddhist humanism, as defined by BSGI.

Innumerable testimonies to the benefits of chanting, which record the interplay between individual and collective success, are recorded in BSGI's monthly newspaper, *Nova Era* (*Brasil Seikyo* since 1966). This newspaper frequently reminded followers of this

---

[29] Ikeda, *Nova revolução humana*, 196.   [30] Ibid.   [31] Ibid.

dynamic, explaining that "Nichiren Daishonin himself demonstrated that only through energetic *shakubuku* was it possible to extinguish all the faults of the past—that is, to change our destiny in order to attain absolute happiness."[32] *Shakubuku* was practiced with such dedication and commitment in São Paulo in the 1960s that, members recall, it was necessary to arrive early for meetings in order to be sure of entry. In hindsight, it is now thought that, in the early years in São Paulo, as in Los Angeles, this method of proselytization was characterized by too much raw energy, too much haste, and too little reflection.[33] There was, however, one difference between the two situations. In Brazil BSGI had to be sensitive to Catholic interests—if not for legal, then for cultural, reasons. The membership in Bahia, in northeast Brazil, where social and economic deprivation is more widely felt than in São Paulo, makes this point even more emphatically.

BSGI in Salvador, Bahia: "A Work of Ants"

In most respects, the city of Salvador, capital of the northeastern state of Bahia, is different from São Paulo. The former has a much larger population of African descent, which has greatly influenced its cultural and religious life, and far fewer Japanese or descendents of Japanese. Moreover, where there has been contact with Japanese culture, the effects, unusually, have been more negative than positive. As one of the pioneers of BSGI in Bahia, who lived near the Japanese *colônia* at Itubera in the south of the state of Bahia, recollected, "I found their habits and customs unattractive."[34] Bahia's levels of literacy, employment, and health care facilities are also lower than those of São Paulo.

BSGI in Bahia is self-made. It was started in 1958 by a Japanese immigrant family, the Kominatu family, who farmed on the Japanese *colônia* of Mata de São João, 100 kilometers south of the capital city, Salvador. Mrs Kominatu, in particular, devoted herself

---

[32] *Nova Era* (1965), 5; my trans. from the Portuguese.
[33] BSGI interviews, São Paulo, Dec. 1998.
[34] BSGI interviews, Salvador, Bahia, Dec. 1998.

to *shakubuku*, among the Japanese immigrants in Mata de São João. It was only in the late 1960s that non-Japanese Brazilians joined the movement. Even with this change in ethnic composition, the ceremonies remained entirely in Japanese for some time. One of the first non-Japanese Brazilians to join recalled that all that she could find as sources of information were a few of President Ikeda's discourses that had been translated into Portuguese. It was through reading these that she came to admire him "as a complete philosopher."[35] Ikeda's stature as a philosopher and teacher in Bahia is high. Though few revere him as a prophet or savior with supernatural powers, he is widely regarded as a great and wise man. One senior member of the BSGI *kankai* (main center) in Salvador places him alongside Nelson Mandela and Mikhail Gorbachev as one of the three most important personalities of the twentieth century.[36]

Far from the center of things the movement in Bahia has not, as yet, received a visit from President Ikeda, who has traveled to Brazil on three occasions and reportedly intends to return sometime in 1999. Over a period of forty years BSGI in Bahia has achieved much with little, or, in the words of one of its pioneers, it has been "um trabalho formiginho (a work of ants)."[37] For several years it consisted of a small group of around fourteen members. The present director joined in 1975 after searching for a cure for paralysis in Catholicism, Spiritualism, and Candomblé, a cure that was eventually to come through chanting.[38] By the beginning of 1999 there were 823 BSGI families in Salvador itself and 8,000 in the northeast of Brazil as a whole.[39]

This growth has been achieved without salaried staff and without any full-time administrators. All events, including ceremonies, *zadankai* (study group) sessions, seminars on Buddhism, and youth activities, are organized by volunteers. The entirely voluntary character of the enterprise generates an atmosphere of authenticity in the *kankai* that is rare and difficult to describe. Participants seem not only to hold genuinely to their beliefs but also to be

[35] Ibid. [36] Ibid. [37] Ibid. [38] Ibid. [39] Ibid.

tightly held by them. Much happens, including chanting, classes on Buddhism, counseling, and youth band rehearsals in a confined space that is carefully looked after and contains only bare furnishings. Those who attend the ceremonies are not comfortably off. Few have cars, and many will have taken half an hour or more to walk to the *kankai*. The director, who displays a clear grasp of Nichiren Buddhist principles and is obviously widely read in general philosophy and psychology, came from a poor family background in the interior of Bahia, where there was no opportunity to attend school. This he did after marrying and moving to the city of Salvador in 1966. Makiguchi's stress on education was of great importance in attracting him to the movement.[40]

Though not comfortably off, neither are members generally from the most materially deprived sections of society. There are a few wealthy and privileged adepts; among them the telecommunications engineer who, born into a rich family, enjoyed the benefits of a private education followed by university. Another member from a similar background is teaching at the Catholic University in Salvador while studying for an MA in Portuguese literature. But few members have been so fortunate. Some are self-employed and run small businesses, others are clerks or in semiskilled work from which they obtain modest incomes. Like Brazil's evangelical Protestants, BSGI members dress modestly and neatly. In other respects they are unlike Protestants; they are less judgmental about matters relating to private morality, going to the beach, smoking, drinking alcohol, dancing, and participating in profane festivals such as carnival. In this respect they resemble Catholics rather than evangelical Protestants.

BSGI is not seen as an easy option. Members confess to being challenged by the movement to realize their own potential. During a certificate-awarding ceremony on December 2, 1998, 120 mothers who had completed courses on Buddhism expressed great satisfaction and pride in their achievement—the first public affirmation of their abilities they had ever received.

[40] BSGI interviews, Salvador, Bahia, Dec. 1998.

What is most noticeable in Bahia, and further distinguishes this branch from BSGI in São Paulo, is the repeated emphasis in interviews, seminars, and sermons on the social dimension of Nichiren Buddhism. In this it echoes liberation theology discourse, though the philosophical paradigms differ greatly. Rather than emphasizing the inner transformations or the material rewards that have been achieved through chanting, BSGI members in Salvador are much more likely to point to the social improvements that have taken place in a particular community where chanting has been introduced. Tenement blocks and even whole neighborhoods, once known as socially unfriendly and dangerous, are said to have seen a marked improvement in interpersonal relationships since the practice of chanting began.[41]

Though its practice generates success in problem areas such as these, to which people despair of finding a solution, and while it displays tolerance of the wider Catholic culture in the ways mentioned above, the question remains as to whether BSGI is not too sharply set apart from the general drift of traditional belief and practice in Bahia, and Brazil as a whole, ever to have a more than marginal influence on its religious and cultural life—let alone bring about the Third Civilization through the human revolution. Moreover, does BSGI's self-definition as a humanist philosophy seriously limit its appeal in a culture where belief in God is taken for granted?

BSGI and Catholicism as a Religion and Cultural System

The problem of the encounter between Buddhist humanism and the existence of God in a Catholic culture is a large one. How it is dealt with by BSGI is discussed separately after examining that movement's interpretation of and response to Catholicism as a religion and cultural system.

Without endorsing relativism in doctrinal matters, BSGI maintained from the outset what might be termed a "politically correct"

[41] Ibid.

attitude toward Catholicism, seeing it as an integral part of Brazilian cultural life. *Brasil Seikyo* carried articles explaining BSGI's approach to other religions, one of which, written by Mr Saito, the then executive director of the movement in Brazil, is worth commenting on at some length. With the title "Sejamos uteis ao Brasil" ("Let us be Useful to Brazil"), the article emphasized that Nichiren Buddhism is the only legitimate and authentic form of Buddhism and the religion that will save humanity; it is "a mais correta e maravilhosa religião entre as demais (the most correct and marvelous of all religions)."[42]

This truth, the article continued, was to be believed and spread with conviction and energy, but without belittling other religions. Moreover, strategically, *hobo-barai* (the elimination of non-Nichiren images or icons[43]), followers were informed, was not to be practiced in Brazil for the time being. That meant that those who possessed them were absolved of the duty to remove non-Nichiren images and icons from their persons or homes, nor need this be demanded of new converts. Such objects could be kept, members were advised, until such time as through the practice of Nichiren Buddhism they acquired their own—presumably a personal copy of the *Gohonzon*.

BSGI placed other limits on exclusivism, granting members the freedom to associate with followers of other religions and even participate in certain of their ceremonies. Thus, if asked by a parent or a friend to attend a baptism or one of the other rites of passage in a Catholic church, members should do so, for "it would be worse for us to belittle them by not going."[44] This sensitivity to Catholic feeling and culture was motivated by more than pragmatism. It was also based on a firm belief in the unique power and efficacy of BSGI's own practice to protect its member from any dangerous influences that contact with Catholicism, or any other

[42] *Brasil Seikyo*, Apr. 15, 1966, 3.
[43] During the 1950s and early 1960s Soka Gakkai interpreted *hobo-barai* to mean that new converts were to remove all other objects of worship from their homes and destroy them, including ancestral tablets, family altars, and Shinto icons.
[44] Ibid.

religion, might bring. At the same time, it rested on the notion of a clear separation between the religious and other spheres of life. Such an outlook allowed for considerable interaction with Catholics in various spheres of life, including the important sphere of education. Members were advised not to worry about their children attending Catholic schools "because this has nothing to do with religion," and the pupils would be protected by the invincible power of the *Gohonzon* even if difficulties over faith were to arise.[45]

Concessions to religious, educational, and social mixing notwithstanding, at no time were theological boundaries blurred. In the following year another article in *Brasil Seikyo* spelled out the criteria according to which the authenticity of other religions should be assessed. Readers were informed of three tests of authenticity: proof from literature, theoretical proof, and proof derived from experience. The first—the proof from literature—was to be found in the *Gosho* (writings of Nichiren Daishonin), which were described as impeccably logical, rational, scientific, and relevant to the modern world. The second was a logical consequence of the first, in that Nichiren Daishonin's teachings provided both a totally comprehensive and appropriate philosophy for the modern world. Christianity, by comparison, was irrelevant to contemporary life because it was based on miracles. Proof from experience, or *prova real*, derived from the principle that belief can either benefit or harm the believer. Nichiren Buddhism's greatest benefit, it was claimed, was the attainment of complete happiness in this life. Readers need not concern themselves with a detailed investigation and analysis of the "scriptures" to confirm all of this, for the most intricate details of true Buddhism, they were informed, were incorporated in the *Gohonzon*, just as the "principles of electricity were incorporated in the various appliances."[46]

During the 1960s BSGI displayed a positivistic and optimistic outlook. While stress was placed on practice, every effort was made by BSGI to demonstrate compatibility between modern scientific thought and Buddhism. *Brasil Seikyo* carried article on article about

---

[45] Ibid.   [46] *Brasil Seikyo*, Nov. 11, 1967, 3.

Buddhism and contemporary science, including features illustrating harmony between the former and the theory of relativity.[47] Another article elaborated on the theory of evolution to demonstrate further the agreement between the Buddhist understanding of the origins of human life and that of modern science.

BSGI was prompt to associate itself with the spirit of the age and to claim credit for contributing to the ideas behind scientific progress, but also realized the importance of introducing the vernacular if it was to attract and retain the allegiance of non-Japanese Brazilians. By 1967 a committee had been formed to oversee the translation of the *Gosho* into Portuguese and English, and by the early 1970s the benefits of this were obvious from the increasing number of Brazilians of non-Japanese origin who were joining. By the late 1980s over 60 percent of the membership were of non-Japanese descent.[48] By the late 1990s that figure had risen to 85 percent, and BSGI had grown to 2,139 local communities, 806 districts, 327 regions, 149 areas, 94 general areas, and 30 metropolitan regions.[49]

With increasing numbers of non-Japanese Brazilian members, BSGI's approach to other religions, and in particular Catholicism, has undergone a process of Brazilianization. It is now more inclusive—to the extent that it not only tolerates but also accepts in principle multiple membership. New recruits are no longer required to reject their previous religion. "Formerly," it was explained by the present BSGI leadership, "there was a lot of this but now it is over. Attending Church, or Umbanda, or a Spiritualist session is a decision for the individual."[50] Those interested in joining Soka Gakkai may decide for themselves what to believe, for "everyone has enough intelligence to know what is best for them."[51] This allows BSGI to compete on more favorable terms with other Japanese new religions in Brazil—in particular with Seicho no Ie and Messianity.

[47] Ibid., Mar. 30, 1968, 3.
[48] Clarke, "Cultural Impact of New Religions," 123.
[49] BSGI interviews, São Paulo, 1998.   [50] Ibid.   [51] Ibid.

The more inclusive approach of BSGI is not simply pragmatism on the part of a minority movement in a religious culture characterized by tolerance and openness, and one in which there is keen competition from other alternative religions, spiritualities, and philosophies, including other Japanese new religions. It is also an expression of confidence in its own methods of socialization—a more appropriate term than "conversion" to describe the process of becoming a member. The main agency of socialization is the family, still largely structured along traditional lines, in which, as in Japan, the religion of the senior member of the household, usually the father, is the religion of the whole unit.

While it espouses traditional methods of socialization, BSGI is insistent that its approach to religion represents a departure from "old" forms of religion, including Catholicism. Many of the young, who are joining BSGI while at university, are attracted by its ecological and human rights programs, which have moved center stage, creating an image of the movement in Brazil as a radical, humanist philosophy derived from Buddhism rather than a religion *per se*. Members themselves stress that it is more than a religion or, as one adept from Rio de Janeiro commented, "nao e religião por ser religião (it is not a religion for the sake of being a religion)."[52] For members the ultimate test of whether BSGI is a religion or not is the impact it makes on individuals and society. If it fails to change people and their environment then it is not, informants stress, a religion.

BSGI and the Problem of God

There is no attempt by BSGI to seek common theological ground with Catholicism or with any Christian Church or monotheistic religion that believes in a personal God. This belief undermines, members explain, the fundamental Nichiren Buddhist principle of self-responsibility and fails to provide any answer to the problems of suffering and inequality.[53]

[52] BSGI interview, Salvador, Bahia, Dec. 1998.   [53] Ibid.

It is widely believed, among BSGI members in Brazil, that whatever else Nichiren Shoshu Buddhism does or does not do in obtaining benefits, its notion of karma renders life less outrageous to reason and more in keeping with common sense. To them, it offers a more compelling, intelligible view of the anomalies encountered at every turn in daily life in Brazil. One long-term member in Salvador explained that, for her, "believing in a personal God as Father is not only incompatible with *Nam-myoho-renge-kyo* and with Nichiren Buddhist philosophy, but brings the whole idea of God into disrepute." She added, "It is incompatible with Soka Gakkai, which is founded on the practice of self-transformation, leaving no room for attributing blame to anyone else."[54]

The director of BSGI in Salvador was convinced of this through personal experience. Chanting motivated him to acquire the skills of literacy and numeracy, and this enabled him to become an effective parent, which he defined as one who realized the value of education for his children. "You cannot," he insisted, "believe in a God outside yourself . . . if God is the Father of all, why so many different races, why do some prosper and others suffer? God is a Law, the Law of *Nam-myoho-renge-kyo*."[55] Looking back, he is certain that it was BSGI that gave him the opportunity and the motivation to accept personal responsibility for his own happiness or unhappiness.

BSGI members are careful not to deny the existence of God in every sense of the term. Aware of the psychological importance of such a belief, BSGI has modified its approach to proselytization. No attempt is made to dissuade people from believing in God. On the contrary, BSGI presents the seeker with a "Buddhist notion of God." The usual practice of a BSGI evangelist, informants explain, is to stress that there are many ways of thinking about God, and that clear similarities exist between saying that God is *Nam-myoho-renge-kyo* and the Catholic notion of God as Creator of the Universe.[56] Moreover, members of religions, including those of

[54] BSGI interview, Salvador, Bahia, Dec. 1998.   [55] Ibid.
[56] Ibid.

the African Brazilian religion of Candomblé, who understand God as Nature are said to be "close to the Buddhist idea of God."[57] Minimalist acceptance of belief in the existence of God protects BSGI from the charge of atheism in a culture where such a belief is regarded as prior to experience.

While there is a Buddhist notion of God, there is no attempt to construct a Buddhist notion of the Devil compatible with the Catholic concept. When discourse moves to the area of belief in the Devil—a belief as important in the folk Catholicism of Bahia as belief in the existence of God—recourse is taken once again to the notion of karma and personal responsibility, and matters are left there. The line adopted on other beliefs central to the religious culture of Brazil, including the belief in Jesus as Savior and in Mary his Mother, emphasizes that BSGI holds these two people in the highest regard and values their contribution to changing the world for the better. At the level of ethos, BSGI retains its distinctiveness. As we have seen, there are no traces of Catholic influence in its rituals. However, BSGI's clear distinction between the "sacred" and "profane" leaves the way open for members to participate in the secular side of religious festivals and public events.

Conclusions

BGSI is a tense intermixture of exclusivism—which, in a global religious market, can have its own special appeal—and tolerance grounded in realism. It has developed a strategy that legitimates crucial elements of Catholic culture, such as belief in God, without itself actually becoming, internally, Catholic. Still, the complete absence of any Catholic ritual may explain why it has not been as successful as movements such as Seicho no Ie. The degree of tension between BSGI and the wider society may be too high.[58]

However, as in the case of Seicho no Ie, BSGI benefits from being both a philosophy and a religion, depending upon the angle from which it is viewed. This dual identity, and BSGI's acceptance

---

[57] Ibid.
[58] Stark, "Why Religious Movements Succeed or Fail," 137.

of multiple religious affiliation, has facilitated the entry of Catholic members in particular. BSGI does not seek, it should be noted, to "convert" all Catholics in Brazil, as this is not considered to be essential to the completion of *kosen-rufu* and its mission to build the Third Civilization. BSGI's millennial dream of a world in which every individual will have experienced human revolution has been tempered by realism, at least in Brazil. Expectations are that, one day, one third of Brazilians will be followers, and that percentage, it is believed, will be sufficient to have a transformative effect on the behavior of all the rest.[59]

It is pointless to try to predict the future; other than to say that, in general, it is rarely unlike the present. What happens next will depend greatly on the way the process of adaptation is handled. This process is a balancing act; it must be neither so thorough as to screen out all distinctive traits of the movement, nor so incomplete as to show a lack of desire or ability to come to grips with more than one highly specific conception of life. The present encounter between Buddhist humanism and Catholic culture suggests that BSGI's adaptive strategy has so far enabled it to retain its distinctive character and pursue specific goals, while at the same time accommodating its key notion of *Nam-myoho-renge-kyo* to the fundamental culture of Catholicism in Brazil. Its steady progress to date rests largely on this foundation.

[59] BSGI interview, São Paulo, Dec. 1998.

13

The British Movement and its Members

Bryan Wilson

T HE success of any new religious movement within a particular national culture depends not only on the features that constitute its specific appeal, vital as they are to understanding the way it is received, but also on the pre-existing character of the host environment. In the early 1960s, when the first Soka Gakkai Buddhists appeared here, Britain was a country still recovering from the effects of war on its economy. A class structure undergoing radical change, a new mood of optimism, belief in prospects of social and economic progress, and the recognition that the nation had now to reshape its role in the wider world were significant elements in the prevailing social ethos. This was the time when a prime minister could refer to the "winds of change," but could also tell the public as a whole that they "had never had it so good."[1]

Despite numerous indications of a growing process of secularization, Britain was notionally a Christian country. Christianity had, for centuries, enjoyed a virtual monopoly as the religion of the Western world, and even though that monopoly concealed—especially in Protestant countries—some divergence of belief and practice, those variations were generally contained within a wider Christian framework. But within the half century immediately antecedent to the emergence on the British stage of Soka Gakkai, new and radically different spiritual perspectives had become

[1] An earlier and shorter version of this chapter appeared in the *Journal of Oriental Studies*, 8 (1998), 3–14. The permission of the editor of that journal for the publication of this chapter is gratefully acknowledged.

evident in Britain, as in other parts of the Western world. By the 1960s an entirely unprecedented diversity of religions was being canvassed in the country. Missionaries (as they may be designated, although by no means all of them were full-time professional agents of the organizations to which they belonged) came from America, Asia, and even Africa to disseminate their particular creeds in the United Kingdom. There were of course other means by which the various new gospels were reaching the British public. Increased travel and tourism, commuting, and the communications revolution were together leading to the relativization of local customs and knowledge, creating publics increasingly willing and sometimes eager to experiment with new life-styles, some of which were far from compatible with traditional mores. One aspect of this cultural revolution was a new openness to imported spiritual ideas and, consequently, the gradual erosion of that ethos that Christianity had engendered and sustained over many centuries.

The Christian ethic, which influenced society far beyond the confines of the Church, was essentially an ethic of self-denial and restraint. It functioned as a powerful agency of social control through self-control. It condemned sloth, self-indulgence, and intemperance. It preached forbearance to the powerful and wealthy; long-suffering to the poor. In reconciling men to their social and material circumstances, the message of Christianity was that the trials of this world were a test of worthiness for salvation in a world to come. The Christian religion never assumed that human happiness in this life was in any sense a laudable or worthwhile goal.

The ascetic ethic of Christendom was, without doubt, largely responsible for the patterns of self-discipline, social order, and civic commitment that enabled Western societies to advance economically and educationally. Protestantism, in particular, promoted rational conduct and rationalized social institutions, eliminating superstition and promoting scientific advance. Christian teachings created a climate, a *mentalité*, of self-restraint and often, it must be said, even of self-repression, in which the individual was urged to sacrifice or at least to postpone personal gratification in response to religious exhortations.

This ascetic ethic was remarkably congenial to social conditions in Western societies. In circumstances of economic scarcity and in a world generally perceived to be a "vale of tears," when life was hard, disease endemic, famine frequent, wars recurrent, and death or bereavement imminent, an ethic that counseled a morally regulated, ordered, and obedient life, offering the possibility of compensation only in the afterlife, was both compatible and auspicious. The model held up by the Church for the population at large was that of the suffering saint. Indeed, suffering and the need to accept it were central motifs of the Christian message— saints suffered as Christ had suffered, and so Christian men and women might also suffer as part of their earthly apprenticeship for a blissful life hereafter. An ethic of austerity reconciled people to the prevailing hardship and conditions of scarcity that prevailed in preindustrial society.

Yet the austere ethic requiring that personal gratification be postponed to an afterlife proved to be the basis for a steady process of capital accumulation and the scientific and technological advances that eventually produced latter-day prosperity for the advancing nations of Europe. In the era of scarcity the prime concern was to produce, and European countries in that phase of development have been not inappropriately designated as producer societies; among which Britain was the first. There was a clear congruity between the religious ethic and economic circumstance. Consider the remarkable convenience of the institution of the season of Lent. At this time of year—the harsh winter months—faithful Christians were not only exhorted to refrain from wanton self-indulgence but also, most conveniently, to accept a regime of abstinence as a religious obligation, obedience to which was claimed to be spiritually meritorious.

From the nineteenth century onwards, at an accelerating pace as the twentieth century advanced, Britain, and subsequently other producer societies in the West, underwent transformation. Religion, however, changed less rapidly. It was entrenched in long-established influential institutions. It had accumulated costly and impressive plant. Over many generations the Church had invested in training and maintaining specialist personnel. These factors provided some measure of immunity for the Church and its faith against the effects of changes in economic and social structure. Since religions almost invariably regard the truths they propound as timelessly valid, the generalized religious ethos was also resistant to change. Thus, in this period of rapid social development, Western Christianity increasingly found itself in a time warp.

The socioeconomic base, which the Christian ethos had found so congenial, was changing. Producer societies were becoming consumer societies, dependent on ever increasing consumption if economic development was not to be disrupted. Thus gradually, the old, religiously canvased asceticism was no longer a suitable ethic. Self-denial, austerity, and the restriction of consumption were dispositions that constituted a hindrance to the new patterns of economic behavior required by unrelenting growth in economic output. The emerging consumer society demanded an ethic that stimulated people to exercise choice and legitimized their desire for enjoyment and gratification. It needed to stimulate a level of demand for the artifacts of happiness that matched the enhanced productive capacity to provide these things. An ethic that endorsed consumption corresponded to the increased productivity of consumer goods, which new technologies and the accumulation of industrial capital had brought into being. Consumption was no longer to be excoriated. Pleasure was not to be condemned. Life was to be more than a period of probation to establish one's credentials for a blissful life hereafter — "Life was for living."

This shift of ethical disposition, conducive to the newly emerging pattern of socioeconomic order, could not but unsettle Christian religion. After centuries of proclaiming its ascetic ethic, Christianity could scarcely go into reverse gear and legitimize consumption, enjoyment, indulgence, and the pursuit of happiness. This growing incongruity between economic well-being and the churches' ascetic moral teaching was of course a gradual process, but in the longer run it may be cited as one factor in the steady decline in the percentage of people choosing to make Christian commitment. New agencies, disseminating new values, were coming into being, which tacitly challenged the moral authority of the churches. The growing advertising and entertainment industries promulgated a message very different from that of traditional morality. It was a message based on a more hedonistic ethic promoted by the powerful devices of the communications revolution. Those industries enjoyed vast resources and had an expenditure utterly incommensurate with anything the churches could muster in response to it. Modern society increasingly came to endorse the new values canvassed by the media, which became imperatives implicit in everyday behavior.

At the same time, open avowal of crude hedonism left a certain vacuum—the whole spiritual dimension, the values of compassion, social concern, civic responsibility, and disinterested goodwill were disregarded by the naked materialism of the new economic climate, entrenched as these values had once been in the old ascetic ethic. As Christian asceticism lost its economic *raison d'être*, so it also lost its old effectiveness in endorsing compassionate values. Thus, the climate was propitious for new types of religiosity which, whilst entertaining an ethic congruent with the new economic impulses, retained a spiritual humanistic orientation.

Into such a situation came Soka Gakkai. It was not, of course, the only religious movement from the Orient newly introduced into Britain. But of the others, some were no less ascetic than traditional Christianity; some even more so. Soka Gakkai represented a different type of moral tradition, positing a new balance between restraint and reward—that is to say, offering a different logic for the relationship between personal comportment and personal gratification. Instead of self-denial and the postponement of gratification to some post mortem experience, Soka Gakkai rejects the validity of inflexible moral rules. The individual is to take responsibility for his own behavior—to be answerable to and for himself—in accordance with very general abstract principles of compassion, integrity, and fortitude. Behaving responsibly, being in charge of his own life, he need not eschew pleasure, but should rather experience happiness in this world and enjoy its good things. Indeed, diligent performance of religious exercises is held to insure that the individual will experience conspicuous or material benefits as well as inconspicuous or spiritual blessings.

Whilst not endorsing all the tenets of philosophical hedonism as such, the teachings of Soka Gakkai are certainly compatible with the ethic required by modern consumer society. Whilst individuals are responsible for their own behavior, each member is left free to determine exactly what, in terms of day-to-day comportment, the cultivation of that responsibility should actually entail. His moral probity is not evidenced by self-abnegation, by adherence to a code that disdains personal pleasure or the pursuit of happiness. Rather, he is enjoined not to forgo the good things of life, which are part of his inherited entitlement. He is encouraged to take a positive attitude to secular culture and to human endeavor in all departments of life; to use his talents; to broaden his vision; and to avoid moral value judgments.

My analysis suggests that it was essentially the moral ethos of Soka Gakkai that induced native Britons to adopt this new faith. The religious teachings of Buddhism may have their appeal, but the teachings of Soka Gakkai Buddhism differ considerably from the Theravada version of the faith with which those sections of the British public at all acquainted with Buddhism were more likely to be familiar. The Lotus Sutra, the text at the heart of this and some other branches of Japanese Buddhism, is not in itself an immediately accessible text for Westerners; the practice of chanting is distinctly exotic; and the *Gohonzon* is in itself an entirely unfamiliar object of worship. None of these fundamental features of the Buddhism propounded by Nichiren was in itself likely to be the primary source of attraction for British converts. The soteriology of this new faith, the moral economy it expounded, and the ethos it engendered were much more likely to capture the imagination of prospective members. Even the person of Nichiren—the monk who revealed himself as the incarnation of the Buddha, superseding in his teachings the provisional doctrines of earlier manifestations of Buddhahood—was not projected as a compelling personal agent of salvation. In essence, the faith reposed in a much more abstract and philosophical conception of the prospects for human well-being. Rather than formal doctrine or practical liturgy, it was the ethic of Soka Gakkai Buddhism with which British converts initially found resonance.

The carriers of the faith to Britain, in 1961, were Japanese, mainly women, the wives of British businessmen with whom they had become acquainted in Japan. The first British converts were their spouses. From this small beginning the membership has grown to some 6,000, spread widely across the country, but with particular concentrations in London and other urban areas. The movement brings together a diverse public, but generally a public that is attracted by Soka Gakkai's specific ethical orientation, its abandonment of rigid moral codes, and its liberal adaptability to circumstance.

It need not then be so surprising, in spite of the exotic character of the religious performances of Soka Gakkai, the use of ancient language, the novelty of chanting, and the reverence for the *Gohonzon*, that increasing numbers of Westerners, no longer able to reconcile the conflicting values promoted by various agencies in modern society, should find this faith to be entirely in harmony with their everyday lives and claim it as a beneficial, life-enhancing practice. Soka Gakkai offers an ethical teaching that is flexible and adaptable to individual circumstances. It does not demand conformity to any narrowly conceived code of specific rules that seek to set forth a prescribed, detailed response to every sort of contingency.

While, in the modern age, the majority of British people find little need for religious expression, there is a sizable minority who have readily accepted some form of guidance in their daily lives. Some within that minority have been drawn to Soka Gakkai, and this despite its exotic character. On the face of it, a religion based in a remote country, which is endued with traditions and procedures entirely unlike those of any Western tradition, and the practice of which requires the acquisition of unfamiliar concepts and the unfamiliar language in which they are expressed, might appear as an unlikely contender for the adhesion of modern Westerners.

Yet, among those who have looked for some new spiritual thera-
peutic experience or for the legitimization of general ethical principles, some have found in Soka Gakkai a new and vibrant faith.
We have some evidence, from research undertaken in Britain, of
what it is that attracts people to this new religion, and which sections of the population are most likely to feel that attraction.

The sources of Soka Gakkai's appeal appear to include various
features. First, it is a lay movement among ordinary people—
unlike other forms of Buddhism, it has nothing monkish about it.
While, until the schism of the early 1990s, Soka Gakkai had the
service of the Japanese priests of the Nichiren Shoshu sect, in
Britain that priesthood played very little part in the operation of
the movement; principally only at the ceremony in which the convert received, from an occasional visiting priest, his copy of the
Gohonzon. In contrast to the situation in Japan, British members
lived in a culture that did not call for the imperative services of
Buddhist priests at funerals, nor did the members become affiliated
to the movement's temples—in the United Kingdom no such temples were established. From its beginnings in Britain and in
response to the specific contingent circumstances prevailing there,
the lay character of Soka Gakkai was more conspicuously evident
than was the case for the movement in Japan. Paradoxically, the
absence of a local priesthood, and—even before the schism—the
fact that the role performed by Nichiren Shoshu priests was minimal enhanced the attractiveness of Soka Gakkai for some.

Second, Nichiren's Buddhism is emphatically pragmatic.
Believers are taught to expect the solution of personal problems as
a significant function of their faith. Chanting is considered to be a
means of realizing one's goals and harmonizing one's dispositions
with the universal law that is thought to operate in the universe.
Since it is held that the individual should experience health, abundance, and every attribute of happiness, and that faithful and systematic chanting is the way these desiderata might be attained,
Soka Gakkai Buddhism is canvassed as a supremely practical means
of ordering one's life. Thus it can offer itself as a religion and an
ethic well suited to practical everyday affairs.

Third, the soteriology of Nichiren's Buddhism embraces multi-form conceptions of salvation. All manner of benefit is to be realized. Thus, chanting may be undertaken for general goodwill, for altruistic ends, or for personal benefit whether material or spiritual; not solely for a blissful life hereafter. Such an afterlife is something in which, we know from opinion polls, fewer and fewer people in the West believe. And among those who do, the prospect of reincarnation is seen increasingly as its preferred form. Such is the enhanced pleasurability of life in this world. Recurrent reincarnation is clearly an implicit part of the theodicy that postulates a karmic law of cause and effect transmitted from one incarnation to another, but it is far from being at the forefront of Soka Gakkai conceptions of salvific benefit. Soka Gakkai Buddhism is an essentially this-worldly rather than an other-worldly religion, with a concept of salvation relevant to the here and now rather than to the hereafter.

A fourth characteristic of this Buddhism is that, unlike many other Buddhist organizations, and some other new religions that have emerged in the West, Soka Gakkai is what sociologists call "world-affirming," which adherents may understand more specifically as "life-enhancing," in that it endorses positive attitudes to social experience. Members are not enjoined to relinquish involvement in the world: on the contrary, their participation in civic, political, artistic, cultural, and social activities is positively endorsed. The "world-denying" attitude of ascetic religions is altogether remote from the perspective on life espoused by this variant of Buddhism. In a period when, from other sources, many new religious movements now burgeoning in the West place a strong emphasis on positive thinking, Soka Gakkai derives from ancient teachings a commitment to exactly the same type of orientation, which is markedly in tune with the times.

Fifth, the teachings of the movement promote a view of religion as an instrument of benefit, not as a compensation for suffering. As we have already observed, the focus is on freedom rather than restraint. Hence it appeals to a public for whom the moral constraints of traditional religion would be a distinct deterrent. In place of a catalog of moral rules there is a commitment to abstract concepts such as compassion, forbearance, fortitude, integrity, goodwill, and a general ethic of responsibility, in accordance with which the individual determines for himself what he should regard as the right course of action.

A sixth source of attraction is that, as a lay society, Soka Gakkai is able to dispense with much of the apparatus of conventional church organization. Many meetings are in homes, conforming to the current trend for religion to become de-institutionalized and privatized. Liberated from ecclesiastical constraints, Soka Gakkai is enabled to present itself as a much more informal, relaxed, and spontaneous worshiping fellowship. In a period when democratic popular styles have displaced or largely discredited hierarchic structures, the typical meetings of Soka Gakkai reflect the style and form increasingly favored by the public at large.

A seventh feature of the movement that probably appeals to prospective members is the fact that its local groups do something to restore a sense of community and identity in a society has become steadily depersonalized. In these groups, a type of what may be termed mutual counseling occurs. From their associates, encountered frequently in chapter meetings, individuals derive support and a sense of shared commitment in the context of rapidly changing society where impersonality undermines other spontaneous agencies of support. Local leaders offer guidance and advice in a concern not to assuage guilt, but to build confidence concerning the practical issues arising in everyday life. Guidance and encouragement are the watchwords in accordance with which local leaders seek to transmit the lessons and examples provided by the writings of Nichiren and by the successive presidents who have led Soka Gakkai since its inception in late prewar Japan.

Soka Gakkai adopts a positive and outgoing orientation toward a wide variety of activities, many of which are ignored as being no concern of theirs by other religious groups. Thus, there is an eighth source of appeal in the support the movement lends to campaigns for the preservation of the environment, for peace, as well as for the more usual candidates of religious concern such as aid for the Third World and care for refugees. Members are encouraged to participate in projects and programs organized by the movement to provide benefit in all of these areas. Chanting and worship are thus not just ends in themselves, but are seen as instrumental in awakening members to their responsibilities to the wider society. Cultural events are no less a feature of this proactive disposition. Concerts, entertainments, and exhibitions are all objects of regular sponsorship to promote the opportunities for artistic expression and creativity.

Not least among the attractions of the movement is the way its members are encouraged to make others aware of the benefits derived from their faith. The result is the creation and maintenance of a vigorous community that seeks, both by a commitment to disseminate Buddhist teachings and by personal example, to bring their religion to the attention of others. This is a means not only of winning new adherents, but also of reinforcing the loyalty of those already enrolled.

Finally, as a tenth item of positive appeal, the whole ideology of the movement legitimizes well-being. Whereas traditional religion, and specifically Christianity, inculcated guilt and preached penitence in the face of life's tragedies and inevitable suffering, Soka Gakkai finds no place for guilt. Being religious is thus not, as in traditional Christianity, virtually tantamount to making an apology for being alive. Soka Gakkai affirms that the individual can transcend suffering, that he has a right to happiness, and that happiness is something that faithful practice can help him to acquire.

These, then, are the features of Soka Gakkai, which, in the prevailing culture of British society, strike the analyst as being likely to attract prospective converts. Clearly, actual attraction must vary for people of different ages, sexes, educational levels, occupations, and general social circumstances. Sociological research has been directed to these very questions, and it is possible to present a profile of the membership of the movement in Britain as it stood at the beginning of the 1990s. The following profile is derived from a sample of 620 SGI-UK members, who at that time were more than 15 percent of the then total listed membership. That survey also explored the points of attraction that had prompted their interest in joining the movement.[2]

The membership was found to be comprised of some 60 percent women, a figure that is probably paralleled or exceeded by many other contemporary religious bodies in Britain. If, in this respect, Soka Gakkai conforms to the general character of religious bodies, in another respect it almost certainly differs. It was found that, even disregarding the Japanese members (who constituted a sizable minority of members, but who were deliberately excluded from the survey), more than 25 percent of respondents had been born overseas. This is a remarkably high figure and (excluding the specifically immigrant religions) probably unparalleled by any other religious body in Britain. These members of overseas origin came from no less than forty countries and confer on Soka Gakkai a more thoroughly international complexion than that of most, if not all, other religious bodies in Britain.

There may be a number of reasons why immigrants are especially attracted to new religious movements. For people who are living in an alien culture, the support that strongly canvased religions offer may have a special appeal. The common circumstance of separation from kinsfolk and countrymen may induce migrants to draw together. In particular, a movement that is detached from the culture of the host country, and has thus a distinctly multicultural complexion such as obtains in Soka Gakkai in Britain, may be especially appealing. The immigrant may find it difficult or even impossible to penetrate, much less to become affiliated with, indigenous communities or institutions. Perhaps it is easier to make common cause with others in a like situation, even though they stem from cultures totally dissimilar to his own. It may also be noted that migrants are often people of independent mind and personal initiative, who have to stand on their own feet in coming to terms with a new and strange environment. That such people

---

[2] Detailed results of this survey will be found in Bryan Wilson and Karel Dobbelaere, *A Time to Chant: The Soka Gakkai Buddhists in Britain* (Oxford: Clarendon Press, 1994), from which the data in the following paragraphs are drawn.

should embrace a religion emphasizing personal responsibility is thus no surprise.

Regardless of the actual source of attraction to a particular movement, an understanding of its success must also take into account the circumstances through which members are first brought into contact with the religious organization. The issue is of importance, not only for a sociological understanding of social influences, but also for the missionary strategy of religious bodies themselves. Religious movements often put considerable resources into making themselves known through publicity, lectures, and the like, but what in fact are the effective means by which the attention of potential converts is actually attracted? The evidence on this subject, for Soka Gakkai-UK, is unequivocal. Over 90 percent of members had been brought into contact with the movement by spouses, partners, relatives, friends, or colleagues. Among these, friends were the largest influence—over 40 percent attributed their first acquaintance with the movement to a friend, while 23 percent attributed it to a spouse, partner, or family member. Only 6 percent had been drawn to the organization by publicity, exhibitions, media presentations, and the like. Personal witness—which some members regarded as *shakubuku*—was clearly the effective method of winning new converts. This finding is consistent with those of other studies in regard to proselytizing techniques used by various religious bodies.

Where Soka Gakkai appears to be quite different from many other religions is the circumstances by which some members had first become acquainted with people who were already in the movement. Among the places where UK members had their own first encounters were a night club; a dinner party in Copenhagen; a pub where a stranger introduced himself; a lecture on macrobiotic diet; and an astrology class. One respondent reported, "My friend's mother met a member at a party, and when she told me, I was intrigued because I thought Buddhists did not go to parties." It may be readily observed that night clubs, alternative medical centers, astrology classes, and pubs are not the sort of locales in which one would expect to get a serious introduction to join the

Church of England, much less the Methodists or Baptists. Another respondent, concerned to show that Soka Gakkai Buddhism was very much at home in the everyday secular world, furthered the point: "Our leaders . . . are not *saintly*—they go to the pub, watch *Neighbors* [a popular television soap opera]. They are ordinary— Buddhas are ordinary people."

First encounter with a movement is one thing, but contact does not necessarily lead someone to join; there has also to be some distinctive initial attraction. That attraction is not normally the movement's doctrines, which are learned only subsequently. The survey of British members sought to discover just what, at the time of joining, had appealed to them about Soka Gakkai. The single most important factor was *the quality of the people they met*. Thirty-seven percent declared this to be the principal initial attraction. There was something about members—often expressed as vibrancy, energy, or vivacity—that led these converts, as outsiders, to want to discover more about the teachings to which the possession of such qualities was attributed. The second most powerful attraction lay in the expectation that chanting was an effective means of realizing benefit—usually the conspicuous benefits of material well-being. Twenty percent of respondents had been drawn to Soka Gakkai as an agency producing tangible benefits.

However, when these same members were asked what was *now* (that is to say, at the time of the survey) the persisting attraction of the movement, the emphasis had changed. Instead of the 37 percent who had initially been drawn by the qualities manifested by the members, only 14 percent declared that this was the attraction now. What had occurred? Was the quality of other members taken for granted once people became inured in the movement? Or had there been disenchantment, even disillusionment, once others members came to be better known? The likely explanation would appear to be that the movement had effectively socialized—educated—a sizable section of its membership to the acceptance of rather different values. In particular, there was a marked rise in the importance they attached to the ethical dimension of Soka Gakkai's mission—to such matters as world peace and ecological concerns. Whereas, in their initial contact with the movement, only 3 percent had suggested that this was the main attraction for them, 18 percent advanced this aspect as the main source of continuing appeal.

Two propositions are often advanced with respect to new religions. One is that the members of such movements may be characterized as "seekers"—people on a personal religious quest, seeking solutions to personal, intellectual, emotional, or ethical problems. The other, an assumption often made by Christian clergymen and by journalists, is that new religions poach people from their previous religious allegiances. On the evidence acquired from the survey of members of Soka Gakkai-UK, neither of these ideas appears to be warranted.

More than three quarters of respondents had not previously belonged to any religious organization. Of those who had a previous affiliation, former Roman Catholics (who constitute only a small minority of the British population) contributed a disproportionately high percentage—8 percent, as against 6 percent who had been Anglicans, and 3 percent Nonconformists. The members generally were not religious seekers. They had not been looking for spiritual solutions, and they had not found Soka Gakkai in religious contexts. Nor had most members come from a religious background—generally they were not people who had been on a specific religious quest. Having belonged to a religious body does not exhaust the potential for religious commitment, of course, and members were asked if they considered themselves religious before they joined Soka Gakkai. Forty-seven percent declared that they had not previously been religious. Only 8 percent said that they had been searching for meaning—only these and a further 6 percent who claimed to have had a previous interest in religion might qualify as having been seekers. The general conclusion is that the members of Soka Gakkai were not previously a religious public, that the movement had not recruited former churchgoers, and that the great majority had not been actively looking for a religion when they first learned about chanting.

Chanting is the core activity of Soka Gakkai, and the survey sought to discover just what place chanting occupied in the lives of members. Not every member claimed to chant twice a day, but some 51 percent claimed to do so on a regular basis. What were they chanting for? That is, what were they seeking in undertaking this rigorous religious exercise? Fully 96 percent affirmed that they chanted for particular goals. Such was the faith in chanting that the British leader had felt the need to warn a group preparing to chant before the *Gohonzon* at Taiseki-ji (in the days before the schism, when British members were eager to go on pilgrimage to the head-quarters of the Nichiren Shoshu sect) that they should "not go in with their shopping lists."

The most frequent objects of chanting were for career improvements or for better employment. More than half the members sought better relationships with spouses, partners, girlfriends or boyfriends, and even work colleagues, and almost as many chanted for material benefits—a better house, a car, or even to win a lottery. Personal health and happiness were mentioned by two fifths of respondents; a fifth sought the well-being of others, and a similar proportion chanted for a change in their own attitudes.

The aim of chanting may not be dissimilar to the aims of prayer in other religions. In the absence of any comparable survey of the things for which people pray, however, one may suppose it to be unlikely that many prayers are directed so specifically at the improvement of interpersonal relationships. Nor does it seem likely that prayerful supplication—prayer for recovery from illness and grief apart—would normally be directed to such highly specific targets. Soka Gakkai members, however, affirm emphatically the practical nature of their faith and have implicit faith in the power of chanting to affect, indeed to achieve, certain highly specific outcomes. Chanting is not only, not even primarily, a device for changing subjective orientations, although it is certainly claimed to have that effect. It is also seen as a way of tapping into the latent power of a universal law that affects objective events and phenomena as effectively as it influences attitudes and subjective dispositions.

Indeed, members claimed that "chanting worked." Fifty-five percent believed that what they had chanted for had been achieved in a direct way. They readily listed the items for which they had chanted and indicated the successes achieved, from suicides averted to financial support suddenly, unexpectedly, and often immediately secured. Of several impressive claims, perhaps the most dramatic was that of the art teacher whose account of success might be given in his own words:

One tends to equate spiritual paths separately from materialism, but it was made clear that if you want something, it will come to you. I chanted for money to begin with, and almost feel guilty about it. I thought "What do I want?" First I wanted money to finish the house. We had the usual mortgage business. We needed a few thousand pounds to finish the extension. Should we remortgage the house? I thought, "I will enter some competitions". We'd never done that before, but we came up in a DIY store—they offered prizes of gold bars in Texas Homes . . . We entered three times. There was a "tie-breaker", and you had to say what you liked about it. We won it. M [my wife] was ill, and reluctantly we'd agreed to get a second mortgage. The letter [for the second mortgage] came at the same time as the announcement of the prize. We'd won £7,000 in gold bars . . . We went to the Hilton Hotel in London—had to take a day off! We had chanted for money, and we won.

Apart from such tangible "conspicuous benefits," there were others—the inconspicuous benefits of the change in personal dispositions. Almost two fifths claimed to have gained in self-confidence, self-control, and the capacity to change their lives, and a fifth specifically referred to the change in their own attitudes to life and to others. Others claimed enhanced compassion, altruism, and peace of mind.

As one might expect from the committed members of a movement, and particularly so among a sample of people all of whom were first generation converts, there was abundant enthusiasm for their faith. Notes of doubt, hesitancy, much less of criticism, were very few. This was a public satisfied with the religion that they had espoused and confident of the benefits it conferred. Even so, members were far from being passive recipients of a faith simply handed down to them. Many recognized that what they achieved depended on the integrity of their own commitment, and some observed that chanting before the *Gohonzon* could sometimes be a challenging experience, bringing them face to face with their own uncertainties and anxieties, and making them aware of their own failings and imperfections.

There were other levels at which some members tempered raw enthusiasm with down-to-earth comments about the movement in which they had enrolled. For British people the dependency and reliance on a master–disciple relationship, such as is common in religious traditions of Asia, was sometimes a difficulty. At the local level this sometimes resulted in a more critical attitude toward local chapter leaders than would have been expected in Japan. At a higher level it led some to question the degree to which the movement elevated its leader, President Ikeda, to a status not commonly conferred on the leaders and officials of Western religions. Some couched this criticism in terms directed less toward Ikeda himself, a man often presenting a modest image, than toward those who surrounded him. In all this, some members appeared to express a cultural predisposition in their dislike for fuss, and a few commented that the movement was too much dominated by Japanese cultural style.

Distinguishing what was explicitly Nichiren Buddhism from the trappings and paraphernalia of Japanese culture was by no means always easy for members. For some, the distinctive Japanese style was undoubtedly an adornment they appreciated, and may, indeed, have been one of the attractions of this new and exotic faith. But a few others expressed the desire to see their adopted religion trimmed of its Japanese-ness, if not shorn of it altogether. For them, the essence of the teachings must transcend what they saw as virtually the adventitious circumstances of its origin. The problem is by no means a new one in the dissemination of religions. The issue of the extent of enculturation troubled Christianity not only in the time of St Paul, but also during the early Christian missions to China, and more recently, in the assimilation of the Unification Church to European cultures. It can scarcely be surprising that a movement with teachings propounded by a thirteenth century Japanese monk, and organized in accordance with the strong principles of master–pupil and parent–child models of Japanese social structure, should awaken some reservations among those espousing it in the climate of individualist, libertarian twentieth century Britain.

Other organizational features of a kind distinctly alien to Britain, and imported from Japan, were the subject of comment, too. Some women, in particular, voiced reservations about the separated men and women's divisions in the movement. A few, more avowedly feminist in outlook, took exception to the stereotyping of sex roles by age and sex in the service activities of the movement; in which men, for example, act as traffic regulators on special occasions, while to women is delegated such tasks as that of providing and serving refreshments.

The very success of the movement in drawing together people of widely differing social class, occupations, and life-styles was, for some, another concern on which they voiced reservations. Middle-class members were not always appreciative of the exuberance and uninhibited style of some fellow members, whose cultural background so much differed from their own that they were not always comfortable in chapter meetings. But for their shared spiritual perspectives, these people would scarcely ever have found themselves in company with one another. That they remained in the fellowship with each other was evidence of the primacy of religious faith over social convention. In spite of all the various sources of complaint, these critics, none the less, considered themselves to be committed members of Soka Gakkai. Criticism and complaint is a normal phenomenon in human enterprises, and had research into the British membership produced no evidence of such reservations, one might have doubted its reliability.

It is not only with respect to their critical acumen that one might recognize the British members of Soka Gakkai to be people of independent minds. This was evident from the very demographic features of the membership. More than half of them had no family members in the movement—they had made their own decisions. They were also predominantly young people—not *very* young like the members of some other new religious movements, which recruit people with an average age of 22 or 23, but young relative to the general population. Three quarters of members were between 25 and 50 years of age, whilst fewer than 6 percent were under 25 years of age.

Independence of mind was also reflected in the untypical range of professions in which members were engaged. Nine percent were in the caring professions, 13 percent were in or associated with the performing arts, and a further 8 percent were in crafts or the graphic arts. When to these were added the teachers, academics, and those working in the media and public relations, they accounted for more than 40 percent of the entire membership. These are all occupations in which the individual has a considerable amount of autonomy in his work or in which he or she undertakes a role that calls for considerable personal responsibility. The impression of independent people standing on their own feet and expressing individual personality dispositions is altogether at variance with the blanket image of members of new religions (of "sects" or "cults" as the media often choose to call them), who are often depicted as virtually brainwashed zombies. Of Soka Gakkai, our research indicates that nothing could be further from the truth.

The average educational level of the respondents to the survey questionnaire reinforces this conclusion. Some 50 percent of the sample had been educated beyond the age of 18; 12 percent had an academic degree; a *further* 7 percent had both an academic degree and some further professional qualification; whilst a still *further* 4 percent had higher degrees. In all, some 24 percent had an academic degree or more. The proportion of the highly educated may well exceed that of any other sizable spiritual movement in Britain.

Why then does Soka Gakkai in Britain attract such a high proportion of highly educated people, concentrated in the professions we have mentioned? At least part of the explanation lies in the fact that many of those who responded to the questionnaire were freelance or self-employed people, working in occupations that made strong demands for personal entrepreneurship, resilience, and self-confidence, and where professional success might often be hazardous and subject to the vagaries of fortune. Such fortune members might see as karma, but karma that was amenable to improvement by dint of conscientious chanting. For such people, the sense that they could take additional measures — spiritual insurance as one might call it — to secure their circumstances has an obvious appeal. If, as members believed, chanting helped in the cultivation of self-confidence, that in itself might indeed be part of the equipment needed for success.

The need to take responsibility for one's own life and circumstances, which Soka Gakkai strongly proclaims, fits exactly the demands of the self-employed professions. Further, whilst its broader educational and ecological concerns coincide with those of the thinking classes in contemporary society, the movement's encouragement of creative and cultural expression complements the concerns of professionals in the graphic and performing arts, and its general ideological orientation of compassion and altruism has a marked affinity with the motivations of people in the caring professions. For perhaps both of these groups of professionals, there is the added impetus of a religion that has disowned guilt as a mechanism by which good behavior is to be stimulated, and has abandoned what members see as the constraints of moral interdictions. The old moral economy of traditional religions — the moral economy of sinfulness, suffering, and repentance — is disavowed to allow positive orientations to be embraced in a way that members regard as liberating the spirit.

At first sight, it may appear surprising that a faith with ancient roots grounded in a distant country, employing what is for most adherents an unknown language, embracing an alien culture, and utilizing strange concepts should exercise an appeal in the contemporary West. Yet, such cultural diffusion has been by no means uncommon in the history of the world's religions. After all, much of the same might be said of Christianity at various points in its missionary history. It is certainly true that the fundamentally spiritual orientation of Soka Gakkai sustains an ethos that accords with the demands of the present-day consumer economy and the licensed hedonism required for its maintenance. The set of values this movement endorses (its name translates, after all, as "the

Value-Creating Society") is readily reflected in some of the major cultural and recreational concerns of modern people. The goals that Soka Gakkai espouses in the fields of ecology, education, peace, and worldwide compassion, as manifested in the relief programs for refugees and victims of natural disasters, find a ready echo among those of enlightened opinion in the Western world. In such a social climate a religion that teaches personal responsibility but which rejects guilt as a negative response, that embraces positive thinking and is concerned for life enhancement, is likely to exercise considerable attraction.

Despite its commitment to what are today recognized as global ethical concerns, Soka Gakkai in Britain has not escaped the opprobrium which has been a widespread response, particularly of the media, to contemporary new religions. Nor, indeed, has such hostile reaction been confined to modern times: generally it was worse in the past. Even so, like other movements—whether themselves new, or merely newly emerging in Western society—Soka Gakkai has been subject both to criticism and to calumny. A principal source for negative press reports in Britain has been the self-styled Cult Information Centre, a so-called 'anti-cult' organization the self-appointed mission of which has been to vilify new religions and to spread alarm about their activities. Thus, such innocent promotions as the sponsorship of a company of Japanese dancers and drummers by the Soka Gakkai Min-On Association (which promotes musical performances) was reported in a northern newspaper, on the basis of information disseminated by the Cult Information Centre, as the work of a "dangerous brain-washing cult."[3] The same organization, using the opportunity to advertise its own activities, alleged that a husband whose wife objected to her husband's commitment to SGI practices was "brainwashed."[4]

These isolated incidents have occasionally been reinforced by the reproduction in the British press of allegations made in the Japanese press against SGI. Thus allegations by a disaffected woman member that she had been raped by President Daisaku

[3] *Northern Echo*, Nov. 15, 1991.
[4] *Woman's Own*, July 18, 1994, 36–7.

Ikeda were reprinted in *The Times* (London).[5] The plaintiff was subsequently discredited, and the allegations were disproved and became the subject of contrite apologies from political opponents who had given wide publicity to these charges. It appears that this rebuttal received no attention from the press in Britain. Even wilder charges appeared elsewhere in Europe and were reproduced by British newspapers. Thus the *Evening Standard*[6] carried a report that French intelligence services suspected that SGI was "attempting to infiltrate the Élysée Palace"—a charge later elaborated by the *Daily Telegraph*, which reported that SGI was recruiting French nuclear scientists and was subject to monitoring by the French secret service "because it has set up bases near nuclear research centres and reactors."[7] All of which—given President Mitterrand's friendly reception of Daisaku Ikeda—verges on the ludicrous.

A more calculated and sensationalist assault came on one occasion from the BBC, which broadcast a program, *The Chanting Millions*, in October 1996, which was biased and ill informed, and which sought, by inserting photographs of the effect of the poison gas attacks on the Tokyo underground perpetrated by Aum Shinrikyo—a movement totally unrelated to Soka Gakkai—to discredit this largest of Japan's new religions. It appeared as an almost racist indictment—that being a *Japanese* new religion was enough to warrant calumny from the mass media.

In contrast to these evidences of negativity, Soka Gakkai has also won some plaudits in Britain. Particularly in the local press, the efforts of local chapters in such matters as organized cleaning up of parks and public spaces, as well as in promoting entertainments and exhibitions, have earned commendation. Events such as the musical production *Alice*, staged in London with an entire cast and supporting technicians drawn from the British SGI, and with profits going to United Nations causes, have received favorable notices.

It is common practice for the media, in their assault on new religions, to lump them together as "sects" or "cults", using these

[5] *The Times*, June 25, 1991.   [6] *Evening Standard*, Apr. 26, 1991.
[7] *Daily Telegraph*, June 19, 1991.

371

designations as openly pejorative terms. Even when these categories are divested of their derogatory connotations, however, and the terms are employed in accordance with the ethically neutral standards of academic analysis, there are no grounds for applying them to Soka Gakkai International in Britain. The term "sect" generally relates to a group of separated believers within the mainstream established religion of a given society. This is not the condition of SGI in Britain or elsewhere in the Western world. It presents a religious inheritance that is different from the indigenous faith and hence defies the categories that have evolved to describe such divisions. The concept of the sect carries connotations of smallness of size; of rejection of the secular culture; of membership confined to those qualified as "religious virtuosi"; of rigorous, rule-bound discipline, with expulsion as the final sanction for infractions of the code. Apart from size, in Britain none of these characteristics of sectarianism, as depicted in the relevant sociological literature, has any application to SGI.

Nor does the movement display any significant congruity with the popular stereotype of what constitutes a sect—a stereotype that emphasizes secrecy, authoritarianism, inflexibility, and entrenched resistance to change. In contrast to these dispositions, one may cite the fact that in 1995 SGI-UK embarked on a conscious exercise of reappraisal in "a dialogue with everyone who wants to take part about the best way forward for the movement . . ."[8] The issues for debate included "leadership [and] how financial matters are dealt with."[9] The debate concluded that hierarchical organization was "becoming ineffective"; that "the rigid structure of SGI-UK creates dependence rather than self-reliance"; that "the public image of SGI-UK is confused and the organisation can appear exclusive and alien," and that "there is an unnecessary tendency towards secrecy and closed decision making."[10] Such issues as these are altogether remote from the sort of self-presentation that might be found in a sect.

[8] *Creating the Future Together*, SGI-UK Circular (1998).
[9] *SGI-UK Bulletin*, no. 168 (Dec. 1, 1995).
[10] Ibid., no. 177, special suppl. (May 3, 1996).

In the wake of these reassessment discussions, the deputy director issued a written statement on the movement's history, purposes, and prospects, declaring, "The ultimate purpose of our movement is to change society and history for the greater good of humanity." He acknowledged that many leaders overseas (himself included) were Japanese, and "have brought with them Japanese Soka Gakkai customs and traditions. . . . it is important that we endeavor now to create a movement that is suited to each country."[11] As an indication of this resolve it may be noted that in some chapters of SGI in Britain the separate age and sex divisions of members—a structure imported from Japan and not infrequently the subject of criticism among British members—have broken down somewhat, and joint meetings have become more common.

Claiming no more than 6,500 to 7,000 members, SGI-UK is certainly a small religious body, but that does not warrant its designation as a sect. The attitude to membership in itself reveals a sharp difference in its orientation from that of the typical sect. Whereas in a sect the individual is either "in" or "out," and promptly expelled for laxity or inactivity, SGI-UK acknowledges that, of its claimed membership, perhaps only 4,000 may be counted as active. Attendance at discussion meetings is estimated at about 3,000; participants in the Kosen-rufu Fund are about 2,000; subscribers to the monthly *UKExpress*, the movement's organ, number about 5,000 (including overseas subscriptions), while sales of its more explicitly "in-house" bulletin number about 1,800.

We can perhaps most readily regard SGI-UK as one among a number of new denominations, as an autonomous movement owing neither provenance nor allegiance to any immediate Western predecessor. In the wider perspective it is clearly a Buddhist denomination, but in Britain it has little if any relation to such other Buddhist organizations as have been introduced there. Its British members are not particularly interested in the wider divisions of Buddhism, nor even of those that prevailed in the

---

[11] Lecture by Kazuo Fujii, July 26, 1998.

Japanese past, except in so far as they illuminate Nichiren's own distinctive teachings. The British adherents have not, after all, "come out" of any of these older or contemporaneous schools of Buddhism.

Soka Gakkai is also one of those mediating agencies between the state and the individual on which modern society depends if it is to function in a humane way. Such mediating structures were precisely what Émile Durkheim envisaged would be needed in advanced industrial societies. A movement like Soka Gakkai is capable of creating new communal responsibility through its own membership in societies where urban development, commuter life-styles, and impersonal role relationships threaten basic human values. By encouraging small groups to form, by reaffirming the value of mutual counseling, by stressing reconciliation between individuals and groups, Soka Gakkai is an agency capable of reinforcing a measure of social cohesion in societies where the level of shared common consciousness has been jeopardized or eradicated. Such endeavors are no less important than the wider and more public canvas of sound environmental policies, the rehabilitation of refugees, the promotion of education, and the concern for world peace for which, as a nongovernmental organization, Soka Gakkai has already become so widely recognized.

14

Buddhism in Action: Case Studies from Italy

Maria Immacolata Macioti

AT the end of 1998 the Italian Soka Gakkai (ISG) was assuredly the most significant presence of the Soka Gakkai International (SGI) in Europe. About 20,000 members out of a total of about 38,000 in Europe attended meetings and took part in the activities of the Istituto Italiano Soka Gakkai. This prompts many questions: given that Italy is traditionally a Catholic country, it might have been expected that here, more than anywhere, it would have been difficult for a Buddhist school—whose very name sounds alien to Italian culture—to penetrate.

It should also be remembered that the present Istituto Italiano Soka Gakkai has a history of trauma and denominational change, its most difficult moment being the break from Nichiren Shoshu by the lay association presided over by President Ikeda. In Italy this separation was deeply felt. Confused accounts of what was happening in Japan were slow to arrive, causing pain and anxiety among those who were used to thinking of the association as strongly linked to the Japanese priesthood. Most members had received their *Gohonzon* from the hands of a priest who had come from Japan specifically for that purpose. The new member of the Soka Gakkai would assure the priest of his readiness to leave "provisional teachings" and to embrace the "true object of worship," to follow the Lotus Sutra as the definitive teaching for the rest of his life. The priest would call out people's names and they would come forward holding an open *gongyo* book. The priest then raised the *Gohonzon* to the height of the new member's head and lowered it into their opened book. At that moment the novice, the *naitoku*, became a new member of the association.

Between the end of 1993 and the beginning of 1994 the split from Nichiren Shoshu and from its head temple became final. The distribution of *Gohonzons* was terminated forthwith. The lay association, which had previously supported the priesthood, had now to explain that the high priest had seriously departed from the teachings of Nichiren, that the priests' behavior no longer reflected the desire to live in the way that Nichiren taught, or was what was expected of those who had great responsibility and such an important tradition behind them. Ikeda was accused by the high priest of running the association in too personalized a way, of having allowed and encouraged too much openness towards the Western world, and of having distorted the Daishonin's teachings.

The association's publications—the monthly *Il Nuovo Rinascimento*, aimed largely at members, and *Duemilauno*, the bimonthly intended for a wider public—took up this unpleasant subject, proposing that the *Gohonzons* received from Nikken should be returned, and others substituted for them. It was explained that the split had been unsought for, but was perhaps an inevitable outcome of the differences between an innovative lay movement and a priesthood that was becoming more and more reactionary. This was a difficult period of maturation and growing autonomy, for which the association paid with a certain amount of political exile, feelings of unease among the leadership for some months, and imputations on the Internet.

More recently there was a second difficult phase: the passage from lay association to religious institute. The Istituto Buddista Soka Gakkai, "which practices the teachings of Nichiren Daishonin," officially came into being on March 27, 1998. The *Newsletter* which accompanied the May issue of *Il Nuovo Rinascimento* expounded the conviction that Soka Gakkai finds "its best expression in both legal propositions and wider social recognition."

For some this was simply an adjustment to the reality of the situation. For others, however, who were more attached to the identity of a lay association, the change was traumatic. Nevertheless, the decision sanctioned a long process that had accompanied the direction of the Soka Gakkai in recent years. It marked its passage away from a nebulous grouping which included New Age types, new religious movements, and various kinds of spiritual aspiration, together with diverse expectations of the apocalypse—to a clearer sense of belonging within the broad context of Mahayana Buddhism.

When sounded out by the directors, who wanted my opinion on the relationship with the Unione Buddista Italiana (UBI), I replied that it was a reasonable decision. UBI unites various beliefs and schools, and in recent years the Soka Gakkai has taken part in various activities with the union. ISG leaders have participated in important Buddhist events with many other schools, for example, in the Vesak festival at Piacenza, with Taiten Guareschi, and with the Zen Institute Soto Shobozan Fudenji of Salsomaggiore.

The movement in Italy, then, appears to have stood up well to difficult times. The organization was for many years faced with a potentially indifferent, if not hostile, context, and is still in search of its own direction amid organizational and doctrinal difficulties. According to research done in 1993, membership is concentrated in the center and south of Italy. It is composed mostly of females (although the male presence is much higher than is usual in other religious movements: 58 percent female to 41 percent male). They are mainly young adults (in 1993, 33 percent were under 29, and 30 years was the modal age) with rather high educational levels (74 percent had a higher educational qualification) and a high ratio of employees (60 percent against 40 percent self-employed[1]).

Three developments that may be observed in ISG in recent years best account for the school's stability and consolidation in the face of wider public opinion: ISG engagement in social causes; events that facilitate the development of organic solidarity among

---

[1] L. Semprini, "Diffusione in Italia e caratteristiche socio-demografiche degli associati," *La Critica Sociologica*, 111–12 (1994–5), 180–6; M. I. Macioti, "Una ricerca sul movimento della Soka Gakkai in Italia: Primi risultati," *La Critica Sociologica*, 111–12 (1994–5), 164–9.

members; and the birth of an organizational body that negotiates relations between the movement in Italy, the Italian state, and the SGI.

Social Engagement

It is important, first of all, to underline the commitment to others that this movement has made its own, which derives from the conception of the bodhisattva—someone who is on the earth to help his neighbor attain enlightenment, and not because he is constrained by the laws of karma.

Among activities with a social purpose, the ISG has in recent years been concerned with refugee camps, supporting, in a variety of ways, the work of the Consiglio Italiano Rifugiati (CIR), which took over the work of the United Nations High Commission for Refugees (UNHCR) after the enactment of the 1991 law on refugees and immigration. As an association the Soka Gakkai offered indirect rather than direct support. That is, it helped CIR economically but did not organize direct support action for the refugees, and no direct contact between members and refugees now living in Italy was envisaged. At the same time, however, recognition must be given to the fact that the association did a great deal to collect funds, which were then administered by CIR. The proceeds from a theater performance put on by ISG, for example, went directly to CIR. Individual Soka Gakkai members also worked in areas of conflict (for example, the former Yugoslavia), reporting their experiences at meetings in the form of testimonies.

Overall, then, ISG's social commitment grew over a prolonged period, though this was not without difficulties. These sometimes occurred within the organization, among members. For example, the issue of requesting asylum is not always immediately comprehensible to people who have perhaps heard about the problem only from distorted news reports. In relationships with people outside the organization, this choice to support refugees and, more generally, the ISG's social commitment caused perplexity and criticism from some ex-members. This response was also apparent on the Internet in regard to the essence of the movement's Buddhist identity.

The Human Rights Exhibition

In addition to refugee relief, the Soka Gakkai has worked in the last few years to encourage reflection on human rights. For instance, a round of conferences and seminars in various Italian cities held by Johan Galtung were supported by the organization. At the suggestion of the Japanese Soka Gakkai, ISG also prepared and sponsored an exhibition entitled "Human Rights in the Contemporary World." This endeavor required much time and energy, particularly in finding a venue and organizing the displays, which had arrived ready-made but were in need of labels. This involved intensive preparatory work, as well as dedicated labor during the exhibition, which was also enriched by members who acted as guides to individual visitors and organized groups. Among other visitors, schools were invited in the hope of awakening children to the problem of human rights.

Although there were many difficulties (hurried phone calls, frantic searches for adequate space), the directors of the Soka Gakkai carried through the initiative and managed to convey it to members as something very much their own. Within only a few weeks of my first hearing it mentioned, the subject of the exhibition was raised in all the meetings, internal debates, and activity, and, naturally, in the chanting. This last was a most efficacious way of internalizing the theme for members, of seeing it as an opportunity worth the expenditure of time and energy, as well as an opportunity to make friends and relatives, acquaintances and strangers, aware of the issue.

The large visitors' book, full of comments, exclamations, and drawings, and the "diary" that was compiled by members who guided visitors through the exhibit, are of great interest to a sociologist and a rich source of material.

The Visitors' Book

The exhibition was held at the Museo Nazionale Delle Arti e Tradizioni Popolari in Rome, between January 26 and February 20. At the end of their tour, visitors were invited to sign a visitors' book. The volume of signatures alone (about 130 pages) is enough to declare the enterprise a success, at least as regards the number of visitors, and leafing through the album a good deal of other information can be gleaned by anyone interested in qualitative analysis.

In the first few pages we find well-known names—scholars and those who have worked for years in the field of human rights, university professors, migration experts, and diplomats.

Shortly after, the signatures of a wider, more varied public begin. Children's names in unsteady handwriting mix with those of adults. There are Italian and foreign names, both usual and abstruse, and dozens of nicknames. At times the names are written at strange angles. Designs occasionally crop up against the names—a swastika, for example, with evident signs of rubbing out on it. There are frequent exclamation marks, which the pupils put after their names as if to emphasize their presence, one or even two or three of them.

Many schools visited this exhibition. There are secondary, middle, and primary schools, as well as various other educational institutes. The names of the schools evoke a world of history, literature, and science—some are surrounded by an aura of memories and emotions; for others, their prestige or fame may have been tarnished by the passing years. Notably, the names of Catholic schools are evident. There are schools from Rome and the surrounding areas.

In addition to school groups, public and private bodies are present, including international organizations such as Amnesty International, the UN Food and Agriculture Organization, Caritas, and Unicef. As the days pass, the places of origin multiply, encompassing both the north and the south of Italy, but also Spain, Great Britain, Greece, Ireland, Portugal, and—to be expected, of course—Japan. There is even someone from Vatican Radio.

It is impossible to say how many of the visitors were Soka Gakkai members, but they are, to some extent, distinguishable by key words and phrases which recur in the writing:

Awareness of human rights will open the door for the "New Renaissance"—THANK YOU.

Happy to be part of the flow of *kosen-rufu*.

A glorious step forward toward *kosen-rufu*! WELL DONE.

I'd have also put some photos showing the hope and the possibility of human revolution.

Giovanni says hello to all the sokahan.

Every now and then we find *Nam-myoho-renge-kyo* written, and pride of belonging is evident in the exclamation marks—up to three—that follow. President Toda is quoted by someone else: " 'Whatever I search for arrives spontaneously' (Toda). What I search for is peace, therefore it will be realized." Some of the members declare themselves as such and add, "Thank you." In other cases, belonging to the Soka Gakkai can be inferred, but without certainty, as in the case of Micol, who writes: "it's over . . . an incredible experience, thanks to which it's worth continuing to hope . . . beyond any pessimism." It seems probable that this was someone who worked on the exhibition, who worked hard, and sees the end of the exhibition with mixed feelings of relief, regret, and hope.

The exhibition was an important opportunity for education and cohesion for the Soka Gakkai. The members were sensitized to a socially relevant theme. They worked in a multitude of ways to support the exhibition and to publicize it. They brought parents, friends, and relatives. They organized school visits and transport services for special guests. They prepared labels for the displays. There were a multitude of activities for a common and commendable end, and the success of the exhibition is demonstrated by the prestige of the people present at its opening, by the shared involvement of teachers and students from all types of schools, and by the presence of members and friends from Italy, other European nations, and Japan.

The Guides' Diary

In addition to the visitors' book, to which I will return, another source is useful in understanding the impact of the exhibition on members. The guides' diary shows the efficiency with which the exhibition was organized. Each day the guides recorded their experiences in this diary. For the most part, these entries consist of a few lines from each person at the end of their shift. There is a definite sense of having contributed to the success of an important occasion, of reflection, and of awareness on the social plane.

Roberto, for example, refers to another guide: "The following guide, a young man, was more cheerful, using the 'practice' as both starting point and return. He had only recently received *Gohonzon*. He was a great guide—joyful and purposeful." Marisa writes:

I'd like to say how happy it makes me to do this activity. Before the opening I didn't feel very well prepared and also, for various reasons, I hadn't been able to attend the rehearsals. I was obviously far from pleased at the thought of not being able to be a guide, but also at not having used the time well in preparation (this, on top of all the various insecurities connected with study). I said to the *Gohonzon* then that I was willing to do any job assigned to me and that I would make an extra effort to study. So the first Sunday I was assigned to the book table, which might seem a rather marginal activity in comparison with that of guide, but I used it to create value. It turned out to be a profound experience of human contact with the visitors, and it also allowed me to make several interesting discoveries on how much is published and read on the subject.

Vanessa's experience was also positive:

I guided a class of 12 year olds. It was a fantastic experience, they were very involved. They had quite a few questions about things that were by no means hypothetical. The teachers were enthusiastic, complimenting us on the organization and me on my enthusiasm and, at the end, they thanked me and were almost moved! Wow!!!

Luca, who took a class of disabled children around, writes: "A rich but testing experience. It was important not to be afraid, but to communicate safety and tranquility." And later: "As usual a demanding activity but greatly satisfying." Daniela, speaking of the people she accompanied, had this to say: "I felt that they really wanted to know more about it because it's important for them too to be aware of the injustice and discrimination that exist on our planet. Today I feel truly useful and that I have contributed something." There is also another Daniela, who writes of having accompanied, on the 27th, four groups, although she isn't sure of a few things. She knows, however, that they asked for clarification and explanation ("HELP") and that at the end they all declared themselves interested and satisfied: "Many of them stopped longer to read the displays with more attention, and they thanked us with all their hearts. It was a wonderful, edifying activity. CIAO." Later, on February 18, she once again clarifies her state of mind:

Today I've done three tours: coach from Naples, mixed group from Naples and Rome, coach from Latina. The people were very involved and attentive. They'd made a great effort to come to the exhibition, and I felt very much the responsibility of having to repay this. Someone asked me where they could get further information on the subject. It was my last tour; it wrung my heart! I've no words to say how much this has opened up my life, how much strength and richness this activity has given me. I feel as if my 11 years of practice and activity have been the preparation for all this, as if it's for this that Sensei [President Ikeda], and before him Toda have always battled. Thank you with all my heart.

Didone, however, found herself having to guide a group of very skeptical children. She writes: "it was truly pleasing to encourage them to be trusting and to be promoters in defense of human rights." Micol, who spoke little English, encountered one girl among some Japanese visitors who spoke English and understood "just two" words of Italian. Yet, she writes enthusiastically: "it went divinely: long live Daimoku." On February 2, another guide writes about visitors from the Soka Gakkai "Light" group from Trastevere, Rome:

It's really great to accompany members—above all those who've made efforts to put into practice Tamotsu's guidance [ISG director] given for the group meetings; that is, to participate as a group, district, etc. One of them asked me if this exhibition was useful, because he thought only members had come to see it. So I showed him the great number of kids filling the hall and explained to him that Sensei's aim was above all to EDU- CATE the YOUNGER GENERATION and that detailed work had been done with the schools in order to achieve this aim. At the end they were motivated to make a contribution and affirm human rights in their own environment. I'm happy to have been able to hold back on the emotion and to have transmitted determination to improve the world starting with ourselves.

If Cinzia on February 3 writes succinctly of having had a "posi- tive experience," a colleague of hers has a little more to say: "I'm continuing to realize the very great value of this initiative: is it not for this that we have done Buddhist activity for the last 15 years in Italy?"

Many highlight the theme of personal enrichment, including Donatella, who writes: "The experience of being a guide has greatly enriched me, thank you!" A not dissimilar reaction is that of Alessandra, who, after two tours as guide, writes:

My personal experience is to feel that I've taken part in this activity of sen- sitizing the hearts of the people who have visited the human rights exhi- bition, concentrating attention on the possibility of taking action in the daily life of every one of them in light of this new awareness. It has been a great opportunity for me for growth and improvement, in developing the empathy necessary to interact with people who are "different" from me. And for this I want to thank everybody.

And, after having been a guide on February 19 and 20:

In these last few days I've felt it easier and easier for me to communicate sincerely what we really felt—with such acute people—and without the amount, the intensity of the rhythm, and the tiredness being able to prej- udice in even the tiniest way the intensity of the experience. It was possible to go faster and more deeply to the heart of the problem. Thank you every- body, I'm very happy, and I don't think I've ever felt so useful in all my life!

Lodo's testimony, also from the final days of the exhibition, is suggestive as well:

From the point of view of my personal experience, this activity has helped me to unearth all those prejudices that had sneakily and subtly insinuated themselves into my cultural baggage. It has further helped me in making me realize how much my actions have got to be sincerely directed at the *Gohonzon*, and I should not do things just in order to be well thought of by others. Finally, I'd like to recount something that happened to me when I began to take this activity seriously: I slowly started to feel a growing sense of gratitude (and therefore incredible joy) for our organization, without which I'd probably never have deepened my knowledge of human rights, and without which I'd never have been able to use my time, and more generally my life, for something of value. Something that without doubt ends up by infinitely enriching my own life.

The exhibition, then, certainly achieved its primary (though perhaps not explicitly stated) objective—that of making the members feel part of a noble common undertaking. It made them feel proud to belong to the Soka Gakkai, an association capable of offering its support in a socially relevant field such as human rights, a socially useful association to which it was worth dedicating one's time.

Furthermore, the exhibition had secondary (unintended) benefits—that is, recognition on the part of some parents who had not necessarily been enthusiastic about their children belonging to the Soka Gakkai of the relevance, the goodness, of their involvement. This important fact is reflected in some of the guides' spontaneous remarks. Didone, for example, writes: "I accompanied groups of women that I knew; ISG members' mothers who were really happy about how the exhibition was presented, the photos and explanations." Francesca notes: "A member's husband who doesn't practice came for the second time, another came with his daughter and was enthusiastic and encouraged us to continue with the exhibition or have others of this kind, because it's very important." Daniela, in her turn, gives the following account:

My mother didn't want to come, but after having seen the exhibition she said to me, "At times we have prejudices which prevent us from going to see things, from being informed, but then, when we finally do go and look, we are very happy. I'm happy to have seen this exhibition!" I'll end this account with this remark because it's what I think too: "I'm really happy that the SGI and the ISG have begun to take the field, socially!" Thank you!

And Marisa, finally, writes:

Last Sunday I took my parents to see the exhibition, and we were immediately taken up by a guided tour. My parents, who didn't think they'd be able to bear the sight of the photos, in fact saw and read everything. They were very happy about my commitment too and complimented us on the initiative and the organization. They suggested more advertising.

Another aim was partially achieved—that of making the Soka Gakkai better known in Italian life. In addition to showing that it had organized a valuable social event, the ISG demosntrated to the Italian public that it has important partners, such as the UN and UNHCR. Again, entries in the guides' diary illustrate the influence of the exhibit on visitors. Alessandra, for example, writes thus: "Reactions of openness and great willingness and interest toward the subject. People who wanted to be furnished with information on who we are, what we do, what kind of answers we have." The next day Valentina notes that visitors had "particular questions relating to the activity of the UN and of the Soka Gakkai." Another guide, Pierangela, writes of an American couple and their son who "paid particular attention to the development of the SGI at world level." And Marisa shares an experience in which "a teacher asked me why the Buddhists were concerning themselves with this theme. I replied briefly on Buddhist philosophy—that it respects life in all its forms, and on the aim of achieving world peace and then I invited her to read President Ikeda's message." Cinzia also had occasion to talk about the Soka Gakkai: "I led a group of adults who followed everything with interest. There were no specific questions except from two people who knew about the ISG and had been to meetings. They were interested in knowing about the dual function of the ISG (as a Buddhist international lay association and nongovernmental organization)."

The content of the exhibition emerges more pointedly from the guides' accounts than from comments written by the public, which as a rule were expressed in rather general terms. One exception to this was AIDS. Another topic, that of old age, was singled out in the words of Giorgio, who in a very young hand writes a poem called "loneliness":

> Loneliness makes old people sad
> who are on their own poor old things waiting lovingly
> for a bit of company
> Loneliness is horrible sometimes,
> I don't like it because
> always being
> alone is like an abandoned puppy
> that gets forgotten by everyone.

One of the recurrent themes in the guides' accounts is that of female circumcision, an interest at times accompanied by strong emotion, especially among girls. Particular interest was shown by refugees from the former Yugoslavia who were in Italy on a humanitarian permit. What happens when their permit runs out? There were also many questions about immigrants, revealing some prejudice and ignorance.

Marisa writes of the questions and interest regarding the work situation of women in Japan, while many guides mention a wider interest in women's problems. Alessandra encountered the theme of kidnapping, and tough polemic about torture and whether or not it was lawful to torture a kidnapper in order to get information about the person who had been kidnapped. Besides this, she took on the issue of the death penalty and life imprisonment. Particular attention was given to the subjects of malnutrition, infant mortality, and *desaparesidos*.

Public Reaction

There was more consensus than dissent in response to the exhibition, as represented by both the guides' and the visitors' books, in which the public had a more immediate chance to represent themselves. There are many emphatic comments such as: "Really great!" "Well done, memorable." "Truly meaningful. To see and to remember." "Moving!"

Special thanks are at times addressed to the Soka Gakkai:

Thanks to the lay association "Soka Gakkai" that has allowed all this, that has so greatly contributed, thanks to its members, to the constant improvement of our society.

We congratulate you along with the association's collaborators and we thank you for having given us a way in which to understand more deeply the meaning of life.

I would like to congratulate and thank the whole organization on the exhibition because it has been truly an inspiration.

At times the congratulations for the Soka Gakkai come from teachers who explained that they were involved in similar initiatives, as, for example, in the case of a teacher who was working with her class on a project called "A Dream that will Change the World." Amongst others thanking the Soka Gakkai we find a teacher from the Virgilio, a well-known old Roman secondary school: "When you have words that are stronger than silence they need to be shouted. This is an example."

At times the comments appear more in the nature of proposals: "Let's begin with our own homes and respect each other every day, respect ourselves and we'll begin to respect the dignity of every human being. CONGRATULATIONS TO EVERYONE WHO COLLABORATED ON THE EXHIBITION." Next to a rubbed out swastika (a curious, but recurring feature), we find written, "PEACE NO WAR." And a boy writes: "WE WANT FREEDOM." At times good proposals for the future are expressed in forms that are personal and incisive:

I'm going to become an expert in human rights.

This exhibition is very significant and we must commit ourselves to solving the world's problems.

I'm 64 years old and a pensioner: I've sworn to myself that as long as I'm alive I'll continue this project with all my strength: create peace, with dedication, love, constancy, and patience.

Many are reflections that point to a new self-awareness:

Thanks for having awoken our consciences.

This exhibition has made us realize how fortunate we are and how many people need our constant help!

Thanks to this exhibition I've discovered the importance of having to look at the world around me!

I've realized my good fortune and I felt impotent when I understood the misfortunes of others.

It's exhibitions like this that show us an unhappy and tough reality that too many of us and for too long have wished to forget . . . to ignore!

There are days like today when I have nothing to do, and honestly this exhibition of photographs and, above all, of thoughts, has enlarged my mind in respect to existence, which at certain times does anything but smile on me. And I'm content, at least for the moment.

Among other considerations, there is the observation that there is not always sufficient knowledge of what is going on in the world. Alessandra says so, shyly, in brackets: "(I didn't think that there were such inhuman areas.)" And Chiara writes: "Moving and shocking to see and listen to, we ought to know how to remember constantly." And a teacher, Teresa, thanks the sponsors for "sensitizing young people to these dramatic problems."

At times the messages are accompanied by drawings, like that of a girl's where beside the word "heart" is drawn the classic, stylized little heart: "Peace begins in our hearts, when we respect the other person as the mirror of ourselves and we consider other people's suffering as our own." And there is someone who recognizes "A kick in the guts that has been really useful for me. Thanks." For some, the exhibition stimulated a sense of commitment: "Congratulations on the great work you've done. It's only the beginning of a deeper understanding in our lives of how to show others the value of life," arranged down the center of the page and flanked by three rows of signatures.

References to tolerance and against racism are also numerous:

Only someone who admits their own mistakes can tolerate those of other people.

Know yourself before judging others.

A few demonstrate less optimistic states of mind: "I hope that all this has some use, even though I think that people don't want to see all the things that might upset their peace of mind." Somebody puts the question: "What's all this for?" Others, instead, deplore the crudity of the pictures: "there are many ways of touching a person's sensitivity: To bombard them with a series of such crude images doesn't seem to me to be the best way." As a rule, however, dissent is mostly absent.

To conclude, the exhibition had a striking impact on both its organizers and the public, and appears to have achieved its declared aim of raising awareness. It probably achieved some goals that were implicit in the undertaking, though perhaps not clearly predictable. It generated a strong sense of solidarity among members, raised public knowledge of the Soka Gakkai, and improved relations between some members and their families.

Despite the fact that this was a sporadic activity, proposed—as too often in my judgment—from above by the international organization, the positive impact on local members is notable. The exhibition gave individual members a sense of making a contribution to important collective goals and improved the organization's public image by publicizing its association with both national and international organizations that share these interests and aims.

Party Time: Garden Party at the Rome Soka Gakkai

The Soka Gakkai does not, however, live by social commitment, meetings, and chanting alone. For some time it has been aware of the importance of friendship events, leaving a certain amount of freedom of action to the local divisions in this respect. Toward the end of the first half of June 1998 there was much talk of a garden party being prepared in Rome, a similar initiative having previously taken place in Florence to celebrate the *kaikan*'s (center's) first ten years. The intention had been to do something together for the Florentine population and, more particularly, for those who had once been members but had distanced themselves from the movement. The idea was to open the center to members' families, as well as to those who lived near the center. It was, therefore, an enterprise aimed at restoring and strengthening good relations with people who, in one way or another, had already had something to do with the Soka Gakkai, and to spend a pleasant, relaxing time together with people whom the Soka Gakkai did not yet know. The idea was taken up again by the members in Rome. The two-day event was organized by the arts division. The public relations team seemed concerned about a certain chaos, a certain lack of preparation. They themselves did not even know the program.

Next to the large *butsuma* (the room where the *Gohonzon* is kept) is an open structure where birds often fly in and out. For that day it became a piano bar, where we would later go and listen to Neapolitan songs. Between this structure and the large *butsuma*, where three talented singers were performing, there is an open construction. Here there were tables with a rich and varied buffet. All along the side of the lawn and in other strategic points were more tables of food and drink.

Many activities were taking place simultaneously. Everywhere there were children with balloons; some tied them to their wrists, others to the back of their jacket, which tended, inevitably, to be lifted up by the breeze. For the children there were special events at the back of the large *butsuma*, such as an excellent storyteller recounting "Beauty and the Beast." The children sat, enchanted, in front of him. Nearby, delightful music came from an old barrel organ. Further on there was a puppet theater. Someone was walking on very high stilts, and clowns, unknown to their victims, followed people, imitating their walk and making faces. In the mêlée there were fairies, all in blue with flat blue hats wrapped in blue tulle, although one had the classic cone-shaped hat. They carried large baskets and handed out poetry, well known or written by members, on blue, white, or yellow pieces of paper. One little girl received Schiller's "Hymn to Joy."

The members' poetry was particularly interesting. A fairy offered me one; another fairy offered a second. When I went home

I would have a sackful! The poems, both handwritten and typed, were signed by their authors; most were dated. The same author may have given different dates; I chanced to have two poems by the same person but written many years apart. One read:

> I want a friend.
> I want a black friend
> Who'll take me on his horse;
> Down the road on his horse.
> And we'll go silently among all kinds of people,
> Me and my black friend.
> We'll sit together at sunset
> And chat about things with all kinds of people.
> We'll eat cabbage soup out of coconut shells,
> And we'll drink fresh wine at the roadside bars;
> Me, the horse, my friend, and all kinds of people.
> He'll take me to places and to cities
> To talk and to hear what it's good to know.
> I'll learn a thousand languages.
> From time to time,
> The road,
> Another sunset,
> Sitting and chatting,
> Waiting for evening and the night,
> Sleeping,
> Those you can trust outside the door,
> Warm dreams,
> And you'll be rested tomorrow
> To go on again.

> (Francesca Ventricelli, 1981)

Among other items there were poems by young members (aged between 6 and 12). One of these, by an Alessandra Zoia, was entitled "The Flower and the Sun":

> Once upon a time there was a piercing sun.
> Once upon a time there was a weeping flower.
> They greeted each other sadly.
> The flower danced.

The sun moaned.
The flower smiled,
and the sun smiled.
In chorus they cheerfully said,
"We'll be friends for ever."

From a young age, the message that it is necessary to regard reality with a certain optimism, and to be ready to change poison into medicine, is internalized. Thus, the sun stops "moaning" and welcomes the flower's smile, which leads to an amicable understanding between the two.

Members at the party were extremely busy and cheerful. Those in difficulty, such as a couple who had just lost a child, were surrounded by an network of evident solidarity. There was a woman who had been through a difficult operation and an even more difficult postoperative period. Many were cheered to see her there. They celebrated and hung around amicably. The solidarity and the attention directed toward the other members appeared without pause on these festive days.

Everywhere there were women, young and not so young, in flowery or colorful dresses, straw hats with flowers, or baseball caps to give some respite from the strong afternoon sun. The choir Sing to Pass By involved the public, encouraging them in all sorts of ways to sing, to take up a refrain. There was a youth choir, grouped as "flowers," "records," "sweets," and "bathers." One of the flowers, a girl, was wonderfully decorated in green crepe paper with garlands of flowers around her neck and waist.

Attendants assisted at the striptease of a young man covered in ample swathes of white crepe paper. All around people encouraged him with yells and clapping. At the end he was left wearing only his socks. Moving here and there were boys and girls with purple or yellow tufts in their hair, a popular trend that confirmed that they were modern kids. Older members, there to give information should it be needed, were dressed completely in white. The information stand was constantly surrounded.

A more serious option was provided by an exhibition of photographs, the meaning of which was not very clear, inside the *butsuma*. The subject was various Soka Gakkai edifices around the world. Nearby there was a slide show. Besides these, there was a photo exhibition in a yellow tent on the lawn on the theme of "Peace not War." Under each of the seven pictures was a phrase from a well-known personality, such as Bertolt Brecht, Primo Levi, Ungharetti, or Soka Gakkai leaders. Such serious matters, however, were an aside to the main purpose of the event, which was fun.

An eclectic mix of musical styles were offered by artists, many of whom had traveled a long way to act, to dance, and to sing. People might listen to jazz or Latin American music, or delight in the tango. There were people listening to guitars, while others opted for violin and cello; there were also clarinets and flutes for the lovers of wind music. People commented on the *butho* dance, remarking on its solemnity, the slowness of its movements. The dance took place around a water container, in and out of which the dancers very, very slowly moved.

In all, there were sixteen areas of interest, each with its own program. Truly this was an example of "Stendhal syndrome," which means being faced with too rich a cultural offering. The event illustrated the wise alternation between activities initiated from above, by the international organization, such as the exhibition, and more organic activities coming, as it were, from below, such as this garden party. The result is a consolidation of knowledge and mutual solidarity. From this dialectic between direction from above and spontaneous action at the popular level, ISG promotes collective, social undertakings while also providing a free space for creative self-determination. At this time it appears to have achieved a balance that is decidedly functioning.

From Voluntary Society to Religious Organization

In the late spring of 1998 there were 20,719 members of the Soka Gakkai not including those newcomers whose adherence was still uncertain. This number is based on June 1998 attendance at the *zadankai* (group meetings). The members were overwhelmingly female (67 percent), as is often the case in spiritual and religious movements. This is a rather diffuse movement, then, with a strong youthful component—a larger component today than in 1993. The youth component is strong above all in central Italy, where it accounts for 8,895 attendances, and relatively weaker in the north, where attendances number 5,634.

The fact remains that the Soka Gakkai, as I mentioned earlier, seems to have overcome several traumatic periods and, for the time being, to be affirming a presence that is substantially close to that of the UBI as a whole. In particular, it has been able to reemerge from the inevitable polemic accompanying the break with the Japanese priesthood of Nichiren Shoshu. It seems to have overcome the war of defamatory bulletins and communications that, after appearing in Japan, arrived in Italy via the Internet. It has even seen its own president, Daisaku Ikeda, put in difficulty many times and finally, in 1991, excommunicated. Yet, it seems to have stood up to all this. Some members left the organization at the time. Many, though, remained and worked to create a better climate, to lessen the polemic, to clarify the situation within the association.[2]

Again, the Soka Gakkai has got through the difficult moment of passage from lay association to religious institute—for a scholar, an interesting passage to follow, but certainly not a pain-free one for all the members who today find themselves part of a different reality than that which they had initially joined.

The special edition of *Il Nuovo Rinascimento* dedicated to this change presented it as a way of harmonizing substance and form: the legal recognition of Soka Gakkai as a religious body better reflects the reality of the situation, since it has always been typically and essentially religious. Dadina Miglionico, on the day of the garden party, had this to say: "We have always been a religion—in reality this is what Buddhism has always been. Instrumentally, in the beginning we had to avoid highlighting this aspect in order to avoid too much difficulty in a predominantly Catholic country."

---

[2] M. I. Macioti, *Il Buddha che è in noi: Germogli del Sutra del Loto* (Rome: Seam, 1996); K. Dobbelaere, *La Soka Gakkai: Un movimento di laici diventa una religione* (Turin: ElleDiCi, 1998).

In recent years, then, the Soka Gakkai, at least in Italy, has decisively taken the path of alignment with other Buddhist schools: it has chosen to portray itself as a Buddhist movement. The relationship with UBI is much closer and more cordial than it was ten or so years ago. And we know very well that Buddhism is one of the great world religions, as defined also by Émile Durkheim who suggested that the characteristic element of a religion was belief in the sacred.

How will adherents take this change, however? Up to now they have belonged to a lay association that has become emptied of content, at least at the economic level. I am given to understand from a national summer course at Chianciano that the property that belonged to the Association Soka Gakkai passes, if it has not already done so, to the institute—and therefore to the religious form, legally codified. Many things change, from the possibility of marriage ceremonies to that of teaching in schools.

There could be advantages to this, including possible recognition on the part of the Italian state. This is already prefigured in the special edition of *Il Nuovo Rinascimento*, according to which "this new legal form will confer greater social recognition on our movement and will allow us to enjoy those rights and prerogatives that the Italian State reserves for established social realities, specifically religious bodies." Another new entity has also been instituted: a board of ministers of religion, whose list includes the names of some who were at one time lay leaders.

What changes, in general terms, will occur in daily life? Does a religious body, for example, dedicate itself essentially to helping its own members, or should it not rather be open to a wider social perspective? The charitable activities of the Catholic Church, for example, are not only and should not only be directed exclusively toward Catholics. Certainly, this cannot be a statutory obligation. The statute, in fact, says, in point 3: "The institute is a body of religion and of faith, and pursues educational, cultural, and humanitarian aims coessential with the Buddhist concept." It does not stipulate *who* should be the object of the educational, cultural, and humanitarian ends. It would, however, be reductive to think that everything ends with the members who head the institute. On the other hand, it is a fact that their commitment to the other members of the Soka Gakkai is already heavy, in terms of time and energy.

At Chianciano I realized that there were many doubts, even though nearly all the membership declared itself in agreement with this decision. Their discussion at Chianciano was to some extent too late, since the decision had already been made and practical steps to implement it had already gone ahead. The decision was taken at the top, after legal consultation with regard to the form. The substance of it was discussed with members only after the fact.

It was discussed, however. Fabio Massimo Orlando gave a precise introduction to the normative picture, insisting on the concept of freedom of religious expression, reminding us of Article 19 of the Constitution. He dwelt on the aims of a religious body (either of faith or confessional). He confronted the problem of recognition yet to come on the part of the Italian state, that would confer "visibility" and "legal recognition." The aims of a religious body, he explained, were considered to be "of public interest," though they were not properly "the State's own ends." We were talking, in other words, of "constitutional importance." What would an agreement with the Italian state, a "further step in respect to obtaining recognition," bring? It would open up the possibility of recognition, the speaker explained, as a "religious confession . . . with full entitlements at the legal, social, and cultural levels." The agreement, it follows, "would be sanctioned by a law of the State."

Francesco Geracitano offered a historical comparative analysis of the other religious confessions existing in Italy that had obtained recognition, reflecting on the accomplishments of the religious bodies. He also mentioned the issue of endowments, which was important to gaining recognition. With the institute, the old compulsory contribution for associate members ceased and was to be substituted by "spontaneous, variable contributions," or "offerings." However, in order to guarantee an adequate endowment, in the coming month of September the ISG would go ahead with a donation to the institute. At the time about 90 percent (18,500) of the members of the ISG were members of the institute. It was predicted that the principal activities as regards faith would be assumed by the religious body.

Mr Tamotsu (one of the two vice-directors of the old association, the other being Mr Kansaki) took up the theme of the consequences of the inauguration of this body, underlining the many benefits that would be derived from recognition by the state. Tamotsu added, however, that Italy was a special case:

This doesn't mean that in all the other European states the Soka Gakkai has to follow the same route as the Italian one—that is, become a religious body . . . the choice to become a religious body is a typically Italian choice that comes from the maturing of our movement in our country and from the Italian normative reality. We must not forget that Italy is one of the leading countries in the *kosen-rufu* movement in Europe, as well as being numerically the most consistent.

Yet, Tamotsu recognized that "recognition of the Soka Gakkai as a religious body operating from one of the member states of the European Union will increase awareness of our movement in the other member states too."

There was much curiosity, and many concerns. We were informed about the economic aspects: had the running costs of the *kaikans* in Florence and Rome already passed to the institute? Someone asked why this initiative was being undertaken alone and not with UBI. The immediate answer was that the Soka Gakkai has its own specific goal—the aim is always to achieve *kosen-rufu*; the numbers were such that entry into UBI would create too many difficulties.

Further doubts arose from the example of the Catholic Church, which has a special relationship with Italy. The questions addressed the possible privileged status of the present ministers of faith, and whether the *kaikans* would have special privileges. Would recognition of the *kaikans* have any effect on the *zadankais* (group meetings)?

The debate concluded with some reassuring phrases: "We're what we've always been," "We've always carried out religious activity." "We'll stay the same." And Tamotsu said: "we must decide democratically what we need to do," which will be, besides action for the members, action directed outwards from the organization toward society as a whole. Someone had already had the idea of doing something for peace and against the nuclear threat; others returned to the issue of refugees. "There are many things to do. But we've only just been born, and it's difficult to do everything, isn't it? I hope that proposals will continue to be put forward as much as they did before."

Conclusion

From this analysis of some of the most significant moments, various tendencies emerge.

The Soka Gakkai maintains a high number of members and a strong internal cohesion, calling its members to a firm commitment. This is directed firstly toward themselves, second toward other members, and third toward society at large. There is no ethic of isolation and renunciation, as has already been noted by Karel Dobbelaere.[3] Cohesion up to now has been such as to overcome particularly traumatic difficulties such as the split with Nichiren Shoshu, uncontrolled attacks on Ikeda on the Internet, and the passage from lay association to religion.

In this sense, one can perhaps hypothesize for the years to come an intensification of the efforts relative to society at large of what Karel Dobbelaere calls "pillars." Probably, the ISG will meet some difficulties here too. Already there has been polemic on the Internet in this regard, in which an ex-member has noted that social commitment (which is very much part of the integration of the Soka Gakkai in an Italian context) has little or nothing to do with the definition of Buddhism by the more consolidated schools.

Third, it seems worth underlining the intelligent alternation and coexistence of moments of strong commitment and moments of "escapism," such as the shows that end the days of reflection, and the courses, or the garden party itself.

---

[3] Dobbelaere, *La Soka Gakkai*.

I highlight once again the management, both elitist and demo-cratic, of the Soka Gakkai. From Japan comes the basic direction, the cultural approach, such as the decision on the human rights exhibition (in this case the displays, too, arrived from Japan: explanatory material and organization was left to the ISG), and the decision to pass from a lay movement to a religion. But, this input is then discussed in all the meetings, members being heard on the matter, being able to express their own opinions (the only excep-tions being in cases of total dissent, when they leave), being involved in preparation and action. Now that the Italian institute has come into being, this was talked about at Chianciano and also in the individual *zadankais*, where ideas for the future are solicited in relation to the new role of the movement. Even the children assist in building the common structure. For example, in "The Future and Beyond" one of them writes under the headline "Useful News": "What is Buddhism? Buddhism is a religion that instead of talking about God talks about Buddha." As a rule, reli-gions are institutional forms with a hierarchical structure and a wider base. In this sense, the Soka Gakkai seems to be taking the route from small or relatively small movement to institutional reli-gion. Until now the coexistence of a pyramidal structure and of a horizontal network organization has proved productive.

It should be mentioned that the Soka Gakkai in Italy meets with difficulties relating to its links with Japan and the SGI. Its organ-izational structure still envisages the presence of a Japanese president of the institute, Mr Kaneda, and of two Japanese vice-presidents, Mr Tamotsu and Mr Kanzaki—all greatly esteemed and loved. Yet their presence at the top reveals a foreign origin that has still not been fully overcome, with all the problems of sepa-rateness that this brings. The Catholic Church, for example, knows this very well, having with difficulty and over time established itself in far-off contexts like those of Asia and Africa. If today it is reap-ing the fruits of these operations, it is because these contexts have acted as reservoirs of vocation, which in Europe has diminished. It is also true that belonging to a vast international organization can imply a sense of security, of greater solidity than there would be if these links were broken. There is also the fact that such an organization can achieve things that a small one would be unable to accomplish or perhaps even conceive of. But it is certain that the challenge for Soka Gakkai in Italy in the future will be to manage that near–far dialectic.

The challenge ahead for the ISG is above all that of consolidation of its identity, in a complex game at both national and international level. It is also challenged by links with other Buddhist schools and its own specific definition: a Buddhism of action, a Buddhism that provides support for daily life, as against other types of Buddhism that are directed more to introspection, to meditation and detachment from context. Will the ISG be able to accomplish this without losing the close contact with its own base which is, today, the reason for its strength?

15

The Expansion of the Soka Gakkai into Southeast Asia

Daniel Metraux

IN recent years Japanese new religions have manifested strong growth in Asia. Among them, Soka Gakkai International (SGI) alone has a strong organizational base in virtually every Asian country.[1] Of these countries, Malaysia, Singapore, and Hong Kong parallel each other as "newly industrializing countries" with significant ethnic Chinese populations. Because of their similarities in ethnic composition and history the SGI organizations in these three states may be compared and contrasted to great effect.

The Success of Japanese Religions in Modern Asian Societies

The transplantation of Japanese religions to other societies is a comparatively recent phenomenon. Japan has long been the recipient of religious and cultural influences from outside sources, but since the 1960s several of Japan's new religions have successfully reversed this process. They have achieved their greatest success in Korea, Taiwan, Hong Kong, Southeast Asia, Brazil, and the United States. There are also scattered groups of followers in Canada, Europe, Africa, and Oceania.[2]

---

[1] The Soka Gakkai strongly rejects the idea that it is a "new religion." It argues that it is promoting the spread of the 700-year-old teachings of Nichiren. The Soka Gakkai prefers to call itself a "new religious movement."

[2] Tokyo University professor Susumu Shimazono provided the following statistics for the foreign membership of Japanese new religions in 1991. In

Although these new religious movements reflect their Japanese origins in some aspects of their ideology and organizational structure, they address questions and problems affecting people in industrializing and postindustrial societies worldwide. These issues include peace and war, a declining environment, conditions at work, family relations, matters of individual health, psychological well-being, and prosperity.[3]

Tokyo University professor Susumu Shimazono writes:

One of the common characteristics of the New Religions is their response to strongly felt needs of individuals in their daily lives, their solutions to discord in interpersonal relations, their practical teaching that offers concrete solutions for carrying on a stable social life, and their provision, to individuals who have been cut off from traditional communities, of a place where congenial company and a spirit of mutual support can be found. As capitalistic industrialization and urbanization advance, large numbers of individuals are thrown into new living environments, thus producing conditions that require spiritual support for the individual. . . . Japanese religions are abundantly equipped with cultural resources that answer the needs of just these people in treading the path towards the urban middle class.[4]

Japan was the first Asian nation to experience industrialization and urbanization. New religions grew rapidly in response to the

Brazil Seicho no Ie had 2.5 million members; Sekai Kyuseikyo and Perfect Liberty Kyodan had 250,000 each; and Soka Gakkai had 150,000. Sukyo Kyuseikyo had several tens of thousands, and Reiyukai claimed 44,000. Soka Gakkai claims 333,000 adherents in North America, mainly in the United States. Hammond and Machacek estimate a much smaller active membership. In Asia SGI easily surpasses other Japanese religious organizations. Seicho no Ie, Tenrikyo, and Sekai Kyuseikyo also have significant followings. See Susumu Shimazono, "Expansion of Japan's New Religions," *Japanese Journal of Religious Studies*, 18/2–3 (1991), 105–32; Nobutaka Inoue, *Umi o watatta Nihon shukyo* ("Japanese Religions Overseas") (Tokyo: Kobundo, 1985); Phillip Hammond and David Machacek, *Soka Gakkai in America: Accommodation and Conversion* (Oxford: Oxford University Press, 1999).

[3] Peter B. Clarke and Jeffrey Somers, "Japanese 'New' and 'New, New' Religions: An Introduction," in Clarke and Somers (eds.), *Japanese New Religions in the West* (Sandgate, Folkestone: Japan Library/Curzon Press, 1994), 1.

[4] Shimazono, "Expansion of Japan's New Religions," 116.

problems facing many Japanese living within this environment. Later, when other East and Southeast Asian cultures experienced parallel forces of urbanization and industrialization, many people there felt a need for religions responsive to their circumstances. Their new lives forced a break with the cultures, religions, and traditions that had held fast for thousands of years. Social change in Asia has included rising demands for the democratization of society and individual rights. There is increased emphasis on the role of the individual and the importance of individual initiative. This idea of self-empowerment, where the individual bears total responsibility for his successes and failures, is closely in tune with capitalist societies, where the individual is supposed to flourish or fail based on his own merits and efforts.

The new religions preach the mutual support of equal partners in a nuclear rather than a patriarchal family. They sustain a strong ethic that emphasizes hard work, honesty, and integrity as well as the need to work for the welfare of others in the local community and for the benefit of the nation and mankind.[5] Veteran members often affirm that they entered the religion to satisfy personal needs, but that, as a result of their new religion, they gradually began to see themselves as transformed and more altruistic than before. Indeed, researchers who reconstruct preconversion attitudes with subsequent change have discovered that converts, including several hundred interviewed by me in Southeast Asia, do in fact "perceive themselves as transformed and more altruistic than before because of the resources they believe they have discovered" in the new religions.[6]

The Soka Gakkai in Southeast Asia

SGI claims a following of 800,000 to 900,000 in Asia. Its initial growth in Southeast Asia started in ethnic Chinese communities in

[5] Shimazono, "Expansion of Japan's New Religions," 120.
[6] Mark Mullins and Richard Young, "Editors' Introduction," *Japanese Journal of Religious Studies*, 18/2–3 (1991), 99.

Hong Kong and Thailand[7] in the early 1960s, and spread to Chinese communities in Malaysia, Singapore, and elsewhere by the mid-1960s. Today ethnic Chinese constitute an overwhelming majority of SGI members in Malaysia, Singapore, and Hong Kong. There is also a minority ethnic Indian membership and a scattering of other Asian and Western members.

Shimazono's thesis concerning the appeal of Japan's new religions to upwardly mobile urbanites also applies quite well to younger SGI members in Malaysia, Singapore, and Hong Kong. Career-oriented SGI members in these countries maintained that SGI's emphasis on individual responsibility and initiative, together with the organization's ability to provide them with a strong sense of optimism, happiness, and a meaningful "extended family," were things which made membership in the organization very appealing. Another key factor in SGI's success in many Asian states, however, is that as a strong Buddhist movement it represents one of the largest and most traditional of Japan's schools of Buddhism. Most Asian countries have strong Buddhist traditions of their own and almost half of SGI members surveyed indicated that their families were Buddhist and that they had actively practiced some form of Buddhism in the past, usually as children. Many SGI members suggested that when they joined SGI, they felt that they had found a deeper and more relevant form of Buddhism. They had not left their Buddhist tradition; rather, they had found an enhanced version of it.

Why should a Japanese-based Buddhist movement be so successful among ethnic Chinese in Malaysia, Singapore, and Hong

[7] There are many Thai members as well, especially in less urban and more rural areas. Interviews with three Thai members in Japan in Nov. 1998 indicate that except for the fact that SGI has a lower percentage of ethnic Chinese members than in other countries studied in this chapter, its basic characteristics are very similar to SGI elsewhere in Southeast Asia. Most members grew up as Buddhists and regard SGI as a reaffirmation of their Buddhahood. They appreciate SGI because of its focus on the needs and desires of the individual and because Nichiren Buddhism in their opinion not only provides a clear explanation of why they suffer, but also provides a clear path to greater happiness, personal transformation, and satisfaction in life. SGI in Thailand is very community-oriented and has excellent ties with the government.

Kong? Memories of Japanese World War II military atrocities against Chinese in each of these areas remain very vivid, especially among the elderly. Still, SGI has won broad official and public acceptance in these countries, and most SGI members indicated that they had only rarely received criticism from friends and relatives when they joined. There are apparently several reasons for this ready acceptance. The Soka Gakkai strongly opposed the war effort, and its leaders at the time—Tsunesaburo Makiguchi and Josei Toda—were imprisoned when they refused to cooperate with government authorities. The Soka Gakkai also has a long and genuine record of friendship with cultural, educational, and political leaders in the People's Republic of China. SGI's Buddhist identity, however, is the most important factor.

SGI's success in Southeast Asia may thus be attributed to a combination of factors: its ability to provide members with a strong Buddhist foundation in their lives and its appeal to individuals living in rapidly urbanizing and industrializing societies. Interviews with members indicated that they had experienced a strong spiritual vacuum before joining SGI and that their membership had helped them to fill this void. Every member expressed satisfaction with their new lives and alleged that a positive transformation of personality was the source of their increased happiness.

The keys to this transformation are the twin concepts of karma and responsibility for one's own actions. SGI leaders stress that Buddhism is not for those people who like to be told how to order their lives, who look constantly for guidance from an outside authority, whether in the form of a priest, scripture, or ritual. Throughout the Gakkai's teaching, along with the insistence on a balanced life and common sense, there is a stated obligation for each person to think things out for himself, to make up his own mind and to make his own decisions. The doctrine of karma requires each believer to be responsible for his own salvation.

No matter how bad things have been in the past, the SGI faithful see a bright future *in this lifetime* for those who demonstrate strong faith, work hard for their own career development, demonstrate compassion, and offer a helping hand to others. People who are convinced that they can wipe away the burdens of the past and improve their lot in life will take positive action to upgrade their existence and will take risks for success in a free enterprise economy. A pioneer female member in Hong Kong exclaimed:

Becoming a Soka Gakkai member was like emerging out of a cold dark tunnel into the bright sunshine. I had been a prisoner of my past, but then I joined a loving family whose members genuinely enjoy taking care of each other. Trivial matters that used to worry us about our own lives pale into significance compared to the problems facing society as a whole.

SGI works hard to make members feel comfortable with its Buddhism. For example, the Singapore Soka Association (SSA) reports that a number of older members left the movement in the early 1990s when Soka Gakkai broke with the Nichiren Shoshu priesthood. Older ethnic Chinese Buddhists in Singapore had always maintained close relationships with Buddhist priests and temples and were not entirely comfortable when SGI broke its ties with the priesthood. Some of these older members returned to the Soka Gakkai in 1997 when it opened a modern temple and brought in a "reformed" Nichiren priest from Japan who is a strong supporter of the Soka Gakkai.[8]

Local chapters are fully organized, financed, and led by local nationals. They receive publications, doctrinal documents, and writings by and about Daisaku Ikeda, but little else. An SGI leader in Hong Kong stated proudly, "We are a Hong Kong-based Buddhist organization serving Hong Kong people. We work very

---

[8] The priest, Yuhan Watanabe, is a 40-year-old graduate of Soka University whose parents are Soka Gakkai members. He had received training as a Nichiren Shoshu priest before breaking with the sect when it expelled the Soka Gakkai in the early 1990s. Watanabe reports that some conservative Singapore members were offended by the fact that Nichiren Shoshu priests often married and had large families. Watanabe is single and was hired in Singapore on the condition that he will remain celibate. Watanabe criticizes the traditional Nichiren Shoshu priesthood because it allegedly places itself "above" the people, insisting that priests alone have the power to alter people's karmas. He asserts that priests are in every respect equal in status with the lay believer and that the role of the priest is to assist the lay believer in strengthening his faith. Watanabe left Nichiren Shoshu and joined a small group of "reformed priests" willing to work together with Soka Gakkai.

independently of Tokyo. . . . The key links between us and Tokyo are our faith in Nichiren Daishonin's Buddhism and our deep respect for Daisaku Ikeda. We finance all of our own operations."

Profile of SGI Members in Malaysia, Singapore, and Hong Kong

Although each SGI organization has its own distinct characteristics, there are significant similarities in membership. Extensive surveys conducted by me among SGI members in Malaysia, Singapore, and Hong Kong reveal a Soka Gakkai the membership of which is at the same time quite stable yet changing rapidly. It is stable in that followers have always been almost entirely ethnically Chinese (about 98 percent in each of these countries), but it is changing in that the movement, initially consisting of not very well-educated adult females, is becoming increasingly young and well educated with an even distribution of male and female members. The founding members of SGI in Southeast Asia were overwhelmingly older women; there were very few young members. A rapid jump in youth membership in the 1970s came as a result of the willingness of children to follow their parents into the organization, and their presence attracted other young members recruited from among their peers. Today, SGI membership in Asia has become quite young; most are in their twenties, thirties, or very early forties. They are virtually all high school graduates, and most have attended some college. A large percentage of members in Malaysia and, to a lesser extent, in Singapore have done graduate work as well. While many older members were housewives or involved in some form of small business or traditional occupations such as teaching, younger members are more likely still to be students or have professional careers in business, high tech, accounting, and teaching.

There is every indication that most members were satisfied with their lives before joining SGI. Only about a third report having been decidedly unhappy. Indeed, members of all age groups in Asia also report highly optimistic worldviews. Over 98 percent of members felt that both the short-term and long-term future of the world looked very bright and that the Soka Gakkai, with its programs fostering "peace, education, and culture," was a "precious vehicle" for peace.

There were, however, a few active members with more cynical perspectives. They speculate that the world outside their movement had become so corrupt that not even Nichiren Daishonin's Buddhism could ultimately save the world. One youth division member even called Daisaku Ikeda a "sincere idealist" who "meant well," but whose peace proposals were out of place in a "Machiavellian" world.

Questions concerning religious activity and concerns about religion before joining SGI indicated strong differences between Malaysian and Singapore members on the one hand, and Hong Kong members on the other. A majority of Singapore and Malaysian members followed their parents' beliefs and practices in traditional Taoism and Buddhism, while a large majority of Hong Kong members were previously "free thinkers"—people without any active religious beliefs.

Motivation for Membership

Respondents in all three countries (N = 305) were asked to write brief essays explaining their motivations for joining SGI. This approach has the advantage of providing believers with an opportunity to express themselves freely rather than forcing them to choose from preselected categories. The disadvantage, of course, is the large number of varying responses. Still, most of the essayists provided two or more factors that brought them into the Soka Gakkai movement. Table 15.1 gives the most frequently mentioned circumstances.

The most noteworthy statistic is the number of believers who joined because of family relations. The leading source of conversions is within individual families. A middle-aged mother in Hong Kong, for instance joined because she was distressed over her husband's acute illness and the financial panic that ensued once her

Table 15.1. Reasons for joining SGI

Reason	Number
Parents, family members already belonged to SGI	96
Family illness	38
Personal illness	33
No direction in life	29
Poor personal, family finances	27
Disharmony in family	24
Relative cured of illness	21
Searching for meaning in life	21

husband's paycheck disappeared. The husband recovered, and credited his wife's new religion with this "miracle." Able to resume work, he joined immediately, and the couple's three children, the wife's parents, and the husband's two brothers and one sister also joined. Thus, the typical pattern is for the new faithful to convert members of their immediate families, while the children, when they reach their mid-teen years, convince some of their own peers to join.

The survey and interviews indicate that people who joined on their own often spoke of problems related to health, human relations, occupation, and anxiety ("peace of mind") that led them to Soka Gakkai. Family health problems were more numerous than personal illness, but both were quite often accompanied by financial problems and, not surprisingly, these circumstances often led to family stress. The few people who wrote that they were searching for a new religion when they joined SGI were a distinct minority.

Benefits of SGI Membership

Respondents to the survey of SGI members in Southeast Asia were also asked what benefits they had derived from their faith and membership in the organization. The respondents could check off as many items as they pleased from the list in Table 15.2.

Table 15.2. Benefits of membership

Benefit	Number
Improved health	117
Better financial situation	156
Happiness, more confidence	221
Hope for the future	210
Happier family	100

Respondents were also asked to provide essay responses concerning their benefits. The following four responses are representative:

It is very easy to explain the benefits of SGI membership. I have cut down on BAD CAUSES and instead channel my resources (time, energy, and money) for one GOOD cause: HAPPINESS of my family, friends, people in my town and country, and the world. These changes are reflected in my daily life. No more night-life, no more drinking, no more movies or TV. Instead, more time with my family, building friendships with others, helping others to improve themselves, reading more, being less stressed in daily life. I am happier because I know that I am the cause of what I am and what I am not. I can be what I want to be. (40-year-old male businessman in Malaysia)

My kidney problem became so severe that my doctor advised against marriage and bearing children, but when I joined the Soka Gakkai and started chanting there was rapid improvement in my condition. I married happily, gave birth to two children, and am still healthy. I am happy because my practice gives me the life force to sustain a healthy constitution even though my kidney problem still exists.

Buddhism also taught me not to be an escapist, but to face all of my problems squarely and to overcome them happily. It also taught me not to depend on outside stimuli to be happy. Happiness must be found from within. My family life is also happy because I really do not attach myself to love, but instead thrive on compassion and the love generated spontaneously from the love of a harmonious family. (30-year-old female office worker in Hong Kong)

I was once a stubborn and argumentative person, but after studying Nichiren Daishonin's writings, I came to understand my weaknesses and decided to improve. I give much of my time and resources for the benefit of others. Life has much more meaning now. My husband's once severe health problems have also improved.

This Buddhism gives me the courage and wisdom to face the realities of life. Although life is always changing, we must work hard to bring happiness to others. Life is meant to be enjoyed—materialism cannot guarantee our happiness. It all depends on our hearts to feel joy, but that joy depends on how much we do for others. In the past I had no goals in life. I never thought about value or human potential, but having joined in SGI activities, I now understand that each one of us has unlimited potential. SGI activities have shown us the courage and care needed to live (40 year-old female in Singapore).

I am happier. My family members are all very happy and harmonious. Everyone in the family is very happy, positive, and possesses a strong life force. They possess the Buddha's wisdom to overcome all obstacles. That is what we call absolute happiness, not relative happiness. (A general contractor in Hong Kong)

While roughly half of the SGI members surveyed said that membership had brought them better health, fewer financial worries, and improved family relations, an overwhelming majority felt that they have undergone a deep positive transformation that had made them happier and more confident as individuals. There was constant reference to their belief that they were no longer lonely, that they could enjoy the benefits of a genuinely caring extended family. There was a feeling that they had a greater degree of control over their own lives, that they had been empowered with the ability to maximize their own potential.

Devotion to the movement also implies financial support. Members give generously not only to support day-to-day activities, but also to special fundraising campaigns to build large community centers. Malaysian SGI leaders reported, for example, that when they formulated plans for a new community center and inaugurated fundraising drives, the response had always been rapid and strong. A successful ethnic Chinese businessman and Soka Gakkai Malaysia (SGM) leader in Kuala Lumpur explained: "I have profound happiness through Nichiren Daishonin's Buddhism. My business career has also prospered since my entire family joined SGM. It is a Chinese custom to enthusiastically support an organization that has brought one so much good fortune."

Nurturing and Leadership

SGI thrives as a voluntary association, many of the leaders and active members of which volunteer considerable amounts of their free time to the welfare of the organization and its members. The concept that the Soka Gakkai in Southeast Asia is every member's extended family is very real. The heart of the movement is a system of nurturing, where each member is, in essence, responsible for the health and welfare of other members.

The role of an SGI leader at any level is to provide and organize care for a group of members. The leader is supposed to nurture the member, encourage study, and chant with and for him, but making home visits, attending study meetings, and involvement in activities takes up much of one's free time. The leader must keep in constant touch with members, and if she or he sees any hint of trouble, the member will almost certainly receive a phone call or, more commonly, a home visit. One leader stated that on average she made up to three or four home visits each week. The same leader recalled how she had helped a family suffering from financial stress, another household in which a housewife was receiving physical and mental abuse from a violent husband, and a mother whose child had just developed cancer. A member who had been in the hospital for a difficult operation reported that many members visited him to boost his spirits and to chant together with him before the day of the operation.

The care and devotion that a troubled member receives is very personal. An important objective is to let the person know that he is not alone, that he does not have to face a difficult situation without the devotion and support of other members. A leader in Hong Kong reported how she had just visited a fellow member who had suffered considerable verbal and physical abuse from her husband, a successful businessman who was suddenly doing badly during an economic recession. She had several children, no money, very little education, and no place to escape. She felt trapped and isolated. Her SGI comrade's main initial task was to be a good listener, reassuring her that her many friends in the Soka Gakkai sympathized with her plight and would do anything possible to boost her morale:

A group of fellow members went to her house and chanted with her before the family *Gohonzon*. Later I reminded her of the karmic law of cause and effect and that it was up to her to change the family karma for the better. She seemed to gain strength and resolve through her chanting and the encouragement we gave her. Her husband was so deeply moved by her strength and tenacity that he joined her in chanting. His anger seemed to subside, and gradually he apologized to her for his former conduct and became a kinder person.

Qualifications for leadership include strong spiritual commitment and genuine or "spontaneous" devotion to the movement—and especially to the welfare of other members. A leader should also have experienced success in his career, and his family should manifest well-being. Malaysian leaders said that their husbands or wives have to adapt themselves to these circumstances as part of their commitment to the Soka Gakkai movement. When both parents are leaders, older children must look after themselves and their younger siblings, or accept or receive care from grandparents or other family members.

A lengthy discussion with a group of twelve Malaysian women leaders indicated that they were out five or six evenings a week and all day Sunday. As a group they estimated that they spent up to 80 percent of their free time in SGI-related activities. There was little time for non-SGI-related activities such as longer vacations, visits to restaurants, or even downtime with other family members. They insisted that SGI was their life work and source of enjoyment, and that their family lives had actually improved because many, if not all, family members had dedicated their lives to the movement and had found great joy in their ability to help others.

Other SGI leaders indicated, however, that while there were many individual SGI leaders and members who devoted most of their free time to the movement, such time-intensive commitments were not the norm. Leaders throughout the movement work long hours to further the movement and assist other members, but they are also expected to spend quality time with their families, get adequate rest, and to pursue other hobbies and activities.

The large amounts of time and devotion expected of an SGI member and leader, however, may cause problems for future generations of SGI leaders. Some younger leaders clearly must devote fewer hours to the movement because of tremendous time commitments at work and a desire for some quality time with their families. While there is clearly a core of young leaders and members who make extraordinary efforts to further the cause, Bon Chai Ong, general director of the SSA, openly chided a large gathering of youth leaders in July 1998 for an attendance rate at SSA meetings of only 32 percent over a recent period. An SSA youth leader confided that it had taken an inordinate amount of time to find about ninety-six youth members to take part in the 1998 national youth festival celebrations. A youth leader in Hong Kong confessed that youth today have to work so many long hours at school or for a company that they have very little time or energy for SGI events: "Members such as myself deeply care about the future of SGI, but we have professional careers that simply wear us out. There is no such thing as the forty-hour work week here—especially during the current recession. Our faith is strong, but we must manage our time very carefully."

Despite the problem of free time, it does appear that the average member in Southeast Asia devotes more of his time to SGI than his counterparts in North America. A key factor is that chapters in the West tend to be much smaller and thus offer far fewer activities for members. SGI community centers in Asia are humming all day seven days a week, but SGI culture centers in such places as Toronto and Montreal are generally quiet during the day.

Education and "Cultural Activities"

Soka Gakkai organizations throughout the world perform a variety of activities to promote "Peace, Education, and Culture." The Gakkai is an "engaged" Buddhist movement that seeks to influence major social institutions with "Buddhist values." Education, for example, is important not only for the teaching of basic facts or concepts, but also for inculcating in students a sense of tolerance, compassion, and respect for the dignity of life. Peace activities include exhibitions to remind citizens of the horrors of war, and events to bring together people of different cultures and backgrounds to establish common bonds. Cultural activities include a wide variety of activities from music and dance groups to garden clubs to help members find greater enjoyment in the movement, to establish friendship among members, to study and practice the faith together, and to deepen a sense of commitment to the organization.[9]

The SGI organizations in Hong Kong, Malaysia, and Singapore have built large and very successful kindergartens for the children of both members and others in the community.[10] The schools are housed in modern, spacious, and colorful buildings that create an ambience to delight the minds of the students. Classes are small, teachers are well trained and benevolent, and students appear to be delighted to be where they are. When asked how education in a Soka Gakkai school system differs from other schools in her country, a teacher at the Soka kindergarten in Malaysia described SGI's view of "humanistic education":

[9] Cultural groups in the SSA are organized by the various divisions. For example, the men's division choir and drum groups; the women's division dance and choir groups; the young men's division brass band, lion dance, choir, and calisthenics groups; the young women's division fife and drum corps, choir, and dance groups. The SSA Chinese orchestra and the symphonic band comprise members from all divisions. These cultural groups perform at certain SSA activities and cultural shows. Since 1975 SSA has staged many cultural shows. Besides these, the groups are occasionally invited by other organizations to perform.

[10] Children of nonmembers outnumber children of members in Malaysia and Hong Kong.

Every child in Malaysia learns reading, writing, math, science, and other subjects in school to help them earn a living. But these same schools are often lacking in their ability to teach youngsters about daily life in society—how to deal with anger, how to reconcile conflicts, how to breathe, smile, and get along. We offer a revolutionary approach to education. Our "humanistic education" focuses on training students in the art of living in peace and harmony. Our students learn about courtesy, compassion—it is perhaps even more important for a child of 5 to learn how to play and share with other 5 year olds than it is for him to pass a test in math. But, as it turns out, our children go on to do very well in primary and secondary school.

Religious Life

The Soka Gakkai, however, is specifically a religious movement, so it is hardly surprising that worship and Buddhist practice occupy most of the time and attention of Southeast Asian SGI members. Members pray at home in front of a Buddhist altar (*butsudan*) for a period of time every morning and night. Each community center has a room or—in the case of Singapore—a temple where members and visitors can drop in for a period of chanting with other members.

Discussion and dialogue meetings (*zadankai*) are held regularly at members' homes or, in the case of Hong Kong, at Soka Gakkai community centers, where friends and relatives come together on a regular basis to study Buddhist philosophy, discuss problems in their daily lives, and enjoy each other's company. Members often bring nonmember guests to acquaint them with the movement and teachings.[11]

I attended a number of discussion meetings in Malaysia and Hong Kong. The typical Malaysian *zadankai* was a congenial gathering of members. Approximately fifty residents of a middle-class neighborhood gathered in the spacious family room of a member. It was a noticeably relaxed family affair. Most of those in attendance were young or middle-aged couples and their children, but

---

[11] Bringing nonmember guests to meetings and activities is the most common form of proselytization.

there were also a representative sampling of older women and men and a larger number of teenagers and young adults. Parents with children too young to leave at home brought them to the host's home. While the meeting progressed, small children ran back and forth from the kitchen to their parents. It was a congenial, warm atmosphere.

The meeting opened with the entire group chanting in unison before the host's *butsudan*. Members then rose to sing two rousing Soka Gakkai songs, which seemed to put the group into a joyful mood. There followed the reading and discussion of a passage of the sacred writings of Nichiren as well as a reflective essay on the reading composed by SGI president Daisaku Ikeda. Two members provided testimonials in which they told how the "Daishonin's Buddhism" had brought joy and health to their lives. The meeting ended with another song and a brief period of chanting. Friends gathered into small groups for a few moments of small talk before taking their leave.

These meetings are central to the activities of SGI members worldwide. The purpose of the *zadankai* is to cultivate a feeling of solidarity and harmony among local members and to provide a time when they can socialize and pray together and hear about each other's triumphs, hardships, and concerns. A Singapore member aptly described these meetings as a "wonderful form of group therapy." It is also a time when local SGI members and leaders can discuss issues facing SGI and make announcements about forthcoming events.

SGI–Community Relations in Southeast Asia

Since their inception in the 1960s SGI organizations in Southeast Asia have worked hard to build strong ties with their communities and local and national governments. SGI leaders continually stress that Buddhism emphasizes both personal gain and service for the benefit of society, the nation, and the world. SGI sponsors publicly visible programs in each of these countries with the hope of playing a meaningful role in community and national events, and building a solid relationship with the outside world. It is also apparent that local and national governments and communities surrounding SGI community centers generally have a positive view of SGI. An important factor in this development is that each of the three national SGI organizations consists of, and is led by, local nationals with a strong accommodating stance. Each SGI organization is very independent of Tokyo.

The SSA performs regularly in annual national New Year's Day and in National Day parades and in biannual Singapore youth festivals. There are also highly effective community programs, including one that brings elderly citizens for a month-long "course" designed to help them make the transition into retirement. Participants, most of whom are not SGI members, declared that the SSA program had helped them build new and quite active social lives.

The SGI organizations in Malaysia and Hong Kong are equally involved in local and national activities: Hong Kong SGI members played a highly visible role in ceremonies marking Hong Kong's 1997 return to Chinese rule, and over 5,000 Malaysian members performed in the opening and closing ceremonies of the September 1998 Commonwealth Games in Kuala Lumpur.

The following sections portray the close relationship between SGI organizations in Southeast Asia and their respective communities and governments. In 1999 SGI had approximately 20,000 members in Singapore and 40,000 to 50,000 followers each in Malaysia and Hong Kong.

The Singapore Soka Association: A Patriotic Civic Organization

Patriotism and national service are important themes in all Southeast Asian SGI organizations, especially in Singapore. Singapore today is both an immigrant society and a Chinese city state. When Great Britain acquired the island in 1819, Singapore had a population of several hundred Malays living in small simple fishing villages, but by the year 2000 it had become a thriving nation of about 3 million citizens with the highest per capita income in Asia outside of Japan. There is a significant Indian minority population and a much smaller Malay community, but political, commercial, and cultural power are in the hands of the ethnic Chinese majority.

One of the major themes in Singapore history since World War II has been the effort to create a distinct Singapore identity. What does it mean to be a Singaporean? How can the dominant Chinese cultural heritage be transformed into a distinctly Singaporean culture? How can minority populations be successfully incorporated into this new culture? How can a small, predominantly ethnically Chinese city state learn to get along with much more populous but less prosperous Malay Muslim neighbors in Malaysia and Indonesia?

SSA responds by emphasizing its role as a patriotic organization working to enhance Singaporean nationhood. A 1996 SSA publication emphasized this point, describing the role SSA played in making that year's National Day parade a success despite terrible weather conditions at the National Stadium:

Despite the overwhelming obstacles, the spirit to persevere, to give one's best and succeed for our nation, for the people of Singapore prevailed. Driven by the sense of mission, 520 performers and another 235 working behind the scenes displayed the kind of pioneering spirit and resolve that our forefathers possessed to build the nation we proudly call, Singapore. Their valiant struggle was based on resolute faith and a harmonious unity that was imbued with the spirit of mutual care and support.[12]

The Singaporean government in turn has praised SSA for its service to the nation. The prime minister made the following observations when he attended the opening ceremony of the new Soka culture center in January 1993:

We have made a conscious effort to separate religion from politics. Religious leaders in Singapore understand why we have the Religious Harmony Act. Many, like the Singapore Soka Association, have contributed to better national understanding, over and above their usual religious teachings. I congratulate the Singapore Soka Association for its

---

[12] *Eternal Aurora* (Sept. 1996), 27.

consistent efforts in promoting social, cultural, and educational activities for the benefit of all Singaporeans.

This identification with both community and nation has helped SGI place itself as an acceptable—even positive—force in every Asian society it has entered. SGI's native membership, its hard work to foster good relations in local communities, and its active participation in national events in Malaysia, Hong Kong, and Singapore indicate that SGI organizations in Asia ironically have achieved a degree of national acceptance never found in Japan despite the organization's Japanese origins.

Soka Gakkai Malaysia: Chinese Buddhists in an Islamic Nation

The key social factors in Malaysia are ethnic division and a delicate balance among ethnic groups that is needed to form a united nation. There are more than sixty ethnic or culturally differentiated groups among Malaysia's population of about 20 million, but the most critical population division is between Bumiputera and non-Bumiputera people. The Bumiputeras are those with cultural affinities indigenous to Peninsular and Bornean Malaysia and the surrounding region. Malays constitute the main Bumiputera group and account for around 55 percent of Malaysia's population. Non-Bumiputeras are people whose cultural origins lie outside Malaysia—principally people of Chinese and Indian descent. Chinese constitute about 32 percent of Malaysia's population and Indians about 8 percent.

Malaysia is anything but a "melting pot." Each of the major cultural groups maintains its own linguistic and cultural traditions even today. Thus, ethnic Chinese still communicate among themselves in one of several Chinese dialects and have their own Chinese newspapers, although most Chinese Malaysians also speak Malay and English. Ethnic Indians maintain their own traditional communities as well, and Malays have their own distinct cultural identities. One can walk down any street in Malaysia and quickly find Hindu and Buddhist temples blending with mosques.

The ethnic division of Malaysia was strengthened by economic stereotyping during the British colonial era, which extended from the mid-nineteenth to the mid-twentieth centuries. Chinese dominated such areas as finance, transportation, construction, small-scale industry, and retail trading. Upper-class Malays entered professional careers in law and government, while ordinary Malays worked as rice farmers and fishermen. Most Indians labored on rubber estates.

Terrible racial riots in May 1969 led to the conclusion by all parties that each cultural group must learn tolerance and must work together for the salvation of the nation. Malay and Chinese leaders saw the need to tackle vigorously the economic and social disparities that had fueled racial antagonism. Measures were adopted to facilitate quality universal education, and to encourage the participation of all ethnic groups in the rapidly modernizing economy. Wealthy Chinese had to agree to considerable government control over business, and favoritism shown to Malays in such areas as education and employment. Malays in turn learned to be more tolerant of Chinese participation in the economic and political life of the nation. The result is that all of Malaysia's ethnic groups have gained significantly from the nation's rapid economic growth of the 1980s and 1990s.

Religion, however, is still a critical issue in Malaysian society. With government patronage, Malaysia is a much more insistently Islamic society than it was even a generation ago. The entire Malay population is Islamic, and it is very much against the law for any person to even attempt to convert a Moslem to another faith. Most of the Chinese in Malaysia are either Taoists or Buddhists. Some are Christians, and a small percentage follows Islam. A vast majority of the Indians are Hindus, although a few embrace other faiths including Islam, Sikhism, Buddhism, and Christianity.

Although there is a tiny Indian membership in SGM, the membership is essentially Chinese. The fact that ethnic Chinese introduced the SGI movement to other Chinese and that Malays are forbidden by law to convert to Buddhism has meant that SGM has remained a Chinese-based religious and civic organization.

Malaysian constitutional guarantees of religious freedom mean that SGM members can practice their faith without fear of government interference as long as SGM makes no attempt to win converts from the Malay majority. The survival of the Malaysian nation, however, depends on more than just simple tolerance. Wherever one goes in Malaysia, there is a deliberate effort by many groups to work together for the benefit of the whole country, and SGM is an active partner in this process. An SGM leader stated emphatically that while SGM projects itself as a social organization "based on the life philosophy of Nichiren Daishonin, we respect the cultures, customs, traditions and religious practices of other groups."

There is a long history of SGM members learning cultural dances of other ethnic groups and inviting non-Chinese individuals and organizations to participate in SGM cultural events. SGM has been invited to perform at various functions organized by the government or government agencies at the district, state, and national levels including National Day celebrations, state ruler birthday celebrations, and multinational sports events. The SGM Soka kindergarten has also hired two Malay teachers to teach their language to the mainly Chinese group of students.

SGM thrives not only because of the many benefits members feel that they derive from Nichiren Buddhism, but because it is also a cooperative and patriotic civic group that participates in important local and national activities, strongly respects the cultures, customs, and religious practices of other ethnic groups, and, perhaps most importantly, respects laws forbidding the attempted conversion of Malays. This respect, and its contributions to the welfare of other cultures, has led to SGM's general acceptance in Malaysian society.

SGI-Hong Kong and the Chinese Community

Unlike Singapore and Malaysia, both full-fledged nations with distinct characters, Hong Kong is a political entity in search of its identity. The British have left, and the Chinese government is maintaining a very low profile, so to a certain extent the people of Hong Kong have the city to themselves, but when I asked them of which nation they considered themselves citizens, I got confused, startled looks and blank stares. "Although we are proud to once again be together with China, we identify ourselves with Hong Kong."

SGI-Hong Kong (SGI-HG) faces some of the same problems as the city itself. It lacks the characteristic patriotic demeanor of Singapore and even Malaysia, but there is a sense of civic pride. SGI-HG identifies itself with Hong Kong and specifies that a crucial goal is the enrichment of the lives of Hong Kong people, but it is more inwardly directed than other Asian SGI groups. More of its cultural events seem to be for its own members than for outsiders. Although SGI-HG played an important role in the July 1997 celebrations marking the return of Hong Kong to China as well as other important local civic events, a younger SGI leader noted: "We are in fact comparatively little involved in community affairs. We need to play a more visible role in public events."

SGI-HG has experienced explosive growth in Hong Kong since the 1960s. Since 1961, when President Ikeda inaugurated the first district of eight members, Hong Kong has developed into an organization consisting of eleven community headquarters, fifty-three chapters, and 40,000 members. Ten of the headquarters serve a Chinese membership that demographically resembles Hong Kong as a whole. SGI-HG's headquarters #10 serves as an umbrella organization for non-Chinese members. Meetings are held in a variety of languages including English, Tagalog, and Korean.

SGI-HG makes no attempt to extend its organization and proselytization into mainland China despite the proximity of the People's Republic. The Japanese Soka Gakkai has carefully built up a long-term relationship with various Chinese political and cultural leaders and institutions over four decades. There is a strong desire to refrain from any activity that might jeopardize these relations by running afoul of Chinese laws forbidding proselytization on Chinese soil by nonresident Chinese or foreigners.

SGI-HG is also unique because a few of its leaders are also foreign. General Director Kong Sau Lee is a Japanese national who has helped to lead the organization since the mid-1960s, and several other members of the SGI-HG staff are also Japanese. Several Chinese SGI-HG staffers attended university in Japan (primarily Soka University) and speak fluent Japanese. President Ikeda has made more than twenty official visits to Hong Kong, whereas he has visited Singapore only twice and Malaysia only once. Although SGI-HG is in an overall sense a very Chinese and Hong Kong-based organization, its ties with the Soka Gakkai in Japan are extraordinarily close.

There are notable socioeconomic differences between Hong Kong members and those in Singapore and Malaysia. The Singapore and Malaysian members are generally better educated, hold better jobs, and have higher incomes than their counterparts in Hong Kong. The SGI in Malaysia in particular has attracted a number of extraordinarily wealthy members. SGI-HG has its share of wealthy leaders and members, but one cannot compare them to Malaysia.

When SGI-HG got its start in the early 1960s, members were mostly middle-class proprietors of shops and small company proprietors. Vigorous propagation activities succeeded in building a strong membership base in the poorer sections of Hong Kong, including many who lived their lives on boats in the harbor. The living conditions of members improved dramatically in the 1970s and 1980s, but there is still a high percentage of middle-aged and older women members who have received very little education. Indeed, older women members outnumber their male counterparts by a ratio of about three to one. Younger members, on the other hand, are far better educated, have rising career prospects, and have a much stronger male–female ratio.

Of the three organizations, SGI-HG most nearly fits the image of a religious organization that attracts alienated people living in an urban industrial environment. A majority of members had no strong religious background and lacked a sense of direction or confidence before they joined SGI-HG. Their strong dedication to the movement, their current happiness with their lives, and their renewed optimism and confidence indicate that SGI-HG plays a constructive role in the Hong Kong community.

Soka Gakkai International Indian Minority

The SGI organizations in Malaysia, Singapore, and Hong Kong are overwhelmingly Chinese, but there are several hundred Indian members in each organization. Most are the children or grandchildren of Hindu Indian immigrants from southern India who arrived in Southeast Asia earlier this century. SGI Indian members in Asia were typically brought up within the social caste and Hindu traditions of their parents, but became dissatisfied with the role of religion in their lives until they found Nichiren Buddhism.

Indian members in Singapore and Malaysia have their own chapters within both SGI organizations, where they meet with other Indians and converse in their own languages. This cultural–linguistic division of membership, which is quite common among SGI organizations worldwide, is said not to be seen as discrimination against minority members or as a way of segregating them from the mainstream. Indeed, various scholars have found that one of the most noteworthy aspects of SGI is the excellent relationship that exists among people from different races, cultures, and linguistic groups worldwide within each organization. Indeed, the creation of separate units for minority members is strictly voluntary and largely for the convenience of members. When anglophone members meet in Quebec or Tamil-speaking Indians gather in Penang (Malaysia), they can converse in their own language and relate to other people from their own culture. Multicultural meetings where translators are continually at work are slow and cumbersome. An Indian not fluent in Chinese would feel isolated in a Chinese-only meeting but would benefit from hearing testimonials and lessons in Tamil. He might also feel more comfortable discussing personal problems with people from his own culture. On the other hand, members from different cultural backgrounds do meet frequently at larger cultural activities and study or prayer meetings.

I held a long discussion with a Singapore-born descendent of Indian immigrants, who plays an important role in SSA. He was a 43-year-old manager in a construction company and father of two young children. His father was a devout Hindu, and his son had strong religious interests since youth. He recounts going to a local temple, where he would ask religious authorities to explain the causes of certain events and was told that what happens is always the will of god. Since Hinduism failed to provide a rational explanation for hardships in his and his family's life, he left the religion and became a skeptic and "free thinker." He went on to describe the attraction of SGI for him:

I eventually found a copy of the SGI publication *Seikyo Times* where I read that suffering is caused by karma and that we are responsible for our own actions. Indians traditionally believe that good fortune comes as a result of their own actions while bad luck is the "will of the gods." But if you realize that you are fully responsible for your conduct, you can create an entirely new life for yourself and your family.

Nichiren Daishonin's Buddhism teaches us compassion for others and helps us find happiness here and now. SGI encourages each of us to foster our own cultures while gaining respect for others. All Nichiren Buddhists are equals and even though we are a minority, we never experience any form of discrimination. Singapore is a nation built on the compatibility of different cultures, and SGI is a living model of what our nation must develop.

Because we all have inherent Buddha-nature, we can overcome our suffering and help others overcome theirs. We bring happiness to others and in so doing enrich our own lives.

Another Indian member in Penang made these comments:

Nichiren's Buddhism strengthens our own community, but also helps us to bridge the gap to the Chinese community. When I realized that my destiny in life was entirely in my own hands, I became free to develop my own career and to help other people find their own happiness.

Many younger Indians, like their ethnic Chinese counterparts in Southeast Asia, have found their traditional cultural life including the caste system to be irrelevant in a modern urban capitalist environment. They are attracted to a new religion which closes the gap between different cultures and encourages them to work hard to develop not only their own lives, but also those of their friends and family members.

Conclusion

SGI organizations flourish in Asia because, to their members, they represent a form of extended family. There is extensive caring and concern for fellow members. There is also a genuine sense of warmth and kindness—a sharing of all the ups and downs of the lives of all members—and a spirit of joy and warmth. One sees a sense of purpose and hope, a certainty that they live in a good world, which, despite all of its problems, can become better. There is a strong desire for peace and harmony and a realization that even the most difficult problems can be solved for the best. SGI members are happy and successful; they feel full of confidence and manifest a sense of optimism.

The Soka Gakkai has also succeeded in Southeast Asia because, in a context of rapid socioeconomic change, many people have felt a need for new religious inspiration. Many of Japan's new religions thrived because they satisfied the spiritual needs of people living in the midst of postwar Japan's urbanization and industrialization. When a number of these religions expanded to Southeast Asia in the mid to late 1960s, they encountered people likewise experiencing socioeconomic change.

Professor Bryan Wilson has noted:

Nichiren Buddhism is a strongly individualistic religious orientation: one takes responsibility for oneself, and chanting has a powerful, albeit not exclusive, role in self-transformation. Realizing one's true identity, transcending one's karma, coming to terms with reality by using the *Gohonzon* as a mirror of one's own individuality—all of these central preoccupations reflect the extent to which Nichiren Buddhism focuses on self-improvement and self-help.[13]

[13] Bryan Wilson and Karel Dobbelaere, *A Time to Chant: The Soka Gakkai Buddhists in Britain* (Oxford: Clarendon Press, 1994), 186–7.

This sense of an individualistic orientation and responsibility for oneself is ideally suited for younger upwardly mobile members of Southeast Asia's increasingly educated and professional emerging middle class.

The Soka Gakkai has succeeded in Asia also because it provides members with a new extended family. Ethnic Chinese are traditionally family-oriented, but many younger members of the new middle class have moved away from their traditional families and now live alone or as part of their own nuclear families. Nevertheless, a number of members interviewed by me expressed a strong need for "family" and proudly stated that SGI had become their new family.

The Buddhist background of many members made it easier for them to accept a movement that is itself Buddhist. Virtually all members interviewed stated that their strong desire for some degree of religious practice and/or spirituality in their lives made the Soka Gakkai attractive to them once they came in contact with the organization and its members. The fact that many of them had Buddhist backgrounds and that the Soka Gakkai is itself a Buddhist movement made SGI inherently more attractive than Christianity or other "foreign" faiths. Religious and racial tolerance in Singapore, Malaysia, and Hong Kong permits new faiths a chance to develop strong local roots.

Beyond these considerations lies a further contributing factor in SGI's success in these countries—virtually all SGI leaders are natives who have strong ties with the local community. Their willingness to work closely with local leaders and with the government enhances their prestige and facilitates their endeavor.

Further Reading

BABBIE, EARL T., "The Third Civilization: An Examination of Soka Gakkai," *Review of Religious Research*, 7 (1966), 101–21.

BENZ, ERNST, "Buddhism in the Western World," in Heinrich Dumoulin and John C. Maraldo (eds.), *Buddhism in the Modern World* (New York: Collier, 1976).

BETHEL, DAYLE M., *Makiguchi the Value Creator* (New York: Weatherill, 1973).

Buddhism and the Nichiren Shoshu Tradition (Tokyo: Nichiren Shoshu International Centre, 1986).

CAUSTON, RICHARD, "Freedom and Democracy: To Be or Not to Be," *Issues between the Nichiren Shoshu Priesthood and the Soka Gakkai*, i (Tokyo: Soka Gakkai International, 1991).

—— *Nichiren Shoshu Buddhism* (New York: Harper & Row, 1989).

ELLWOOD, ROBERT S., *The Eagle and the Rising Sun: Americans and the New Religions of Japan* (Philadelphia: Westminster Press, 1974).

FUJIWARA, HIROTATSU, *I Denounce Soka Gakkai* (Tokyo: Nisshin Hodo Co., 1970).

HAMMOND, PHILLIP, and MACHACEK, DAVID, *Soka Gakkai in America: Accommodation and Conversion* (Oxford: Oxford University Press, 1999).

HOURMENT, LOUIS, "Transformer le poison en élixir: L'Alchimie du désir dans un culte néo-bouddhique, la Soka Gakkai française," in Françoise Champion and Danielle Hervieu-Léger (eds.), *De l'émotion en religion: Renouveaux et traditions* (Paris: Centurion, 1990).

HURST, JANE, *Nichiren Shoshu Buddhism and the Soka Gakkai in America: The Ethos of a New Religious Movement* (New York: Garland Press, 1992).

IKEDA, DAISAKU, *The Human Revolution.*, 5 vols., condensed version of the Japanese original (New York: Weatherhill, 1972, 1974, 1976, 1983, 1984).

INOUE, NOBUTAKA, "NSA and Non-Japanese Members in California," in Kei'ichi Yanagawa (ed.), *Japanese Religions in California: A Report of*

Research within and without the Japanese-American Community (Tokyo: Department of Religious Studies, University of Tokyo, 1983).

Issues between the Nichiren Shoshu Priesthood and the Soka Gakkai, i–iii (Tokyo: Soka Gakkai International, 1991).

KISALA, ROBERT, "Soka Gakkai, Komeito, and the Separation of Religion and the State," *Bulletin of the Nanzan Institute for Religion and Culture*, 18 (1994), 7–17.

The Liturgy of the Buddhism of Nichiren Daishonin (n.p.: Soka Gakkai International, 1992).

The Liturgy of Nichiren Shoshu (n.p.: Nichiren Shoshu Temples, 1972, 1979).

METRAUX, DANIEL, *The History and Theology of Soka Gakkai* (Lewiston, NY: Edwin Mellen Press, 1988).

—— "The Dispute between the Soka Gakkai and the Nichiren Shoshu Priesthood: A Revolution against a Conservative Clergy," *Japanese Journal of Religious Studies*, 19/4 (1992), 325–36.

—— *The Soka Gakkai Revolution* (Lanham, Md.: University Press of America, 1994).

—— "The Soka Gakkai: Buddhism and the Creation of a Harmonious and Peaceful Society," in C. S. Queen and S. B. King (eds.), *Engaged Buddhism* (Albany: State University of New York Press, 1996).

MORGAN, PEGGY, "Methods and Aims of Evangelization and Conversion to Buddhism, with particular reference to Nichiren Shoshu Soka Gakkai," in Peter B. Clarke (ed.), *The New Evangelists: Recruitment, Methods, and Aims of New Religious Movements* (London: Ethnographica, 1987).

MULLINS, MARK R., SHIMAZONO, SUSUMU, and SWANSON, PAUL L. (eds.), *Religion and Society in Modern Japan* (Berkeley: Asian Humanities Press, 1993).

Myodo, 1–3 (Pinole, Calif.: Nichiren Shoshu Temples of the United States, 1991–2).

NATTIER, JAN, "Visible and Invisible: On the Politics of Representation in Buddhist America," *Tricycle: The Buddhist Review* (Fall 1995), 42–9.

NICHIREN DAISHONIN, *The Major Writings of Nichiren Daishonin*, i–vi (Tokyo: Nichiren Shoshu International Centre, 1979, 1981, 1985, 1986, 1988, 1990).

—— *Nichiren: Selected Writings*, trans. Laurel Rasplica Rodd (Honolulu: University of Hawaii Press, 1980).

—— *Selected Writings of Nichiren*, ed. P. B. Yampolsky, trans. B. Watson *et al.* (New York: Columbia University Press, 1990).

—— *Letters of Nichiren*, ed. P. B. Yampolsky, trans. B. Watson *et al.* (New York: Columbia University Press, 1996).

Nichiren Shoshu and Soka Gakkai (Tokyo: Seikyo Press, 1972).

Nichiren Shoshu Ceremonies (n.p.: Nichiren Shoshu Temple, 1990).

PALMER, ARVIN, *Buddhist Politics: Japan's Clean Government Party* (The Hague: Martinus Nijhoff, 1971).

Questions and Answers on the Temple Issue (Santa Monica, Calif.: SGI-USA, 1997).

Reaffirming our Right to Happiness: On the Gohonzon Transcribed by High Priest Nichikan (Santa Monica, Calif.: SGI-USA, 1996).

SHIMAZONO, SUSUMU, "The Expansion of Japan's New Religions into Foreign Cultures," *Japanese Journal of Religious Studies*, 18/2–3 (1991), 105–32.

SHUPE, ANSON D., "Militancy and Accommodation in the Third Civilization: The Case of Japan's Soka Gakkai Movement," in Jeffrey K. Hadden and Anson D. Shupe (eds.), *Prophetic Religion and Politics* (New York: Paragon House, 1986).

—— "Globalization versus Religious Nativism: Japan's Soka Gakkai in the World Arena," in Roland Robertson and W. R. Garrett (eds.), *Religion and Global Order* (New York: Paragon House, 1991).

SNOW, DAVID A., "Organization, Ideology, and Mobilization: The Case of Nichiren Shoshu of America," in David G. Bromley and Phillip E. Hammond (eds.), *The Future of New Religious Movements* (Macon, Ga.: Mercer University Press, 1987).

TAMARU, NORIYOSHI, and REID, DAVID (eds.), *Religion in Japanese Culture* (New York: Kodansha International, 1996).

VAN BRAGT, JAN, "An Uneven Battle: Soka Gakkai vs. Nichiren Shoshu," *Bulletin of the Nanzan Institute for Religion and Culture*, 17 (1993), 15–31.

WILSON, BRYAN, and DOBBELAERE, KAREL, *A Time to Chant: The Soka Gakkai Buddhists in Britain* (Oxford: Clarendon Press, 1994).

Internet sources

Official Soka Gakkai Sites

<www.sgi.org>
<www.sokagakkai.or.jp>
<www.sgi-usa.org>

< www.brc21.org >

Official Nichiren Shoshu Sites

< www.nstmyosenji.org >

Unofficial Soka Gakkai Sites

< members.aol.com/watchbuddh/link.htm >
< members.aol.com/kachiyuke/nichiren-shoshu-corruption/index.htm >
< www.sokasprit.com >

Unofficial Nichiren Shoshu Sites

< coyote.accessnv.com/tamonten/discus/index.htm >
< www.cebunet.com/nst/ >

Glossary

daimoku	see *Nam-myoho-renge-kyo*
Gohonzon	the sacred scroll inscribed by Nichiren, and the object of worship
gongyo	recital of two chapters of the Lotus Sutra, a ritual undertaken morning and evening
Gosho	the collected writings of Nichiren
Komeito	literally "clean government party"
kosen-rufu	the spread of Buddhism in the world
mappo	the latter day of the law (namely, the present age)
Nam-myoho-renge-kyo	the invocation of the Lotus Sutra
obutsumyogo	the union of worldly matters and Buddhist teaching
shakubuku	literally "break and subdue" (false teachings) — the vigorous method of proselytizing
shoju	the "show by example" approach to recruitment
Soka Gakkai	Value Creation Society

Index

AIDS 387
Akiya, Einosuke 77, 109, 251
Albanese, Catherine 282
Alice 246, 371
Allied Occupation 211
American Academy of Religion 91
Amida Buddha 20
Amnesty International 380
Asahara, Shoko 228
Asahi 207
Aum Shinrikyo 143, 144, 209,
  218–19, 228, 371

Baba, Tetsuji 306
Baldschun, Dave 310
Berman, Morris 65
Bonnell, Stephen 318
Boston Research Center for the 21st
  Century 91, 250, 289
Boston University 91
Bowers, Chet 55
Braddock, Shoko 319
Brecht, Bertolt 394
British Broadcasting Corporation
  (BBC) 228
Broadcasting Law 208, 222
Buddha, *see* Shakyamuni Buddha
Buddhist Churches of America 300,
  see also Jodo Shinshu
Bungei Shunju 213

C. Itoh Corporation 214
Candomble 339, 347
Caritas 380
Carpenter, Robert 328–9, 330
Carroll, Lewis 246
Catholic Party 236
Center for the Study of Religion 9
Chateau des Roches 245
Chih-i 20
Children's Rights Treaty 182
Christian Democratic Union (CDU)
  124, 127
Christian People's Party 233

Church of Perfect Liberty Kyodan
  327, 329–33, 336
Church of World Messianity 327–33,
  335–6, 344
Clark Edward 306, 308
Columbia Teacher's College 91
Commonwealth Games 419
Communist Party 218
Confucianism 18, 29
Consiglio Italiano Rifugiati (CIR)
  378
Counter-Reformation 85
Cult Information Centre 370

Daalder, Hans 234
Dalai Lama 317
Day of Chicago 316
Delmar, Linda 311–12
Democratic Party of Japan (DPJ)
  134, 142, 147, 148, 149
Democratic Socialist Party (DSP)
  119, 135, 136, 138, 139, 251
Dentsu Incorporated 222
DePaul University 317
Derrett, E.M.A. 328
Dewey, John 43, 44, 60–1
Divine Light Mission 281
Dobbelaere, Karel 79, 197–8, 399
Dogen 20
Domei 87, 92
Durkheim, Emile 374, 396

Earth Charter 91, 250
Elysee Palace 371
Endo, Otohiko 135, 145, 151, 152
Enlai, Zhou 118
Evans, Christopher 65
Florida Culture Center 289
Florida Marlins 317
Froebel, Friedrich 43
Fromm, Erich 61
Fudo-myo-o 328
Fujikura, Y. 330
Fujioka, Ted 306, 308

437